Trees & Shrubs For Dummies®

D0507561

Assessing Your Planting Site

Match trees and shrubs to your planting site by first taking an inventory of what your site has to offer. Choose only those plants that can grow to their full potential where you plan to put them. See Chapter 2 for more details.

- **Sun and shade:** Duration and time of day and year that sun shines directly on the site.
- **Soil:** Structure, texture, pH, drainage, and moisture.
- **Views:** Unsightly views to screen; pleasant views to enhance or preserve.
- **Slope:** Steep, flat, valley floors.
- **Wind:** Speed and direction at different times of year.
- **Hardiness zone:** Average winter low temperatures.
- **Obstacles:** Locations of buildings, overhead and buried utilities, roads, and property boundaries.

Choosing Healthy Trees and Shrubs

Before laying down your hard-earned cash, check your plants for the following attributes (see Chapter 11 for more information and for definitions of some of these terms):

- **Trunk:** Straight, unless intentionally otherwise, and tapered gently from top to bottom. Bark free of cuts, bad pruning, and constricting ties. Able to stand without a stake, except for grafted weeping trees.
- **Branching structure:** Limbs evenly distributed and in proportion to each other and to the trunk. Free of breakage, damaged bark, evidence of disease, or pests.
- **Foliage:** Size and color normal compared to others of same cultivar. No evidence of insects, disease, or wilting.
- **Roots:** Bare-root plants have moist, evenly distributed, unbroken roots. A balled and burlapped tree has a firm, unbroken root ball that shows evidence of regular watering. Container grown plants feel well-rooted in the pots, but don't have roots circling inside container or growing out the bottom holes.

Knowing When to Prune

Prune your trees and shrubs at the proper time of year, using this chart.

Type of plant	When
Spring-blooming shrubs	Just after flowering
Summer or fall-blooming shrubs	Late winter while dormant
Rhododendrons and azaleas	Just after flowering
Conifers	In spring as the shoots elongate
Sheared hedges	Late spring and as needed to mid-summer
Deciduous shade trees and shrubs	Late winter or early summer
Trees that bleed sap	Mid to late summer

For Dummies™: Bestselling Book Series for Beginners

Trees & Shrubs For Dummies®

Cheat Sheet

Average Annual Minimum Temperature by Zone

Use the following chart and the color maps near the center of this book to find your USDA Hardiness Zone.

Temperature F	USDA Zone	Temperature C
−50°to −40°	2	−45.5° to −40.1°
−40° to −30°	3	−40.0° to −34.5°
−30° to −20°	4	−34.3° to −28.9°
−20° to −10°	5	−28.8° to −23.4°
−10° to 0°	6	−23.3° to −17.8°
0° to 10°	7	−17.7° to −12.3°
10° to 20°	8	−12.2° to −6.7°
20° to 30°	9	−6.6° to −1.2°
30° to 40°	10	−1.1° to 4.4°
40° and above	11	4.5° and above

Mulch to Cover a 100 Square Foot Area

Use the following table to determine the amount of mulch you need to cover 100 square feet of planting area:

Inches of mulch (depth)	Amount of material needed to cover 100 ft²
4" (.34 feet)	34 cubic feet
3" (.25 feet)	25 cubic feet
2" (.17 feet)	17 cubic feet

For areas other than 100 square feet, use the following formulas to determine the size of your planting area and the amount of mulch you need:

- Area of a rectangle (in square feet) = length (in feet) x width (in feet)

- Area of a circle (in square feet) = radius (in feet) x radius (in feet) × 3.14

   Note that the radius is one-half the diameter of a circle.

- Cubic feet = area (in square feet) × depth (in feet)

Conversions

Use the following chart to convert U.S. and metric measurements. In each case, the conversions are approximately equal.

1 centimeter ≈ 0.4 inches	
1 meter ≈ 39 inches ≈ 1.1 yards	
1 kilometer ≈ 0.6 mile	
1 liter ≈ 1.1 quarts	
1 kilogram ≈ 2.2 pounds	
1 gram ≈ 0.04 ounce	
1 inch ≈ 2.5 centimeters	
1 yard ≈ 0.9 meter	
1 mile ≈ 1.6 kilometers	
1 quart ≈ 0.9 liter	
1 pound ≈ 0.4 kilograms	
1 ounce ≈ 31 grams	

IDG BOOKS WORLDWIDE

For Dummies™: Bestselling Book Series for Beginners

Trees & Shrubs FOR DUMMIES®

by Ann Whitman and the Editors of the National Gardening Association

IDG Books Worldwide, Inc.
An International Data Group Company

Foster City, CA ◆ Chicago, IL ◆ Indianapolis, IN ◆ New York, NY

Trees & Shrubs For Dummies®

Published by
IDG Books Worldwide, Inc.
An International Data Group Company
919 E. Hillsdale Blvd.
Suite 400
Foster City, CA 94404
www.idgbooks.com (IDG Books Worldwide Web site)
www.dummies.com (Dummies Press Web site)

Library of Congress Catalog Card No.: 99-67264

ISBN: 0-7645-5203-1

Printed in the United States of America

10 9 8 7 6 5 4 3 2 1

1B/SS/RS/ZZ/IN

Distributed in the United States by IDG Books Worldwide, Inc.

Distributed by CDG Books Canada Inc. for Canada; by Transworld Publishers Limited in the United Kingdom; by IDG Norge Books for Norway; by IDG Sweden Books for Sweden; by IDG Books Australia Publishing Corporation Pty. Ltd. for Australia and New Zealand; by TransQuest Publishers Pte Ltd. for Singapore, Malaysia, Thailand, Indonesia, and Hong Kong; by Gotop Information Inc. for Taiwan; by ICG Muse, Inc. for Japan; by Intersoft for South Africa; by Eyrolles for France; by International Thomson Publishing for Germany, Austria and Switzerland; by Distribuidora Cuspide for Argentina; by LR International for Brazil; by Galileo Libros for Chile; by Ediciones ZETA S.C.R. Ltda. for Peru; by WS Computer Publishing Corporation, Inc., for the Philippines; by Contemporanea de Ediciones for Venezuela; by Express Computer Distributors for the Caribbean and West Indies; by Micronesia Media Distributor, Inc. for Micronesia; by Chips Computadoras S.A. de C.V. for Mexico; by Editorial Norma de Panama S.A. for Panama; by American Bookshops for Finland.

For general information on IDG Books Worldwide's books in the U.S., please call our Consumer Customer Service department at 800-762-2974. For reseller information, including discounts and premium sales, please call our Reseller Customer Service department at 800-434-3422.

For information on where to purchase IDG Books Worldwide's books outside the U.S., please contact our International Sales department at 317-596-5530 or fax 317-596-5692.

For consumer information on foreign language translations, please contact our Customer Service department at 1-800-434-3422, fax 317-596-5692, or e-mail rights@idgbooks.com.

For information on licensing foreign or domestic rights, please phone +1-650-655-3109.

For sales inquiries and special prices for bulk quantities, please contact our Sales department at 650-655-3200 or write to the address above.

For information on using IDG Books Worldwide's books in the classroom or for ordering examination copies, please contact our Educational Sales department at 800-434-2086 or fax 317-596-5499.

For press review copies, author interviews, or other publicity information, please contact our Public Relations department at 650-655-3000 or fax 650-655-3299.

For authorization to photocopy items for corporate, personal, or educational use, please contact Copyright Clearance Center, 222 Rosewood Drive, Danvers, MA 01923, or fax 978-750-4470.

is a registered trademark under exclusive
license to IDG Books Worldwide, Inc.
from International Data Group, Inc.

About the Author

Ann Whitman grew up in an extended gardening family and fondly remembers picking berries and bouquets of flowers with her grandmothers. She learned the finer points of growing vegetables from one grandfather and reverence and appreciation of trees from the other, a county forester. Her parents continued their traditions with bountiful gardens of their own and summer vacations spent camping, hiking, and canoeing in the forests of eastern Canada and New England.

Ann hopes to someday organize her own orchard, perennial, fruit, and vegetable gardens in a style that reflects her education instead of her spontaneous nature and compulsive plant collecting habits. She earned a Bachelor of Science degree in Plant and Soil Science at the University of Vermont and completed a Master of Arts in Landscape Design from the Conway School of Landscape Design in Massachusetts.

Considering herself a "jack of all trades and master of a few," Ann has enjoyed an eclectic job history involving everything from clearing trails, managing greenhouses, and conducting apple orchard research for the University of Vermont to sales, management, and staff training for several major retail stores. When her first child was born, she discovered that writing was a great way to stay home with the kids and still keep in touch with the world of grownups. She lives, gardens, and writes in Vermont.

National Gardening Association: The National Gardening Association is the largest member-based, nonprofit organization of home gardeners in the United States. Founded in 1972 (as "Gardens for All") to spearhead the community garden movement, today's National Gardening Association is best known for its bimonthly publication, *National Gardening* magazine. Reporting on all aspects of home gardening, each issue is read by some half-million gardeners. For more information about the National Gardening Association, write to 180 Flynn Ave., Burlington, VT 05401 USA; or visit its Web site at www.garden.org.

ABOUT IDG BOOKS WORLDWIDE

Welcome to the world of IDG Books Worldwide.

IDG Books Worldwide, Inc., is a subsidiary of International Data Group, the world's largest publisher of computer-related information and the leading global provider of information services on information technology. IDG was founded more than 30 years ago by Patrick J. McGovern and now employs more than 9,000 people worldwide. IDG publishes more than 290 computer publications in over 75 countries. More than 90 million people read one or more IDG publications each month.

Launched in 1990, IDG Books Worldwide is today the #1 publisher of best-selling computer books in the United States. We are proud to have received eight awards from the Computer Press Association in recognition of editorial excellence and three from Computer Currents' First Annual Readers' Choice Awards. Our best-selling ...*For Dummies*® series has more than 50 million copies in print with translations in 31 languages. IDG Books Worldwide, through a joint venture with IDG's Hi-Tech Beijing, became the first U.S. publisher to publish a computer book in the People's Republic of China. In record time, IDG Books Worldwide has become the first choice for millions of readers around the world who want to learn how to better manage their businesses.

Our mission is simple: Every one of our books is designed to bring extra value and skill-building instructions to the reader. Our books are written by experts who understand and care about our readers. The knowledge base of our editorial staff comes from years of experience in publishing, education, and journalism — experience we use to produce books to carry us into the new millennium. In short, we care about books, so we attract the best people. We devote special attention to details such as audience, interior design, use of icons, and illustrations. And because we use an efficient process of authoring, editing, and desktop publishing our books electronically, we can spend more time ensuring superior content and less time on the technicalities of making books.

You can count on our commitment to deliver high-quality books at competitive prices on topics you want to read about. At IDG Books Worldwide, we continue in the IDG tradition of delivering quality for more than 30 years. You'll find no better book on a subject than one from IDG Books Worldwide.

John Kilcullen
Chairman and CEO
IDG Books Worldwide, Inc.

Steven Berkowitz
President and Publisher
IDG Books Worldwide, Inc.

WINNER

*Eighth Annual
Computer Press
Awards ≥ 1992*

WINNER

*Ninth Annual
Computer Press
Awards ≥ 1993*

WINNER

*Tenth Annual
Computer Press
Awards ≥ 1994*

WINNER

*Eleventh Annual
Computer Press
Awards ≥ 1995*

IDG is the world's leading IT media, research and exposition company. Founded in 1964, IDG had 1997 revenues of $2.05 billion and has more than 9,000 employees worldwide. IDG offers the widest range of media options that reach IT buyers in 75 countries representing 95% of worldwide IT spending. IDG's diverse product and services portfolio spans six key areas including print publishing, online publishing, expositions and conferences, market research, education and training, and global marketing services. More than 90 million people read one or more of IDG's 290 magazines and newspapers, including IDG's leading global brands — Computerworld, PC World, Network World, Macworld and the Channel World family of publications. IDG Books Worldwide is one of the fastest-growing computer book publishers in the world, with more than 700 titles in 36 languages. The "...For Dummies®" series alone has more than 50 million copies in print. IDG offers online users the largest network of technology-specific Web sites around the world through IDG.net (http://www.idg.net), which comprises more than 225 targeted Web sites in 55 countries worldwide. International Data Corporation (IDC) is the world's largest provider of information technology data, analysis and consulting, with research centers in over 41 countries and more than 400 research analysts worldwide. IDG World Expo is a leading producer of more than 168 globally branded conferences and expositions in 35 countries including E3 (Electronic Entertainment Expo), Macworld Expo, ComNet, Windows World Expo, ICE (Internet Commerce Expo), Agenda, DEMO, and Spotlight. IDG's training subsidiary, ExecuTrain, is the world's largest computer training company, with more than 230 locations worldwide and 785 training courses. IDG Marketing Services helps industry-leading IT companies build international brand recognition by developing global integrated marketing programs via IDG's print, online and exposition products worldwide. Further information about the company can be found at www.idg.com. 1/24/99

Dedication

I devote this work to my husband, Don, and our children, David and Kate, for their support and patience with "Mom's book," and to Mari-Beth DeLucia, our true friend and family fairy godmother who fixed dinner and made me go to the gym even when I said I didn't have time.

Acknowledgments

The message on the back of my son's favorite soccer shirt reminds me that "you can't win without your teammates." That universal truth holds true for publishing, as well. I am grateful to my teammates on this project who shared one common goal — to give readers a truly useful book. It's been my good fortune to work with talented people throughout this labor of love and I thank each of them for their important role.

Michael MacCaskey, Editor-in-Chief at *National Gardening* magazine, talked me into tackling this book by assuring me that he and the rest of the National Gardening Association (NGA) staff would support my efforts along the way. True to his word, Mike has my utmost appreciation for his guidance, for believing in me, and encouraging me when my own enthusiasm flagged. Linda Provost, Art Director at NGA, lent her keen eyes and vast experience to the selection of the color photos in this book and taught me a few things in the process. Thank you, too, JoAnn Gaye for always answering the phone with a smile.

Tere Drenth, Project Editor at IDG Books, deserves a big hug and huge round of applause for her excellent editing skills and good humor. She was the center of the cyclone on this project and managed to keep us all on track. I also wish to thank Patricia Yuu Pan, Editor and Master Gardener, who asked many thought-provoking questions, and Denny Schrock, for his careful attention to detail and accuracy that saved me from embarrassment. I also appreciate Mary Goodwin, who got this book off to a good start and gave me thorough coaching on how to write a ...*For Dummies* book.

Lance Waltheim carved time out of his own busy writing schedule to help with this book. Thanks, Lance, for your time, contributions, and considerable expertise. And thanks, DD Dowden, for your wonderful illustrations.

I also wish to acknowledge a few unsung heroes — teachers who expected excellence from their students and worked miracles to help them achieve it; Kirk Bosworth, Randy Griffith, Don Walker, and Walt Cudnohufsky. To borrow from the words of Sir Isaac Newton — truly, I have stood on the shoulders of giants.

Publisher's Acknowledgments

We're proud of this book; please register your comments through our IDG Books Worldwide Online Registration Form located at http://my2cents.dummies.com.

Some of the people who helped bring this book to market include the following:

Acquisitions, Editorial, and Media Development

Project Editor: Tere Drenth

Acquisitions Editor: Holly McGuire

General Reviewers: Denny Schrock, Patricia Yuu Pan

Editor Director: Kristin A. Cocks

Editorial Coordinator: Jill Alexander

Special Help
Mary Goodwin, Michelle Hacker, Jonathon Malysiak

Production

Project Coordinator: Maridee Ennis

Layout and Graphics: Amy Adrian, Karl Brandt, Angela F. Hunckler, Clint Lahnen, Shelley Norris, Tracy Oliver, Jill Piscitelli, Brent Savage, Jacque Schneider, Maggie Ubertini, Dan Whetstine, Erin Zeltner

Proofreaders: Laura Albert, Corey Bowen, John Greenough, Marianne Santy, Kathleen Sparrow, Charles Spencer

---

General and Administrative

IDG Books Worldwide, Inc.: John Kilcullen, CEO; Steven Berkowitz, President and Publisher

IDG Books Technology Publishing Group: Richard Swadley, Senior Vice President and Publisher; Walter Bruce III, Vice President and Associate Publisher; Joseph Wikert, Associate Publisher; Mary Bednarek, Branded Product Development Director; Mary Corder, Editorial Director; Barry Pruett, Publishing Manager; Michelle Baxter, Publishing Manager

IDG Books Consumer Publishing Group: Roland Elgey, Senior Vice President and Publisher; Kathleen A. Welton, Vice President and Publisher; Kevin Thornton, Acquisitions Manager; Kristin A. Cocks, Editorial Director

IDG Books Internet Publishing Group: Brenda McLaughlin, Senior Vice President and Publisher; Diane Graves Steele, Vice President and Associate Publisher; Sofia Marchant, Online Marketing Manager

IDG Books Production for Dummies Press: Debbie Stailey, Associate Director of Production; Cindy L. Phipps, Manager of Project Coordination, Production Proofreading, and Indexing; Tony Augsburger, Manager of Prepress, Reprints, and Systems; Laura Carpenter, Production Control Manager; Shelley Lea, Supervisor of Graphics and Design; Debbie J. Gates, Production Systems Specialist; Robert Springer, Supervisor of Proofreading; Kathie Schutte, Production Supervisor

Dummies Packaging and Book Design: Patty Page, Manager, Promotions Marketing

◆

The publisher would like to give special thanks to Patrick J. McGovern, without whom this book would not have been possible.

◆

Contents at a Glance

Cartoons at a Glance

By Rich Tennant

page 293

page 101

page 47

page 177

page 5

Fax: 978-546-7747
E-mail: richtennant@the5thwave.com
World Wide Web: www.the5thwave.com

Table of Contents

Introduction

*1*f you don't know the difference between a maple and an oak, and can't tell a rhododendron from a rose bush, this book is for you. This book assumes that you have no prior knowledge of trees and shrubs or how to care for them, but that you need to know enough to keep your property looking respectable and your plants alive. If this sounds like you, tote this book to the cash register right now. You can read the cartoons while you stand in line.

Growing trees and shrubs isn't rocket science and it isn't magic. But, unlike the petunias that you pull up at the end of the summer and toss on the compost heap, trees and shrubs live a long time. Planting them carries with it a responsibility to the people who will live with your decision for years to come. In this book, you can find enough information to make responsible choices about what to plant and where to plant it.

How to Use This Book

Feel free to dive into chapters that contain the information you need right now, and skip ones that you don't need yet. Thumb through the chapters to get a feel for the layout and location of interesting topics. Take a look at the Table of Contents or skip to the Index. Or just open the book randomly and see where it takes you.

Everything you need to know about a particular subject is contained in the corresponding chapter. Really. ...*For Dummies* books are designed that way, so that you don't have to search all over the place to find answers. However, when another part of the book can shed additional light on the subject at hand, I suggest where to look for more information.

Conventions Used in This Book

The plants in this book are arranged into two parts: Part II for trees and Part III for shrubs. Within each part, I've divided the plants into chapters based on their major attributes, such as whether they're grown mainly for foliage and flowers. Each chapter lists the plants within it alphabetically by botanical name — and that's where it gets tricky. Chapter 1 can help.

Throughout the plant descriptions in Parts II and III, I refer to the USDA Plant Hardiness Zone Map, which is based on the average minimum temperatures of an area. Where I've listed temperatures, they are given in degrees Fahrenheit. See the color photo section, near the center of this book , for a look at your hardiness zone.

How This Book Is Organized

I organize this book into parts that follow a logical sequence. In the first part, I introduce the whole idea of trees and shrubs and how to use them. In Parts II and III, I go on (and on) about the trees and shrubs themselves. The fourth part helps you choose plants and keep them healthy after you get them home. Finally, the book ends with five chapters full of useful lists and landscaping ideas.

Part I: Adding Trees and Shrubs to Your Landscape

Like getting a tattoo, deciding where to plant a tree is a momentous occasion that you may celebrate or regret for years to come. In this part, you get a feel for what makes a shrub a shrub and a tree a tree and how to use each type in the landscape. I also discuss the nitty-gritty of planning landscapes and making wise plant choices. Read this part before you take up your shovel!

Part II: Selecting Trees for All Seasons

The chapters in this part showcase the best and brightest trees for your landscape. Whether you want a flowering tree or something for shade; an evergreen or a tree with part-time leaves, you can find it here. Each chapter is organized alphabetically by fancy botanical names (see Chapter 1 for more information), but I list the common names of each tree first to making finding your favorites easier.

Part III: Choosing Shrubs for Any Location

If you're overwhelmed by all the different shrubs at the garden center and don't know where to begin — start here. In this part, I separate the shrubs into easy-to-handle groups. Look to evergreen shrubs for good hedge plants and shrubs that keep their foliage year round. Deciduous shrubs lose their leaves, but offer attractive foliage from spring to fall. Flowering shrubs add sparkling color and heavenly fragrance to your landscape.

Part IV: Buying, Planting, and Caring for Your Trees and Shrubs

In this part, you get the scoop on how to select a healthy tree or shrub at the garden center and know what to do with it after you get it home. Turn to this part to keep it happy and healthy with food and water and mulch; clip it into shape with the right pruning cuts; and ward off bad bugs, noxious diseases, and environmental hazards. This part even tells you know when and who to call for help.

Part V: The Part of Tens

When you go shopping, you always take a list — right? What better way to end this book than with a set of handy-dandy lists that you can consult before you head over to the garden center? Look in this part for trees and shrubs suitable for every situation, as well as a few to avoid. If you need landscaping ideas, you can find some here, too.

Color photo section

Fitting all the plants in this book into 24 color pages near the center of this book was impossible, no matter how hard we tried. We did manage to squeeze in several dozen important and common landscape trees and shrubs, however. These photos show the wide range of forms and foliage, from which you can choose when making decisions about your own landscape. Use them for inspiration! To help you figure out if a particular tree or shrub will grow in your area, we also include USDA Zone Maps that give the average winter minimum temperatures for the United States, Canada, and Europe.

Icons Used in This Book

To help you find some of the really important ideas and facts more quickly; I have put icons on the page margins. An *icon* is a little picture that tells a bigger story. Here's what they mean:

I can't refrain from offering friendly advice from time to time. This icon alerts you to a good idea — something that saves you time or money, helps you make a better decision, or is good for the environment.

With this icon, I introduce and define some words that may be unfamiliar to you. Use this icon to increase your vocabulary!

This icon gives you fair warning. When you spot it, stop and consider the consequences. It alerts you to actions that may be dangerous to you, your trees and shrubs, or the environment.

When you want more information about where to find particular plants, equipment, or help, look for this symbol.

For detailed descriptions of the largest and most important tree and shrub groups, look for this icon in the margins.

When I give an important fact or bit of useful information that you need to keep in mind, I use this icon.

Where to Go From Here

Not sure what to do next? I suggest picking a hot topic (say, the one that caused you to pick up this book in the first place), and flipping to the chapters that covers that information.

Whether you have a blank-canvas landscape or a yard full of mature trees and shrubs, you should find the answers to your questions in this book. Part I gives you all you need to know to plan your landscape and choose the right plants. Parts II and III describe the most common trees and shrubs. Turn to Part IV for tips on picking out healthy plants and keeping them that way. And I bet you've already looked at the Part V, the Part of Tens, but that's as good a place to start as any. Happy reading!

Part I

Adding Trees and Shrubs to Your Landscape

The 5th Wave   By Rich Tennant

In this part . . .

When is a tree not a tree? When it's a shrub! In Chapter 1, I magically demystify the anatomy of these plants. (No, Toto, don't look behind that curtain!) If you regret not taking Latin in high school when you had the chance, you can get a painless glimpse of what you missed here. And if that's not exciting enough for you, skip to the end of Chapter 1 for the "what's in it for me" section.

If you plan to plant shrubs and trees, organize your yard, or just get a grip on your landscape, stroll on over to Chapter 2. That's where you get to play with crayons and paper and scissors. You'll be talking like a designer when you're done.

Chapter 1

Trees and Shrubs from the Roots Up

- -

In This Chapter

▶ Recognizing the difference between a tree and a shrub

▶ Identifying the useful and ornamental parts of trees and shrubs

▶ Understanding the lingo of plant names

▶ Knowing what trees and shrubs can do for you and your landscape

- -

T rees and shrubs form the permanent parts of your landscape, unlike the annual and perennial plants that fade away between seasons. These permanent elements provide the structure around which you plan and plant everything else. Landscaping with trees and shrubs can save you money, too, by reducing your heating and cooling costs.

If you don't know a tree from a shrub, read on. Getting to know the parts of plants helps you choose the right plant for your site and ask the right questions at the garden center. Knowing the lingo also helps you understand the salesclerk's answers.

If the names written on the plant labels look like Greek to you, this chapter gives you an explanation of how to decipher those tongue-twisting appellations.

Examining the Anatomy of Trees and Shrubs

Trees and shrubs share several characteristics. For example, trees and shrubs have hardened stems and trunks that survive from year to year in favorable environments. These *woody stems* also increase in diameter as the plant grows. Some shrubs die to the ground each year if you plant them in unsuitable climates, but in their *natural range,* where they normally grow, their stems endure from one year to the next.

Historic and social heritage

Trees form a living link to personal and collective histories. Old trees serve as points of reference in neighborhoods where residents sorely miss them if they die or must be removed. Whenever diseases or insects threaten trees, such as elms that shaded so many city streets and rural farmyards, communities make heroic efforts to preserve them.

Trees and shrubs often memorialize special events — famous battles, births, and deaths. You can purchase young trees grown from seeds that flew to the moon on Apollo XIV or were harvested from trees growing at the John F. Kennedy Memorial Gravesite. My family prizes a white pine that we planted as a seedling when my son was born. We have buried beloved pets beneath its roots and watch for nesting birds in its branches each spring.

Ancient cultures worshipped trees and the spirits within them. While most people don't view trees quite that reverently anymore, trees do contribute to your living history and connection to the past and to the future. Local organizations all over the country are dedicated to planting and preserving trees. Contact the nonprofit American Forests organization at www.amfor.org or call (800) 368-5748 for more information about purchasing trees from famous and historic sites, Global ReLeaf, the National Register of Big Trees, and other community forestry programs they sponsor.

Trees and shrubs, which are often called *woody plants*, also share some anatomical features. Knowing something about the structure of trees and shrubs helps you make better decisions about which plant to buy and where to plant it to get the effect and level of maintenance you can live with. (See Chapter 11 for more information on purchasing trees and shrubs.)

Bottoms up

Trees and shrubs start underground with roots that anchor them to the soil and collect water and nutrients, as shown in Figure 1-1. *Anchoring roots* come in two basic forms:

- **Taproots:** Long, thick roots that grow vertically, deep into the soil. Some, but not all, trees and shrubs have taproots.

- **Perennial branch roots:** These roots grow horizontally under the surface of the soil.

Feeder roots absorb and transport nutrients and water to the rest of the tree or shrub. These small fibrous feeder roots grow mostly in the top 6 to 12 inches of the soil and can spread out two or three times wider than the aboveground branches.

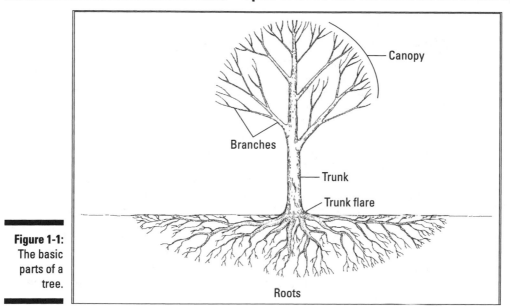

Figure 1-1:
The basic parts of a tree.

 The place where the roots meet the trunk of a tree is called the *trunk flare* because the trunk spreads out at this point. In shrubs, the root-shoot meetingplace is called the *crown*, shown in Figure 1-2. You find trunk flares and crowns right about ground level on healthy trees and shrubs. I talk more about planting trees and shrubs and the correct placement of their trunk flares and crowns in Chapter 11.

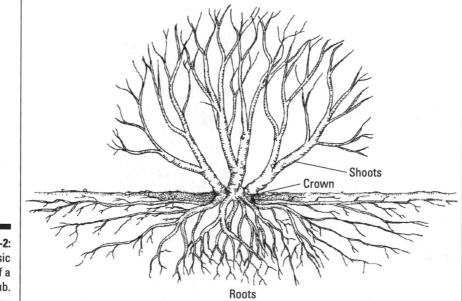

Figure 1-2:
The basic parts of a shrub.

Barking up a tree and around a shrub

Tree trunks and shrub stems rise directly from the roots and support the branches that grow from them. Like the shell of a clam, *bark* covers trunks, branches, and stems. The bark itself isn't alive — its function is to protect the living occupant that it surrounds.

If you scrape off the bark, you find the living layers of the trunk, branches, and stems called the *inner bark* and *cambium*. The cambium is a thin layer of xylem that's immediately inside. Food and water in the form of *sap* travel in the inner bark to the tips of every branch. The cambium is the part of the woody plant that causes its stems and trunk to increase in diameter each year.

You can see how much a stem or trunk has grown each year by looking at the width of its *growth rings*. For each year that a woody plant lives, it adds a new ring of wood. In years when a tree grew rapidly, such as when water, food, and sunlight was plentiful, the rings are wider than in years when the tree grew slowly due to drought, disease, or crowding from other trees. You can determine the age of a tree branch or trunk by counting the number of its growth rings.

Bark can have deep grooves in it or be smooth. The bark can wrap tightly to the trunk or peel off in papery pieces, a process known as *exfoliating*. (See Figure 1-3.) Colors can range from chalky white through nearly every color of the rainbow to black. When the leaves fall off your shrubs and trees in the autumn, the color and texture of their bark become important features in your winter garden.

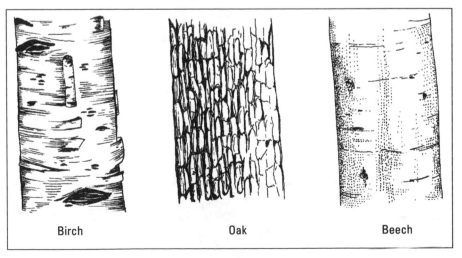

Figure 1-3: Bark protects the living wood underneath it and adds texture to your yard or garden.

Birch   Oak   Beech

Out on a limb

Plants grow new branches, leaves, and flowers from *buds* on the twigs or shoots, as shown in Figure 1-4. As the buds at the tips of the twigs expand, the branches grow longer and the new growth is frequently a different color than the older wood. When buds below the branch tip expand, they form new branches. Between each year's growth on a shoot, you often can see a raised ring of bark. The length and number of new shoots that a plant makes each year is called its *vigor*. Some very vigorous trees can grow more than 2 feet per year.

The way that branches grow gives a tree or shrub its character. Some branches grow nearly straight up like a military procession, some spread out horizontally like fence rails, while others weep and cascade like a waterfall.

The size and number of a plant's branches and twigs make a difference, too. Thin twigs have a lacy, fine-textured appearance, but plants with fewer, larger twigs often look bold or coarse.

Figure 1-4:
Branches, flowers, and leaves of trees and shrubs grow from buds on the twigs.

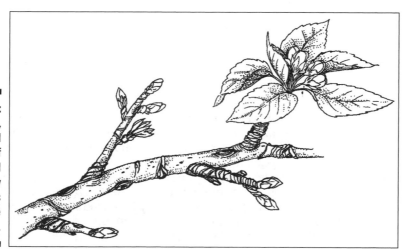

Leafing out

Woody plants come in a few basic flavors, and you can tell what flavor you're dealing with by knowing about its *foliage,* or leaves. At the most basic level all the leaves either fall off the tree or shrub in the autumn or they don't. *Deciduous* trees and shrubs go naked for part of the year. *Evergreen* plants modestly hold on to their foliage, dropping just a few leaves at a time, but never all of them at once.

Evergreens have two different kinds of foliage — narrow needle-like foliage and wide, flat leaves. The trees and shrubs with needles that remain green year round are called *coniferous evergreens.* Plant people refer to evergreens with wide, flat leaves as *broad-leaf evergreens.* (See Figure 1-5.)

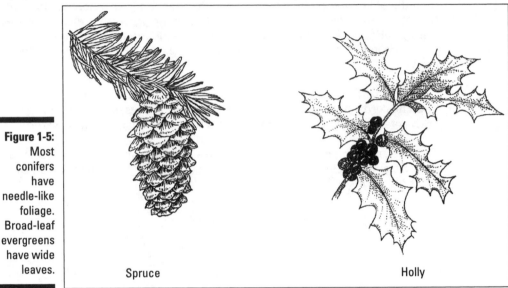

Figure 1-5:
Most conifers have needle-like foliage. Broad-leaf evergreens have wide leaves.

Spruce   Holly

Leaves come in so many different shapes that plant people have given each shape a name. The name often describes how the leaf looks; for example, a *serrated leaf* has an edge that resembles the notched edge of a knife.

Compound leaves have three or more *leaflets* combined to form one big leaf. You can tell the difference between a leaf and a leaflet by looking at how each is attached to the plant. Leaves attach directly to a perennial woody branch or shoot and have a bud at the point of attachment, but leaflets attach to a bud-less stalk that falls off when the plant sheds its foliage. Figure 1-6 shows a few of the basic shapes that you can read more about in Parts II and III of this book.

Colorful foliage turns a plain-Jane plant into a showstopper. Thanks to plant breeders, many trees and shrubs now come in designer colors such as red, purple and pink, light green, dark green, and various shades of golden yellow. *Variegated foliage* combines green with white, yellow, or other-colored streaks and edges. Plant breeders have also enhanced the naturally vivid autumn colors of some deciduous trees.

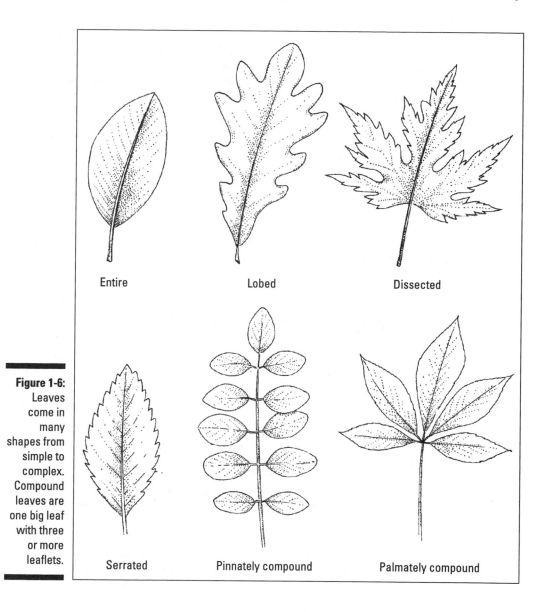

Figure 1-6: Leaves come in many shapes from simple to complex. Compound leaves are one big leaf with three or more leaflets.

Entire   Lobed   Dissected

Serrated   Pinnately compound   Palmately compound

Flowers, fruits, and nuts

Visitors flock to Washington, D.C., each spring to witness the spectacle of cherry trees in bloom. Roses — celebrated in festivals and parades — are Americans' favorite flowering shrubs. Flowering trees and shrubs add color, fragrance, and drama to your landscape.

If you plan to grow flowering trees and shrubs for their fruits or nuts, however, you need to know that some plants are male, some are female, and some are both. For those plants with separate male and female plants, you need at least one of each sex to produce fruits, but only the female bears fruit. Some plants, such as apple trees, have both male and female flower parts on the same tree, but they are incompatible and can't form fruit. They need the pollen of another tree of a different variety to set fruit. This is called *cross-pollination*. In other words, to get 'Red Delicious' apples on your tree, you need a 'Granny Smith' or some other kind of apple that blooms at the same time planted nearby.

The fruit or flowers of some plants are so messy or foul smelling that you might want to avoid the particular sex of plant that produces them. Plant breeders have been busy working on these problems, too, and have produced many fine plants with better flowers and fruit and without the offending characteristics. Parts II and III offer more details about flowering and fruiting trees and shrubs, especially those with nice flowers or attractive fruit. Chapter 18 lists trees with messy fruits, nuts, and flowers.

Sorting Out the Trees from the Shrubs

Figuring out the difference between shrubs and trees can be confusing. Luckily, plant people have some rules to keep everyone speaking the same language. Plant people love rules and language, as you can see in the section titled, "Naming Names" in this chapter. You can use the following guidelines to distinguish trees from shrubs:

- **Trees:** These plants usually have a single main stem that gets thicker with age and develops large secondary branches and limbs. Some trees appear to have more than one trunk, but often, what you see are actually several trees growing close together in a clump. Trees that have been injured sometimes send up two or more trunks, too, but that is not their usual habit.

- **Shrubs:** By nature, shrubs have lots of woody stems coming from a central growing point under or close to the ground. Shrubs often form a dense tangle of stems called *thickets*. The stems on a shrub usually don't grow large side branches — shrubs generally grow to less than 20 feet high. The line between trees and shrubs gets blurred when a tall shrub is pruned so that it has a single trunk. For the purposes of this book, I consider a plant a shrub if its natural habit is to grow multi-stemmed and shorter than 20 feet.

Naming Names

Plant people are guilty of speaking in garden jargon, going on and on about the latest this and the latest that. These folks toss out words that are as inscrutable as the directions for getting your VCR, satellite dish, TV, and stereo system all working in harmony. If fancy plant names confuse and frustrate you as much as television systems confuse me, this section can help you. I share a few tips about deciphering those unpronounceable names; and in just a few short paragraphs you will understand how plant names work — in plain English.

Common names

Within a region, most people recognize a familiar plant by its *common name* or nickname. When you travel outside of your area, the same plant may have a different common name. To further complicate matters, many plants have several common names within the same region, and sorting out the names gets really confusing.

Plants often get their common name from

- A special characteristic, like the long, flowing limbs of the weeping willow
- A historical use, such as arrowwood
- Its native country, like Japanese maple
- Its habitat, such as swamp maple

Plants that share a common feature or habitat often share a nickname. For example, more than one kind of maple grows in swamps, yet several have the same common name, swamp maple. Who knows whether you will end up with an *Acer rubrum* or an *Acer saccharinum* if you just ask for a swamp maple at a tree nursery?

Common names just aren't precise enough when you're looking for a specific plant. Three different trees share the common name sycamore, for example. If I want to buy the sycamore that has creamy green bark when it's mature, I need to know more than the common name — I have to know its fancy name.

Fancy names

Each plant has a fancy name, called a *botanical name,* which helps keep everyone on the same page about which plant is which. You may have seen some of these botanical names (which are always underlined or in italics) on the front of seed packages, plant labels, and in other books — *Juniperus horizontalis*, *Rosa rugosa*, and *Magnolia stellata*, for example. If these names look like Greek to you, don't worry. They're actually Latin names, and each part of these names has its use. The first part is called the *genus*, the second is the *species*, and the *variety* and *cultivar* parts come at the end. With each added element, the name becomes more specific. For example, *Acer* is the genus that describes all the maples. Adding the second part of the name, such as *palmatum*, specifies just Japanese maple. The cultivar name 'Bloodgood' at the end differentiates a specific kind of Japanese maple with characteristics distinct from other Japanese maples.

Genus names

The first part of a plant's botanical name, the *genus,* always begins with a capital letter. Like the members of a large family, plants that share a genus are related, but not necessarily just alike. You probably have cousins, aunts, and uncles all over the country with whom you share the same last name and family heritage, but you don't look alike or enjoy the same climate or activities. For example, your Aunt Maude likes sunny Florida, Cousin Suzy is a rock climber in Wyoming, and Uncle Harold loves the coast of Maine. Plants in the same genus also may thrive in very different places, but have something in their anatomy that makes them kin. For example, all the maples share the genus name *Acer* whether they grow in Canada or China.

Species names

The second part of the botanical name — the *species* — sets a plant apart from other plants in its genus, like a first name sets you apart from your mother or your Uncle Fred. The species name appears in all lowercase letters; for example, *Acer palmatum*.

When botanists name plant species, they often use the name to describe a characteristic of the plant. This approach is really helpful after you understand the code. Some of the code words are easy to recognize — *canadensis* means the plant came from Canada, while *caroliniana* refers to the Carolinas. If you are looking for a plant that can survive in your frigid winter climate, *Amelanchier canadensis* is probably a better choice than *Prunus caroliniana*. Species names also commonly refer to the color of the plant's flowers, shape of its leaf, or growth habit. *Rubrum* or *rubra* means red, *prostratus* species lie flat, and *palmata* or *palmatum* means palm-shaped. So *Acer palmatum* is a maple with palm-shaped leaves.

Variety names

Plant people keep tinkering with plants and, whenever they invent a new one, they have to name it. Luckily, plant names have to follow some naming rules (although plant people like to argue about *how* to follow them). When one of these new plants is still pretty much the same as the old plant, but with say, a different flower color or leaf shape, the botanical name gets a third part — the *variety* name.

Variety names follow the species name, are written in small letters, and are either italicized or underlined. The "var." part in the middle is the abbreviation for *variety* and doesn't get italicized. For example, Japanese maples that have deeply cleft or *dissected* leaves become *Acer palmatum* var. *dissectum*.

Cultivars

Plant variety parents pass their specific characteristics to their seedling offspring. When the plant tinkering results in a new plant that can pass on its unique characteristics only by cloning, cuttings, or division, the new plant is called a *cultivar*. (In rare instances, cultivars can be propagated by seed.) Cultivar is the abbreviation for cultivated variety.

The cultivar name begins with a capital letter and is enclosed in single quotation marks at the end of the botanical name. This part of the name also does not appear in italics or underlined. An example of a cultivar is *Acer palmatum* 'Bloodgood', a Japanese maple with dark reddish-purple foliage. The whole fancy name for the Japanese maple cultivar 'Garnet', which has reddish-purple, deeply dissected leaves is *Acer palmatum* var. *dissectum atropurpureum* 'Garnet'. Now that's a mouthful!

Abbreviations

Botanical names can get pretty long, so botanists use some abbreviations to cut down on their typing time (people after my own heart!). After the first mention of a genus name, then using just its first letter in all the following references is okay. *Acer palmatum* becomes *A. palmatum*. If I introduce another character from the same genus, I can continue to use the abbreviation, such as *A. rubrum*, the red or swamp maple. If I want to refer to maples in general, I can call them *Acer* species or *Acer* sp., for short.

The benefits of trees and shrubs in the landscape

More than providing aesthetic pleasure, trees and shrubs make several practical contributions to your home's landscape.

- **Defining space:** Walls define the outside boundaries of your house and enclose the private space in which you live. The trees and shrubs in your yard perform similar functions as the walls and ceiling of your house. Shrubs separate your yard from everyone else's and, within your yard, screen private areas from public view. These plants also block unsightly service areas, like dumpsters and gas tanks, from spoiling the beauty of your landscape.

- **Controlling movement:** Trees and shrubs guide the way that people, wind, and sight travel through the landscape. Hedges or groups of shrubs show people where they may or may not walk. The arrangement of shrubs and trees guides our eye through the landscape. You can use plants to block views or call attention to them (see Chapter 2).

- **Environmental benefits:** Trees and the environment go hand-in-hand. Plants improve air quality by absorbing carbon dioxide and other pollutants, such as ozone, carbon monoxide, and sulfur dioxide, and then turning them into food and oxygen. Plantings of trees and shrubs for windbreaks slow the wind, which prevents soil from blowing away and protects crops; prevents drifting and blowing snow along highways; and helps hold the snow and moisture on your property in arid climates.

Trees and shrubs also help control storm run-off and erosion, and bring a natural element to urban landscapes, giving homes to welcome birds and wildlife and providing them with nuts and berries to eat.

- **Show me the money:** Reduce your heating and cooling costs with trees and shrubs. Foliage deflects and absorbs the rays of the sun and, in return, gives off moisture that cools the air — a valuable resource in cities and around paved areas. Studies show that shade on your roof from nearby trees can reduce the temperature in your attic by as much as 40°. Shaded air-conditioning units operate two to four times more efficiently, too.

Attractively landscaped homes are worth 5 percent to 20 percent more than homes without trees and shrubs, according to U.S. Forest Service studies. *The Wall Street Journal* reports that you can expect to fully recover and sometimes double the money you invest in your landscaping by increasing your home's value.

Chapter 2

Mapping Out Your Landscape Plan

. . . .

In This Chapter

▶ Analyzing your yard and planning for your landscape needs

▶ Making your landscape plan

▶ Finding out about climate and its effect on trees and shrubs

▶ Identifying the characteristics of trees and shrubs

▶ Putting the right trees and shrubs in the right places

. . . .

*B*efore you can match the right trees and shrubs to your landscape, you have to know the unique benefits and shortcomings of your site. In this chapter, you get to examine all the parts of your landscape, such as sun, water, soil, views, slopes, and wind, in a process called *site analysis.* As you analyze your site, you can start dreaming about how you want to use your space.

Each tree and shrub also has a unique combination of characteristics, such as shape, size, color, texture, and growing requirements. When you know what your site has to offer, you can match the right plant attributes to suit your site and your goals.

Analyzing Your Site — Appraising and Mapping Your Assets

In many ways, analyzing your landscape is exactly like making a meal plan and checking the contents of your kitchen before heading out to the grocery store. You can skip the inventory and planning, but chances are, you will buy items that you didn't need or forget something important. Unlike groceries, however, trees and shrubs remain a part of your landscape for many years, so figuring out what you need before you take a drive to the garden center really pays off.

Diagram your yard

Your first project is to map and inventory the parts of your landscape and note your site's strengths and weaknesses on paper. Grab an 8½-by-11-inch pad of paper, a clipboard, pencil, and tape measure and head outside. Here's how to do a site analysis:

1. **Make a drawing of your property, including buildings and property lines.**

   Use your tape measure and do your best to draw to scale, with everything in the correct proportion to everything else, but don't worry, neatness doesn't count at this stage. Have a buddy hold the other end of the tape measure to speed this process.

   Record the location of windows and doors; the driveway; pool; and existing structures such as fences, the deck or patio, tool shed, or gazebo; and where you park the boat for the winter. Make an arrow on your map to indicate the direction of north — you'll need that information later.

2. **Walk around your property with your map and take notes about the following natural features.**

   - **Sun and shade:** Label the sunny and shady spots around your yard, especially if you want to change them or take advantage of them. Observe the patterns of sun and shade around your buildings and trees at different times of the day and year, if possible.

   - **Views:** Note the location of nice and not-so-nice views both into and out of your property. Remember to check the views as you look out your windows, too.

   - **Soil, slope, and water:** Draw arrows on your map that point down slopes. Circle areas where water pools or runs after a rainstorm. Note whether your soil stays muddy or drains quickly.

   - **Wind:** Note the direction and strength of the prevailing winds across your site at different times of the year.

   - **Existing plants and natural features:** Use circles to draw existing trees and shrubs. Record the width of the plant *canopy* by measuring from one edge of the *drip line* — where rain drips from the foliage to the ground — to the other. Note the location and sizes of gardens, large rocks, streams, ponds, and other features you want to preserve.

That's it! Your map may look like the example in Figure 2-1 when you're done. Now that you have a rough idea of what you have to work with and have a few goals in mind, look through the next few pages for more detailed information about the features in your landscape and how trees and shrubs fit into the picture.

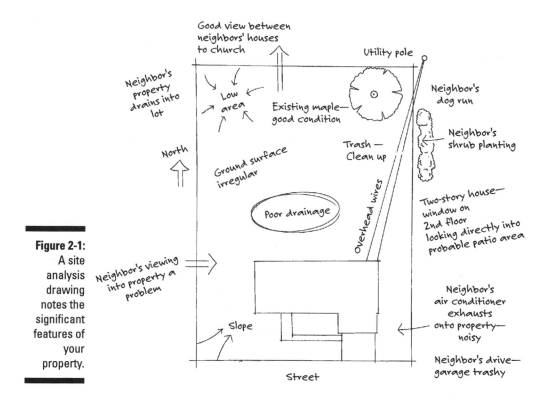

Figure 2-1:
A site analysis drawing notes the significant features of your property.

Sun and shade

Your *latitude* or where you live in relation to the equator determines the sun's intensity, how high it rises in the sky, and how long it shines at different times of the year. The patterns of sun and shade on your property also change throughout the seasons and times of day, as you can see in Figure 2-2. On June 21, the longest day of the year, the sun rises highest in the sky.

The sun shines more strongly in southern latitudes, affecting how plants grow. Some plants that tolerate *full sun* — 6 hours or more of direct sunlight each day — in Seattle, Washington, wither in the full sun of Houston, Texas.

Shade has different intensities, too, depending on its location and when it occurs:

- **Deep or dense shade** occurs where no direct sun shines, such as on the north sides of buildings and under trees with dense foliage.

- **Partial shade** occurs in spots that receive about 4 to 6 hours of direct sun in the morning or afternoon, but none at midday between approximately 10:00 A.M. and 2:00 P.M.

- **Dappled or light shade** falls under trees with sparse foliage or high branches.

Figure 2-2:
Where the
sun rises
and sets
and how
high it rises
in the sky
changes
throughout
the year.

June 21

Dec 21

The longest shadows occur when the sun is low on the horizon — early and late in the day and in the winter months, especially in northern latitudes. Understanding when and how strongly the sun shines on your site enables you to plant trees and shrubs where you can gain the most benefit. Shading your home during the hottest hours and days of the year, but letting in the winter sun's warming rays saves you money and keeps your home comfortable year round.

Views

Note the location of views that you want to preserve — a distant mountain, river, flower garden, skyline, or sunset. Go inside your house and look out the windows and jot down what you see. Also note views that you want to hide, such as the neighbor's compost bin or a busy road. Does the view change when the trees lose their leaves in the fall?

Now consider the views into your property. Can neighbors or passers by look into your windows or patio? Do they see a cheerful garden or your recycling bins? You can use shrubs and trees to increase your privacy and hide or enhance your views, as shown in Figure 2-3. You can find more information about using trees and shrubs to enhance your views in the section titled, "Matching Trees and Shrubs to Your Site" in this chapter.

I used to believe that trees and shrubs blocked sound until I moved to a house near the highway. Even though we have a hedge and lots of trees between the road and us, the sound of trucks, trains, and cars comes through crystal clear. According to the engineers and landscape architects that study how to block sound, you have to install a planting of dense-foliaged evergreens at least a 100 feet wide to begin to make a dent in the noise. Now they tell us. Trees' and shrubs' greatest value is screening the source of the sound from view. Plants also soften the look of barriers, such as solid fences, walls, and earth mounds, which really do block sound.

Figure 2-3:
Screen objection-able views and create privacy with shrubs and trees.

Soil

Plant roots, which may comprise more than half of the plant's structure, absorb water and nutrients from the soil to make food. Most trees and shrubs can adapt to a wide range of soil conditions, but they grow best in soil that closely matches their genetically programmed needs. Completely changing the soil in your yard to suit your plants is impossible; choosing plants to match your soil is easier.

You may be surprised to find that a favorite plant may not grow as well in one part of your yard as it does in another. The answer can lie in the differences in the soil pH, texture, and drainage. All these factors, combined, affect how your trees and shrubs grow. Take a look at what you need to know about your soil:

Soil texture

Soil consists of mineral particles, organic matter, and air spaces. Of the three sizes of mineral particles, sand is the largest, clay the smallest, and silt is in between. The relative proportion of each particle type in your soil determines its texture.

The broad categories of soil textures and their characteristics are

✔ **Sandy:** Water and nutrients drain through sandy soil quickly, making it less fertile and more drought-prone than other soils. Sandy soils feel rough and gritty between your fingers.

✔ **Clay:** Clay particles pack together tightly, causing water and nutrients to pass through them slowly. Soils with a lot of clay in them stick to your shoes when wet and crack when dry.

✔ **Loam:** A mixture composed of sand, clay, and silt in roughly equal proportions, loam soils combine the best qualities of each in that they drain moderately well and hold nutrients. Ideal loam soils contain about 40 percent sand, 40 percent silt, and 20 percent clay.

To quickly identify your soil's texture, take a handful of moist soil, squeeze it into a ball, and work it out in a ribbon between your thumb and your forefinger. Stand the ribbon straight up in the air.

✔ If you can't form a ribbon, the soil is at least 50 percent sand and has very little clay.

✔ If the ribbon is less than 2 inches long before breaking, your soil has roughly 25 percent clay in it.

✔ If the ribbon is 2 to 3½-inches long, it has about 40 percent clay.

✔ If the ribbon is greater than 3½-inches long and doesn't break when held up, it is at least 50 percent clay.

Soil drainage

Soil structure, the way in which sand, silt, and clay particles combine, determines how well soil drains or retains moisture. When the particles clump tightly together — become compacted — with little air space between them, water cannot pass easily through the soil. When the soil contains large air space, such as occurs in sandy soils, water passes through too quickly.

Adding organic matter improves your soil's structure because, as it decays, the organic matter helps form *humus*. Humus enables clay soils to drain more quickly and sandy soils to hold more moisture and nutrients.

You can determine how well your soil drains with the following test.

1. **Dig a hole 1 foot deep by 1 foot wide near where you intend to plant a tree or shrub.**

2. **Cover the hole with a sheet of plastic, if rain threatens, and let the soil dry out.**

3. **When the soil is dry, fill the hole to the top with water and record the time it takes for the water to completely drain.**

   The ideal time is between 10 and 30 minutes.

   • If the water drains in less than 10 minutes, choose shrubs and trees that can tolerate drought.

- If it takes 30 minutes to 4 hours to drain, most trees and shrubs will grow well, but water them slowly to avoid runoff and to allow the water to soak in deeply.

- If your soil takes longer than 4 hours to drain, poor drainage may prevent you from growing all but the most moisture tolerant plants. Sometimes a hard layer of clay or mineral deposits below the surface blocks water movement. Break through this layer, if possible, before planting your trees or shrubs.

Soil pH

Soil pH, a measure of a substance's alkalinity or acidity, is important to your trees and shrubs because certain nutrients are available to plants only within a specific pH range.

Soil pH is measured on a scale of 1 to 14. Most soils fall between pH 5, which is strongly acidic, and 9, which is very alkaline. Neutral soils measure pH 7. Gardeners sometimes refer to alkaline soil as *sweet* and acidic soil as *sour.*

The nutrients that plants need are most readily available in the range from pH 6.0 to 7.0. Some plants, such as acid-loving rhododendrons and blueberries, prefer a pH below 6.0. Usually, areas of high rainfall, such as the U.S. Northeast and Northwest, have low pH soils, while areas with low rainfall, such as the Southwest, have high pH soils.

You can buy a kit to accurately test your soil's pH or do the following fizz test to get a ballpark idea of what you have to work with.

- ✔ To check whether your soil is severely alkaline, take a tablespoon of dried garden soil and add a few drops of vinegar. If the soil fizzes, the pH is above 7.5.

- ✔ To check for acidity in the soil, take a tablespoon of muddy, wet soil and add a pinch of fresh baking soda. If the soil fizzes, the soil is probably very acidic with a pH less than 5.0.

If you find that your soil pH is out of the 6.0 to 7.0 range, you can alter it temporarily by adding lime to make it more alkaline or sulfur to make it more acidic. The best way to determine how much lime or sulfur your soil needs is to bring a sample of your soil to a garden center or send it to a soil-testing lab. You can find a testing lab by calling your local extension service or a garden center. After testing it for pH and soil texture, the lab can recommend the right amendment and amount to apply. You can find out much more about testing your soil in *Gardening For Dummies,* 2nd Edition, by Michael MacCaskey, Bill Marken, and the Editors of The National Gardening Association (IDG Books Worldwide, Inc.). Unless your conditions are extreme, however, choosing trees and shrubs to match your soil gives your plants a better chance of survival in the long run.

Slope and water

The most important aspect of slope in your landscape, as far as trees and shrubs are concerned, is its influence on how water moves across the surface of the soil. On steep slopes, fast-moving water can wash the soil away from their roots. In flat landscapes, water sometimes puddles around them. People who work with soil often describe the steepness of a hill as *percent slope*.

The following steps show you how to measure the percent of a slope. (See Figure 2-4.):

1. **Assemble your tools.**

   You need a carpenter's level, tape measure, a 10-foot straightedge, and a buddy.

2. **Position the straightedge and level.**

   Set one end of the straightedge at the top of the slope and support the other end over the downhill slope. Place the carpenter's level in the middle of the straightedge. Adjust the downhill side of the straightedge up and down until the carpenter's level shows that the straightedge is level. The length of the straightedge is called the horizontal *run*.

3. **Measure the height of the straightedge.**

   Have your buddy measure the distance from the downhill end of the straightedge to the ground. The height of the slope at that point is called its vertical *rise*.

4. **Calculate the percent slope.**

   Use the following formula to calculate the percentage of your slope:

   (vertical rise ÷ horizontal run) x 100 = percent slope

For example, if the rise or distance from the ground to the end of the straightedge is 2 feet and the run or length of the straightedge is 20 feet, your percent slope is 10 percent.

Water moves very slowly and may puddle on grassy, 2 percent slopes. On steeper slopes, however, water moves more quickly and can wash away the soil. Plant roots hold the soil in place while their foliage decreases the impact of heavy rain on the soil surface. On slopes that measure greater than 20 percent, use shrubs or other low maintenance, ground-covering plants that don't require mowing.

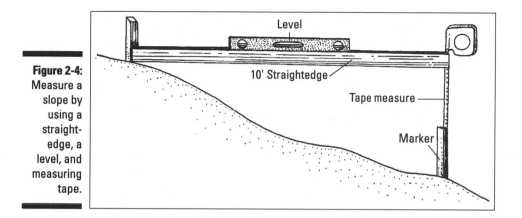

Figure 2-4:
Measure a slope by using a straight-edge, a level, and measuring tape.

Wind

If your site lacks protection from hills or trees or if you live near tall urban buildings, strong winds may blow through your yard. Wind contributes to soil erosion and plays a role in how well plants survive the winter in freezing climates. Gentle breezes cool hot summer days and help prevent some plant diseases, but gusty and stormy winds blow away your patio chairs and break tree limbs.

If you want more protection from the wind, you can plant a *windbreak*. Windbreaks planted perpendicular to the prevailing wind offer the most protection, but they must be at the right height and distance from the place you want to protect. For the most wind protection, use the following guidelines.

✔ Determine the direction of the prevailing winds by noting from which direction the wind usually blows. If you aren't sure, ask a neighbor or call the National Weather Service bureau in your state.

✔ Walk into the prevailing wind and measure the distance from the area you want protected to the place you want to plant a dense hedge or row of trees.

✔ To find the height of the trees or shrubs you must plant, divide the distance by four. That is the tallest height you need. Divide the distance by ten to find the lowest effective height for your windbreak. The taller the windbreak and the closer it is to the protected area, the greater its protection.

✔ The windbreak should extend 50 to 100 feet beyond the area you are protecting for maximum effectiveness.

If, for example, you want to protect your house from a prevailing northwesterly wind, plant a 10- to 25-foot-tall windbreak 100 feet from the northwest side of your house. Extend both ends of the windbreak at least 50 feet beyond the length of your house.

Weathering the Climate

Climate refers to the long-term prevailing weather conditions — temperature, humidity, precipitation, and wind patterns — of a place. Distance from the equator, elevation above sea level, and position relative to mountains and large bodies of water affect climate. Plants genetically adapt to live in certain climates, but not in others. Cacti, for example, survive perfectly well in the hot, arid southwestern deserts, but apple trees do not.

Usually when you consider climate, you may think of large regions such as Florida, the Northeast, the Pacific Northwest, the Midwest, or Southern California. But, smaller climate zones exist within these regions. The climate near the ocean differs from the climate 20 miles inland. The same holds true for a valley location versus the top of a 5,000-foot high mountain above it. The *Sunset National Garden Book* describes and maps 45 different climate zones throughout the United States and adjacent parts of Canada. The climate zone maps differ from the more familiar hardiness zone maps (discussed in the following section) by considering rainfall, humidity, wind, and sun intensity in addition to seasonal temperatures. You can also find information about the climate zone system and descriptions of the western zones (west of the Mississippi River) at Sunset Magazine's Web site at www.sunsetmag.com/magazine/magazineframe.html.

Microclimates

The smallest climates, such as those that exist around your home or neighborhood, are called *microclimates*. You can see and feel microclimates at work by standing on the sunny south side of a building and then walking around to the shady north side, or by facing into the wind and then stepping behind a wall that blocks the wind.

Microclimates differ in some way from the larger climate around them. You can use microclimates to your advantage to grow plants that otherwise might not survive in your climate. For example, if your climate is arid, take advantage of a spring or stream to grow moisture-loving shrubs. In cold climates, plant somewhat tender shrubs near a wall to shelter them from winter cold and wind. Large bodies of water help prevent temperature extremes, so you may be able to grow more tender plants. The bottom of a slope, however, is for extra hardy plants only because that's where cold air collects. (See Figure 2-5). Pushing the limits of your climate doesn't work in every case, but sometimes it's worth a try.

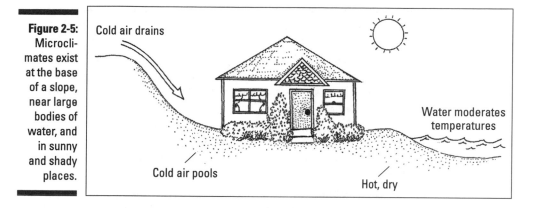

Figure 2-5: Microclimates exist at the base of a slope, near large bodies of water, and in sunny and shady places.

Cold air drains

Water moderates temperatures

Cold air pools

Hot, dry

Plant hardiness

No matter how much I love avocados and mangos, I simply can't grow them outdoors in the northeastern United States and expect them to produce fruit because the plants aren't *hardy* — freezing temperatures kill these tropical trees. When most people talk about plant hardiness, they are referring to a plant's ability to survive the coldest temperatures in a particular area — but it's not quite that simple. The following factors determine plant hardiness:

✔ **Genetics:** Plants inherit the ability to adapt to cold temperatures.

✔ **Stage of growth:** Trees and shrubs acclimate to winter cold by going through a series of physical changes. The timing of *acclimation,* or winter readiness, varies with each species. Early freezing may injure otherwise hardy plants that acclimate too late in the fall due to late-season planting, pruning, or fertilizing. See Part IV for more on caring for your plants.

✔ **Health:** Environmental stress, diseases, and pests weaken plants and make them less able to tolerate cold.

✔ **Plant parts:** Flower buds and roots usually cannot tolerate as cold a temperature as woody stems, and they may be damaged or killed before stem damage occurs.

A plant's ability to withstand the minimum winter temperature is only part of the story, however. The following aspects of climate also affect the hardiness of trees and shrubs:

✔ **Duration of winter:** Some plants are genetically programmed to begin flowering and growing after receiving a particular number of hours of cold temperatures followed by warm temperatures. The plant may *break dormancy* — begin growing — before winter is really over and be damaged by frost and freezing weather.

✔ **Duration of extreme cold:** A single night of unusually cold temperatures usually does less damage to woody plants than prolonged periods of extreme cold.

✔ **Wind:** Woody plants, especially those that keep their leaves all year round, lose moisture through their exposed parts. That lost moisture cannot be replaced while the plant is *dormant*, or not growing. Wind increases the moisture loss.

✔ **Precipitation:** Plants that receive adequate moisture during the growing season are hardier than those that suffer from drought. Snow also provides an insulating blanket that protects plant roots and stems from extreme cold.

✔ **Sun exposure:** Winter sun can thaw the bark of a tree during the day, but when the temperature suddenly drops at sunset, the bark may freeze and then split, damaging the tree. The sun can also increase moisture loss from winter foliage and stems.

Damage to plants caused by cold or excessive moisture loss during the winter is called *winter injury*. Flip to Chapter 15 to find out more about winter injury symptoms and prevention.

You can ensure the hardiness of a tree or shrub in your yard by considering the plant's *provenance* — the genetic adaptability of a particular plant to a specific climate and soils. In simple terms, this means buying plants propagated from plants native to your area or choosing non-native plants from very similar climates. (See Chapter 11 for more tips on buying trees and shrubs.) Unfortunately, finding a plant with the provenance to grow in your area is a bit more complicated because the ancestors of most of the trees and shrubs you find at the garden center originally came from other parts of the world or regions of the United States. Many no longer resemble their wild forebears. How can you determine whether a plant will grow in your location? You can compare the plant's *hardiness zone* to where you live.

What's your zone?

The U.S. Department of Agriculture's Plant Hardiness Zone Map — last updated in 1990 — divides North America, Europe, and China into zones based on the average annual minimum temperature. The USDA zone map is the one that most gardeners rely on, and the one that *National Gardening* and most other magazines, catalogs, and books currently use. The color section of this book shows the zone maps for the United States, Europe, and parts of Canada. For another Canadian zone map, head to the Internet and visit `www.icangarden.com/zone.htm` or pick up a copy of *Gardening For Canadians For Dummies* by Liz Primeau, *Canadian Gardening,* and the Editors of the National Gardening Association (CDG Books Canada, Inc.).

Each of the 11 zones on the USDA Zone map is 10° warmer or colder in an average winter than the adjacent zone. Zone 11 — in which the lowest average annual temperature is 40° or higher — is the warmest. In Zone 1, the lowest average annual temperature is a bone-chilling –50° or colder. Zones 2 through 10 on the North American maps are subdivided into *a* and *b* regions. The lowest average annual temperature in zone 5a, for example, is 5° warmer than the temperature in zone 5b.

Zone maps link regions that share an average winter minimum temperature. The minimum winter temperature in Colorado Springs, Colorado; Albany, New York; and Prague, Czechoslovakia, averages –10 to –20°, for example, so all three cities fall into USDA Zone 5. Although the climate in these distant cities is quite different, they share similar average winter minimum temperatures — one of the key factors that determine whether or not your trees and shrubs will survive.

I indicate the USDA hardiness zones for all of the trees and shrubs listed in Chapters 3 through 10 in their descriptions. If you live in one of the plant's recommended USDA zones, you have some assurance the plant is hardy enough to survive the winter cold.

The question that the USDA map does not address, however, is whether the plant can survive the summer heat. Just as cold limits where plants can grow, so does extreme heat.

In 1997, The American Horticultural Society published *The AHS Plant Heat-Zone Map* (or the *Heat Map*). This map divides the United States into 12 zones based on the average number of days each year that may reach temperatures of 86° or higher. According to the AHS, 86° is the point where many plants begin to suffer damage from heat. Of course, many plants also thrive in hot climates because they are genetically adapted for heat in the same way that other plants are adapted to cold. The AHS zones range from cool Zone 1, in which temperatures at or above 86° almost never occur, through hot Zone 12, which averages 210 days or more per year of 86° or higher temperatures. This book does not use the AHS map, but you can order your own color poster of it for $15 by calling the AHS at (800) 777-7931, ext. 10.

Designing with Trees and Shrubs

Consider the landscape changes that you want to make and how to match the right trees and shrubs to your needs and your site. Each plant offers its own unique contribution to your landscape. Knowing which ones to choose and deciding where to put them can be daunting. Getting familiar with a few basic design rules and the characteristics of the trees and shrubs themselves help you make choices that you — and your plants — can live with.

Making a site plan

If you haven't written down all your great ideas to transform your yard into the perfect landscape, do that now. Your list might include things like summer shade over the patio, more privacy in the backyard, nicer landscaping in the front yard, less weekend mowing, or hiding the view of the neighbor's garage. You can accomplish many of your goals with trees and shrubs. If your landscaping plans involve deck or patio construction, fences, or big gardening projects, check out *Decks and Patios For Dummies* and *Landscaping For Dummies,* both published by IDG Books Worldwide, Inc.

Play time! Get out your site analysis map, a pencil and eraser, and a few sheets of tracing paper. Place a sheet of tracing paper over your map and start doodling. Draw ovals and circles on your dream map to represent ideas and where you want to put them. Label your ideas inside each circle and let your site's existing features guide your plans. For example, the circle over the steep slope might read, "groundcover shrubs" or the oval near the hot, southwest corner of the house might be labeled "shade."

Designer concepts

Before you rush out to buy trees and shrubs to fill in your doodles, consider the following concepts and plant features that professional designers use to plan landscapes:

- **Public, private, and utility areas:** Think of your site as a series of outdoor rooms in which different activities take place, just as they do inside your home. Trees and shrubs form the walls that divide these spaces from each other.

    - *Utility areas,* such as your oil or gas fills, outdoor faucets, and trashcans, should be easily accessible but hidden from view, like the laundry room indoors. Screen these areas with shrubs.

    - *Private spaces* allow family gatherings and personal pursuits, such as vegetable gardening, sunbathing, and barbecues, to occur without neighborhood scrutiny. Most frequently, the backyard, protected by trees and shrubs, becomes the private area that is out of view from the street.

    - *Public spaces* give visitors and passersby an impression of your personality and style. Make the part of your site that faces the street as hospitable and attractive as possible to improve the value of your home and to make guests feel welcome. If you are planning to sell your home in the near future, spend your landscape dollars here — tasteful landscaping improves "curb appeal" and can reduce the time your house spends on the market.

✔ **Form and function:** Trees and shrubs, and all other plants for that matter, grow in specific shapes, called their *form*. The plants may spread or branch horizontally or grow stiffly upright. The branches may cascade or weep or grow in spiky clumps. Plants can grow tall and vase-shaped, creep over the ground, or do something in between. See Figures 2-6 and 2-7 for common tree and shrub forms.

A plant's form suggests its place or *function* in the landscape. Would you choose a low-growing shrub to shade your house? Of course not! The shrub's form may be better suited to a hedge or garden accent. The form you need to fulfill the function of shade is a tall, leafy tree. To refine the form a bit more, you can choose a deciduous tree — one that loses its leaves in the fall — to provide summer shade and let most of the winter sun shine through, as shown in Figure 2-8.

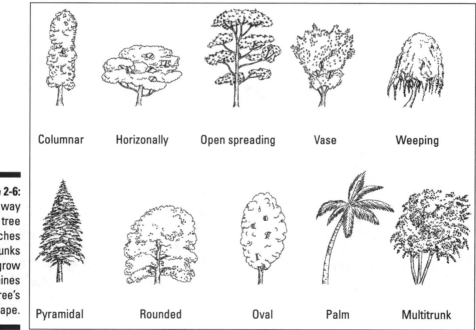

Figure 2-6: The way tree branches and trunks grow determines the tree's shape.

Columnar   Horizonally   Open spreading   Vase   Weeping

Pyramidal   Rounded   Oval   Palm   Multitrunk

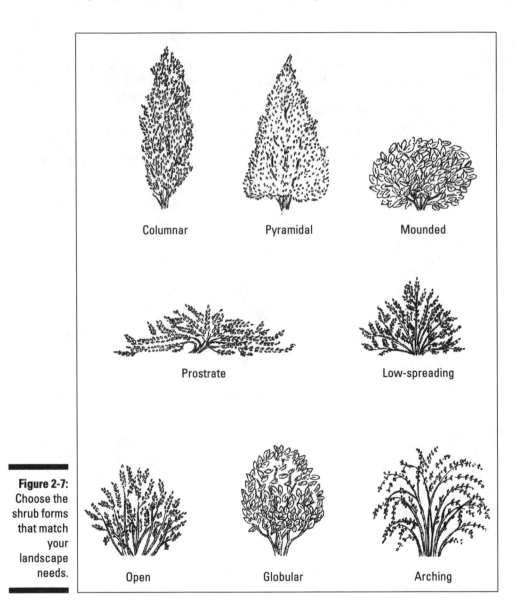

Figure 2-7:
Choose the shrub forms that match your landscape needs.

Figure 2-8:
Deciduous
trees cast
cooling
shade in the
summer, but
let most of
the winter
sun shine
through
their
leafless
branches.

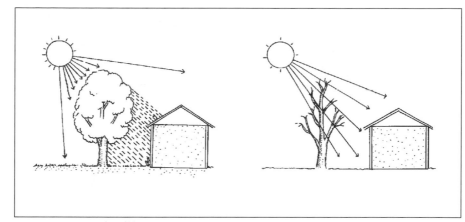

Ground-hugging shrubs and erosion control make another form and function pair. When you think of the functions "privacy" and "blocking views," what form comes to mind? If you answered evergreen hedge, you're thinking like a designer.

✔ **Scale and mass:** *Scale* — the relative size of a tree or shrub — and *mass* — the density of its foliage and branches — determine a plant's appropriate place in the landscape, too. Imagine an adult riding a child's tricycle for a moment. In that ludicrous picture, the adult is out of scale with the vehicle. Trees and shrubs, too, can grow out of scale to the elements around them.

When you choose plants, consider their ultimate size. As a general rule, trees appear in proportion to your house when they grow no taller than approximately one fourth to one third taller than the roof. (See Figure 2-9.) Very large trees, especially ones with dense mass, overwhelm small houses and properties the way a grown-up overwhelms a child's toy. Little trees quickly grow tall, possibly hanging over your roof or car or blocking your sidewalk. Their roots, too, can damage sidewalks and driveways and grow against building foundations.

A plant's mass or density can change your perception of the plant's scale. A tree with high branches and an open canopy dominates the landscape less than a dense, low-branching evergreen of the same height.

Figure 2-9:
Choose trees and shrubs that remain in scale with your home.

✔ **Composition:** Planning a landscape is similar to, in some ways, painting a picture or composing a song. Repetition, balance, and sequence lead the eye and, in the case of music, the ear through the composition. Framing holds all the elements together.

- *Balance* is achieved when opposing elements in the design appear equal in weight. Formal designs often use *symmetrical balance* — when identical elements appear as mirror images on opposite sides of a focal point, such as your front door. *Asymmetrical balance* does not use the same elements on either side of the focal point to achieve balance. The result gives the composition a more casual and welcoming appeal, as shown in Figure 2-10.

- *Sequencing* leads your eye logically through the landscape and creates a sense of movement. Layering short plants in the foreground, medium-height shrubs behind them, and tall trees in the background is an example of sequence, as shown in Figure 2-11.

- *Repetition* or repeating elements in the landscape, such as using the same kind of shrub or tree in several places in your landscape, unifies your design. You can repeat either the plant itself or some aspect of it, such as its form, color, or texture, as in Figure 2-12. For example, if you use a group of dark-leafed evergreens near the end of your driveway, you can repeat the same grouping close to the house or use a tree with similarly colored foliage instead.

Figure 2-10: Formal designs often use symmetrical balance (top), while asymmetrical balance signals a more casual style (bottom).

Figure 2-11: Short plants in front, medium in the middle and tall trees in the back gives your design a logical sequence.

Figure 2-12:
Repeating
elements
in your
landscape
unify your
design.

- *Framing* adds structure, mystery, and drama to your landscape just as it does to photographs and paintings. When you use plants to partially hide a space or view, you create mystery — a compelling desire to look more closely at what is hidden. Viewing a spectacular sunset or skyline from between tall trees gives the vista perspective and scale. Use trees to frame distant views or a gap in the hedge to highlight a focal point or frame an intimate space. (See Figure 2-13.)

✔ **Color, texture, and year-round interest:** When you choose shrubs and trees, consider all their parts — branches, flowers, bark, fruit, and foliage — and what color and texture they bring to your design.

Texture, an often-overlooked feature, depends on the size of the leaves, branches, and twigs in relation to the size of the plant as a whole. Shrubs with a fine texture have thin twigs and small or lacey leaves. Large twigs, branches, and leaves give trees and shrubs a coarse texture. Plants with fewer branches — an open canopy — usually appear more finely textured than one with a densely branched canopy. Mix different textures for variety and interest in your landscape, as shown in Figure 2-14.

Bark adds color and texture to your yard — an important feature in wintry landscapes. Many trees and shrubs also produce colorful fruit that remain attractive long after the petals have fallen. Foliage, however, offers the greatest opportunity for bringing color into your site. You can find a wide range of shrubs and trees with colorful foliage from silvery gray, gold and speckled white, to red, pink, and burgundy, to endless shades of green. Place shrubs and trees with complementary, but different colored foliage together to create depth and contrast.

Take care, however, not to mix too many competing elements into a small space. Plants with brightly colored foliage, for example, stand out in the landscape — use them judiciously. Better to choose one shrub with flamboyant foliage or group several together as an accent than to scatter them around and create visual clutter.

The most useful trees and shrubs combine several appealing features for year-round interest. A shrub that blooms for one week a year is less valuable that one that blooms and offers attractive foliage or bark, for example. If you have room on your site for only a few plants, choose those that offer decorative form, texture, and color in at least three seasons of the year.

Figure 2-13:
Framing intimate and distant views with trees and shrubs brings structure and drama to your landscape.

Figure 2-14: Mixing trees and shrubs with different textures adds visual interest to your landscape.

Choosing Trees and Shrubs to Match Your Site

Knowing what you expect your trees and shrubs to do in your landscape and how much maintenance you're willing to accept helps you match the right plants to the right place. Think about what you want your plants to do — screen the trash cans, shade your patio, decorate your front yard, provide fruit for you or the birds, or cover a steep slope. Also consider what you don't want from your plants — frequent pruning, watering, raking or spraying, blocked views, or sparse lawn.

Each tree and shrub described in Parts II and III has particular characteristics that you can use to determine whether it belongs in your landscape. As you read the plant profiles, consider all the following aspects before making your choices:

✔ **Vigor:** How fast does the plant grow? Very vigorous trees and shrubs quickly fill their allotted space and provide shade and privacy in just a few years. These plants tend to require frequent pruning, however, and have brittle limbs and short life spans. Plants that grow slowly usually live longer and require little pruning.

✔ **Size:** How tall and wide will the tree or shrub get? Consider this aspect carefully if you have limited space or dislike pruning. All too often, shrubs that naturally grow to 8 feet high get planted under low windows, which the shrubs eventually cover. Final width matters, too, especially when choosing shrubs for hedges and groundcovers for which you need to calculate the planting distance between plants. To determine how much space a particular shrub will fill at maturity, take your tape measure with you to the garden center. Use it to do a "reality check" before you bring home a plant that will outgrow your space, as shown in Figure 2-15.

Calculating the height of a mature tree takes more than a tape measure. Here's a simple method of finding the ballpark height of a tall object:

1. **Position a person or other object of known height near the tree.**

2. **Hold a pencil or stick vertically in your outstretched hand and back away from the person until the pencil "covers" the person from head to toe.**

3. **Standing in the same spot, use the pencil as a ruler to measure the height of the tree by eyeballing the number of pencil lengths it takes to cover the height of the tree.**

Multiply the tree's number of "pencil lengths" by the known height of the person, as shown in Figure 2-16. If your friend is 6 feet tall, for example, and it takes four pencil lengths to cover the tree height, then the tree is 24 feet tall.

Figure 2-15:
Consider the mature heights to ensure that shrubs remain within their allotted space and to reduce maintenance and pruning.

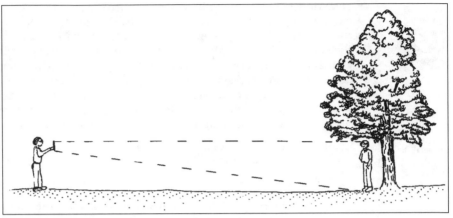

Figure 2-16:
Approxi-
mate the
height of a
tall tree by
comparing it
to the height
of a known
object.

✔ **Form and mass:** Will the plant be mounded or flat, arching or upright, loose and billowy, or dense and formal? Plant forms suggest landscape function. Low, spreading shrubs, for example, make excellent ground covers. Go back to the section titled, "Designer concepts" in this chapter for more information on plant shapes and their uses in the landscape.

✔ **Culture:** Is the tree or shrub adapted to your climate and the sun, soil, and water conditions at the proposed planting site? Previous sections in this chapter give more complete information about climate, minimum cold temperature zones, soil texture and drainage, and sun and shade. Try to match as many of your site's conditions to your chosen plant's cultural needs as possible. Don't throw your money away on a tree or shrub that will die from the cold or require constant watering to stay alive.

✔ **Bad habits:** Does the plant have any habits that could cause problems in your landscape? Find out if the plant will have invasive roots that ruin your lawn, leach field, or driveway; weak limbs that snap in the wind; messy fruit, leaves, or flowers; and particular pests or diseases that frequently shorten its life. Turn to Chapter 18 for mug shots of some common bad actors.

✔ **Ornamental interest:** Does the tree or shrub offer ornamental value for more than one season of the year? Look beyond the obvious flower and foliage colors and consider the texture and color of all the plant parts. Bark, fruit that remains colorful, and branching patterns become important when plants lose their leaves in the autumn. Cones, berries, winter foliage color, and long bloom season make evergreen plants more valuable in the landscape.

Understanding the unique features of trees and shrubs helps you match the best-suited plants to your site and landscape plan.

Considering the Consequences of Inappropriate Placement

More than just a matter of aesthetics, planting the right trees and shrubs in the right place promotes safety; and prevents damage to the plants, nearby buildings and utilities, and relations with the people who live next door. Anticipate the consequences of poorly placed plants — dangerous limbs hanging over your roof or growing into electrical wires, roots clogging your sewer pipe or leach field, inaccessible utility service boxes, unhappy neighbors, and unsafe driving conditions.

Pruning efforts to correct the problems after the trees and shrubs mature can damage the plants and leave them looking unnatural and more prone to pests and diseases. Consider the following situations before you plant.

Overhead power lines and utilities

Before you cross the street, you know to look both ways. Before you plant a tree, however, you have to look up and down. Utility companies spend millions of dollars each year cutting trees away from electric, telephone, and cable television wires because limbs and tree trunks that fall across the wires interrupt customer service and damage equipment.

You cannot safely prune your own trees if they grow too close to overhead wires even if they grow on your property. Limbs that touch or fall across electrical wires can electrocute you. Climbing a ladder or the tree itself with a saw in hand also poses the hazard of falling from a dangerous height.

If you already have trees growing into your overhead wires, call the utility company and ask that they send a pruning crew to your home. *Arborists* — professional people who preserve and care for trees — will also prune your trees for a fee.

The best way to keep your overhead wires clear of tree limbs is to consider the mature height and spread of trees before you plant. The International Society of Arboriculture recommends planting trees that grow no taller than 20 feet directly beneath utility wires. Taller trees should be planted so that their mature canopy grows no closer than 15 feet from the wires. You can contact the International Society of Arboriculture at P.O. Box 3129, Champaign, IL 61826-3129, or visit the Web site at www.ag.uiuc.edu/~isa/.

Buried wires and gas lines

Frequently, utility companies bury electric, telephone, and cable television wires underground, especially in new developments. That tactic makes choosing tree or shrub locations easier because you don't have to worry about overhead wire, but you still need to think about the underground cables. Don't assume that the wires are buried deeper than your planned planting hole — sometimes they are buried just below the surface.

Natural gas pipes pose another problem. Although pipes should be buried at least 3 feet below ground, gas companies prefer a tree-free corridor of 15 to 20 feet on either side of pipes to allow for safety and maintenance. Gas leaks within a plant's root zone can also damage or kill it. If you have a propane tank with copper tubing running underground to your house or another building, be aware that the pipe may be buried very close to the surface.

Cutting through a buried wire or gas line could result in severe injury. The utility company also may charge you a fee for interrupting service and necessary repairs to their damaged property.

To avoid disrupting underground utilities, many states have laws that require you to contact utility companies that may have wires or pipes on or close to your property before you dig. The companies send someone out to locate and mark the path of the wires or give you a toll-free phone number to a regional clearinghouse. The clearinghouse routinely marks underground wires and pipes for the utility companies.

When you know the location of underground utility lines, avoid planting close to them because, when the cables or pipes need repair in the future, digging may harm your trees or shrubs.

Service boxes and wellheads

Your wellhead and the unattractive metal box that the utility company planted in your front yard need disguising, but someone will need access to them someday. After you find out exactly where the wires and pipes are located (see the "Buried wires and gas lines" section, above), plan your shrub plantings so that the mature shrubs will not touch the box or wellhead. Better yet, allow enough space for someone to actually work on the utilities located in the box without having to prune back your shrubs. And have a heart, avoid spiny plants in your planting plan.

Buildings

Insurance companies take a dim view of large tree limbs hanging over their customers' homes and businesses — and with good reason. A strong wind can send branches crashing through your roof. Overhanging limbs also drop leaves that clog your gutters and sticky sap that can stain siding. Dense shrubs planted against your house may grow up to block the view from windows or provide a hiding place for unwelcome intruders. Keep shrubs at least several feet from your house and plant trees that grow to 60 feet or more at least 35 feet away.

Streets, sidewalks, and septic lines

Don't ignore the power of roots when you consider where to plant trees. Some trees, such as poplar and willow, grow large roots close to or on the surface of the ground where they heave paving and everything else out of their path. Shallow-rooted trees also compete with lawn grasses and make mowing a bumpy experience.

Roots cause other problems, as well. To tree and shrub roots seeking out sources of moisture and nourishment, your septic leach field looks like a Sunday buffet. Moisture-loving species cause the most trouble when their roots grow into the perforated drainpipes, clogging them and disrupting the function of the leach field. Plant roots usually grow two to three times farther from the tree trunk than the aboveground branches do, so leave plenty of room between the planting hole and your driveway, sidewalk, or septic field for outward expansion. Check Chapter 18 and the plant descriptions in Part II to see if your chosen tree may be among the shallow-rooted septic or sidewalk saboteurs. Keep in mind, too, that grass and other landscape plants growing in the root zone will have to compete with the tree roots for moisture.

Property boundaries and public rights of way

Before you install a hedge along your property line or plant trees along the sidewalk out front, do a little homework. Your state and municipal governments own the land on either side of all public roads. The width of this *right-of-way* may vary from 50 feet to more than 120 feet, as measured from the road's center line. Many communities and highway departments prohibit planting in the public right-of-way or have regulations that you must follow. Contact your local government office for guidelines or the State Highway Department, if your property borders a state or federal highway.

Homeowners commonly plant privacy hedges along their property boundary. If you plan to plant a hedge or row of shrubs or trees between you and the neighbors, avoid future disputes by hiring a professional surveyor to find the actual property lines. When you plant the shrubs, allow enough space so that, when the shrubs mature, they will not encroach on the neighboring property. You'll also have room to maintain them from your own yard.

Merging traffic

Sitting in the driver's seat of an average automobile, the driver's eye is about 45 inches from the ground. Shrubs and hedges near intersections, such as the end of your driveway, must be lower than that height or planted far enough from the road to allow drivers to see oncoming motorists, bicyclists, and pedestrians. If your street is on a hill, adjust the position of the hedge so that you have a clear view of traffic in both directions. For safety's sake and to avoid possible liability, keep signs and lines-of-sight clear.

Part II
Selecting Trees for All Seasons

The 5th Wave   By Rich Tennant

"Originally we thought of calling a tree surgeon, but then we heard of this new tree chiropractor in town..."

In this part . . .

Live in the desert, windy Plains, sultry South, nippy North? No problem! Turn to this part to find a tree that loves where you live. Whether you want a tree for shade, autumn color, spring flowers, or just to block the view of the neighbor's sculpture garden, this part is where you'll find it.

Chapter 3

Evergreen Trees for Everyone

· ·

In This Chapter

▶ Using evergreens in your landscape

▶ Discovering the most popular needled evergreens

▶ Using broadleaf evergreens in warmer climates

· ·

*E*vergreen trees provide shade, wind protection, and visual screening all year round. They frame the winter landscape with their evergreen boughs when the deciduous world turns brown. In the summer, the dark-leafed trees create a foil for brightly colored perennial flowers and shrubs. Evergreens clearly count among the most majestic of landscape trees.

Year-round foliage can be a disadvantage in some situations, however. Although welcome in the hot summer months, shade from evergreens may prevent winter sun from warming the house. Tall, dense trees can also block desirable views as they mature, and stiffly formal pyramid-shaped conifers often don't blend gracefully into small landscape settings. If you live in a postage-stamp sized yard, look for dwarf conifers and evergreen shrubs instead. This chapter shows you how.

Needling for Attention

Before plopping down a Colorado blue spruce in your front yard next to the mailbox, read this section! You can use needle-bearing evergreen trees for hedges, screens, windbreaks, formal specimens, and, of course, Christmas trees, but remember that they are trees, and therefore will grow to tree-sized proportions. Many of the species in this section have dense, imposing growth habits, and the larger ones really get too big for most home landscapes unless you happen to live on a ranch, estate, or five acres in the country. Many species, however, have great cultivars or varieties with unique charac-teristics that stay compact and within the bounds of most suburban yards. (See Chapter 1 for more about cultivars and plant names.) These make nice additions to a rock garden, shrub border, or foundation planting, especially dwarf conifers, which naturally grow slowly and have interesting shapes and growth habits. You can find more cultivars and information about dwarf conifers in Chapter 7.

In some groups of evergreens, such as pines and cedars, the young, immature trees that you buy in the nursery have very different forms from the full-grown, mature specimens. A compact pyramid may grow into a spreading, open-canopied tree with no limbs near the ground. Although many years may pass before the tree achieves that stature, keep the ultimate size and shape in mind before you buy and plant. The next generation of homeowners and landscapers will thank you.

Needle-bearing evergreens are different from deciduous trees in that, unlike wide, flat leaves that live for only a few months, needles are tough, very narrow leaves that remain on the tree for a year or more before falling off. Evergreens don't lose all their needles at once, but drop some of them every year. (It's no cause for alarm when you notice that your pine tree has yellow needles in the middle of the tree — it's just getting ready to shed.) Some evergreens, like firs, have needles that attach directly to the branch while others, like pines, have needles grouped together in papery coverings that hold them to the twigs. Some have foliage that doesn't look like needles at all: Junipers and cypress, for example, have flat foliage that grows in overlapping scales along the branches.

Needled evergreens produce their seeds in scaly *cones*. Cones of some evergreens, like junipers, look like small berries. Pines, firs, cedars, and spruces and hemlocks have the more recognizable kind of cones — commonly called *pine cones* — that either hang under the branches or stand upright on top of the branches. Some species have very ornamental cones.

Fir better or worse

Firs have short needles, usually about an inch long, that grow straight out from the twigs. Their growth habit is pyramid- to cone-shaped, and their branches grow out in horizontal layers along the trunk — perfect as Christmas trees on which to hang ornaments, but too stiff and formal for small landscapes. Consider the smaller cultivars for specimens in smaller landscapes and for use around your home.

Firs make attractive groupings and screens in large areas and woodland settings that can accommodate their mature size. While those grown as Christmas trees require pruning, the landscape trees rarely need pruning except to remove damaged limbs or undesirable growth. Native to cool humid climates, firs prefer full sun and moist, well-drained, neutral to slightly acidic soils, and protection from strong winds. They don't thrive in hot, dry climates or urban areas.

Needled evergreens produce a sticky sap, called *pitch*. Some species — most notoriously, pines — drop pitch from their branches, making them unsuitable for planting near driveways, patios, and other areas where their hard-to-remove sap is unwelcome.

- **Balsam fir:** *Abies balsamea.* See Chapter 7.

- **White fir:** *Abies concolor.* Zones 4 to 7. This fir tolerates drier soil and more summer heat than most firs, but still grows best in moist, cool climates. It grows 30 to 50 feet tall, and spreads 15 to 30 feet wide in a stiff pyramid that branches to the ground. 'Compacta' is a dwarf cultivar that grows slowly to 10 by 10 feet and has 2-inch long, blue-green needles. 'Candicans' has very blue needles and grows to 30 by 15 feet.

- **Frasier fir:** *Abies fraseri.* Zones 4 to 7. Best known as a beautiful and popular Christmas tree, this species matures at 30 to 40 feet or more and spreads 20 to 25 feet. It prefers cool, humid climates and doesn't tolerate air pollution or city life. Use it as a screen or group planting where it has room to spread.

- **Atlas cedar:** *Cedrus atlantica.* Zones 6 to 9. This cedar has a stiff, open habit and strongly upright growth when young. As it matures, it spreads out into a flat-topped, picturesque specimen 60 feet tall and 40 feet wide. The purplish, 2- to 4-inch cones stand upright on the branches. The cultivar 'Glauca Pendula' has blue-green foliage and a beautiful weeping habit. Long pendulous branchlets hang from the horizontal branches. Stake it until it develops a trunk strong enough to support itself (see Chapter 12).

- **Deodar cedar:** *C. deodara.* Zones 7 to 8. A pyramid with gracefully drooping limbs in its youth, deodar cedar ultimately grows 40 to 70 feet tall after many years and can spread as wide. It's the least cold-hardy cedar. 'Aurea' has yellow needles and tolerates even less cold than the species. Specialty nurseries offer other cultivars with weeping, prostrate, and dwarf forms as well as those with various needle colors.

See here, my dear cedar

Cedars, stately trees that are common in European parks and landscapes, start life as sometimes gangly, upright pyramids, with clusters of needles about one inch long. Don't let early appearances fool you, however. These trees grow quickly into magnificent specimens that can reach 100 feet or more in the right climate, which is why they look best in public parks and large landscapes. Cedars need sun and deep, moderately moist to well-drained soil. Give them plenty of room to spread and protect them from the wind.

- **Cedar of Lebanon:** *C. libani.* Zones 5 to 7. This cedar takes the cold down to –10 to –15°. It grows slowly to 40 to 60 feet high and wide. Although rather open and upright as a young tree, the adult habit is one of grandeur. The branches spread into a flat-topped, horizontally layered habit. Upright purplish cones accent the dark green foliage. Several cultivars make better home landscape specimens than the species. 'Pendula' is often grafted onto an upright trunk from which it weeps gracefully. Give it support until it can stand on its own (see Chapter 12).

- **Lawson falsecypress:** *Chamaecyparis lawsoniana.* Zones 5 to 7. Native to Oregon and northern California, falsecypress grows best in moist, well-drained soils and cool, humid conditions. They don't do well in hot, arid climates or very windy sites. Although the species can grow well over 100 feet tall, many of the more than 200 cultivars remain the size of shrubs. They range in size from low mounds that are suitable for rock gardens to tall narrow columns. Foliage colors include golden yellow, dark green, silvery, blue-green, and variegated. Some have thread-like twigs, while others have flattened sprays of foliage that look like fans. Despite the number of falsecypress cultivars, few are commonly available except from nurseries that specialize in conifers.

- **Nootka falsecypress:** *Chamaecyparis nootkatensis.* Zones 4 to 7. The most commonly available form of this tree is 'Pendula', which has branchlets that hang down from the horizontally spreading branches. The tree grows into a droopy looking pyramid 45 feet or more high and varies in width. The foliage is scaly, giving the twigs a thread-like appearance. It prefers moist, well-drained soils and cool, humid climates. It's native to the west coast of Canada, Alaska, and the Pacific northwest.

A CLOSER LOOK

Impressing cypress and falsecypress

These two closely related groups of evergreens share many ornamental features, but differ considerably in their preferred climates. Falsecypress prefers cool, moist, humid conditions, while cypress enjoys heat and drier soil found in more arid climates. The hybrid between the two groups, Leyland cypress, tolerates a wider range of soils and climates than either of its parents.

These evergreens have flat, scale-like foliage that's compressed against the twigs instead of sticking out the way needles and leaves do. That gives the twigs and branches stringy or fan-like textures, depending on the species and cultivars. Some cultivars retain their natural tree-size growth, while others grow only to dwarf dimensions. (You can find the shrub-size cultivars in Chapter 7.) Use cypress and falsecypress trees as specimens in large landscapes. Some species also make excellent windbreaks and tall hedges.

- **Hinoki falsecypress:** *Chamaecyparis obtusa.* See Chapter 7.
- **Japanese falsecypress:** *Chamaecyparis pisifera.* See Chapter 7.
- **Leyland cypress:** *Cupressocyparis leylandii.* Zones 6 to 10. This hybrid tree and its multitude of cultivars are actually the result of crossing *Chamaecyparis nootkatensis* with a *Cupressus* species over 100 years ago. Now, it is the most popular plant for creating hedges in England. It grows rapidly — up to 3 feet a year — and makes a quick screen, hedge, or windbreak and you can prune it into nearly size or shape you desire. Left unpruned, it forms an upright column or narrow pyramid shape. Leyland cypress grows in any soils except poorly drained ones, and prefers full sun. It is one of the most tolerant conifers of both airborne salt spray and salty soil. Bagworms can cause considerable damage, though (see Chapter 15). Twig blight and canker are also problems in some places, especially if the trees are growing in unsuitable soils or climates. Avoid planting Leyland cypress in wet soils, but provide adequate moisture until they are well established.

  Many of Leyland cypress' cultivars differ from the original hybrid by having gold, variegated, or some other color of foliage. 'Castlewellan Gold' has finely textured golden foliage and grows into a compact column 15 to 25 feet tall. 'Neylor's Blue' has blue-green foliage, while 'Silver Dust' has creamy white foliage mixed with the green. Many other cultivars are available from specialty nurseries.

- **Arizona cypress:** *Cupressus arizonica.* Zones 7 to 9. This is an evergreen tree for hot, dry climates where falsecypress won't grow. Thriving in well-drained soil and full sun, this species grows naturally in Arizona's arid country. It forms a broad pyramid that's 40 to 50 feet high and 25 to 30 feet across when mature. Use it for windbreaks and screens. Several cultivars have foliage other than the standard green, including 'Blue Ice' and 'Blue Pyramid', which have gray-blue foliage and dark red stems.

- **Italian cypress:** *Cupressus sempervirens.* Zones 7 to 9. Tall and very narrow, Italian cypress grows straight up to 20 or 30 feet, but spreads no more than a few feet wide from bottom to top. It has a stiff appearance and looks best in large formal gardens and groupings. The cultivar 'Swane's Golden' has golden yellow foliage, 'Stricta' is deep green, and 'Glauca' has blue-green foliage. Full sun and well-drained soil keep them happy.

- **Norway spruce:** *Picea abies.* Zones 4 to 7. A tall somber tree in its mature form, Norway spruce normally grows 40 to 60 feet tall by 25 to 30 feet wide in the landscape. Branchlets with dark green needles droop from the horizontal branches giving it a somewhat weeping appearance. Young trees have a stiffer, more pyramidal shape. Specialty cultivars with dwarf or pendulous habits are sometimes available and well worth seeking out. The denser growth and smaller habits make them more ideal for landscape focal points and garden specimens than the species.

Sprucing up

Spruces have stiffly formal character and grow into dense pyramids that make them most suitable for large parks and public areas. Although commonly planted in home landscapes (especially the Colorado blue spruce), they soon outgrow their allotted space unless they're carefully sited. If you have a large property, plant spruce species as windbreaks, screens, and specimens. If you have a smaller property, look for dwarf cultivars with habits that match the character and size of your landscape.

Spruce needles are short and deep-green to blue-gray, depending on the species and cultivar. The cones hang from the branches and attract squirrels. Plant spruces in cool climates in well drained, but moderately moist soil. They don't grow well in dry, polluted urban conditions. They are often attacked by aphids, spruce budworm, bagworm, and other pests as well as several serious diseases (see Chapter 15).

- **White spruce:** *P. glauca*. Zones 2 to 6. One of the hardiest evergreens, white spruce grows where few other trees can — on the slopes of craggy mountainsides and near the cold, windy ocean coasts. It adapts well to nearly any site and makes a valuable windbreak or tall screen. Both in youth and maturity, white spruce has a pyramid shape and dense branching habit. It grows up to 60 feet high and 20 feet wide in most landscapes, but can reach 130 feet. 'Conica' or 'Dwarf Alberta Spruce' is a dwarf cultivar that grows slowly into very dense 10-foot pyramid. 'Densata', also called 'Black Hills Spruce', also grows very slowly into a compact cone that can eventually reach 20 feet.

- **Oriental spruce:** *P. orientalis*. Zones 4 to 7. This species takes up less room in the landscape than most spruces because it forms a narrower pyramid. It has dark green, very short, ½-inch long needles and dense branching all the way to the ground. The branchlets droop slightly from the horizontal branches giving the trees an elegant appearance. It grows slowly to 50 to 60 feet by 25 feet wide, and tolerates a very wide range of well-drained soils. Plant it away from sweeping winds.

- **Colorado spruce:** *P. pungens*. Zones 3 to 7. This popular tree has stiffly spreading branches with sharp needles. Colorado spruce prefers rich moist soil and full sun, but will tolerate drier soil. Several insects and diseases, including spruce gall aphid, spruce budworm, canker, and twig blight, cause serious damage.

Pining away

Pines grow in a wider range of climates than any other conifer group, tolerating hot deserts and frigid mountainsides alike. They range in size from dwarf cultivars that don't grow any higher than your knee to towering 100-foot giants. Most species start out as cone or pyramid-shaped, but many gradually mature into rounded adults. Pines make excellent landscape trees for large spaces where their size and form can be appreciated. The dwarf cultivars make better plants for smaller, residential yards.

Pines have the longest needles of the evergreens — up to 18 inches long in the longleaf pine — giving them a softer texture than many other conifers. The needles occur in bundles of two, three, or five. Pines with the same number of needles in a bundle often share other common characteristics, such as growth habits and cultural requirements. *Two-needled pines,* such as Scotch pine, for example, tolerate drier soil and more heat than the *five-needled species,* such as white pine.

Many insects, diseases, and environmental conditions cause serious and often fatal damage to pines. Some of the most common include salt and ozone damage to trees near highways, white pine blister rust, spruce budworm, and white pine weevil. Pines, in general, don't tolerate air pollution well and suffer when planted near heavily traveled roads or in urban areas. All prefer well-drained soil with adequate moisture and full sun.

Colorado spruce grows 30 to 50 feet high and about half as wide, making it difficult to use in small residential landscapes. Fortunately, many cultivars exist that remain much smaller and have more interesting shapes. The word 'Glauca' in the plant name differentiates Colorado *blue* spruces from plain Colorado spruces. If you want a really blue-colored Colorado blue spruce, choose a cultivar grown from cuttings in a nursery instead of one grown from seed, because the foliage color of this species varies from one tree to the next, from plain green to silvery blue-green. Cultivars offer uniformity, so that you know what to expect. 'Hoopsii' is considered one of the best blue-white, tree-sized cultivars, because it grows to 30 feet and has dense branching and typical pyramid form.

✔ **Japanese red pine:** *Pinus densiflora.* Zones 4 to 7. A two-needled pine with reddish-orange bark when young. It develops a picturesque, open, flat crown with horizontally spreading branches as it matures. It grows 40 to 60 feet high and wide and prefers well-drained soil and full sun. Smaller cultivars include 'Pendula', which is a weeping form that either grows prostrate on the ground or grafted to an upright trunk, and 'Umbraculifera', another dwarf form with an umbrella-shaped canopy that grows slowly to 15 to 20 feet. 'Umbraculifera Compacta' is similar, but grows only 5 feet tall.

- **Limber pine:** *P. flexilis.* Zones 4 to 7. A five-needled pine that grows into a flat-topped tree 30 to 50 feet high and half that in width, limber pine prefers moist, well-drained soils. It also adapts to drier conditions and tolerates wind and cold. A number of cultivars offer different growth habits for smaller landscapes.

- **Mugo pine:** *P. mugo.* See Chapter 7.

- **Austrian pine:** *P. nigra.* Zones 4 to 7. A two-needled species, this pine works well as a windbreak or screen. It matures at 50 to 60 feet and develops a round-topped canopy. It lives in a wider range of soils than most species and tolerates urban conditions. Many cultivars exist.

- **Japanese white pine:** *P. parviflora.* Zones 4 to 7. This pine has twisted, five-needled tufts of foliage that give it a lumpy, but attractive habit. It grows 25 to 50 feet high, but many cultivars remain smaller. 'Glauca' in particular is used extensively for training into bonsai. This species has good salt tolerance and a small size, which makes it better for residential landscapes than most other pines.

- **White pine:** *P. strobus.* Zones 3 to 7. A five-needled pine with many cultivars, white pine grows 50 to 80 feet high and spreads its mature crown half that width. Much too large for average home landscapes, white pine looks at home in parks, open public lands, and forests, and on large estates and country homes. It has a soft, graceful texture. Many small and elegant cultivars exist, some with variegated foliage.

Unfortunately, five-needled pines are subject to white pine blister rust, a fungus that spends part of its life on the trees and part of its life on *Ribes* shrubs, such as currant and gooseberry. The rust looks like orange-yellow blisters on the pine bark or around the needle clusters and appear in spring to early summer. The disease is fatal to pines — that's why nurseries cannot ship *Ribes* species into many parts of the country.

- **Scotch pine:** *P. sylvestris.* Zones 3 to 7. A two-needled pine with orange-red young bark, this tree grows up to 60 feet tall. It has an irregular and picturesque growth habit, and tolerates dry soils. Existing cultivars include those with yellowish foliage and unusual growth habits.

- **Japanese black pine:** *P. thunbergii.* Zones 5 to 8. A small, two-needled tree that grows 20 to 40 feet high, this pine has very good salt tolerance, making it useful for seaside planting. Like other two-needled pines, it grows in dry soil and full sun. The cultivars make good landscape and bonsai specimens.

- **Podocarpus.** *Podocarpus species.* Zones 8 to 11. Evergreen trees or large shrubs grown for their dense, fine-textured, needle-like foliage. *P. gracilior*, the fern pine, grows 20 to 60 feet high with a round, sometimes-weeping habit. Yew pine, *P. macrophyllus,* is more upright and grows 40 to 50 feet high. Both are easy to grow and can be pruned to maintain size, making them good hedges, screens, or container plants. Grow in full sun or part shade in moist but well-drained soil.

- **Douglas fir:** *Pseudotsuga menziesii.* Zones 4 to 6. Although not really a fir, this species shares true firs' tall pyramid shape, short needles, and cultural requirements, which are discussed in the "Firs" sidebar, earlier in this chapter. One of the most important timber trees in North America, it's also grown extensively for Christmas trees. Douglas fir can reach over 200 feet high in the Rocky Mountains and along the West Coast where it grows wild, but rarely gets more than 40 to 80 feet in landscape situations. Give it plenty of room to spread — a mature landscape tree may become 20 feet wide at the base. The variety *glauca* has blue-green foliage and is hardier in the north.

- **California redwood:** *Sequoia sempervirens.* Zones 7 to 9. These grand and awe-inspiring trees grow to 300 feet tall in their native California habitat and can live for over 2,000 years. In other areas, the trees usually grow much smaller, reaching 50 to 60 feet. Pyramid-shaped when young, the trees lose their lower limbs as they mature. Some cultivars have dwarf habits that differ from the species and these make better home landscape specimens. Redwood needs a humid climate and deep, moist, acidic, well-drained soil to thrive.

- **Eastern white cedar, arborvitae:** *Thuja occidentalis.* Zones 3 to 7. Although most commonly grown as a landscape shrub, eastern white cedar is actually a large tree in its native habitat. As it matures to its full 50 foot height, it loses its lower limbs and develops a somewhat open, rounded to cone-shaped canopy. It grows best full sun. Its foliage turns brownish in the winter in windy sites.

- **Western red cedar:** *Thuja plicata.* Zones 5 to 7. Although native to the damp, humid climate and moist soils of the Northwest, it grows rapidly in the U.S. southeast on clay soils, too. Use this tree for large hedges, screens, or specimen plants. Naturally growing 100 to 200 feet tall in the wild, it stays half that size in the landscape. It retains good dark green winter color and resists most insect pests. Many beautiful cultivars exist.

A CLOSER LOOK

Adventures with arborvitae

The *Thuja* and *Platycladus* species of arborvitae, also commonly called *cedar* (unrelated to the true cedar), serves as one of the most important evergreens for hedges, screens, and specimen plants. The smaller cultivars also make useful foundation plants, and are covered in Chapter 7. Although they prefer deep, moist, cool soils, they grow in a wide variety of situations without complaint. Common from lowlands to craggy mountainsides, arborvitae survives where you plant it. It even tolerates part shade, but grows faster and more compactly in full sun. The fine-textured foliage of this group is scaly and pressed tightly against the branches. It often forms flat, fan-shaped branches that have a vertical or scalloped effect. The reddish bark is attractive, too.

A CLOSER LOOK

Unlocking hemlock

Hemlocks, which are graceful, deep-green trees with short needles, grow best in cool, humid climates. They also grow well in shade unlike most other needled evergreens. Give them moist, well-drained, slightly acidic soils. Although they grow to large tree status, you can keep them smaller by pruning or choosing smaller cultivars. Like yews, they make good hedges, although they look better if pruned informally instead of sheared. Turn to Chapter 14 for details about creating informal hedges.

Unfortunately, hemlocks have a serious problem with an insect called the *wooly adelgid,* especially in the eastern United States. Call your county extension office to inquire about the pest in your area before planting a hemlock.

- ✔ **Canadian hemlock:** *Tsuga canadensis.* Zones 3 to 7. This hemlock has graceful, pendulous branches that arch horizontally before drooping downward. It can grow to 40 to 70 feet, but you can easily prune it to stay much smaller. Its fine texture helps it blend into nearly any landscape. Many cultivars are naturally dwarfed. 'Pendula' takes several forms, depending on its source, but commonly grows about 5 to 10 feet tall and twice as wide and has long trailing branches.

- ✔ **Carolina hemlock:** *Tsuga caroliniana.* Zones 4 to 7. This tree is similar to Canadian hemlock, but has a stiffer, less weeping habit. Its size, hardiness, and growing needs are the same, however.

- ✔ **Western hemlock:** *Tsuga heterophylla.* Zones 6 to 8. Native to the western United States, this tree grows taller than the other two species of hemlock, and forms a broad pyramid with weeping branchlets that hang from spreading branches.

Broadleaf Evergreen Trees

Mild winter climates far from ice, snow, and freezing winds are home to broadleaf evergreen trees. Through all the seasons, these evergreens hold their foliage, making them valuable for shade and year round greenery — the backbone of warm-weather landscapes. Unlike broadleaf evergreen shrubs, however, broadleaf evergreen trees rarely grow where winter temperatures are likely to drop below 10 to 15 degrees. You can find many more broadleaf evergreen trees in Chapter 5.

- ✔ **Carob tree:** *Ceratonia siliqua.* Zones 8 to 11. The foot-long fruit pods of this small tree are ground and used as a chocolate substitute. You can grow this fast-growing 30 to 40 foot evergreen as a large, dense hedge or prune it into a round-headed tree with a single trunk. It has dark green, pinnately compound leaves (see Chapter 1 for a detailed explanation) and small red flowers. Carob has male and female flowers on separate trees — try to get a male tree if you don't want the messy fruit pods dropping on your lawn. Plant in full sun and well-drained soil, but keep it away from sidewalks, driveways, and patios — its shallow roots can damage the pavement.

- ✔ **Sweet bay:** *Laurus nobilis.* Zones 8 to 11. This aromatic tree is the source of bay leaves used in cooking. Where temperatures don't drop below 20°, you can grow it as a formal clipped hedge, topiary, informal hedge, or small tree. If your winter temperatures don't allow you to grow this lovely evergreen outside year round, plant it in a container and move it into a cool, well-lit spot when necessary. Sweet bay has a cone to pyramid shape when left unpruned, and grows slowly to 20 to 35 feet tall and 15 to 20 feet wide. Give it well-drained soil and full sun to part shade. The species tends to send up lots of suckers and shoots, making it good as a hedge, but the cultivar 'Saratoga' grows more like a tree.

- ✔ **Japanese silver tree:** *Neolitsea sericea.* Zones 9 to 11. Growing quickly to 25 to 40 feet by 20 to 35 feet, this ornamental tree likes fertile, moist soil and a sheltered place out of the wind. Its 6-inch long leaves emerge bronze-colored and mature to leathery, glossy green with silver undersides that give the tree its common name.

- ✔ **Evergreen pear:** *Pyrus kawakamii.* Zones 9 to 11. A lovely deep green, glossy leafed tree where it can be grown, evergreen pear is covered with white flowers in the early spring. The drooping branches are attractive when planted against a wall or trellis and specially trained as a two-dimensional espalier, as described in Chapter 15, or you can prune it into a small 12- to 25-foot multi-trunked tree. Stake the trunks until they can support themselves and prune the long limbs to keep the crown more compact and upward growing. Grow in any soil except poorly drained and full sun. In colder climates, the foliage may drop in the winter. This species is prone to fireblight, a serious and easily spread disease that affects pears, apples, and hawthorns. (See Chapter 15 for more information.)

- ✔ **California live oak:** *Quercus agrifolia.* Zones 9 to 11. Small oval, leaves with serrated edges grace this dense, round-headed shade tree. This oak grows 50 to 70 feet tall and spreads wider in the hot southwestern U.S. zones. The spreading limbs and rough gray bark add interest to the mature specimens. It tends to shed leaves in the spring.

- ✔ **Holly oak:** *Q. ilex.* Zones 7 to 9. This Mediterranean native grows to 40 to 70 feet and develops a round canopy of equal width. The deep green leaves are 2- to 3-inch long ovals with silvery undersides. It tolerates seaside conditions and salty air.

Evergreen oaks from little acorns grow

With life spans measured in centuries, broadly spreading oaks with massive trunks grow slowly, taking their time to build strong wood and deep roots. Evergreen oaks grace old plantations and parks all across the southern United States, where they provide cool and welcome summer shade. Most oaks sold in nurseries are grown from acorns, and the source of these seeds determines the *provenance* or natural cold- and heat-hardiness of the tree. If you want to grow a species in the extremes of its comfort zone, seek trees grown from seed collected from trees in your climate and avoid those trees that are native to the opposite extreme. See Chapter 2 for more about provenance.

Many oaks have long, vertical taproots (as described in Chapter 1) that grow deep into the soil and break easily when transplanted. For that reason, plant young trees and stay patient! Although many oaks grow slowly, some can put on a foot or more of new growth per year, especially when young. Many insects, including gypsy moth, oak moth, and hosts of others, attack oaks and cause significant damage (see Chapter 15).

✔ **Live oak:** *Q. virginiana.* Zones 8 to 10. Massive, sprawling limbs above the heavy, checkered trunks of this oak mark the entrance to numerous estates and public parks from the Atlantic coast to Texas. Growing 40 to 80 feet tall and spreading 60 to 100 wide, give this tree plenty of space. Live oaks have dark green leaves 3 inches by 1 inch wide, prefer deep, fertile soils, and tolerate salt spray.

✔ **Texas mountain laurel:** *Sophora secundiflora.* Zones 8 to 10. A low, spreading tree that grows 20 to 30 feet high, this species thrives in well-drained to droughty soil in hot climates. It grows slowly and can be pruned to several trunks, making a valuable addition to smaller yards. Left unpruned, it's useful as a screen. In addition to its attractive pinnately compound foliage, Texas mountain laurel, also known as *mescal bean,* has fragrant hanging clusters of bluish-purple flowers in late winter to early spring. The seeds, borne in long pods, are poisonous.

✔ **Brush cherry:** *Syzygium paniculatum.* Zones 9 to 11. A medium-sized, single to multitrunked tree for the warmer climates, brush cherry also makes a good screen or hedge if pruned. The reddish new leaves mature to glossy deep green, and the tree has white flowers in summer followed by edible purple fruit. It grows 30 to 60 feet high and has a narrow habit and full crown.

Chapter 4

Made in the Shade — Deciduous Trees

Losing all their leaves in an often-fiery display each autumn, deciduous trees mark the cycles of the seasons. From spring through summer, they provide shade and ornament, and even in leafless winter, their bark and branches decorate the landscape. From weeping limbs to those that stretch upward, straight trunks to gnarled, smooth bark to furrowed, and bold leaves to daintier foliage, a tree exists to fit any desire. Spring through fall, many trees also have foliage colors that rival the showiest flowering perennial.

Foliage helps moderate the climate under a tree's spreading branches or *canopy*. The size and quantity of leaves as well as the branching structure of each tree determines the density of its shade. Trees with branches close to the ground and those with the densest canopies often prevent other plants, including grass, from growing beneath them. High-branched trees and those with sparse limbs, on the other hand, create light shade that allows lawn grass and other ground-covering plants to survive.

Falling for Deciduous Trees

Many of the trees in this section are among the most widely grown plants for home and public landscaping. Others are less familiar, but deserve greater use. To help you find your way through this long list, I describe the characteristics of the major tree groups in sidebars.

Mainly maples

Maples are among the most widely planted and useful landscape trees for shade, street-side planting, and ornamental specimens. Large, mature specimens lend elegance and a sense of permanence to landscapes that can be matched by few other trees. When I think of brilliant fall foliage color, maples come first to mind. Although many deciduous tree species contribute to the blaze of autumn color, maples' unmatched orange, scarlet, and yellow blends add depth and fire to the annual display.

As a group, maples tolerate a very wide range of soils and growing conditions. Some survive the harshest winter climates while others bask in southern heat. Some live at the edges of acidic lowland swamps while others tolerate hot, dry, alkaline city soils. From full sun to full shade, from bonsai specimens to 100-foot species, you can find a tree from this diverse and useful group to match any situation. Other than removing damaged or poorly placed limbs, maples require little pruning.

Many insects and diseases, such as leaf spots, cankers, caterpillars, borers, leaf hoppers, and scales injure maples, and trees growing in stressed conditions at the edge of their hardiness range or in unsuitable soils face the most risk. Some species are also more insect- and disease-prone than others and each locality has its own pests. In cold climates, maples can suffer severe damage from ice and snow build-up. In hot, dry climates, look for brown leaf edges that signal leaf scorch.

✔ **Trident maple:** *Acer buergeranum.* Zones 5 to 8. An excellent tree for small yards, under utility wires, and along a street, this small maple grows only 25 to 30 feet high and 15 to 20 feet wide. Its leaves are lustrous dark green in summer and turn yellow to orange in the fall. Bark becomes scaly with age. It tolerates dry, infertile soils, but prefers moist, well-drained, acidic soil. Grow trident maple as a multitrunked tree or prune to a single stem. The trident maple has few pest or disease problems.

✔ **Hedge maple:** *A. campestre.* Zones 5 to 8. Used extensively as a hedge plant in Europe, this maple also makes a fine specimen tree. It grows slowly up to 35 feet high and wide, forming a rounded canopy. The deeply lobed leaves turn yellow in autumn. This maple tolerates nearly any well-drained soil, including alkaline, and air pollution and has few pests. It tends to branch close to the ground, so that you can shear it into a hedge.

✔ **Paperbark maple:** *A. griseum.* Zones 5 to 7. Peeling cinnamon-red bark and good red fall color makes this small maple attractive all year 'round. It has three leaflets on each leaf, and reddish brown twigs. This maple grows upright and rounded with many upward reaching limbs, reaching a height of 20 to 30 feet and spreading 10 to 15 feet. This is one of the most attractive maples for a wide range of soils and either full sun or part shade.

✔ **Fullmoon maple:** *A. japonicum.* Zones 5 to 7. Named for its rounded, slightly lobed leaves, fullmoon maple grows 20 to 30 feet tall. In spring, purplish flower clusters hang from the limbs. The light green foliage turns brilliant crimson and yellow in the autumn. This lovely rounded tree makes a good substitute for Japanese maple, especially the cultivar 'Acontifolium'. This tree grows only 10 feet high and has deeply cut, fern-like foliage.

✔ **Boxelder:** *A. negundo.* Zones 2 to 9. No matter where you live, you can grow boxelder, which is sometimes called ash-leaved maple. This tree withstands nearly any soil and situation from Texas to the Canadian interior. Unfortunately, this adaptability comes at a price. Boxelder is one of the messiest, most prolifically seeding, and pest-prone trees around. Considered a "weed tree" in vacant lots, roadsides, and wastelands, boxelder nevertheless does have some attractive cultivars. The species grows up to 50 feet high and wide and has pinnately compound leaves with 3 to 5 leaflets that turn yellow in autumn. (Flip to Chapter 1 for an illustration of leaves.) The cultivar 'Flamingo' has creamy white and green variegated foliage that emerges pink in the spring. It grows up to 20 feet and shows the best color when pruned heavily to maximize new growth.

✔ **Japanese maple:** *A. palmatum.* Zones 5 to 8. These beloved maples serve many landscape uses from garden specimens to groves, and even find their way into bonsai collections. They make perfect landscape accents for any size yard. Hundreds of cultivars exist, each with unique foliage form and color, plant habit, and size. They need moist, well-drained, slightly acidic soil with plenty of organic matter, and prefer light shade in hot summer climates and protection from wind and late frost in cooler zones. The leaves are shaped somewhat like a hand with 5 fingers, and have spectacular fall color. The seeds, called *samaras,* often turn red in the fall. Forms vary from shrubby to broadly rounded, multi-stemmed trees up to 25 feet tall. The branching habit is beautiful in its own right, often twisting and spreading gracefully. Plant them far enough away from sidewalks and driveways — at least 6 to 8 feet — so that you won't have to prune the lower limbs as they grow and spread.

Japanese maple cultivars fall into broad groupings based on their leaf color and form. Those belonging to the *dissectum* group, sometimes called *laceleaf* or *threadleaf maples,* have very deeply cut leaves that appear finely textured and fernlike. The *atropurpureum* group has reddish purple foliage. (See Chapter 1 for information about plant names.) Specialty nurseries offer dozens of cultivars.

✔ **Norway maple:** *A. platanoides.* Zones 4 to 7. One of the most commonly planted landscape trees in the United States, Norway maple grows in a wide range of climates and soils. It casts dense shade under its large canopy and has shallow roots that often defeat turfgrasses. This maple typically grows 40 to 50 feet tall and 30 to 40 feet wide, but cultivars vary considerably in their habits. Foliage is usually deep green and lobed, although variegated and purple-red leafed cultivars exist. Norway maple is too large for smaller yards, but it makes a grand presence in parks and large properties.

You can choose from nearly 100 cultivars of Norway maple, including purple-leafed 'Crimson King', 'Drummondi', which has green leaves edged in white, column-shaped 'Columnare', and dwarf 'Globosum', which grows 15 feet high. 'Emerald Queen', a popular cultivar for planting along streets, grows slowly to 35 by 20 feet and has dark green leaves. 'Summershade' resists leaf scorch.

✔ **Sycamore maple:** *A. pseudoplatanus.* Zones 4 to 7. Although subject to many pests and diseases that shorten its life and boost it into the "messy tree" category, this maple is salt tolerant and makes a magnificent specimen where space allows. It can grow 60 feet or higher and is slightly narrower, forming an upright oval or round canopy. The bark of older trees exfoliates to expose orange to brown inner bark. This maple grows in windy areas and in acidic to alkaline soil, as long as it's well drained.

✔ **Red maple:** *A. rubrum.* Zones 3 to 9. This maple has some of the best fall color of any deciduous tree. Although individual trees vary considerably, they range from bright yellow to apricot to orange to scarlet. Red maple grows best in moist acidic soil, including low swampy spots, which earned it the nickname of *swamp maple.* The trees have a fuzzy red appearance when they bloom early in the spring, and the bark of young trees is smooth and silvery gray. Their shallow roots compete with lawn grasses, however, and can crack nearby asphalt. These maples grow 60 feet or higher with equal spread and have smaller leaves and more open canopies than some other maples. Some cultivars have especially good fall color, including 'Autumn Flame', 'October Glory', and 'Red Sunset'. Crosses between this species and silver maple are referred to as *A.* × *freemanii* and have resulted in some excellent cultivars, such as column-shaped 'Armstrong'.

✔ **Silver maple:** *A. saccharinum.* Zones 3 to 9. This fast-growing maple has weak wood and, as a result, often suffers from broken limbs and split trunks that shorten its life. Its deeply lobed foliage is light green with silver undersides and turns yellow in the fall. Very showy red flower clusters appear in very early spring even before red maple's bloom. It has an upright oval form and grows 70 feet or more tall. Give this tree plenty of room — it spreads 50 to 60 feet wide and often loses limbs to snow, ice, and wind. Its shallow roots will lift sidewalks and driveways and clog septic lines. It is also subject to many insect and disease problems.

- ✔ **Sugar maple:** *A. saccharum.* Zones 4 to 8. The source of maple syrup and splendid autumn color, sugar maple has significant economic importance in the northeastern United States and nearby Canada. This majestic tree can reach 100 feet high, although it usually stays half that size and forms a round to upright oval crown of deep green leaves. Sugar maples show their most brilliant fall colors of red, orange, and yellow in the cooler parts of their hardiness range. It prefers moist, well-drained, slightly acidic soil, but grows in more alkaline soil, too. It does not tolerate salt, however, and declines along roads where winter road salting is common. Plant this large tree where it has room to spread. A few of the many cultivars include 'Bonfire', which tolerates poor environmental conditions better than the rest of the species. 'Green Mountain' is hardy in zone 3, while 'Legacy' grows best in zones 5 and warmer.

- ✔ **Amur maple:** *A. tataricum* ssp. *ginnala.* Zones 3 to 8. This is one of my favorite small trees because it packs a lot of value into a small package. Its small pointed, lobed leaves change from shiny dark green to bright red in the fall. You can prune this 15- to 20-foot tree to one or several trunks or let it become shrubby, depending on your landscape needs. It makes a great street tree, specimen, screen, or mass planting in nearly any well-drained, moist soil. Try cultivars 'Flame' or 'Embers' for reliable autumn color.

- ✔ **Three-flower maple:** *A. triflorum.* Zones 5 to 8. Although not commonly available, this maple is worth seeking out if you want a good four-season tree. It grows only 15 to 20 feet high and has peeling bark on its multi-stemmed trunks. Pinkish flower clusters appear in early spring before the deeply lobed green leaves emerge. It has good fall color. Sometimes trees are grafted, but these are less hardy on clay soil and in hot climates than those grown on their own roots.

- ✔ **Shantung maple:** *A. truncatum.* Zones 4 to 8. This small tree has many fine features that make it useful in home landscapes, streetside, and grouped in large areas. It grows only 20 to 25 feet high and wide, forming a dense, round crown. The foliage emerges reddish purple, changes to dark glossy green for the summer and changes again in the fall to orange-yellow. It grows in a wide range of soils and environmental conditions.

- ✔ **Italian alder:** *Alnus cordata.* Zones 5 to 7. Italian alder grows 30 to 50 feet high and develops a pyramid-shaped to rounded crown and smooth brown bark. It tolerates urban conditions and is widely used in Europe as a street tree.

- ✔ **Black or common alder:** *A. glutinosa.* Zones 4 to 7. This alder grows 2 feet or more per year, ultimately reaching 40 to 60 feet with an upright oval habit. The female flowers develop into persistent brown, ½ to one inch long, pine-cone-like fruits. This tree is especially useful in wet sites and infertile soils.

Respect your alders

If you need a tough tree for tough situations, take a close look at alders. Whether acidic or slightly alkaline, most alder species take wet and dry soils in stride. They grow fast in full sun to part shade, and make useful screens, wind- breaks, and massing plants for highways and waste areas. Some cultivars have finely cut, fern-like foliage. You may find other alder species locally available.

- **Himalayan birch:** *Betula jacquemontii.* Zones 5 to 7. This species has very white bark and dark green shiny foliage that turns yellow in the fall. It has an upright oval habit and grows 35 to 40 feet high and 25- to 30-feet wide. Japanese beetles and leaf miner insects love its foliage.

- **Paper birch:** *B. papyrifera.* Zones 2 to 6. This lovely birch is native in much of North America and resists bronze birch borer better than other white-barked species, although it is still susceptible to attack in some areas. (See Chapter 15 for more on insect pests.) It grows 50 to 70 feet high and 30 to 40 feet wide, forming a rounded upright oval shape, and often appears as a multitrunked specimen in garden centers. You can also grow them with a single trunk, if space is limited. The peeling white bark is a favorite of children and vandals who must be discouraged from damaging the trunks. The foliage turns bright yellow in the fall and the bark brightens the landscape year 'round, especially when planted against a backdrop of evergreens or a dark building. Give this tree moist, acidic, well-drained soils.

- **European white birch:** *B. pendula.* Zones 2 to 6. This once-popular birch has been so severely decimated by the bronze birch borer in North America that most nurseries now offer only specimen-type cultivars. Trees develop white bark at a young age and tolerate a wide range of soil types, but prefer conditions similar to those of paper birch. If borers are prevalent in your area, consider these trees as short-term investments. Cultivars include 'Laciniata' and 'Dalecarlica', which have deeply lobed foliage that gives them the common name of *cutleaf birch.* 'Purple Rain' has a weeping habit and purple foliage. 'Purpurea' also has purple foliage, but is quite variable in habit, leaf color, and insect resistance. 'Youngii' has a weeping habit, grows 15 feet high, and spreads wider.

- **Asian white birch:** *B. platyphylla japonica.* Zones 4 to 6. The cultivar 'Whitespire' resists borers and has become an important landscape tree where other white-barked birches can't grow. It grows 40 to 50 feet high and half as wide and enjoys the same soils as paper birch. Stressed and unhealthy trees are still subject to insect infestation.

A CLOSER LOOK

Bravo for birches

Although clumps of white-barked birches take center stage in many landscapes, other ornamental birch species actually make better specimens in some areas. These less showy birches feature fall color, peeling bark, disease and insect resistance, and hardiness among their attributes. Use birches as specimens, for light shade, and in natural areas. Most birches thrive on moist, well-drained, acidic soils, but some live in drier situations while others don't mind seasonal flooding. Prune birches in late spring to early summer after the leaves have fully emerged. If pruned too early or late in the season, they bleed sap excessively.

As a group, birches are subject to attack from many insects and several diseases, including leaf miners, canker, and leaf diseases. The bronze birch borer decimates the white-barked birches, especially the European white birch, throughout the eastern and midwestern United States, targeting stressed trees and older specimens first. The first symptom of infestation is dead branches near the top of the tree. Maintaining tree health by providing adequate water during dry spells and mulching around the trees helps birches ward off this deadly pest. Also avoid using herbicides, including lawn weed and feed products, around birches, because they have shallow, easily damaged roots.

✔ **Gray birch:** *B. populifolia.* Zones 3 to 6. This small, native North American birch grows naturally in abandoned fields, clear-cut and burned forests, and at the edges of woods throughout its range. It commonly grows 20 to 30 feet high in multistemmed clumps. This small tree has triangular-toothed leaves that turn bright yellow in the autumn and a light, airy texture that make it useful in smaller landscapes. Use it as a specimen or in a grove in nearly any soil — even dry and infertile ones. Gray birch does have some serious problems, especially leaf miner and canker, but resists bronze birch borer. It usually lives only 15 to 25 years.

✔ **River birch:** *B. nigra.* Zones 3 to 9. My favorite birch, river birch has reddish-brown peeling bark; grows happily on poorly drained, acidic soils; and is unaffected by the dreaded bronze birch borer. It tolerates heat better than any other birch species. At maturity, river birch reaches 40 by 30 feet and has a spreading rounded canopy that turns yellow in autumn. Multistemmed specimens are the most appealing and look best in spaces where they have room to spread their limbs. The cultivar, 'Heritage', grows more vigorously; has whiter bark that begins peeling at an earlier age; and has darker, thicker leaves than other birches.

✔ **European hornbeam:** *Carpinus betulus.* Zones 5 to 8. This handsome and versatile tree is useful for shade, screening, and planting in large parks, yards, and other open spaces. It grows into a fine-textured, rounded tree 30 to 60 feet high and wide in all soils except excessively wet or dry ones. It has no serious pests or diseases, and tolerates urban shopping mall conditions and severe pruning. The bark is smooth, gray, and rippled like muscles. The cultivar 'Fastigiata' grows into a compact upright oval 35 feet high and 25 feet wide. 'Frans Fontaine' remains narrower at 15 feet wide.

- **American hornbeam, blue beech:** *Carpinus caroliniana.* Zones 4 to 9. Less commonly available, but no less attractive than its European counterpart, this North American native grows only 20 to 30 feet high and wide. It, too, has muscle-like gray bark, fine texture, and good reddish to yellow fall color. It prefers moist, acidic, fertile soil, but can tolerate drier sites.

- **Catalpa:** *Catalpa* species. Zones 5 to 8. These large-spreading trees have bold, heart-shaped leaves and showy clusters of 2-inch white flowers in early summer. Although catalpa is handsome in large landscapes, the trees drop flowers, foot-long seedpods, and foliage from spring to fall. They grow up to 60 feet high and 40 feet wide in nearly any soil.

- **Sugar hackberry:** *Celtis laevigata.* Zones 5 to 9. This tree has smooth gray bark and tolerance for adverse conditions that make it valuable as an urban species. It grows 40 feet tall and wide in a spreading vase shape. Its fruit attracts berry-eating songbirds.

- **Common hackberry:** *Celtis occidentalis.* Zones 3 to 9. Similar to sugar hackberry, this species is cold hardier and tolerates the Midwestern wind. It is prone to a disfiguring disease that makes the twigs grow abnormally. The cultivar 'Prairie Pride' resists the disease. Use hackberry for screens and street trees.

- **Katsura tree:** *Cercidiphyllum japonicum.* Zones 4 to 8. Rounded leaves, (2 to 4 inches across) and spreading limbs grace this 40 to 60 foot tree. Usually a multitrunked specimen, katsura tree has a rounded crown that is as wide as it is tall. The foliage emerges reddish purple, darkens to blue-green, and then turns yellow to orange in autumn. Plant katsura tree in any open area or yard where you want some trouble-free shade from a magnificent specimen tree. It prefers moist, slightly acidic, well-drained, fertile soil, and full sun. Keep the soil moist, but not saturated, for the first year or two after transplanting. The beautiful cultivar 'Pendula' is grafted onto a straight trunk from which it grows cascading limbs. It reaches 15 to 25 feet high and spreads wider.

- **White ash:** *Fraxinus americana.* Zones 4 to 9. A large and beautiful tree native to the United States, white ash grows 50 to 80 feet tall and wide. Its hard, straight-grained wood is prized for tools and furniture. It grows best on deep well-drained soils, preferring moist soil, but tolerating dry conditions. Autumn color ranges from reddish purple to yellow. This tree is best suited to parks and large landscapes, although many improved cultivars work as street trees. Seedless cultivars include 'Autumn Applause' (zones 5 to 8) with deep burgundy fall color that grows 40 to 50 feet tall and wide. 'Autumn Purple' is similar and won the 1998 Michigan Growers' Choice Award. 'Rosehill' grows quickly in an upright oval to 50 by 35 feet and tolerates infertile, alkaline soils. 'Skyline' has a very uniform habit, reaching only 45 feet tall and 35 feet wide.

Ashes, ashes, we all fall down

Ashes are among the most commonly planted street trees as well as the usual source for base-ball bats and tool handles. Ash species occur on all kinds of soils in temperate climates from North America to China and Europe. They have large, pinnately compound leaves and generally form rounded to upright oval canopied trees. Ashes are valuable shade trees for difficult sites throughout the midwestern United States and the plains states, and are commonly used along streets throughout the U.S.

Ashes have a number of serious pests and dis-eases, however, such as borers, leaf miners, caterpillars, and cankers. The seeds of some species cause a litter problem, but many seed-less cultivars exist. Check your local nursery for ash species and cultivars adapted to your local climate.

✔ **Flowering ash:** F. ornus. Zones 5 to 6. Although not commonly available, this medium-size tree is worth seeking out for its fragrant white flower clusters and attractive growth habit. It grows 40 to 50 feet high and wide and has smooth gray bark. This species is used as a street tree in Europe.

✔ **Green ash:** *F. pennsylvanica.* Zones 3 to 9. Since the demise of the American elm, this tree has been commonly used for planting along streets, in parks, and other public areas. It grows in nearly any soil and situation from moist, fertile soil to parking lot planters. A very rapid grower, some cultivars can add more than 3 feet per year. The mature species forms an upright, rounded canopy 50 to 60 feet high and 30 to 40 feet wide. Many cultivars exist, however, and they vary in size and growth habit. 'Fan-West' is best for zones 7 and 8, grows 50 by 40 feet, and has a round canopy. 'Marshall', grows in zones 4 to 7, and is used extensively for street planting. It grows 50 by 40 feet. 'Patmore' is hardy to zone 2, and has little problem with disease or insects. It grows 50 by 35 feet with upright branching and is seedless. 'Summit' is hardy in zones 4 to 7, and grows quickly to 50 to 60 feet tall and half as wide.

✔ **Maidenhair tree:** *Ginkgo biloba.* Zones 4 to 8. This prehistoric tree species dates back 150 million years when it once grew throughout North America. A testament to its hardiness, *Ginkgo* continues to thrive in nearly every climate and soil, making it useful for urban conditions, street plantings, shade trees, and groves. It can grow 50 to 80 high and spreads 30 to 40 feet or more. The fan-shaped leaves turn bright yellow in the fall, but may drop off suddenly in freezing weather. If you need to prune *Ginkgo*, do it in early spring. This species has male and female flowers on separate trees and it's important to know which is which — females produce very messy and malodorous fruit. Trees commonly don't begin blooming until they are 20 years old, so it pays to buy a named male hybrid instead of an unknown seed-grown sapling. Good male cultivars include 'Autumn Gold', 'Fairmount', and 'Princeton Sentry'.

- **Thornless honeylocust:** *Gleditisia triacanthos* var. *inermis*. Zones 4 to 9. Long compound leaves with small oval leaflets cast light, dappled shade under this tree. Honeylocust has an open, spreading canopy that has an airy and graceful appearance. It grows in nearly any situation, including urban streets, although it doesn't perform well in the hottest parts of the United States. The foliage shrivels and turns brown in droughty soil and very hot weather. Unfortunately, many serious pests and diseases also affect this tree, including borers, webworm, and canker. Cultivars have various growing habits and mature sizes and include 'Halka', which grows vigorously to 40 by 40 feet and has a rounded crown, 'Moraine' and 'Shademaster' with upright branches and rounded vase shapes 45 high by 40 feet wide. 'Skyline' is one of the most popular cultivars and grows 45 feet by 35 feet wide. 'Sunburst' has yellow foliage on the growing tips that turns green as it matures.

- **American sweetgum:** *Liquidambar styraciflua*. Zones 5 to 9. Well-known for its lobed, star-shaped glossy leaves and excellent red to purple fall color, sweet gum makes a good landscape tree for large areas. It grows in a pyramid shape while young and spreads as it matures to 60 to 75 feet tall and 40 to 50 feet wide. It prefers moist, slightly acidic soil and full sun and doesn't tolerate urban conditions very well. Caterpillars, webworm, and scale insects attack it and the trees also shed spiny fruit capsules that require regular raking up. Many cultivars exist. 'Rotundiloba' has rounded leaf lobes instead of pointed, rarely produces fruit, and is hardy to zone 6.

- **Tulip tree:** *Liriodendron tulipifera*. Zones 4 to 9. Also called yellow poplar and tulip magnolia, this large species can grow 70 to 90 feet tall and spread more than half that in width. It grows quickly and, as a result, has weak wood that tends to break up in storms and under heavy snow. Grown in wide-open spaces, tulip tree develops a broad, spreading crown. The tulip-shaped leaves are glossy and dark green, turning golden yellow in autumn. The 2- to 3-inch, cup-shaped cream and orange flowers appear in early summer. Plant in deep, moist soil and full sun where it can spread its limbs.

- **Tupelo:** *Nyssa sylvatica*. Zones 4 to 9. Known for its flaming orange-red fall foliage, tupelo, also called black gum or sour gum, makes a good specimen tree for modest landscapes, rural to suburban streets, or for grouping in large spaces. It grows 30 to 50 feet by 20 to 30 feet in a rounded-pyramid shape, and has lustrous deep green leaves and attractively ridged bark. Tupelo grows best in fertile, moist, acidic soil, and full to part sun. It has a deep taproot, which makes transplanting difficult, so start out with small trees. If necessary, prune in the fall.

- **Hophornbeam:** *Ostrya virginiana*. Zones 4 to 9. A North American native that's not common in nurseries, but is worthy of greater acclaim, this 25 to 40 foot by 15 to 30 foot tree has a rounded to pyramid habit and attractive scaly bark. It grows in dry, acidic to alkaline soils, and in sun to part shade. You can plant hophornbeam along streets, as lawn specimens, or in groves. The seeds are borne in clusters of little oval to heart-shaped pods that turn from mint green to brown as they mature.

A CLOSER LOOK

Life's a beech

One of the grandest trees in the wild or cultivation, beech lives for hundreds of years, forming groves of gray, smooth-barked trunks with broad, spreading crowns of slender twiggy branches. The toothed, lance-shaped leaves turn bronze yellow in the fall and then to brown, hanging on the youngest limbs through most of the winter. The edible nuts, relished by many birds and animals, are borne in ¾-inch, spiny round pods.

Beeches tend to branch close to the ground and have shallow roots — the combination spells doom for lawn grasses that cannot compete. Planted on moist, acidic, humus-rich soil, beeches grow 70 feet tall and wide. They also can grow in less favorable circumstances, tolerating dry, but not droughty, soil and a pH on the alkaline side. Both the American (*Fagus grandiflora*) and European (*F. sylvatica*) beeches are hardy in zones 4 to 7. The American beech can grow into zone 9.

The European beech has many cultivars with unusual habits and foliage. 'Pendula' is a weeping form that grows into a mound 50 feet high and spreading wider. You can walk under the limbs of mature specimens and feel like you're in a leafy cave. 'Purpurea Pendula' also weeps, but has purple foliage and grows only 10 feet high. 'Riversii' has purple foliage. 'Tricolor' is similar, but has purplish leaves with pink and cream margins. Other beech cultivars include those with fern-like leaves, round leaves, yellow foliage, twisted limbs, and column shapes.

✔ **Persian ironwood:** *Parrotia persica.* Zones 5 to 8. The glossy, ruffled oval leaves of this small tree emerge reddish, mature to dark green, and turn yellow, orange, and red in the fall. It grows 20 to 40 feet tall by 15 to 30 feet wide and develops a spreading, arching crown. The gray bark flakes off to show mottled green and white patches. They bloom in late winter and have small ½-inch clusters of maroon flowers. Use this tree as a specimen in any landscape situation where you can provide well-drained, loamy, slightly acidic soil. It tolerates urban conditions and has no serious pests or diseases.

✔ **Chinese pistachio:** *Pistacia chinensis.* Zones 7 to 9. This tough tree has a lot going for it — drought tolerance, attractive flaky bark, good fall color, and no serious pests or disease. It grows only 30 feet high and wide, making it useful for small yards and planting under utility wires as well as in urban situations. The 10-inch long compound leaves turn bright orange-red in autumn, even in warm climates. Stake the tree after planting, and prune it in its youth to shape its crown.

✔ **London planetree:** *Platanus × acerifolia.* Zones 5 to 8. The flaky olive green and cream bark of this tree is handsome year 'round. Because it grows in any soil and in polluted environments, London planetree has been used as an urban street tree and in parks throughout Europe and North America. It grows quite large, however, reaching 100 feet high and

80 feet wide, and has messy 1-inch round fruits. It is also susceptible to some serious diseases, including anthracnose and canker. Disease-resistant cultivars include 'Columbia', 'Liberty', and 'Yarwood'. 'Bloodgood' is the most commonly available cultivar, but it's only somewhat resistant to anthracnose.

✔ **American sycamore:** *Platanus occidentalis.* Zones 4 to 9. This native American tree is one of the parents of the London planetree (see previous bullet) and grows to the same size. It prefers moist, deep, fertile soils and doesn't tolerate the wide range of conditions that its offspring does. It is also more prone to disease and insect infestations and, as a result, drops more leaves, twigs, and fruit throughout the growing season. Although sycamore is a beautiful and majestic native tree, London planetree makes a better landscape specimen.

✔ **White poplar:** *Populus alba.* Zones 3 to 8. This species has lobed, maple-like leaves with grayish white undersides and cream-colored bark. They grow 40 to 70 feet high and wide with a rounded open crown. It can tolerate damp and dry soils, air pollution, and salt spray. They live longer given moist, well-drained soil, and full sun. Use white poplar in situations where little else will grow, but don't plant it where its roots can invade septic lines or where its falling limbs can cause damage in storms or high wind. This tree also tends to send up suckers from its roots that can make mowing and yard maintenance difficult.

✔ **Eastern cottonwood:** *P. deltoides.* Zones 3 to 9. This large tree is unsuitable for planting in most situations except as a naturalizing tree for large landscapes where few other large trees will grow. It grows very fast (4 to 5 feet per year) up to 100 feet tall and 50 to 75 feet wide, and prefers moist, fertile soil, such as that found along rivers. Its bark develops very deep fissures and fall color is golden yellow. It drops leaves, twigs,

A CLOSER LOOK

Pop-up poplars

Members of the poplar group share several traits: Nearly all grow rapidly and have the associated problem of weak wood; they have shallow, aggressive roots; and they attract many, many insect and disease problems that make them unwelcome near leach fields, lawns, driveways, and buildings. Poplars also tend to scatter their seeds far and wide and sprout wherever they land. Their rapid growth, however, does make them useful wherever you need a quick effect. Prune poplars in the summer or fall to prevent excessive sap bleeding.

flowers, and seeds in all seasons. The cottony seeds fill the air like snow in early summer and germinate vigorously. Several cultivars, such as 'Siouxland', are seedless.

✔ **Lombardy poplar:** *P. nigra.* Zones 3 to 9. This tree's main appeal lies in its tall, narrow growth habit and speed with which it grows. It can grow 50 to 70 feet tall and 8 to 12 feet wide within 15 to 20 years, but it's prone to canker and other diseases that significantly shorten its life.

✔ **Quaking aspen:** *P. tremuloides.* Zones 1 to 6. This poplar grows from the coldest regions of North America to zone 6. It's not usually planted in the landscape, but often occurs naturally. The rounded, toothed leaves tremble in the breeze, giving it its common name. It grows in any soil and attains heights 40 to 50 feet. The bark is yellow to green to tan and the yellow fall foliage glows, especially against an evergreen background.

✔ **Callery pear:** *Pyrus calleryana.* Zones 5 to 8. One cultivar of this tree, 'Bradford', has been widely planted as a street tree in communities all over the United States. Unfortunately, it is quite disease prone and has a branching habit that shortens its useful life. The limbs tend to crowd each other and form narrow, V-shaped crotch angles, often causing the tree to split apart. (See Chapter 11 for more information.) It has a uniform pyramid habit, however, and glossy deep green leaves that turn yellow to red to purple in the fall. It grows 30 to 50 feet by 20 to 35 feet and resists fire blight disease better than other pears. It has showy white flowers in the early spring. Some other cultivars of callery pear, such as 'Aristocrat', 'Chanticleer', and 'Cleveland Select', are more disease resistant and have better branching habits.

✔ **Sawtooth oak:** *Quercus acutissima.* Zones 6 to 9. This oak is easy to transplant and grows fairly fast for an oak, adding as much as 2 feet per year. It reaches 50 feet or so in height and width. The toothed leaves emerge yellow, maturing to dark green, and are 4 to 8 inches long and 1 to 2 inches wide. Sawtooth oak prefers acidic, well-drained soils, and full sun.

✔ **White oak:** *Q. alba.* Zones 3 to 9. This tree grows throughout the eastern half of the United States and reaches 50 to 80 feet tall and wide. It prefers deep, fertile, moist, acidic, well-drained soils, and full sun. White oaks have deep taproots and are difficult to transplant except when young.

✔ **Swamp white oak:** *Q. bicolor.* Zones 4 to 8. Growing along rivers and near swamps, this oak tolerates moister soil than do most oaks. It grows 60 to 80 feet high and wide and transplants easier than white oak. It needs acidic soil and full sun.

✔ **Scarlet oak:** *Q. coccinea.* Zones 4 to 9. The common name of this oak comes from its excellent autumn color. It grows 75 feet tall and 40 to 50 feet wide. It doesn't tolerate urban conditions as well as some other red oaks.

A CLOSER LOOK

Mighty oaks

Oaks are among the longest lived and grandest trees alive today. In England, where some ancient trees date back to medieval times, they chronicle the life of an oak as "three hundred years growing, three hundred years living, three hundred years dying."

All oaks have acorns that, although they make quite a mess on mowed lawns, are an important food source for large and small wild animals and birds. Some oaks have evergreen foliage (see Chapter 3), but most are deciduous. The leaves of some oaks are lobed and either pointed or rounded; others have oblong or narrow oval leaves, either with or without serrated edges. Fall foliage colors ranges from brown to red.

Most oaks prefer deep, fertile, acidic soil. Some grow in very moist soil and others in droughty conditions — the majority of oaks require moisture levels somewhere in between. Some have taproots that make them difficult to transplant except when very young, but others have a more shallow and fibrous root system that makes planting easy. Oaks don't tolerate soil compaction, changes to soil level, or other common construction-related injuries (see Chapter 15). Nearly all oaks have devastating insect pests that defoliate them in different regions of North America. Gypsy moth, oak moth, mites, borers, and various fungus diseases infect oak, but rarely kill otherwise healthy trees.

✔ **White oaks:** The oaks in this group have leaves with rounded lobes. White oaks grow slowly, forming wide-spreading, majestic crowns that need plenty of room to grow. They are suitable for planting only in large landscapes, but should be preserved wherever they grow naturally.

✔ **Red oaks:** These oaks have leaves with pointed lobes, and they tend to grow faster than white oaks, have more fibrous, easy-to-plant roots, and tolerate urban conditions.

✔ **Narrow-leafed oaks:** These oaks don't have lobed leaves. Instead, the leaves are long, narrow, and pointed, with either smooth or serrated edges.

✔ **Bur oak:** *Q. macrocarpa.* Zones 3 to 8. This oak resembles white oak and has a similar native range, but prefers well-drained limestone soils and tolerates urban conditions. It grows 70 to 80 feet high and wider and is best suited to parks and other open spaces.

✔ **Pin oak:** *Q. palustris.* Zones 4 to 8. This is the most commonly planted landscape oak because it has fibrous shallow roots that transplant easily and it tolerates seasonally flooded soils. It prefers moist, fertile, acidic soils — in alkaline soil, the leaves turn yellow and unsightly. The pyramid growth habit is unique with the lower branches arching downward, the middle branches growing horizontally, and the upper limbs reaching skyward. The mature size is 60 to 70 feet tall and 25 to 40 feet wide.

✔ **Willow oak:** *Q. phellos.* Zones 5 to 9. The narrow 2- to 5-inch leaves of this oak give it a fine texture and good yellow-red fall color. It grows especially well in zones 7 to 9 and prefers moist, well-drained soil, but tolerates nearly any soil. Willow oak has a pyramid shape when young and develops a rounded crown as it matures, reaching 50 feet tall and almost as wide. It grows quickly and may need some pruning when young to develop a good branching structure.

✔ **English oak:** *Q. rober.* Zones 4 to 8. This mighty oak is legendary in the country of its common name. Individual specimens that were planted on estates near medieval castles still cast shade on the surrounding pastures and cemeteries. They prefer well-drained soil and full sun and aren't fussy about pH. They grow slowly to 75 to 100 feet high and wide. The columnar cultivar 'Fastigiata' grows 50 feet high and 10 feet wide.

✔ **Red oak:** *Q. rubra.* Zones 3 to 7. This tree can grow 2 feet per year, ultimately reaching 60 to 75 feet high and wide with a spreading, rounded canopy. It prefers well-drained to sandy, acidic soils, and full sun.

✔ **Shumard oak:** *Q. shumardii.* Zones 5 to 9. This massive oak grows in moist to well-drained, acidic to alkaline soils, and full sun. It can grow 100 feet tall with a wider spread, although it usually stays half that size.

✔ **Black locust:** *Robinia pseudoacacia.* Zones 4 to 8. Although this species occurs wild from the midwestern U.S. to the Atlantic coastal states, it is not usually planted as a landscape specimen for several reasons: Individual trees tend to form groves by sending up root suckers and dropping seeds, it's susceptible to many diseases and pests, and it has sharp thorns along its limbs similar to those of roses. Trees grow 30 to 50 feet tall and have a narrow crown about 20 to 30 feet wide. On the positive side, black locust has very fragrant clusters of white flowers in early summer, the bark is deeply furrowed, and the wood strong and durable enough for use as fence posts. It grows in any soils, except for poorly drained ones. Prune in summer to avoid excessive bleeding.

Black locust has a number of cultivars and hybrids with attractive features that make them better landscape trees than the species. 'Frisia' has golden yellow foliage, 'Purple Robe' has rose to pink flowers and a compact growth habit. It grows only 30 to 40 feet tall. 'Idaho', also known as *R. × ambigua* 'Idahoensis', has fragrant pink flowers, too. It grows only 25 to 40 feet high and half as wide and does well in arid climates afflicted with temperature extremes.

✔ **Sassafras:** *Sassafras albidum.* Zones 4 to 9. Bright autumn foliage, attractive berries and stems, and golden spring flowers make this native to the eastern United States a winner. It grows 30 to 60 feet high and 25 to 40 feet wide, and has contorted, gnarly limbs that spread horizontally. The flowers emerge in clouds of yellow in early spring, followed by small purple berries on red stalks in midsummer. The mitten-shaped foliage is fragrant when crushed and turns spectacular yellow, orange, and red in autumn. Trees tend to send up root suckers that form thickets around them — pull the suckers to maintain a single specimen. Transplant seedlings, not suckers, in late winter to establish trees in natural settings and open areas. Sassafras grows in any soil after it's established, and needs full sun.

Leaning toward lindens

These excellent shade trees are common in parks, open spaces, and as street trees in much of temperate North America. They form densely branched, gracefully mounded trees that cast deep shade. The species listed in this chapter have toothed, heart-shaped leaves and very fragrant cream-colored or yellow flowers in early summer that serve as an important nectar source for honey bees.

They tolerate a wide range of soils from moist to dry, sandy to clay, acidic to slightly alkaline. Unfortunately, Japanese beetles, leaf rollers, aphids, and gypsy moth plague its leaves. Ice storms and deer frequently damage the soft wood. Most linden species tend to sucker profusely from the base of their trunks, especially when damaged, and often branch close to the ground or form multitrunk trees.

✔ **American linden or basswood:** *Tilia americana*. Zones 3 to 8. This large tree grows naturally throughout eastern North America. A mature tree often reaches 60 to 80 feet tall or more, and its wood is valued for woodworking and cabinetry. Although less commonly planted as a landscape tree than other lindens, some cultivars exist that have smaller or more compact habits.

✔ **Littleleaf linden:** *T. cordata*. Zones 3 to 7. One of the most commonly planted street trees, littleleaf linden has a neat pyramid shape when young, and spreads into a rounded, broad pyramid 60 to 80 feet by 40 to 60 feet wide as it ages. Use this linden along streets, in yards and open spaces as a shade tree, or as a large, pruned hedge. Avoid planting where bees could be a problem. Japanese beetles devour the lustrous dark green foliage. Common cultivars usually grow up to 40 feet tall and include 'Chancellor', 'Glenleven', and 'Greenspire'. 'June Bride' has 3 to 4 times more flowers than other cultivars.

✔ **Crimean linden:** *T.* × *euchlora*. Zones 3 to 7. This hybrid linden is noted for its glossy dark green leaves and graceful branching habit. It grows 40 to 60 feet tall and 20 to 30 feet wide in a broad oval to pyramid shape and the lower limbs often reach the ground.

✔ **Silver linden:** *T. tomentosa*. Zones 4 to 7. Growing the same size and shape as littleleaf linden, this species distinguishes itself by its dark green, shiny leaves (with white undersides) that shimmer in the breeze. The silvery gray bark resembles beech when young. These trees often grow more than one main trunk and have an upright pyramid to rounded habit. It flowers in midsummer about two weeks later than littleleaf linden.

✔ **Camperdown elm:** *Ulmus glabra* 'Camperdownii'. Zones 4 to 6. This is actually a grafted cultivar of the Scotch elm. The tree, grafted onto an American elm trunk, grows into a spreading, weeping mop 15 to 25 feet high and growing wider. The branches are attractive in winter after the leaves fall. It is susceptible to elm leaf beetle, aphids, Japanese beetles, Dutch elm disease, and many other diseases. It tolerates a wide range of soils.

✔ **Lacebark elm:** *Ulmus parvifolia.* Zones 5 to 9. This elm resists the devastating diseases and insects that wiped out American elms as ornamental trees in North America. It resembles its famous relative, however, and is useful as street trees and specimens for parks, large properties, and open spaces. It grows 40 to 50 feet high and wide although its size and habit depends on the cultivar. It grows best in moist, fertile soils, but tolerates urban conditions. It has grayish scaly bark that flakes off to reveal mottled orange-brown patches. Many cultivars exist including 'Drake' and 'Sempervirens', both of which grow in zones 7 to 9 and often remain semi-evergreen. 'Allee' closely resembles the American elm and grows 50 to 70 feet high in zones 5 to 8. 'Athena' has a rounded spreading habit and grows 40 feet high and 55 feet wide.

Deciduous Evergreens

Some trees have needles and cones like evergreens, but they drop all their foliage in the fall just like deciduous broadleaf plants. These *deciduous evergreens* usually have bright green spring foliage that turns yellow to golden brown in the fall. Use them wherever you want the look of an evergreen for the summer, but want to avoid winter shade. They also look great in groves that you can appreciate from a distance.

✔ **European larch:** *Larix decidua.* Zones 3 to 6. A member of the pine family, larch grows 70 to 75 feet tall and 25 to 30 wide in a pyramid shape with slender, drooping branches. The emerging foliage in spring is bright green and spectacular, as is the luminescent yellow it becomes in the fall. Use larch in large landscapes, especially in groups. It grows best in moist to well-drained, but not dry, soils and full sun. It doesn't do well in dry or alkaline soils. Prune, if necessary, in midsummer. The cultivar 'Pendula' is grafted onto an upright trunk from which it weeps gracefully.

✔ **Dawn redwood:** *Metasequoia glyptostroboides.* Zones 5 to 8. Scientists knew about this cone- to pyramid-shaped tree because fossil records showed that it existed 100 million years ago, but many thought it was extinct. Surprisingly, an explorer found living specimens in China in 1941. It bears cones and needled foliage, but drops all its ½- to one- inch needles after a golden to brown display each autumn. These trees can grow up to 3 feet per year, ultimately reaching 100 feet tall, in slightly acidic, wet to dry soil. It tends to continue growing late into the season and is often nipped by early frosts. Use dawn redwood along streams and ponds, in groves, parks, and other large landscapes.

✔ **Golden larch:** *Pseudolarix amabilis.* Zones 5 to 7. This tree grows in an open pyramid shape 30 to 50 feet tall and 20 to 40 feet wide and prefers moist, well-drained, fertile soil on the acidic side. It resembles European larch, and has bright yellow fall color. Use it in groves or as specimens where it has room to spread.

✔ **Common baldcypress:** *Taxodium distictum.* Zones 4 to 11. Forming a pyramid of loose, feathery branches, this tree grows in anything from standing water to well-drained streetside plantings. In and near water, it grows *knees*, woody stump-like projections, around its base. It grows 50 to 70 feet tall and 30 feet wide. Use it in wet, swampy locations or as a street tree. Plant it in groves or as specimens. The cultivar 'Shawnee Brave' has a narrow pyramid shape, growing 50 to 60 feet tall and only 20 feet wide.

Chapter 5

Fabulous Flowering Trees

*F*lowering trees are among the most revered and beloved of all landscape plants — often, individual trees are known for miles around for their seasonal displays. Many of the trees in this chapter also emit a heavenly fragrance as they cover themselves with bloom in their seasons.

The Budding Talent of Flowering Trees

In addition to giving you and your neighbors a few weeks of beautiful flowers, some trees offer attractive form, foliage, and bark, as well. The best of these trees continue the show with colorful or edible berries or fruit.

When you choose a flowering tree, look for one that has year-round features, and plant it where you can best enjoy the tree: Put those with fragrant flowers, for example, near a patio, window, sidewalk, or garden path. Light-colored flowers show best against a dark background and dark blooms against a pale one. Choose flower colors that complement your home and those of other landscape plants.

Horsechestnuts of a different color

Big, palm-shaped compound leaves; clusters of white to red flowers; and smooth, shiny brown nuts typify this group of trees and shrubs. They prefer deep, moist, fertile, well-drained, acidic soils. Some species are prone to several serious leaf diseases and many insect pests. Often messy trees, horsechestnuts drop fruit capsules, nuts, and large leaves, requiring extra raking — and making mowing around them difficult. The seeds are toxic to humans, but not to squirrels.

✔ **Red horsechestnut:** *Aesculus carnea.* Zones 4 to 8. One of the handsomest and best-sized trees of this group, the red horsechestnut grows 30 to 40 feet high and wide. It has spectacular spiky clusters of rose-red flowers in late spring. Use it as a specimen tree or for planting roadside. The cultivar 'Briottii' has deep-red flowers in 10-inch spikes.

✔ **Horse chestnut:** *A. hippocastenum.* Zones 4 to 7. A very large tree that's best left for large properties, this species also has a number of serious pests and diseases. It can grow to 100 feet high and nearly as wide, forming a mounding tree that branches nearly to the ground. Mature specimens are spectacular when the creamy white flowers bloom in late spring.

✔ **Red buckeye:** *A. pavia.* Zones 4 to 8. This very beautiful tree grows only 15 to 20 feet high, has glossy leaves, and develops deep rose-red flowers in mid-spring that attract hummingbirds. It branches near the ground and can be grown as a large multistemmed shrub or pruned as a small, rounded tree. It prefers light shade and moist, well-drained soil. This species received the Pennsylvania Horticultural Society Gold Medal in 1995.

✔ **Silk tree:** *Albizia julibrissin.* Zones 6 to 9. This fine-textured small tree has clusters of reddish pink, fragrant, brush-like flowers in late spring through summer. It grows 20 to 30 feet tall in a spreading vase shape and often has multiple trunks. The 20-inch long leaves are doubly compound — each leaflet is divided into more leaflets — giving the tree a tropical look. Silk tree grows in most soils and tolerates drought, alkaline soil, salt, and wind. Unfortunately, a wilt disease often kills these trees, and several insects infest it.

✔ **Shadblow serviceberry:** *Amelanchier canadensis, A. laevis,* and *A. arborea.* Zones 3 to 7. Also called *shad, shadblow, service tree,* or *saskatoon,* these species resemble each other so closely that one is often sold as another. They grow about 20 feet high and have upright, spreading crowns. They often sucker or form multiple trunked trees with silvery bark. They produce clouds of white flowers in spring, which ripen to delicious deep red to black fruits similar to blueberries by June. The specimen I planted outside my office window feeds a flock of appreciative catbirds as I write. They have glossy, deep green, oval foliage that turns brilliant yellow to orange in the fall. They have a few diseases, such as leaf spots and rust, and insects that pester them, but none serious. Shadblow serviceberry trees prefer moist, acidic soils.

- **Apple serviceberry:** *Amelanchier × grandiflora*. Zones 4 to 9. This hybrid grows 20 feet tall, spreads about 15 feet wide, and has a number of cultivars. A few of the best include 'Autumn Brilliance', which grows upright and has bright red fall color in zones 3 to 8, and 'Cole Select', which has an upright, spreading habit and red to orange fall foliage. 'Princess Diana' has a graceful spreading habit, bright red fall color, and is hardy in zone 3.

- **Eastern redbud:** *Cercis canadensis*. Zones 5 to 9. This 20 to 25-foot, multitrunked tree has graceful, wide-spreading, horizontal limbs. Before the heart-shaped leaves appear, pink flowers open in clusters all along the branches, followed by 2-inch pods, which remain through winter. They adapt to full sun to part shade and prefer moist, well-drained soils, but tolerate dry soil and aren't fussy about soil pH. Canker is the only serious problem in areas where the disease is common. Prune to remove diseased, damaged, and poorly placed limbs. Mulch to protect its shallow roots from weed competition and to keep the soil moist and cool.

White-flowered 'Alba' and 'Royal White' are hardy in zone 5 and parts of zone 4, while 'Texas White' grows only through zone 6. 'Flame', which has semi-double to double rosy-pink flowers and few pods, and pink-flowered 'Rubye Atkinson' are hardy to zone 5. 'Oklahoma' bears loads of purple-red flowers through zone 6. Cultivars with unusual foliage include 'Forest Pansy', which has dark purple new leaves that mature to deep burgundy to zone 6, and 'Silver Cloud' with creamy-white, variegated leaves.

- **Chinese redbud:** *C. chinenesis*. zones 6 to 9. This species has a more upright, but shrubby, habit than redbuds native to North America. It grows about 10 to 15 feet high, with bright rose-pink flowers and heart-shaped leaves. The cultivar 'Avondale' blooms heavily with deep lavender flowers and grows more tree-like than the species.

- **Western redbud:** *C. occidentalis*. Zones 7 to 10. This species is native to California and the west coast of the United States. It resembles eastern redbud except that the leaves differ in that the tips of the smaller leaves are notched instead of pointed. It grows 10 to 15 feet tall.

- **Chinese fringe tree:** *Chionanthus retusus*. Zones 6 to 8. You can grow this plant as a large shrub or small tree and the leathery foliage varies from nearly round to lance-shaped, depending on the source of the plants. Those with rounded foliage are more common in southern U.S. zones, and tend to be shrubby. Multitrunked trees grow to 15 to 20 feet tall by 20 to 25 feet wide. Clusters of white flowers appear at the tips of the new branch growth in May and June, followed by attractive dark blue fruits on female trees. Plant in acidic, moist to well-drained soils with plenty of organic material in full to part sun. It tolerates urban conditions. Prune in winter, if necessary.

- **White fringe tree:** *Chionanthus virginicus*. Zones 4 to 9. When this small tree blooms in late spring, it looks as though it's covered with white lace. The flowers, borne on the previous year's growth, have long, narrow petals — male trees have even longer petals. Female trees have blue fruits that are relished by birds in the fall. The multitrunked trees grow 20 to 25 feet high and spread wider, maturing to a rounded habit. It has no serious pests or disease and enjoys the same growing conditions as Chinese fringe tree (see previous bullet). Prune after flowering, if necessary.

- **Yellowwood:** *Cladrastis lutea*. Zones 4 to 8. Foot-long clusters of fragrant, white, pea-like flowers dangle from the limbs of this beautiful tree in May and June, followed by tan pods that remain on the tree through autumn. This 30 to 50 foot by 40 to 55 foot wide tree also has smooth, silvery bark and clear yellow autumn foliage. Use this graceful tree in any open area or landscape as a specimen or shade tree. It prefers well-drained alkaline to acidic soils, and full sun. It doesn't have any significant pests or diseases, but does have weak wood that tends to break under ice and snow buildup. Prune in summer after flowering, if necessary.

- **Flowering dogwood:** *Cornus florida*. Zones 5 to 9. Truly a tree with year-round appeal, flowering dogwood is one of the most widely planted flowering trees. From the early spring floral display to the fiery autumn color, attractive bark, and winter branches, dogwood is hard to beat. The only drawback to this lovely tree stems from its intolerance of urban conditions and harsh climates. Drought and air pollution and winter temperatures below −20° spell doom for most specimens. Insects and disease also take their toll, although some cultivars resist disease better than others. A few of the best cultivars from among the many available include 'Cherokee Chief' and 'Rubra', which have red flower bracts, and 'Cloud Nine', which is very cold hardy. 'Welchii' has white bracts and white, pink, and green variegated foliage that turns red to purple in the fall. 'Cherokee Princess' has large white bracts, is very cold hardy, resists disease, and is considered one of the best cultivars.

- **Kousa dogwood:** *C. kousa*. Zones 5 to 8. This Asian native deserves greater use in landscape, especially where disease decimates flowering dogwood. Kousa dogwood resists most of the worst diseases and is less bothered by borers. It grows 20 to 30 feet high and wide with a distinct horizontal habit. It blooms several weeks later than flowering dogwood and is a little cold hardier. The red fruits also make a good display in late summer and fall foliage ranges from scarlet to purple. Its low mature height makes it ideal for small properties and planting near buildings and under utility wires. The variety *chinensis* has larger flowers than the species and grows 30 feet tall. The cultivar of this variety, 'Milky Way', blooms very heavily and early in its life. 'Satomi' has pink to red flower bracts.

A CLOSER LOOK

Flowering dogwood

The flowers of this small tree define the arrival of spring in areas where it can be grown. The showy dogwood "flowers" are actually *bracts* or modified leaves, however, that surround the true flowers, which are small and greenish yellow. Although usually white, many cultivars have pink to red bracts. Bright red fruit, eagerly eaten by birds, form after the flowers drop. Flowering dogwoods grow 20 to 40 feet tall, forming small, single to multistemmed trees. Their slender twigs zigzag and spread horizontally from the trunk, giving the crown a layered look. These elegant trees look best planted against a dark-colored background that serves as a foil for their spectacular spring flowers, attractive summer foliage, and red autumn color.

Native to cool, moist woods and rocky hillsides, flowering dogwoods need well-drained, moist, humus-rich soil to prosper. They enjoy part shade in hot summer climates to full sun in cooler and cloudy areas. Drought and soggy soil can quickly send dogwoods into decline and leave them open to infection from disease or attack by stem-boring insects. Canker, twig blights, and insects frequently damage these trees and shorten their lives. Prune dogwoods to shape the trees and remove undesirable trunks and branches right after they flower in the spring. Take out dead or diseased wood as soon as you see it. Turn to the Chapter 14 for details. Keep the area under dogwoods well-mulched to hold moisture and cool the soil.

✔ **Pacific dogwood:** *C. nuttallii*. Zones 7 to 9. This tree grows all along the coast of western North America from Canada to Mexico. It grows 20 to 40 feet tall and has a pyramidal habit. Six to 8 rounded, white bracts surround its purple and green flowers. Attractive reddish-orange berries develop after the petals fall. It grow best in the moist, well drained, slightly acidic soils of its native habitat where its cold-sensitive flower buds are less subject to the vagaries of winter. Foliage turns orange to scarlet in the winter.

✔ **Cockspur hawthorn:** *Crataegus crus-galli*. Zones 4 to 7. This tree has classic, widely spreading horizontal branches that look attractive whether placed in an open field or in front of a tall building. It grows 20 to 30 feet tall and spreads wider. The glossy oval leaves turn red in the fall when the clusters of red-orange berries mature. The variety 'Inermis' is similar to the species, but is thornless.

✔ **English hawthorn:** *C. laevigata*. Zones 4 to 7. This small, round-headed tree has lobed leaves, clusters of small white to pink flowers, and red fruits. It grows 15 to 20 feet high and 12 to 20 wide and has an attractive branching habit. It is particularly prone to leaf diseases, although cultivars vary in their resistance. 'Crimson Cloud' is resistant to leaf blight and has red flowers with white centers. 'Paul's Scarlet'or 'Paulii' is very susceptible to blight, but has loads of double rose-colored blooms. 'Autumn Glory' is susceptible to leaf rust and fire blight, but has white flowers and lots of large red fruits in the fall.

Stuck on hawthorns

Hawthorns tolerate hot, dry conditions and urban pollution that many other flowering trees cannot. Wild specimens are also a common sight in pastures where grazing animals leave their thorny branches alone. This group of trees is prized for abundant spring bloom followed by attractive small red fruits that resemble ½-inch crabapples. Plant them in any well-drained, moist soil. Many serious diseases and insects plague these trees, however: Fireblight, leaf rusts, blights and spots, apple scab, leaf miners, aphids, and other insects are all too common. Most species also have dangerous 1- to 2-inch long thorns that make them unsuitable for use in many public areas. Use them in landscapes where they can by viewed at a distance or at least where people won't pass close by their well-armed limbs.

✔ **Lavalle hawthorn:** *C. × lavellei.* Zones 4 to 7. This hybrid is mostly thornless, and has handsome fall foliage color. It grows 15 to 30 feet by 10 to 20 feet wide, has orange-red fruits, and resists leaf rust disease.

✔ **Washington hawthorn:** *C. phaenopyrum.* Zones 4 to 8. This deservedly popular tree is also grown as a large shrub. It usually branches close to the ground and reaches 25 to 30 feet by 20 to 25 feet wide with a rounded crown. It is very heat tolerant and has glossy lobed leaves that turn orange to scarlet in autumn. Heavy clusters of small red fruits persist all winter, making this an attractive tree in all seasons.

✔ **Green hawthorn:** *C. viridis.* Zones 4 to 7. The cultivar 'Winter King' is among the most popular hawthorns for landscape use. It grows 20 to 25 feet tall and spreads wider in a rounded vase shape. It is fairly resistant to rust disease and has loads of persistent, ½-inch. red fruit. The flaky bark is attractive, too. It has shiny dark green foliage and thorns.

✔ **Franklin tree:** *Franklinia alatamaha.* Zones 5 to 8. This tree no longer exists in the wild, but has been cultivated for its 3-inch, fragrant white, cup-shaped flowers for over 200 years. Flowers appear in mid to late summer on the upright stems. The multitrunked trees reach 10 to 25 feet tall and spread 6 to 15 feet wide, with spectacular red to plum-colored autumn foliage. Franklin tree has some serious diseases that limit its growth in most of the South. It's also fussy about growing conditions and is often short-lived unless given full sun and acidic, moist, fertile, well-drained soil.

✔ **Carolina silverbell:** *Halesia tetraptera.* Zones 4 to 8. White cherry-like flowers about one inch across bloom in April and May before the leaves emerge. This multitrunked, low-branched tree grows 30 to 40 feet by 20 to 35 feet and has a rounded crown. The dark-gray bark has darker vertical ridges that add winter interest. Use silverbell in natural settings or as a specimen tree. Plant container-grown specimens in acidic, well-drained, moist, highly organic soils in part shade to full sun. It has sparse roots and doesn't like to be transplanted after it's established. Mountain silverbell, sometimes called *H. monticola*, is a larger tree, growing 60 to 80 feet tall.

- **Chinese witchhazel:** *Hamamelis mollis.* Zones 5 to 8. This species has particularly fragrant yellow flowers in February to March and yellow to orange fall foliage in late autumn. It grows 10 to 15 feet tall and wide in a vase shape. Cultivars include 'Goldcrest', which has yellow flowers with a hint of red, growing 12 feet high. 'Pallida' has flowers 1½ inches across, with orange to red fall foliage.

- **Vernal witchhazel:** *H. vernalis.* Zones 4 to 8. Native to the central United States, this species has very fragrant ½- to ¾-inch wide yellow to red flowers in mid-winter starting in January in the warmest regions and March in colder climates. The yellow fall foliage remains showy for 2 to 3 weeks and sometimes the dry leaves hang on the tree through the winter. Vernal witchhazel grows 10 feet high and spreads wider.

- **Common witchhazel:** *H. virginiana.* Zones 3 to 8. This native of the eastern United States is the cold hardiest of the witchhazel species and one of the largest, growing, reaching 20 to 30 tall and nearly as wide with a rounded, spreading crown. Its fragrant, 1-inch, yellow flowers open in late autumn, usually before the yellow fall foliage drops. Common witchhazel prefers moist, acidic, well-drained soil, and tolerates urban conditions if you provide adequate water.

- **Witchhazel:** *H. × intermedia.* Zones 5 to 8. This group of hybrids grows 15 to 20 feet tall and spread about the same in width. They bloom in colors from yellow to orange-red between January and March, depending on the cultivar and climate, and flowers may be 2 to 3 inches wide. Some of the most commonly available cultivars include 'Arnold Promise', which has fragrant, 2-inch, yellow flowers and grows up to 20

A CLOSER LOOK

Which witchhazel?

Witchhazels bloom at the most unusual time of year — autumn and winter — depending on the species and the climate where they grow. Their yellow to red petals look like narrow, twisted strips of crepe paper radiating out like spokes of a wheel — they hang on the tree for several weeks, and some are fragrant. Their autumn foliage is often spectacular, too, in shades of yellow through bright orange-red. They usually grow as multistemmed small trees or large shrubs with spreading, upright branches.

Plant witchhazel in moist, well-drained soils with lots of organic matter in the light shade of natural, woodland settings; against an evergreen backdrop; or near a patio or walkway where you can enjoy their flowers close up. They have few serious pests or diseases. If necessary, prune after flowering.

feet, and 'Diane' with coppery red, 1½-inch flowers, and good yellow-orange autumn foliage. 'Jelena' or 'Copper Beauty' has 2-inch, red-orange-yellow twisted flowers and yellow-orange fall color. 'Primavera' has fragrant soft yellow flowers, and blooms heavily.

✔ **Chinese flame tree:** *Koelreuteria bipinnata.* Zones 6 to 8. This tree blooms in late summer, when its upright 1- to 2-foot high, 1-foot wide clusters of yellow flowers are especially welcome. Shortly after the spectacular bloom ends, the seed heads turn pinkish and can be cut and dried for use in long-lasting dried floral arrangements. If not removed, the seeds spread and sprout readily in surrounding soil. The trees grow 20 to 30 feet tall by 10 to 20 feet wide in an upright, spreading habit. The large compound leaves have pointed oval leaflets, unlike its relative, the goldenrain tree (see the following bullet). It needs full sun and adapts to nearly any well-drained soil.

✔ **Goldenrain tree:** *Koelreuteria paniculata.* Zones 5 to 8. Prized for its yellow flowers in midsummer, and tolerance of difficult sites, this tree looks good in small yards and parks alike. It grows quickly and matures into a rounded tree that grows 30 to 40 feet tall by 30 to 50 feet wide, with 18-inch long compound leaves that have lobed leaflets. The small flowers grow in foot-long clusters from the branch tips and cover the tree with bloom. Attractive green seedpods turn brown and papery by autumn. Goldenrain tree adapts to nearly any well-drained soil, including drought-prone acidic or alkaline conditions, as well as urban conditions and wind. Prune in winter, if necessary.

✔ **Goldenchain tree:** *Laburnum × watereri.* Zones 5 to 7. This small tree has a rounded, upright habit and grows 15 to 20 feet high and wide. It puts on an amazing display of cascading yellow flower chains in May and June that covers the tree. It grows best in cooler climates and prefers moist, well-drained soils and tolerates high pH and light shade. The cultivar 'Vossi' has flower chains up to 24 inches long and a compact habit. Use as a specimen tree or group several in a mass planting.

✔ **Crape myrtle:** *Lagerstroemia indica.* Zones 7 to 9. A classic small tree for warm climates, crape myrtle has year-round ornamental appeal. The smooth, muscular trunks and peeling gray and reddish-brown bark look attractive in all seasons. From midsummer into autumn, they cover themselves with 4-inch by 8-inch flower clusters of crinkled petals in colors from white through red. Flowering occurs on the current season's growth. Deadhead the spent blooms to encourage a longer flowering season (see Chapter 15 for more information on deadheading). Fall foliage colors range from orange-red to maroon, depending on the cultivar. Prune into a 15- to 20-foot specimen tree or train 5- to 10-foot dwarf cultivars for hedges and screens. They prefer moist, well-drained soil and full sun, but tolerate drought when established. Grown as a shrub in zone 6, crape myrtle will regrow from the roots if the branches die in cold weather.

So many exquisite cultivars exist for this plant that it's best to narrow your choice by considering only disease-resistant plants. Powdery mildew and leaf spot cause serious damage, as do aphids, Japanese beetles, and scale. The National Arboretum introduced many mildew-resistant hybrids with the names of American Indian tribes, such as dark purple-flowered 'Catawba', pink 'Seminole', red 'Cherokee', and white 'Natchez'. Mildew-resistant shrub-sized cultivars include bright lavender 'Centennial' and dark red 'Victor'.

✔ **Yulan magnolia:** *M denudata*. Zones 5 to 8. This small, deciduous tree grows to 30 feet tall and wide, and blooms in early spring. The white, fragrant, tulip-shaped flowers spread open to 6 inches across. Although the early flowers are frequently frosted, the tree can survive through zone 5.

✔ **Bull bay or southern magnolia:** *M. grandiflora*. Zones 6 to 9. The undisputed queen of the southern flowering trees, this magnolia grows 60 to 80 feet high and 30 to 50 feet across. It has 5- to 10-inch, evergreen leaves, often with fuzzy, rusty-colored undersides. The creamy white, very fragrant blooms up to 12 inches in diameter appear in early summer and continue sporadically throughout the season. The growth habit of this tree varies from wide spreading to columnar depending on the cultivar. Some, such as 'Little Gem', stay much smaller than the species. This cultivar forms a 15 to 20 foot shrub. Other popular cultivars include cold hardy 'Bracken's Brown Beauty', 'D.D. Blanchard', classic 'Edith Bogue', 20-foot 'St. Mary', and 'Samuel Sommer'.

✔ **Lily magnolia:** *M. liliiflora*. Zones 5 to 8. This species grows 8 to 10 feet tall and produces loads of 3- to 4-inch, tulip-shaped fragrant flowers in early- to mid-season. The most commonly available cultivars include 'Nigra', a compact, purple-flowering shrub that blooms in late mid-season, and 'O'Neill', another dark purple-flowered shrub that is hardier than the species but prone to mildew fungus. 'Holland Red' has dark red flowers with a watermelon fragrance.

✔ **Kosar-DeVos hybrids:** *M. liliiflora* × *M. stellata*. Zones 4 to 7. This group of eight cultivars originated at the U.S. National Arboretum and each bears a girl's name. They grow 8 to 10 feet high and have fragrant, cup-shaped flowers that bloom in early- to mid-season. Unfortunately, they are prone to mildew. The 4- to 6-inch flowers range in color from violet to deep purple. 'Ann', widely considered the best of the cultivars, has deep rose buds that open to pink blooms. 'Betty' has the largest violet-colored flowers, at 8 inches.

✔ **Loebner magnolia:** *M. × loebneri*. Zones 4 to 8. This group of deciduous hybrids grows 25 to 30 feet by 30 to 35 feet wide, with a nice, rounded form. They bloom in early- to mid-season, usually in March or April, and have fragrant white to pink flowers about 4 inches across. The flowers resemble those of star magnolia, one of this hybrid's parents, and bloom when only 2 to 3 years old. They are among the cold hardiest magnolias. The best cultivars include 'Ballerina', purple-pink 'Leonard Messel', and white-flowering 'Merrill' and 'Spring Snow'.

A CLOSER LOOK

Magnificent magnolia

Most magnolia species have evergreen foliage, but the most popular and cold-hardy hybrids are deciduous. In general, the deciduous magnolias usually bloom in early- to mid-spring while evergreen species bloom from early summer to autumn. Low winter temperatures and early spring frosts limit magnolias' northern range. Choose cultivars that bloom when the coldest weather has passed in your area or plant them in a protected microclimate (see Chapter 2). Plants on the north side of buildings, for example, usually bloom later than those exposed to full sun on the south side.

Magnolias prefer moist, well-drained, slightly acidic soil with plenty of organic matter, and full sun to light shade. The tricky part about growing magnolias is getting them planted — after they're established, they grow vigorously in tough conditions. Magnolias have fragile root systems that break easily and they resent transplanting. Choose container-grown plants and leave the bare-root magnolias to the experts to grow. Some can take many years from transplanting until they produce their first blossom, while others bloom when barely knee-high. If you just can't wait for flowers, choose a blooming plant from a local nursery. Mulch after planting to protect the shallow, easily damaged roots.

✔ **Shrub-sized magnolias:** If you have a small space or just want to keep the gorgeous flowers right up close and personal, try some of these magnolias that grow less than 20 feet tall. You can keep them as multi-stemmed shrubs branched to the ground or prune them into small single or multi-trunked trees.

✔ **Larger magnolias:** Most magnolias attain tree-sized proportions and, when they bloom, the sight is unlike any other flowering tree. The smaller species and cultivars suit most home landscapes, while the largest look best in big landscapes where they can spread their branches.

Magnolias require very little pruning. Shape trees and shrubs as they grow by removing small branches right after flowering. If you develop the plant's habit while it is young, you can avoid major renovations when the plant matures. Turn to Chapter 14 for details. For more information about magnolias, contact the American Magnolia Society at 907 South Chestnut St., Hammond, LA 90403-5102.

✔ **Saucer magnolia:** *M. × soulangiana.* Zones 4 to 9. This deciduous hybrid has been around since the early 1800s, and many fine cultivars now exist. The tulip or saucer-shaped flowers appear in white through cream and many shades of pink and purple. Fragrance varies with the cultivar. They bloom early and are frequently devastated by late freezes that turn the blossoms to mush. They grow 20 to 30 feet tall. The cultivars that regularly appear in garden centers and nurseries include 'Alexandrina', 'Lennei', 'Rustica Rubra' (which is hardy to zone 5), and 'Verbanica'.

✔ **Star magnolia:** *M. stellata.* Zones 4 to 8. This wildly popular deciduous species explodes with spreading, starry flowers in early spring, long before the leaves unfurl. The 4- to 6-inch wide fragrant flowers have

15 to 18 strap-shaped petals. The leaves are oval and 3 to 4 inches long. Grow this 5 to 20 foot shrub either branched to the ground or limbed up as a multistemmed small tree. Popular cultivars include 'Centennial', 'Jane Platt', early-flowering 'Royal Star', 'Rubra', and late-flowering 'Waterlily'.

✔ **Sweetbay magnolia:** *M. virginiana.* Zones 5 to 9. Evergreen to deciduous depending on the climate, this small tree or large shrub grows native from Florida to Massachusetts. It has fragrant, lemon-scented, cup-shaped, white flowers that appear on and off from late spring to late summer and its long, lance-shaped leaves have silvery undersides. The species grows 10 to 20 feet high and wide. Many cultivars exist with various growth habits and all have 2- to 4-inch white flowers.

✔ **Magnolia hybrids:** Many, many magnolia hybrids exist, each with unique flowers, habits, and hardiness. Some of the favorites frequently found in garden centers and recommended by magnolia experts include the following:

- 'Athene', a 20- to 25-foot, upright-growing, deciduous tree for zones 7 to 8. It has 8- to 10-inch, saucer-shaped pink and white, fragrant blooms.

- 'Elizabeth', one of the first truly yellow-flowered magnolias. The tulip-shaped blooms appear in early- to mid-spring on upright 20-foot trees in zones 5 to 9.

- 'Galaxy', which grows 30 to 35 feet tall and produces large, red-purple flowers late in the season in zones 5 to 9.

- 'Royal Crown' has crown-like flowers with flat red-purple petals surrounding upright petals in the center. It blooms in the spring and again in the summer in zones 6 to 10.

- 'Wada's Memory' has white flowers and grows to medium-sized, deciduous trees. It performs well in the coastal areas of California in zones 7 to 10.

✔ **Sourwood or Lily-of-the-valley tree:** *Oxydendrum arboreum.* Zones 5 to 9. This tree grows naturally through the southeastern United States in gravelly, moist soils. Its lustrous, pointed, oval leaves turn from dark green to yellow, red, and purple in the fall. It blooms in midsummer, sending out 10-inch long clusters of small, white, bell-shaped flowers from the branch tips. When it's in bloom, this tree looks truly exotic. It grows into an upright, rounded oval 25 to 30 feet by 20 feet wide. Grow it in acidic, moist, well-drained soil with plenty of organic matter, in full sun to part shade. Use it as a specimen tree.

✔ **Carolina cherrylaurel:** *Prunus caroliniana.* Zones 7 to 10. This broadleaf evergreen grows readily throughout its natural range from Virginia to Florida. Attaining heights of 20 to 30 feet and spreading 15 to 20 feet, it makes a fine large hedge or small tree. Its shiny, dark-green foliage looks good year 'round, and it produces fragrant white flowers in early spring. Birds relish the black fruits. It prefers moist, well-drained soils, but adapts to nearly any situation including part shade. The cultivar 'Compacta', also sold as 'Bright 'n' Tight', has a denser habit and pyramid-shaped form that's better for landscape use.

✔ **Cherry plum:** *P. cerasifera.* Zones 5 to 8. Most of the cherry plum cultivars offered for sale have purple leaves and small, pink flowers in mid-spring. These trees grow 15 to 30 feet tall and 15 to 25 feet wide, depending on the cultivar. Unfortunately, they are subject to all of the pests and diseases common to *Prunus* species. Plant in moist, well-drained soil in full sun and keep them growing vigorously to help them avoid most problems. The best cultivars include 'Krauter's Vesuvius', also known as 'Vesuvius', 'Thundercloud', 'Mount St. Helens' and 'Newport' can grow in zone 4.

✔ **Sargent cherry:** *P. sargentii.* Zones 4 to 7. Of all the flowering cherries, this one has the most to offer in all seasons of the year. It has shiny, reddish-brown bark, and lustrous deep green leaves that turn red in the autumn. Trees typically grow 20 to 30 feet high and wide, and blossom in early spring. The pink flowers open before the leaves emerge and mature into small black fruits. Sargent cherry is the cold-hardiest of the flowering cherries. The cultivar 'Columnaris' blooms a little later than the species and has a more upright, vase shape.

✔ **Japanese flowering cherry:** *P. serrulata.* Zones 5 to 9. This popular cherry covers itself with pink to white, single or double flowers in early spring. Its numerous cultivars grow 20 to 30 feet tall and have a spreading, vase-shaped, or weeping habit, depending on the cultivar. Nurseries frequently graft cherry cultivars onto a tall, straight trunk of another species of cherry, so you must be sure to prune off any limbs or suckers that grow below the graft. (See the Chapter 14 for more information.) A few of the many available cultivars include 'Amanogawa', which grows very upright and narrow with fragrant pink flowers, and 'Royal Burgundy', with reddish purple foliage. 'Kwanzan', the most widely planted cultivar, has clusters of double pink flowers. 'Shirofugan' and 'Shirotae' or 'Mt. Fuji' have double to semi-double, fragrant white flowers.

✔ **Higan cherry:** *P. × subhirtella.* Zones 5 to 8. You will find this cherry offered usually in two different forms — weeping or upright spreading. The weeping forms have 'Pendula' in their names and are commonly grafted onto a 6-foot tall trunk of a different cherry. 'Pendula' has single pink flowers in early- to mid-spring, while 'Pendula Plena Rosea' has double flowers of a deeper pink color. 'Autumnalis' opens its double pink blooms in the fall and again in the spring. It has a spreading habit and grows 25 feet high and wide. 'Rosy Cloud' has double pink flowers and a spreading upright habit.

✔ **Yoshino cherry:** *P. × yedoensis.* Zones 6 to 8. This is the cherry famous for its spring display in Washington, D.C. These magnificent trees grow quickly up to 50 feet tall by 30 feet wide. Clusters of white to pale pink flowers turn the limbs into clouds of bloom in early spring. The deep green leaves turn orange to gold in the fall.

A CLOSER LOOK

Cheering for flowering cherries

The genus *Prunus* is home to more than 400 species of shrubs and trees, and includes peaches, plums, apricots, and almonds, as well as cherries. Most people, however, grow the elegant flowering cherry species for their flowers, not their fruit. The flowering display of some species and cultivars is so spectacular that it attracts crowds of tourists, as in the case of Washington, D.C., in the early spring.

Unlike some fussy landscape plants, cherries make few demands. They enjoy moist, well-drained soil, but put up with a wide range of soil pH and texture. Full sun is best, but some species tolerate part shade. Despite their ease of culture, though, cherries host a large number of pests and diseases, many of them serious. They include aphids, stem borers, and leaf-eating insects plus cankers and leaf spots. Prune cherries after they flower in the spring to shape the trees and remove undesirable branches. Prune out any diseased or damaged limbs whenever they occur.

✔ **Korean mountain ash:** *Sorbus alnifolia*. Zones 3 to 7. The leaves of this hardy tree resemble those of beech, change from bright spring green to dark green, and then yellow to orange in the fall. The combination of fall foliage with red berries is quite a sight. The trees grow 40 to 50 feet tall and 20 to 30 feet wide in a rounded pyramid, spreading with age. Plant them in well-drained, moist soil and prune in early spring.

✔ **European mountain ash:** *S. aucuparia*. Zones 3 to 6. This widely grown tree has feathery compound leaves that give it a tropical look and orange-red berries in autumn. It grows 20 to 40 feet by 15 to 30 feet, frequently branches into multiple stems a few feet from the ground, and has a rounded habit. Numerous cultivars include 'Cardinal Royal', which has leaves with silvery undersides, and 'Blackhawk', an upright 30-foot by 20-foot tree that grows well in the midwestern United States.

✔ **Stewartia:** *Stewartia koreana, S. pseudocamellia*. Zones 5 to 7. Small stature, mid- to late-summer flowers, reddish-purple fall foliage, and beautiful flaky bark make this a tree for all seasons. The 2- to 3-inch flowers resemble camellias, while the bark flakes off to reveal orange to cinnamon colors underneath. They have few pest or disease problems. Stewartias like moist, well-drained, acidic soil with lots of organic matter, and full sun to part shade in hot climates. They dislike transplanting. Use these 20 to 40 foot trees as specimens in any landscape — they make good companions for rhododendrons and other species with similar cultural needs.

✔ **Japanese snowbell:** *Styrax japonicus*. Zones 5 to 8. A small, graceful tree for any landscape situation, snowbell grows 20 to 30 feet high and wide with horizontally spreading branches. It has ¾ to 1-inch, white bell-shaped flowers that hang below the branches in May to June. Grow this tree in moist, acidic, well-drained soil with plenty of organic matter. Use it near patios, in small yards, under utility wires, and in groups.

Mountain ash

These small trees offer graceful leaves and very showy white flower clusters in May, followed by spectacular red to orange berries. Unfortunately, some species are very disease and insect prone. Fireblight, borers, and cankers cause the most damage. Keep the trees growing vigorously and away from urban conditions of pollution and drought to help ward off problems. Use mountain ashes as specimen trees where you can enjoy their spreading habit and seasonal displays.

✔ **Japanese zelkova:** *Zelkova serrata.* Zones 5 to 8. Like its relative, the American elm, zelkova grows in a vase shape with a rounded head, making it an excellent street tree. It reaches 50 to 80 feet tall and prefers deep moist soil, but tolerates drought, wind, and a wide range of soil pH, including alkaline. Although not completely immune, zelkova resists the devastating Dutch elm disease, as well as infestation from the Japanese beetle and elm leaf beetle. If necessary, prune in the fall. The cultivar 'Green Vase' grows vigorously to 65 feet tall and 35 feet wide and is especially tolerant of urban conditions. It received the Pennsylvania Horticultural Society's Gold Medal in 1988.

Investigating the Flowering Crabapple

Crabapples (*Malus* species) reign as one of the premier deciduous flowering trees in zones 4 to 7. In May, the trees burst into clouds of bloom from purest white to darkest red. But beyond the spring bloom that all crabapples share, the range of habits, sizes, fruits, and cultural needs diverges dramatically. So much variation exists in the world of flowering crabs that you could easily think they all belonged to entirely different species. The best way to sort out the 900 or so named species, hybrids, cultivars, and varieties is to choose the characteristics you want for your landscape and then look for matching plants. Consider the following attributes:

✔ **Flowers:** The color range includes white, pale to deep rosy pink, and red. The buds also range in color and are often a contrasting color to the open petals. Some flowers are single and cup-shaped, while others are fluffy doubles. Others still fall somewhere in between. Some have fringed petals, although most are rounded, and some are fragrant.

- ✔ **Fruit:** One of crabapples finest features, fruit can remain attractive for months and create a lasting focal point for a winter display. Fruit size ranges from miniature (¼ inch across) to large (2 inches) in colors from yellow to gold, from orange-red to crimson. Birds love the smaller sizes and humans, too, can eat the fruit, especially when made into jelly or preserves.

- ✔ **Foliage:** Most have green pointed oval leaves, but some have lobed foliage or reddish-green leaves. Texture ranges from delicate to leathery.

- ✔ **Habit:** Round-headed and spreading, upright and vase to column-shaped, or weeping — take your pick. Sometimes the upright forms that you see in the garden center become more spreading as the tree grows and matures.

- ✔ **Height:** Small flowering crabs grow 10 to 15 feet tall and many make suitable container specimens. Medium-sized, 15 to 25 foot trees, look good in the average home landscape, while larger trees up to 40 feet in height are best suited to parks and other large display areas.

- ✔ **Disease resistance:** Crabapples suffer from several serious diseases that make them unsightly at best and sometimes kill them outright. Many newer cultivars resist infection and are always a better choice. All the cultivars listed in this section are disease resistant, unless otherwise noted.

- ✔ **Hardiness:** Crabapples can live in zones 3 to 8, but individual cultivars grow better in some climates than others. If you live at either end of the climate extreme, look first for plant hardiness before any other feature.

Crabapples need full sun and well-drained soil, but, beyond that, they aren't too fussy. Any soil with a pH between 5.5 and 7.5 — whether clay or loam — suits them just fine. In cold climates, avoid planting flowering crabs in frost pockets where late spring frosts can ruin the bloom. Diseases can devastate susceptible crabs, ruining their foliage and fruit, and killing limbs. Apple scab, cedar-apple rust, powdery mildew, and fire blight are the worst and most common offenders. Insects, such as aphids, mites, and caterpillars, as well as rodents and deer, love to chew on crabapples.

Most flowering crabapple cultivars are grafted onto rootstocks of another cultivar that give them uniform height and wider tolerance to soil and climate conditions. Prune off any suckers or branches that grow below the graft union. Usually grown as multitrunked trees, flowering crabs require some pruning to shape and maintain. (Turn to Chapter 14 for tips.)

Hundreds of flowering crabs exist for every landscape situation. The following cultivars all remain under 25 feet tall, have ¼ to ½-inch wide red fruit, are disease-resistant, and are hardy in zones 4 to 7 unless otherwise noted.

✔ **Upright vase to column-shaped** cultivars include 'Adirondack', which has white flowers; 'Centurion', which has red buds that open to rose-red flowers; and 'Harvest Gold', with white flowers late in the season that mature into golden fruit. 'Madonna' has fragrant, double white flowers and golden fruit blushed red. 'Red Baron' has reddish new growth that matures to bronze-green and dark red flowers and fruits.

✔ **Round to spreading** cultivars include 'Adams', which has dark pink buds, pink flowers, persistent red fruit, and orange-red fall color; 'Brandywine', with fragrant, deep pink, double flowers and yellowish fruit; 'Christmas Holly', with red buds opening to white flowers and loads of small bright red fruit; and 'Coralburst', which has deep red buds, semidouble pink flowers, reddish-orange fruit, and is hardy in zone 3. 'Dolgo', hardy to zone 2, grows up to 40 feet high and has large, red fruit that make wonderful jelly. 'Indian Magic' has red buds, deep pink flowers, and red to golden-orange fruit, while 'Liset' has very deep red flowers and ½ to 1-inch red fruit. 'Robinson' has deep pink flowers and bronze-green foliage. 'Royalty' has outstanding purple foliage, red flowers, and red fruit — it is quite susceptible to scab and fireblight, however. 'Snowdrift', hardy to zone 3, has tiny ¼-inch orange fruits, red buds, and white flowers.

✔ **Weeping** cultivars include 'Molten Lava', which has abundant ½-inch orange-red fruit and white flowers; 'White Cascade', with white flowers and yellow ½-inch fruits; and 'Weeping Candied Apple', with pink flowers and bright red ½-inch fruit. 'Red Jade' has pink buds, white flowers, and loads of small red fruit, but isn't disease resistant.

Although not truly weeping, 'Pink Princess' has a low, spreading habit and is very disease resistant. The first leaves of spring are purple, maturing to bronze-green. Flowers are rose pink and mature to tiny deep red fruits.

If you find yourself hooked on flowering crabapples and want to know much more about them, read *Flowering Crabapples* by Fr. John L. Fiala.

Chapter 6

Great Adaptations: Tropical and Desert Trees

In This Chapter

▶ Choosing trees for hot, dry climates

▶ Taking a look at spectacular trees for tropical gardens

▶ Introducing a few of my favorite palm trees

---

*W*herever you live, you can grow plants that have adapted to your climate. Unlike the more widely acclimated trees and shrubs described throughout this book, the trees in this chapter live only in subtropical climates where temperatures rarely fall below 20°. Some of them need moist soil year 'round while others thrive in arid climates where rainfall is scarce. If you call one of these special places home, consider some of the special trees in this chapter.

Where Sun Scorches the Earth

Plants that grow in arid climates must be able to withstand long dry seasons that have little rain or water for months, low humidity, and intense sunlight. Not all arid climates are the same, however. Some, like those of the plains states in the U.S., have cold winters where temperatures dip down below 0°. Many of the plants described in Chapters 3 through 5 grow well in such areas. Other arid regions, like the true deserts of the southwestern U.S., have scorching, bone-dry hot weather and a plant palate all their own. The trees in this section are adapted mostly to those subtropical regions.

When you choose trees for areas where water is a limited resource, select only species that remain attractive with minimal water, such as the ones in this section. Even though they need less water than many other plants, most of these plants still need some water during the growing season, however, to look their best in your landscape. When you do water your trees, take advantage of water-conserving strategies like mulching, drip irrigation, and proper soil preparation, which are covered in Part IV.

Native plants — those that grow naturally in a region — are superbly adapted and, after they're established, Mother Nature provides for most of their needs. Even tough plants, however, are vulnerable to drought when newly planted. In most arid regions, autumn is the best time for planting because the trees have the coming cool (and hopefully, moist) season to get their roots in the ground. Regardless of when you plant them, water the new transplants enough to keep the soil slightly moist for at least the first year, until they can get their roots firmly established. But take it easy with the water — some arid climate plants suffer more from overwatering than underwatering!

The following trees and shrubs thrive in the arid, dry summer climates typical of much of California and the southwestern United States. Although quite a few other trees described in Chapters 3, 4, and 5, including junipers, Chinese pistache, and privets, can grow in drought-prone areas, the trees that follow grow almost exclusively in arid climates. Choose these plants for subtropical, low-water landscapes.

- **Acacias:** *Acacia* species. Zones 8 to 11. Most members of this large family of tough, fast-growing evergreen trees and shrubs have fragrant yellow flowers in late winter or early spring and finely cut foliage. *A. baileyana*, one of most common species, grows 20 to 30 feet high and at least as wide. It's good on slopes, but isn't appropriate for small gardens. The cultivar 'Purpurea' has purplish new growth. For smaller yards, try pearl acacia, *A. podalriifolia*, which grows only 10 to 20 feet high and has silvery foliage.

- **Peppermint tree:** *Agonis flexuosa*. Zones 10 to 11. This tough evergreen Australian native reaches 20 to 40 feet high with a spreading crown. It has white flowers in late spring to early summer and its leaves smell like peppermint when crushed.

- **Strawberry tree:** *Arbutus unedo*. Zones 8 to 11. This lovely evergreen, multitrunked tree has dark green leaves with red stems. It has shiny, reddish-brown bark and white spring flowers, followed by showy red fruit. It grows 10 to 25 feet high and wide. A related hybrid, *A*. 'Marina' is more upright, up to 40 feet high, with equally attractive bark, flowers, and fruit — it's a good substitute for the harder-to-grow western native, madrone (*A. menziesii*).

- **Blue palo verde:** *Cercidium floridum*. Zones 10 and 11. This southwestern desert native has an airy canopy of small leaves and thorny, blue-green branches with bright yellow flowers in spring. It grows fast to 25 feet high and wide and tends to branch low.

- **Desert willow:** *Chilopsis linearis*. Zones 6 to 11. Desert willow is a deciduous desert native that grows into a 20- to 25-foot tall shrub or small tree and needs pruning to looks its best. Trumpet-shaped flowers come in many shades of white, pink, and purple in spring and fall.

✔ **Gum:** *Eucalyptus* species. Zones 9 to 11, but varies by species. Widely planted in California and Arizona, this large family of fast-growing, ever-green trees is mostly native to Australia. Many are quite large and upright, reaching upwards of 100 feet high. Smaller species include *E. nicholii*, Nichol's, a willow-leafed peppermint, which grows nearly 40 feet high and has a willowy upright habit, rough dark red bark, and incon-spicuous white flowers. The silver dollar gum, *E. polyanthemos*, reaches 20 to 60 feet high, with silver foliage that's great for arrangements. Coral gum, *E. torquata,* has bright-red flowers and a narrow habit, growing 15 to 20 feet high. Red-flowering gum, *E. ficifolia,* is popular in coastal areas, producing bright orange to red flowers on a rounded tree, 30 to 40 feet high. Eucalyptus long-horned beetle can be a problem.

✔ **Australian willow:** *Geijera parviflora.* Zones 9 to 11. Australian willow is a tough, willow-like, evergreen tree with long narrow leaves and droop-ing habit. It grows 25 to 35 feet high with a narrow crown and is good for small yards.

✔ **Silk oak:** *Grevillea robusta.* Zones 9 to 11. This fast-growing, narrow, upright, evergreen tree has bright-green leaves and orange-yellow flow-ers in spring. It grows 50 to 100 feet high and is useful as a screen, but quickly outgrows most yards and tends to be messy.

✔ **Cajeput tree:** *Melaleuca quinquinervis.* Zones 9 to 11. This distinctive upright, often multitrunked, evergreen tree with spongy white bark pro-duces white, yellow, or pink flowers in summer and fall. It grows 20 to 40 feet high and looks delightful when planted in groves or groups of sev-eral trees. Cajeput tree is a good birch substitute for arid areas. Flaxleaf paperbark, *M. linariifolia,* is similar but is slightly smaller and rounded, with puffy white flowers.

✔ **Jerusalem thorn:** *Parkinsonia aculeata.* Zones 9 to 11. This deciduous desert tree grows 15 to 30 feet high and wide and has wiry, greenish yellow branches covered with small, scale-like leaflets and thorns. It pro-duces yellow flowers in the spring and sporadically throughout the year.

✔ **Mesquite:** *Prosopis* species. Zones 9 to 11. Mesquite is a tough, desert tree with an airy canopy and many trunks. Small, greenish-yellow flow-ers are followed by seedpods. You can find several species to choose from, all about as tough as desert plants come.

✔ **Chinese tallow tree:** *Sapium sebiferum.* Zones 9 to 10. Chinese tallow tree is one of the few deciduous trees that has good fall color in arid areas. Poplar-like leaves turn bright shades of orange and red in fall. Whitish fruit follows small yellow flowers. It grows 30 to 35 feet high with a rounded crown and prefers slightly acidic soil. It spreads its seeds around, so it's not recommended for areas with summer rainfall, where it becomes weedy.

- **Pepper trees:** *Schinus* species. Zones 9 to 11. Pepper trees include two species of beautiful evergreen trees:

    - *S. molle,* the California pepper tree has small divided, bright-green leaves on weeping branches that grow from twisting, gnarly branches. Small, yellowish flowers are followed by bright-red, pepper-like fruit. It grows 30 to 40 feet high and needs lots of room to spread, so it's not recommended for small gardens or near paving.

    - *S. terebinthifolius,* the Brazilian pepper, makes a smaller, stiffer tree with a spreading crown, 20 to 30 feet high. This tree has red fruit, and works well in small gardens. But beware: This tree spreads its seeds with careless abandon and is considered a noxious and invasive weed in Florida and other moist parts of zones 9 to 11.

- **Brisbane box:** *Tristania conferta.* Zones 10 and 11. This evergreen tree has peeling brownish-red bark, bright-green foliage, and white flowers, followed by woody seedpods. It grows upright or rounded to 30 to 60 feet high.

Tropical Beauties

If you live where winter temperatures rarely go below freezing and the weather is generally warm, you can grow a unique world of spectacular plants. Even if you live where the weather gets a little colder, you can grow some of these tropical trees and shrubs in containers and protect them indoors during the winter. Here are some of the best tropical trees — most need frequent watering and well-drained soil:

- **Brazilian butterfly tree:** *Bauhinia* species. Zones 9 to 11. These spectacular evergreen or briefly deciduous trees have lovely, lobed foliage that looks like two kidneys joined along half their length. Hong Kong orchid tree, *B. blakeana,* produces huge orchid-like flowers in shades of pink, red, and purple — mostly in winter. It drops some of its leaves during bloom and grows 15 to 20 feet high and wide.

    Purple orchid tree, *B. variagata,* produces pink or purple flowers in winter and spring, followed by a rather messy, bean-like fruit. It drops its leaves in winter and grows 20 to 35 feet high and wide. Prune it to maintain a single trunk. 'Candida' has white flowers.

- **Floss silk tree:** *Chorisia speciosa.* Zones 9 to 11. This evergreen to briefly deciduous tree has a thick, heavily thorned trunk that grows upright, 30 to 60 feet high. It has large, glorious pinkish to purplish, narrow-petaled flowers. The cultivar 'Majestic Beauty' has pink flowers. 'Los Angeles Beautiful' has deep-red blooms.

- **Carrot wood:** *Cupaniopsis anacardioides.* Zones 10 to 11. This tough evergreen tree grows 30 to 40 feet high in dry or wet soils and is native to Australia. Its leathery, glossy green leaves are divided into leaflets. Some trees produce messy marble-like fruit. It tolerates seaside conditions.

- **Coral tree:** *Erythrina* species. Zones 10 to 11. This bold evergreen or partially deciduous tree has large, eye-catching spikes of orange or red blooms. Kaffirboom coral tree, *E. caffra*, grows 20 to 40 feet high and nearly twice as wide. Dark orange-red flowers appear on its leafless branches in winter. Naked coral tree, *E. coralloides*, has red blooms on top of twisting, leafless branches in spring and its leaves turn yellow before dropping. Naturally, it grows 30 feet high and almost as wide, but can be kept smaller with pruning. Cockspur coral tree, *E. crista-galli*, is a multitrunked, deciduous, small tree or tall shrub, 15 to 20 feet high and wide. It has large clusters of pink to red flowers on and off from spring to fall. Natal coral tree, *E. humeana*, produces orange-red flowers late summer to fall on a 25 to 30 foot, often multitrunked, deciduous tree.

- **Ficus:** *Ficus* species. Hardiness varies. This useful group of evergreen and deciduous trees includes the edible fig. Some evergreen types, such as the weeping Chinese fig *(F. benjamina)*, the fiddleleaf fig *(F. lyrata)*, and the rubber plant *(F. elastica)*, are grown for their attractive foliage in frost-free climates and as houseplants elsewhere.

  The Indian laurel fig, *F. microcarpa*, and its more densely branched variety, *F. m. nitida*, are hardier (zones 9 to 11) and often grown as street trees, hedges, and screens. But, beware — this species has strong roots that crack pavement and clog septic systems. They reach 20 to 25 feet high when unpruned. The variety 'Green Gem' resists attacks by damaging insects called thrips and is recommended for planting in California.

- **Jacaranda:** *Jacaranda mimosifolia.* Zones 10 to 11. This beautiful, evergreen or partially deciduous tree has feathery, deeply divided leaves and stunning clusters of blue flowers, usually in early summer. It grows 25 to 40 feet high with a spreading crown. Prune to enhance its shape.

- **Trumpet tree:** *Tabebuia* species. Zones 9 to 11. This colorful deciduous or partially evergreen tree has large clusters of trumpet-like flowers and divided leaves. Golden trumpet tree, *T. chrysotricha*, bears orange flowers with purple stripes, mostly in spring, and grows 25 feet high. Pink trumpet tree, *T. impetiginosa*, is more upright and a bit taller, and less likely to lose its leaves. Its late winter flowers are pink with white throats and yellow markings.

Palms Trees Swaying in the Breeze

Palms add unique character to any landscape. Perfect for planting around pools, they help create an oasis in arid climates or add the perfect "island" touch when combined with more tropical plants. Here are some of my favorites for home landscapes:

- **King palm:** *Archontophoenix cunninghamiana.* Zones 10 to 11. The graceful, arching, feather-like leaves of the king palm can reach 10 feet long. The tree grows quickly to 30 to 40 feet, eventually getting even taller. It needs moist soil and protection from wind.

- **Bamboo palm:** *Chamaedorea species.* Zones 10 to 11. This elegant, multi-trunked palm is often grown as a houseplant. Bamboo palm is frost-tender, so plant in the shade and water often.

- **Mediterranean fan palm:** *Chamaerops humilis.* Zones 8 to 11. This hardy palm has survived temperatures as low as 10°, but tolerates heat and drought, as well. Its blue-green, fan-like leaves have thorns. This palm usually grows in clumps and can reach 20 feet high.

- **Paradise palm:** *Howea forsteriana.* Zones 10 to 11. This well-known palm is often seen as a houseplant. It grows slowly to 20 to 25 feet, prefers moist soil, and can't take frost. It's best grown in the shade.

- **Pygmy date palm:** *Phoenix roebelenii.* Zones 10 to 11. This slow growing, 5- to 6-foot high palm has wonderfully textured, plume-like foliage, and is usually multitrunked. It grows best with some shade and regular water.

- **Lady palm:** *Rhapis excelsa.* Zones 9 to 11. This thick, clumping palm has smooth, bamboo-like stalks that grow 6 to 12 feet high. Plant in shade and keep its soil moist. Lady palm makes an excellent houseplant.

- **Queen palm:** *Syagrus romanzoffiana.* Zones 9 to 11. The glorious, feather-like leaves, called *fronds*, of this tree can reach 15 feet long. Tall, straight trunk grows to 30 to 50 feet high. The queen palm likes protection from wind, and needs lots of water and fertilizer.

- **Windmill palm:** *Trachycarpus fortunei.* Zones 8 to 11. Stiff, fan-shaped fronds arch from the top of hairy looking, black fiber-covered trunks. It grows 20 to 30 feet high and looks best when planted in groups.

- **Mexican fan palm:** *Washingtonia robusta.* Zones 9 to 11. This classic California palm can climb to upwards of 100 feet tall atop a slender trunk. The tree tolerates drought, but grows faster with water. Plant in full sun.

Part III
Choosing Shrubs for Any Location

The 5th Wave   By Rich Tennant

"Most of our shrubs are used to hide unsightly areas like the garbage cans and trash bins. C'mon inside and I'll show you the shrubs in our son's bedroom."

In this part . . .

"**B**ring me a . . . shrubbery!" I always wondered what kind of shrubbery Monty Python was looking for. Evergreen or deciduous? One with flowers or without? If you are looking for shrubbery — er, shrubs — you've come to the right place. I've described hundreds of the shrubs you're most likely to find in your local garden center, no matter where you live. This part covers shrubs for hedges, foundation planting, groundcovers, flowers, and foliage. From roses to rhododendrons, from holly to hibiscus, this part has it covered.

Chapter 7

Evergreen Shrubs for Year-Round Foliage

. . . .

In This Chapter

▶ Distinguishing between needle-bearing and broadleaf evergreens

▶ Understanding dwarf conifers

▶ Selecting popular evergreen shrubs with needles

▶ Choosing broadleaf evergreen shrubs

. . . .

*E*vergreens give your landscape green foliage in every month of the year. You just can't find better plants for year-round windbreaks, screens, and sheared hedges than the shrubs in this chapter. Their versatility as ground covers, hedges, foundation plants, rock garden and container specimens, and garden accents make them the understated stars of the show.

Evergreens come in two flavors — those with needles and those with wide leaves and flowers. The *needled evergreens* produce their seeds in cones and don't have showy flowers. Their narrow needle or scale-like leaves help them survive in dry soil and snowy, windy winter climates. *Broadleaf evergreens* have wide leaves and often, very attractive flowers. They lose more water through their foliage than do needled evergreens and, for that reason, usually need moister soil and protection from harsh winter weather — turn to Chapter 15 for more on that subject.

Favorite Needled Evergreens

Shrubs and trees that carry their seeds in cones are called *conifers* and most of them have evergreen needles. Most conifers, unlike some other kinds of woody stemmed plants, grow just one main trunk instead of multiple trunks or stems. So, despite their size, many conifers act more like trees than shrubs. The plants in this chapter are called shrubs because most of them grow less than 20 feet high. Keep in mind, though, that a 20-foot-high shrub will cover the second-story windows of a house. It pays to buy shrubs that naturally stay within their allotted landscape space.

Dwarf conifers grow very slowly — usually no more than 3 to 6 inches per year — and reach their mature height at just 3 to 6 feet. Dwarf conifers usually cost more at the nursery because they take a long time to grow to a saleable size. But, if you want a small evergreen for a rock garden or small landscape or one that won't cover your windows, consider one of these compact shrubs. Large nurseries and garden centers usually sell several different dwarf conifers, but specialty nurseries offer a much wider selection. For more information and sources of dwarf conifers, contact the American Conifer Society at P.O. Box 360, Keswick, VA 22947-0360, or on the Web at www. pacificrim.net/~bydesign/acs.html.

Some conifers creep along the ground or cascade over walls. Some of these make durable ground covers because they root wherever their branches touch the soil; others branch close to the ground and send their arching or spreading shoots up in vase or mound shapes or have a horizontally layered look. Evergreen needles range in color from golden yellow and silvery gray to purple-green, mint green, blue green, and dark green. Some pines have long, soft needles, while junipers and arborvitae have short scaly foliage that doesn't look like needles at all.

You can find a conifer to suit nearly any landscape situation. Take your pick from the following favorite needled evergreens and their most popular cultivars.

- ✔ **Balsam fir:** *Abies balsamea*. Zones 3 to 5. A needle-bearing tree, naturally growing from 45 to 75 feet high by 20 to 25 feet wide, the dwarf cultivar 'Nana' grows slowly to a 3- by 3-foot shrub. Somewhat tolerant of airborne salt but prone to insect damage, balsam firs grow best in cooler climates. Grow firs in full sun to part shade in moist to well-drained soil.

- ✔ **Japanese yew plum:** *Cephalotaxus harringtonia*. Zones 6 to 9. This needle-bearing evergreen looks similar in appearance to yew or *Taxus* species, with flat 1- to 2-inch long, dark green to golden-yellow needles, depending on the cultivar. Unlike *Taxus* species, however, yew plum resists deer browsing. Yew plum grows best in mild coastal climates and the southeastern states, where it grows in difficult, shady to partly sunny sites. It also tolerates heat and drought after it's established, but needs moist, well-drained soil for the first season or two. Cultivars range in size from 2- to 10-feet high and from 3- to 8-feet wide.

A CLOSER LOOK

True or falsecypress

Fine texture and gracefully arching, weeping, or plumed branches and foliage are the hallmark of the species and many cultivars of falsecypress. They have scale-like evergreen foliage in colors that often change with the seasons. Although best suited for the cool, humid climates of the U.S. northwest and northeast, some cultivars can grow well in southern and midwestern U.S. gardens as well. Most of the species grow into towering trees, but the cultivars in this chapter remain under 20 feet in height. Give falsecypress full sun to part shade, and moist to well-drained soil. Protect plants from drying winter wind, especially in climates where the ground freezes.

- **Hinoki falsecypress:** *Chamaecyparis obtusa.* Zones 5 to 8. Cultivars of this species prefer humid climates where they grow slowly into dense mounds, which are suitable for foundation and specimen plantings and hedges. 'Filicoides' becomes a pyramid that's 8 to 10 feet high by 3 to 4 feet wide with fern-like foliage. 'Gracilis' grows into a slender column, 10 to 20 high by 4 to 5 feet — its foliage is dense and deep green in summer, bronze colored in winter. Cultivar 'Nana Gracilis' has similar characteristics to 'Gracilis', but grows about half its size. 'Kosteri' grows slowly into a dense 4- to 5-foot globe. 'Pygmaea Aurescens' grows slowly to a 2- by 5-foot mound. Color varies from golden-bronze in spring and fall to green in summer. 'Nana Lutea' remains golden year round. For gardeners who want something different, 'Tortulosa' grows slowly to 9 by 9 feet and has twisted branches.

- **Threadleaf falsecypress:** *C. pisifera.* Zones 4 to 8. This falsecypress remains hardier further north, but tolerates less southern summer heat than Hinoki false cypress. Despite the common name, the foliage of the different cultivars varies from threadlike to plumed. If you see the word 'filifera' in the name, the branches have a threadlike weeping habit. Those with 'squarrosa' or 'plumosa' in the name have a more upright and fuzzy appearance. 'Aurea', 'Golden Charm', and 'Sungold' have golden-yellow, drooping, cord-like foliage. They grow about 5 to 6 feet high and 7 to 8 feet wide. 'Squarrosa Minima' has billowy blue-green foliage and grows into a 2- to 3-foot mound.

- **Atlantic white cedar:** *C. thyoides.* Zones 4 to 8. Most cultivars of this species have an upright or column-shaped habit, similar to arborvitae (*Thuja* species), and fast growth rate especially useful for hedges. It grows well in damp — even boggy — soil, and offers the best choice for the southeastern U.S. The foliage of many cultivars turns plum colored in winter. 'Heatherbun' forms a soft, rounded column that grows 6 to 10 feet high and half that width. It tolerates shearing and makes a nice hedge.

Jumpin' junipers

Junipers rank at or near the top of the list of most versatile and widely planted shrubs — and for many good reasons: Depending on the species and cultivar, juniper's growth habits range from low and spreading to tall and columnar and any shape in between. Among the toughest of plants, most junipers tolerate poor, dry soil, and city conditions. Their sharp needles to soft, scale-like, evergreen foliage appears in colors from golden yellow to bright green, dark green, and gray green. Junipers rarely need pruning except to remove damaged limbs or enhance the natural shape of the plants. Junipers can suffer from a number of insect pests and diseases. Bagworm, scale, webworm, and borers may cause problems, as can twig blight and cedar-apple rust (see Chapter 15).

You can find a juniper to fit almost any landscape situation. The lowest-growing cultivars make excellent drought-tolerant ground covers that landscapers frequently use along roadsides and in other low maintenance situations. They make a neat, attractive lawn substitute for slopes and raised beds, and on poor soil that won't support lawn grasses. Some forms spread long branches from the center of the plant, while others root along the ground where the branches touch the soil. Medium-height cultivars, in the 2 to 5 feet high range, make dense, impenetrable, mass plantings and hide building foundations admirably. You can use taller junipers for hedges and specimen plants.

✔ **Chinese juniper:** *Juniperus chinensis* and *J. × media*. Zones 4 to 9. From ground-hugging forms to upright pyramids that are suitable for hedges, you can take your pick from more than a hundred different cultivars of Chinese juniper. Some have prickly needle-like foliage while others have scaly foliage that feels softer to the touch. Cones of these species look like small grayish berries, which add an attractive accent to some cultivars. Plant these junipers in full sun and keep their soil slightly moist until they become established, usually a season or two. They can tolerate drier soil after that.

Juniper cultivars come in several basic shapes. Those that grow less than 3 feet high and have a spreading habit are considered ground-cover shrubs. Listed in order of height from the lowest at 12 inches to the tallest at 36 inches, cultivars include 'Prostrata' or 'Parsonii', 'San Jose', *sargentii* 'Glauca' and 'Viridis', 'Old Gold', 'Holbert', and 'Armstrong'. A related species with similar characteristics, *J. procumbens* 'Nana', grows 1 to 2 feet high and spreads up to 10 feet wide.

Arching and vase-shaped shrubs have limbs that grow out at a 45° angle from the base. They grow from 4 feet to 15 feet tall. In order of height from short to tall, a few cultivars include 'Sea Green', 'Mint Julep', 'Pfitzeriana', and 'Hetzii'.

Column-shaped shrubs and small trees have upright growth habits. Some, such as 'Blue Point', 'Hetzii Columnaris', 'Robusta Green', and

'Spartan', grow into columns 10 to 20 feet tall and 3 to 6 wide. 'Keteleeri' grows into a small pyramid-shaped tree about 15 to 30 feet high and 5 to 10 feet wide. 'Tortulosa' or 'Kaizuka' has twisted branches that make it effective in Japanese gardens or as a specimen plant. It reaches up to 20 feet high and 10 to 12 feet wide.

✔ **Common juniper:** *J. communis.* Zones 2 to 6. If you have a brown thumb, this plant's for you. This juniper grows nearly anywhere except in hot southern climates (zones 7 and higher) and in every kind of soil except poorly drained and waterlogged. Common juniper, unfortunately, shares the insects and diseases that plague other juniper species. Bagworm and twig blight are the most common problems.

Common juniper cultivars range in habit from ground hugging to columnar, but all grow slowly. Their foliage tends to turn brownish in the winter. Common cultivars include 'Effusa' which grows 9 to 12 inches high by 4 to 6 feet wide, and 'Repanda' which matures at 15 inches and forms slowly spreading circular mats. 'Compressa' grows very slowly into a compact 3 to 4 feet high cone. 'Sentinal' or 'Pencil Point' has silvery foliage and forms a narrow column 5 feet high and 1 to 2 feet wide.

✔ **Shore juniper:** *J. conferta.* Zones 6 to 9. Excellent for sandy, dry, seaside conditions, shore juniper also tolerates heavy clay soils as long they are well-drained. It's probably the best species for the southern United States. Cultivars grow slowly and remain prostrate, creeping along the ground and sending up densely plumed shoots less than 2 feet high. 'Blue Pacific' grows to about 1 foot high with blue-green plumed foliage. 'Emerald Sea' grows 12 inches high and spreads slowly to 8 feet across. It's hardy to –10° and tolerates salty soil.

✔ **Creeping juniper:** *J. horizontalis.* Zones 4 to 9. About a bazillion cultivars of creeping juniper exist, making it the most popular and commonly used ground cover in the United States. It grows just about anywhere and easily qualifies as a brown thumb plant. Its most common cultivar, 'Blue Rug' juniper, is practically a household word in many areas. Juniper blight, which causes the branches to die, can be a serious problem for this species, however.

All of the cultivars remain relatively low growing and prostrate — most stay less than 2 feet tall. Their long, trailing branches spread about 8 feet. The prickly foliage tends to turn purplish in the winter. In areas where snow covers the plants in winter, many cultivars can survive in zone 3. Popular cultivars that grow less than 12 inches tall include 'Bar Harbor', 'Blue Chip', 'Blue Rug' or 'Wiltoni', 'Hughes', and 'Icee Blue'. 'Prince of Wales' remains hardy into zone 3 and grows only 4 to 6 inches high. 'Youngstown' grows 8 feet across and has upswept branches up to 2 feet high.

✔ **Savin juniper:** *J. sabina.* Zones 3 to 7. An arching, vase-shaped species, savin juniper, has much to recommend it. Many of its cultivars remain low to the ground with upswept plumes of foliage that make them valuable as ground covers and for covering large areas. This species does well in urban areas where poor, dry soil prevails. It also tolerates alkaline soils. It grows best in cooler climates and some cultivars remain cold hardy to −40°. Some popular cultivars, however, including 'Tamariscifolia', are highly prone to juniper blight. The cultivars that resist this devastating disease include 'Calgary Carpet', 'Arcadia', 'Scandia', and 'Blue Danube', and 'Broadmoor' (zone 4).

✔ **Rocky Mountain juniper:** *J. scopulorum.* Zones 4 to 7. This is the juniper for the upper midwestern U.S., the plains states, and Rocky Mountain states. Although the species attains 30- to 40-foot tree stature and serves well as a windbreak, many cultivars remain much smaller. Use this juniper for hedges, screens, and foundation plantings. Although prone to the same pests and diseases as other junipers, it does survive at temperatures as low as −30 to −35°.

Cultivars include 'Blue Creeper' which grows 2 feet tall; 'Tabletop Blue' (5 to 6 feet high by 8 feet wide); columnar 'Welchii' and 'Medora'; 15- to 20-foot, pyramid-shaped 'Blue Heaven', 'Gray Gleam', 'Wichita Blue' and 'Moonglow'. 'Tolleson's Blue Weeping' and 'Tolleson's Green Weeping' are hardy from zones 3 to 10, and both grow up to 20 feet high and 8 to 10 feet wide. Long, dangling foliage from arching branches makes these specimen shrubs for landscape accents.

✔ **Singleseed juniper:** *J. squamata.* Zones 4 to 7. Prickly, bright blue-gray and blue-green cultivars of this species can really brighten up your landscape. They enjoy the same soil and sun conditions as the other junipers, but are particularly unhappy in hot, humid climates. 'Blue Carpet' grows slowly to 8 to 12 inches high and 4 to 5 feet wide, with blue-gray foliage. 'Blue Star' has bright silvery blue tufted foliage and grows to 3 feet tall by 3 to 4 feet wide. 'Holger' has yellow new growth that matures to gray green. It grows more upright than other cultivars to 3 feet or more tall and 4 feet wide.

✔ **Eastern redcedar:** *J. virginiana.* Zones 4 to 9. This common juniper that's native to the United States is actually a 40- to 50-foot-tall tree, but some of its cultivars remain much smaller. Redcedar thrives in the poorest of conditions, putting up with dry, gravelly soils, a wide range of soil pH, and sunny conditions. Use the species and tall cultivars for windbreaks and screens. Shorter cultivars make nice hedges and can be pruned into ornamental shapes. The fine-textured, plumed, green foliage may turn brown or yellowish in the winter. Some of the best cultivars include 'Burkii' which grows into a narrow, pyramid-shaped, small tree 10 to 25 feet tall, 'Hillspire', and 'Manhattan Blue' which forms a blue-gray pyramid that's 10 feet tall and 6 feet wide.

✔ **Russian cypress:** *Microbiota decussata.* Zones 3 to 7. The flat, spreading sprays of bright-green, scale-like foliage make an attractive ground cover. The foliage resembles arborvitae or eastern white cedar. Although this shrub only grows 1 foot high, it spreads indefinitely, but gracefully. It's especially useful in cold climates where many other evergreens don't survive. Russian cypress needs full sun to dappled shade and well-drained, but moist, soil to grow its best.

A CLOSER LOOK

Getting loose with dwarf spruce

Normally large trees, some spruce species have dwarf cultivars that stay as small as shrubs. Spruces prefer well-drained, moist, neutral to acidic soil and full sun. All are subject to canker disease and many insect pests. Although most don't require pruning (see Chapter 14), the best time to trim these trees is in the spring when the new growth is still soft.

- **Norway spruce:** *Picea abies*. Zones 4 to 7. This species has a number of dwarf cultivars. 'Little Gem' grows slowly to 2 to 3 feet tall and 3 to 4 feet wide. 'Nidiformis' or 'Bird's Nest Spruce' forms a low, round, spreading shrub with a depression in the center — it grows slowly to 3 feet or more high and wide. 'Pendula' has long, trailing limbs and is often grafted onto an upright trunk to form a weeping shrub. If left on its own stem, it trails over the ground and makes a good rock-garden specimen. 'Pumila' has spreading lower branches and erect upper branches that form a compact globe that's 3 to 4 feet high and 4 to 5 feet wide.

- **Mugo pine:** *Pinus mugo mugo*. Zones 3 to 7. Although technically small trees, mugo pines are all relatively small, reaching up to 20 to 30 feet tall. The best mugo pines, however, are the many cultivars that grow slowly into dense mounds with 1- to 2-inch long needles. You can usually find these at nurseries specializing in dwarf conifers. The widely available variety *P.m. pumilio* forms a prostrate ground cover that grows up to 10 feet across. Plant mugo pines in moist, well-drained soil in full sun to part shade. They tolerate calcareous soils and a range of soil pH. Scale insects and borers may attack them. Prune the soft, new growth to keep the plants more compact.

- **White pine:** *P. strobus*. Zones 3 to 7. You can find more about white pines in Chapter 3. The most common shrub-like cultivars include column-shaped 'Fastigiata', weeping 'Pendula', and 'Torulosa', a specimen shrub with twisted needles and limbs that reaches 25 feet high. 'Nana' forms a compact feathery globe that grows 6 to 8 feet tall.

A CLOSER LOOK

Snow White and the dwarf pines

Like spruces, pines are needle-bearing evergreen trees, but some species have dwarf cultivars. Pines have long needles that are usually bundled into a papery sheath at their base. Plants have a fine, tufted look and often have a soft texture. The dwarf cultivars make good foundation plants and attractive specimens. Flip to Chapter 3 for more information on this large and important genus.

A CLOSER LOOK

Yew asked for it!

The glossy, dark green needles, uniformity, and tolerance for pruning make yew among the most commonly used landscape shrubs for foundation plantings and hedges. But beware — many yews actually grow into trees if left unpruned. Yes, those cute little green mounds may someday obscure the view from your windows and hide your house. I've seen magnificent, 10- to 15-foot-high, tightly clipped hedges that formed the walls of private outdoor rooms and secret gardens. Fortunately, yews tolerate severe pruning, and some cultivars also naturally stay smaller. If your yews do get out of hand or you inherited a window-covering forest, you can reduce them to manageable size and expect them to look respectable again (see Chapter 14).

In the right climate and soil, yews make outstanding landscape plants. They require well-drained, fertile, moist soil and full sun to part shade. Yews need protection from the wind in colder climates and don't tolerate hot, muggy southern U.S. summers. Browsing deer can also take their toll — they love to munch yew branches.

- **English yew:** *Taxus baccata*. Zones 6 to 7. European gardeners have used this yew for centuries for hedges and topiaries, although it's less common in American nurseries than are other yew species. It grows best in mild climates where it can reach 30 to 60 feet high. The cultivar 'Fastigiata' (or Irish yew) matures at 10 to 15 feet and has red, berry-like fruit.

- **Japanese yew:** *T. cuspidata*. Zones 4 to 7. This tough plant withstands urban pollution, sun and shade, and most soils, although it prefers well-drained loam. Its dark, year-round color, and uniform habit make it useful for any landscape use. The common cultivar 'Capitata' can grow to 40 to 50 feet, but is easily maintained at a much smaller size by pruning. 'Nana' grows very slowly into a spreading 10-foot-high shrub.

- **Yew:** *T. × media*. Zones 4 to 7. By crossing English and Japanese yew species, plant breeders developed many new yews with better cold hardiness and improved growth habits. These hybrid yews are among the most commonly available cultivars: 'Brownii' grows slowly to 10 by 12 feet and makes an ideal hedge; 'Densiformis' stays even smaller, reaching 3 by 5 feet; and 'Hicksii' forms a 10- to 20-foot-high column. Gardeners in the mid-western and midsouthern United States should look for cultivar 'Tauntonii' — it resists winter damage and summer heat better than most yews, and spreads slowly to 3 to 4 feet high.

- **Eastern white cedar:** *Thuja occidentalis*. Zones 3 to 7. The hardiest of the arborvitaes, eastern white cedar grows in a wide range of conditions with little complaint. It prefers full sun and tends to turn brownish in the winter, especially in windy sites. Nurseries and garden centers offer many cultivars of this species ranging from dark green to yellow; low, spreading, and globular to upright. The yellow cultivars really draw attention in the landscape where their foliage sometimes looks sickly, so take care where you plant them.

These common cultivars have habits and foliage color to match nearly any landscape need. 'Danica' grows into a 12- to 18-inch mound, while 'Golden Globe', 'Hetz Midget', and 'Little Giant' form 3- to 4-foot globes. 'Filiformis' is an 8-foot-tall weeping form. Pyramid to cone-shaped cultivars include 'Holmstrup', 'Brandon', and 'Rheingold'. 'Smaragd', also sold as 'Emerald', has vertical sprays of emerald green foliage all winter and grows 10 to 15 feet tall by 3 to 4 feet wide. 'Nigra' can reach 20 to 30 feet tall and 5 to 10 feet wide. 'Sunkist' is a yellow cultivar that forms a broad pyramid, 5 to 8 feet high. 'Techny' is one of the most useful northern cultivars due to its attractive, dark-green, year-round foliage. It grows 10 to 15 feet tall and 6 to 8 feet wide.

✔ **Oriental arborvitae:** *Platycladus orientalis* (formerly *Thuja orientalis.*) Zones 6 to 11. Although less hardy in the northern zones, this evergreen can grow as far south as southern Florida. It tolerates any soil except poorly drained, wet spots. It's less commonly available than eastern white cedar, but worth seeking out, especially the cultivars 'Aurea Nana', 'Minima Glauca', and 'Westmount'.

✔ **Western arborvitae:** *Thuja plicata.* Zones 5 to 7. This western U.S. native grows to tree stature, as do most of its cultivars. It prefers the damp humid climate and moist soils of the Northwest, although it grows rapidly in the Southeast on clay soils, as well. Western arborvitae makes a beautiful hedge, screen, or specimen plant. Most cultivars attain heights up to 40 feet or more, although many, such as 'Hillier', 'Stribling', and 'Pygmaea', stay under 10 feet. Several golden and variegated cultivars also exist.

A CLOSER LOOK

Arresting arborvitae

Arborvitae, another shrub that wants to be a tree, grows throughout the northern United States in all kinds of soil and sun conditions. Although it prefers moist, fertile soil, I've seen wild arborvitae or eastern white cedar growing out of rocky ledges and in swamps. Few pests and diseases cause it serious harm.

Cultivars of both native and Oriental arborvitaes make useful hedges, specimens, screens, and foundation plants, but it's best to choose culti-

vars with characteristics that meet your needs. If you want to plant an arborvitae under the windows of your house, for example, choose a cultivar that remains naturally small. Their scale-like foliage often forms flat fan-shaped branches that add a unique vertical accent. Although you can prune or shear arborvitae early in the spring, their natural form is compact and graceful.

Broadleaf Evergreens for Fundamental Foliage

Shrubs with wide leaves that remain on the plant — called *broadleaf evergreens* — give you color, shade, and privacy all year round — not just in the summer. If you live in a warm climate, most of your landscape plants probably fall into this category. If you live in frigid winter zones (as I do!), you have fewer broadleaf evergreens to choose from, however, with good reason: Those wide leaves lose moisture in the winter (especially in windy or sunny locations), which frozen roots can't replace. So, the leaves dry out and turn brown — it's called *leaf burn* — and look miserable by the time spring rolls around.

Plants with big leaves also suffer more when the ice and snow begin to pile up. As the load accumulates, the branches snap off — a heartbreaking sight. You can grow many broadleaf evergreens in cold climates, though, if you protect them from sun, wind, and frozen precipitation. Turn to Chapter 15 for some pointers.

Most broadleaf evergreens have thick, glossy, leathery leaves. Some of the classic formal hedge plants fall into this category. Boxwood and holly tolerate shearing into geometric hedges and other fanciful shapes. (Flowers, too, abound and often appear later in the season when the deciduous shrubs have finished their show. You can find the most popular flowering evergreen shrubs in Chapter 9.) Colorful berries extend the ornamental show and provide food for the birds.

- **Bearberry:** *Arctostaphylos uva-ursi.* Zones 2 to 6. Growing only 6 to 12 inches high, bearberry forms large evergreen ground covers that turn an attractive red in winter. It requires no fertilizer and tolerates even salty seaside conditions with aplomb. Bearberry may suffer from leaf spot disease, but some cultivars are resistant, such as 'Vancouver Jade', which grows 20 inches tall, and 'Massachusetts', a 6-inch-tall spreader with pink flowers. 'Point Reyes' tolerates heat and drought tolerant especially well. The dwarf of the bunch, 'Woods Compacta', remains a diminutive 2 to 3 inches high. Plant bearberry in full sun to light shade in fertile, well-drained, sandy, acidic soil.

- **Marlberry:** *Ardisia japonica.* Zones 7 to 9. An excellent ground-covering shrub with leathery, oval, bright-green leaves, marlberry stems grow upright, but only 6 to 12 inches high. Plants spread via creeping underground stems and produce clusters of white flowers late summer. Shiny, persistent, red berries carry the show into winter. The hardiest cultivar is 'Chirimen'. Plant it in moist soil to well-drained soil in partial to full shade.

↙ **Gold dust plant:** *Aucuba japonica*. Zones 7 to 10. Often grown as a houseplant in cold climates, the brightly colored leaves of gold dust plant brighten dark corners of warm-climate gardens year 'round. Although it can grow 5 to 10 feet high and wide, you can keep it smaller by pruning. Commonly available cultivars include 'Variegata' which has small yellow freckles on green leaves, 'Mr. Goldstrike' featuring intense gold markings, and 'Picturata', which has a gold blotch in the center of each leaf surrounded by smaller freckles. Give this plant moist, well-drained soil and shade for the brightest colors.

↙ **'William Penn' barberry:** *Berberis × gladwynensis*. Zones 7 to 9. This beautiful evergreen barberry has lustrous, dark foliage that turns to bronze in the winter and yellow flowers in the spring. Its arching branches grow quickly into dense mound about 4 feet high and 4 to 6 feet wide. Use it for a natural low hedge or foundation plant in full to part sun and in moist, well-drained soil.

↙ **Warty barberry:** *B. verruculosa*. Zones 6 to 9. This dense, prickly, finely textured evergreen shrub has small, dark-green leaves with whitish undersides that turn mahogany red in the winter. Its arching shoots grow 3 to 5 feet tall and wide, making an excellent natural barrier plant or low to medium height hedge. After the ¾-inch, yellow blooms arrive in late spring, dark purple berries follow. Plant in a sunny spot in any moist, well-drained soil.

↙ **Korean boxwood:** *Buxus microphylla* var. *koreana × sempervirens*. Zones 4 to 9. The hardiest of the boxwoods, most cultivars, such as 'Green Mountain', 'Green Gem', and 'Green Velvet', can tolerate winter temperatures as low as –25 to –30°, although their foliage may turn bronze-colored in the winter. 'Green Gem' grows slowly to a compact 2- by 2-foot mound, while 'Green Velvet' grows about twice that size. 'Green Mountain' eventually forms a dense oval that's 5 feet high and 3 feet wide.

↙ **Common boxwood:** *B. sempervirens*. Zones 5 to 8. Although widely grown, this boxwood grows best in climates and gardens with moist, neutral to slightly acidic soil. 'Suffruticosa', the most common cultivar, grows very slowly to about 3 feet tall, but you can keep it clipped to just a few inches high for a formal garden border or design. 'Graham Blandy' forms an upright, 7- to 9-foot-high and 1-foot-wide column that's ideal for narrow hedges. 'Elegantissima' has small, variegated, green leaves with white edges, and grows into a compact 5- by 8-foot-high shrub.

↙ **Littleleaf boxwood:** *B. microphylla*. Zones 6 to 9. Grows slowly into compact shrubs suitable for nearly every imaginable landscape purpose. Choose from among the many named cultivars for the best results. Most cultivars remain hardy to –10°, and some, such as 'Winter Green', can tolerate temperatures about 5 to 10° lower. This cultivar has light-green foliage and grows into a 3- to 5-foot mound. 'Winter Gem' retains its dark green color through the winter and grows to 4 to 6 feet high and wide.

Thinking outside the boxwood

Small, dark-green leaves and close branching habit make boxwood the quintessential shrub for tightly clipped formal hedges. Boxwood tolerates shaping into every form imaginable, from tall privacy hedges to low herb garden edges and fanciful topiaries animals and geometric shapes in-between. Dwarf cultivars even make wonderful bonsai subjects. Leave them unclipped for billowy, finely textured mass plantings, accents, and natural hedges. If browsing deer make your landscaping life miserable, try planting a boxwood hedge — deer don't like it.

Several species and dozens of cultivars offer wide ranges of leaf color, growth habit, mature size, and winter hardiness, too. You can grow boxwood throughout most of the United States, as long as you provide the moist, fertile, well-drained soil and sunny to partly shady exposure that they prefer. Mulching around the plants also keeps their shallow roots cool and moist, and protects them from grass and weed competition. Boxwoods are prone to root diseases, especially on poorly drained soils, and can suffer from many insect pests. Healthy, well-grown plants, however, generally have fewer problems. In climates where the ground freezes, boxwood, like most other broadleaf evergreens, benefits from protection from winter sun and wind (see Chapter 15). Choose from the following boxwood species — listed in order of cold hardiness — and cultivars to suit your climate and landscape needs.

✔ **Bearberry cotoneaster:** *Cotoneaster dammeri.* Zones 5 to 7. This species has cultivars that creep vigorously only a few inches off the ground and root wherever they contact the soil. It looks terrific on slopes and embankments, in the front of shrub borders, and as a foundation plant. Prune it to keep it more compact and neat. The cultivar 'Canadian Creeper' has red berries and reaches only 6 inches high. 'Coral Beauty' grows about twice that high and has coral-red fruits.

✔ **Parney cotoneaster:** *C. lacteus.* Zones 7 to 9. More shrub-like than other cotoneasters, you can grow this one into an informal hedge from 8 to 10 feet high and wide. This beautiful shrub has arching branches with bright green oval leaves up to 3½ inches long with fuzzy whitish undersides. Attractive red berries follow the clusters of white flowers borne in May. It is more resistant to drought, fireblight, and some insects than other cotoneasters.

✔ **Little-leaf cotoneaster:** *C. linearifolius.* Zones 5 to 7. Growing about 1 foot high, its arching branches root wherever they touch the ground, ultimately spreading from 5 to 6 feet. Tiny leaves give this low-spreading shrub a very finely textured appearance and help it withstand dry soil conditions. Although prone to fireblight disease, it makes an attractive rock garden specimen and ground cover.

A CLOSER LOOK

Taking a cotton to cotoneaster

Pronounced ka-TOE-nee-aster, some members of this large genus make useful ground covers for difficult, low-maintenance hillsides, while others grow tall enough to make an effective screen. Some cotoneasters have evergreen or semi-evergreen leaves; others lose their leaves in the fall. You can find more species in Chapter 8.

Attractive foliage, profuse small, white or pinkish flowers borne in the spring, and persistent red or black berries that remain on the plants for months make these plants attractive in all seasons. Most have a naturally graceful branching habit and fine texture, and usually require pruning only to remove dead or damaged limbs. The dense branching habit of the low-growing species makes them a catchall for wind-blown debris, however. They prefer full sun, grow in most well-drained soils, and even tolerate drought-prone soils after they become established.

✔ **Willowleaf cotoneaster:** *C. salicifolius.* Zones 6 to 7. This species remains close to the ground — 2 to 3-inch-long, willow-shaped leaves and arching branches give this species a graceful look. The cultivar 'Repens' grows vigorously to 1½ to 2 feet high and 8 to 10 feet wide, and bears clusters of white flowers in spring followed by shiny round red berries.

✔ **Hop bush:** *Dodonaea viscosa.* Zones 8 to 11. Hop bush is a dependable evergreen shrub that stands up to heat, drought, and poor soil. Its narrow leaves are olive green. This shrub grows 10 to 15 feet high and almost as wide, with upright branching, which makes it effective as an unclipped hedge or screen. Plant in full sun or light shade. 'Purpurea' has bronzish-green foliage.

✔ **Thorny elaeagnus:** *Elaeagnus pungens.* Zones 6 to 9. This vigorous shrub tolerates all sorts of soils, pollution, and sun conditions. It grows and spreads rapidly to 15 feet and sports 2- to 3-inch-long spikes and shiny, dark green leaves along its stems. It has small, fragrant flowers in the autumn. Use thorny elaeagnus in barriers, mass plantings, and for hedges. Several cultivars have very attractive variegated foliage and smaller stature. Look for 'Variegata', which has creamy gold-center leaves, or 'Hosoba-Fukurin' with white-margined leaves.

✔ **Evergreen wintercreeper:** *Euonymus fortunei.* Zones 5 to 9. This species excels as a fast-growing shrub, ground cover, climbing vine, and even a low hedge, depending on the cultivar. Grown mainly for their attractive foliage, most have 1-inch-long oval leaves with scalloped margins. Leaf colors range from dark lustrous green through various patterns of white, gold, and pink variegation. Most cultivars remain hardy to winter temperatures as low as −20° and some, such as 'Sunspot' and 'Golden Prince', can tolerate minimums about 5 to 10 degrees lower. Scale insects and some diseases bother wintercreeper, especially in warmer climates. They grow in full sun or shade and nearly any soil, as long it isn't waterlogged.

If you need a vigorous ground cover or wall-hugging vine, choose one of these popular low-growing cultivars. 'Coloratus' grows about 1 foot high by 15 feet wide and has deep green leaves that turn plum-colored in winter. 'Emerald 'n Gold' grows to 2 to 3 feet high and wide and sports dark green leaves heavily edged and variegated with gold that turn pinkish-red in winter. 'Emerald Gaiety' forms a low, spreading mound that grows 2 to 3 feet high. This cultivar, especially, will climb trees and nearby structures, if permitted. Its white leaf margins turn pinkish in winter.

Some wintercreeper cultivars behave more like shrubs and the most popular have gold and green or white and green foliage. 'Sunspot', for example, grows into a 3-foot-high by 6-foot-wide compact shrub. Its dark green leaves have yellow centers. 'Golden Prince' forms a 4-foot mound with gold-tipped new foliage that turns green when mature. 'Canadale Gold' grows into a compact shrub 4 feet tall and 3 feet wide. Its light-green foliage has golden-yellow borders. 'Green Lane' has thick, rich-green leaves and bright orange berries in the fall. It grows 4 to 5 feet high and wide.

✔ **Japanese euonymus:** *E. japonicus.* Zones 7 to 9. A versatile shrub that adapts to nearly any soil type and sun exposure, Japanese euonymus also tolerates salt spray and seaside conditions. Unfortunately, it is prone to insects and diseases, although full sun and good air circulation can help prevent some problems. It's best for the southeast and western coastal United States. Variegated leaf forms include 'Aureo-marginatus', 'Silver King' (which grow to 6 feet by 3 feet wide), and 'Microphyllus', a slow-growing dwarf that reaches only 1 to 2 feet high and wide. 'Grandifolius' grows quickly into a 6- to 8-foot by 4- to 6-foot shrub that's ideal for hedges. 'Greenspire' remains a narrow 1 to 2 feet wide, but grows 6 to 8 feet tall.

✔ **Spreading euonymus:** *E. kiautschovicus.* Zones 5 to 8. Lustrous 2- to 3-inch long oval leaves remain on this plant year 'round in warm climates, but fall in the autumn in colder areas. Its small white flowers attract bees and flies in the summer, making it a nuisance by the pool or patio, but the orange-red fruit remains attractive into winter. The cultivar 'Manhattan' grows into an informal spreading mound 4 to 6 feet high and 6 to 12 feet wide.

✔ **Lemon leaf:** *Gaultheria shallon.* Zones 6 to 8. Also known as salal, this native from the west coast of the U.S. grows from 4 to 10 feet tall and 5 feet wide, but spreads by sending up new shoots around the mother plant. Its reddish shoots and glossy, nearly round, 2- to 4-inch leaves make it useful in floral arrangements as well as in the landscape. Lemon leaf has clusters of white flowers in the spring followed by black berries that are relished by birds. It prefers part shade and moist, acidic, well-drained soil with plenty of organic matter.

↙ **English holly:** *Ilex aquifolium.* Zones 6 to 7. The classic, British, tall hedge plant, this species actually grows to a tree-sized 30 to 50 feet high, but is often pruned to much smaller dimensions. Some of its cultivars remain naturally smaller. It has the classic holly-shaped leaf with spines at each of its points. The best places to grow English holly in the United States include the mild climates on the west coast, Long Island, and southern coastal New England. English holly tolerates salt and seaside conditions and grows best in full to part sun and well-drained, but moist, soil.

Its many cultivars include 'Argenteo-marginata', a column-shaped female tree with white edged foliage and red berries, and 'Ciliata Major', which has purplish new growth and green leaves with long curved spines and persistent red berries. 'Gold Coast', a male cultivar that grows slowly to 4 to 6 feet high and wide and has leaves with gold edges, makes a nice hedge and can pollinate the female English hollies. 'Silver King' is a male cultivar that forms a dense, upright tree that grows 30 feet tall. Its has purple stems and spiny leaves with cream-colored margins.

↙ **Chinese holly:** *Ilex cornuta.* Zones 7 to 9. If you need a foolproof, broadleaf evergreen shrub, look no further. After it's established, Chinese holly can withstand drought and flooding, summer heat, and zealous pruning. Its spiny leaves make an effective barrier hedge, too. Male and female flowers appear on the same plant, so you only need one shrub to get attractive fruit.

'Berries Jubilee' bears a large crop of bright-red berries on a compact, 6- to 10-foot-high shrub. 'Burfordii' can grow 10 to 20 feet high and makes an attractive small tree if you remove the lower limbs. It produces a heavy crop of red berries. The dwarf form, 'Burfordii Nana', grows to about 8 feet tall. 'Rotunda' forms a compact 3- to 4-foot-high mound that spreads from 6 to 8 feet wide. 'Willowleaf' has attractive long, narrow leaves with smooth edges and no spines. It grows about 15 feet tall and produces lots of red berries.

↙ **Japanese holly:** *Ilex crenata.* Zones 5 or 6 to 8. The ½- to 1-inch-long, oval leaves of this species resemble those of boxwood, and lack the spines of some other hollies. The female cultivars produce black berries that attract birds. They offer a fine texture in the landscape, serving well as hedges, foundation plants, and mass plantings. Give these plants winter protection in the colder parts of zone 5, especially if your site is windy. They adapt to full sun or part shade.

↙ **Inkberry:** *Ilex glabra.* Zones 4 to 9. A native species with many outstanding cultivars, inkberry deserves greater landscape use. It has lustrous, longish, oval leaves and branches that grow upright. Although plants can tolerate zone-4 winters, they need some protection in these harsher climates to prevent leaf damage from drying wind and sun. The species grows 6 to 8 feet high and 8 to 10 feet wide. It resists deer damage more than Japanese holly and tolerates a wide range of soil conditions.

Happy holly days

As much a part of the Christmas holiday as evergreen wreaths and poinsettias, spiny green holly leaves with clusters of red berries decorate festive homes. But hollies have much more to offer than seasonal décor — hundreds of holly species and cultivars exist, and you can find them in nearly every part of the country. The range of forms varies from deciduous to evergreen, low shrubs to stately trees. Some have serrated leaves with spines at every point while others have smooth oval foliage. Leaf colors range from deep lustrous green and blue-green to white, cream, and yellow variegations. Although some of the following evergreen species attain tree-like stature, I keep them together in this chapter with their shrubby cousins. You can find deciduous *Ilex* species in Chapter 8.

Many species and cultivars produce clusters of attractive red or orange fruit, but most hollies bear male and female flowers on separate plants. If you want ornamental berries, you must have female plants with at least one male plant of the same species for pollination, in most cases. Within a species, some cultivars are female and others male. In some cases, the plants have male or female distinguishing names, such as 'Prince' or 'Princess', to make it easier to know which you're buying.

Although some evergreen hollies remain hardy to –20°, most appreciate protection from winter sun and wind in colder climates where the ground freezes. Useful for hedges, screens, specimen plants, and shrub borders, you can find a holly to suit nearly any landscape. The descriptions in this chapter list the sex of each cultivar, unless the species produces male and female flowers on the same plant.

Female cultivars have attractive, round, black berries in the autumn, which often remain through the winter. 'Compacta', a female, grows to about half the size of the species and remains more compact, but becomes leggy at the base. 'Shamrock' has bright new green leaves that mature to glossy dark green. It grows slowly to 3 to 5 feet and remains compact.

✔ **Meserve hybrid hollies:** *Ilex* × *meserveae* hybrids. Zones 5 to 9. This important group of holly hybrids, sometimes called blue hollies, originated with an amateur gardener, Mrs. F. Leighton Meserve, in New York state in the early 1950s. Many of her hybrids have become important landscape plants, especially in the northern growing zones. The toothed, oval leaves have spines — the female cultivars (indicated in their names) produce attractive red berries. For best berry set, plant one male for every few female plants. Protect plants from winter sun and wind wherever the ground freezes, especially in exposed sites. Turn to Chapter 15 for more information on protecting shrubs from weather.

'Blue Boy', a male, grows 10 to 15 feet high with the dark-green foliage. 'Blue Girl', its female counterpart, grows to 8 to 10 feet tall and 6 to 8 feet wide, and is one of the cold hardiest cultivars. 'Blue Prince', another hardy cultivar, grows about 8 to 12 feet high and is an excellent pollinator for 'Blue Princess', which is similar to 'Blue Girl', but grows a few feet taller and produces more berries. 'China Boy' and 'China Girl' form compact mounds, 10 feet high by 8 feet wide, and are cold hardy and heat tolerant.

✔ **Hybrid hollies:** *Ilex* hybrids. Zones 6 to 9. Plants in this group are the result of crosses between *Ilex* species. They range in habit, but all enjoy full sun to partly sunny sites where the soil remains moist, but well-drained. 'Ebony Magic' is a female with spiny leaves and red-orange fruit. It grows into a 20- by 10-foot pyramid. 'Ebony Male' can serve as its pollinator. 'Foster's Hybrid #2' grows to 25 feet high in a narrow pyramid shape. The foliage is lustrous green and oval with pointed tips and no spines. This female cultivar produces bright red fruit. 'Little Rascal', a male holly, grows slowly to 2 feet tall and 3 feet wide. It tolerates cold into zone 5. Foliage becomes purple in the winter. 'Nellie R. Stevens', one of the most commonly grown hollies in the southeastern U.S., grows quickly into a 15- to 25-foot, pyramid-shaped tree. Its female flowers can be pollinated by male cultivars of Chinese holly, *I. cornuta*.

✔ **Yaupon holly:** *Ilex vomitoria*. Zones 7 to 10. An excellent holly for warm climate gardens, yaupon has few pests and tolerates salt and heat and soils from wet to dry. It has attractive small, oval leaves, and the female plants produce beautiful scarlet or yellow fruit, depending on the cultivar. Yellow-fruited cultivars usually have the word yellow or gold in their name. Use yaupon for screens, hedges, and specimen plantings and for pruning projects, such as topiary and espalier.

'Jewel', a female cultivar that produces heavy crops of red berries, remains compact and rounded. 'Stokes Dwarf' or 'Schillings' is a male cultivar that grows slowly into a densely branched, dwarf mound 3 to 4 feet high with small leaves and purplish new shoots. 'Will Fleming' becomes a narrow 12 to 15-foot-high by 18-inch-wide column.

✔ **Lantana:** *Lantana montevidensis*. Zones 8 to 11. This spreading evergreen shrub has a long, generous bloom that lasts almost year-round in mild winters. Small flower clusters in shades of white, yellow, orange, red, and purple cover the dark-green leaves. Most varieties, of which there are many (choose by flower color), grow 2 to 3 feet high and spread up to 4 feet, which makes it a useful ground cover. Plant in full sun; grows best with occasional water. Use as an annual in cold winter climates. Lantana tends to mildew in cool summer climates.

- **Drooping leucothoe:** *Leucothoe fontanesiana* Zones 5 to 8. Looking for a graceful shrub for a cool, moist, shady spot? Leucothoe's long, arching branches and long, pointed leaves can light up the area, especially when the new, light-green or purplish foliage emerges in the spring. Growing into a 3- to 6-foot mound, this plant makes a nice middle-of-the-border filler in front of leggy or overgrown rhododendrons and azaleas. Two- to 3-inch long hanging clusters of small white flowers bloom along the stems in spring. Plant leucothoe only in moist, humus-rich, acidic soil in the shade and protect it from drying winter winds. Some cultivars have especially attractive variegated or purple foliage. 'Girard's Rainbow' has creamy white, pink, and green splashed leaves. 'Scarletta' has scarlet-red new growth that matures to dark green and turns a lustrous plum burgundy in the winter.

- **Privet:** *Ligustrum japonicum.* Zones 7 to 9. One of the most commonly used shrubs for shearing into hedges, the privet group has both evergreen and deciduous members. In warm climates, evergreen *L. japonicum* can hold its own in any landscape situation as a hedge, specimen shrub, or small tree. The dark-green, shiny, pointed leaves densely clothe the 6- to 12-foot by 6- to 8-foot, upright-growing shrubs. In May, showy plumes of white flowers appear. Privet enjoys full sun to shade and can grow in any soil except boggy — it even tolerates roadside salt. The cultivar 'Suwannee River' stays more compact than the species and grows only 3 to 5 feet tall. 'Nobilis' is more cold hardy. 'Texanum' has larger leaves, grows to 10 feet tall, and flowers in mid- to late-summer. See Chapter 8 for more cold-hardy, deciduous privet shrubs.

- **Oregon grape holly:** *Mahonia aquifolium.* Zones 5 to 9. This common mahonia grows slowly to 3 to 6 feet high and wide and blooms in the spring. The cultivar 'Compacta' only reaches 2 to 3 feet and is hardy to zone 6. Plant in shade in moist, acidic, well-drained soil, and protect from wind.

- **Leatherleaf mahonia:** *M. bealei.* Zones 5 to 8. Fragrant yellow flowers grace this bold-textured shrub in early spring. It grows 6 to 10 feet tall (in the same soil as you would plant Oregon grape holly) and its berries attract birds all summer long.

- **Chinese mahonia:** *M. fortunei.* Zones 8 to 9. The fern-like leaves of this southern species give it a more graceful look than the other mahonias. It reaches 3 to 6 feet and blooms in late summer. Plant in the same soil as you would plant Oregon grape holly.

- **Creeping mahonia:** *M. repens.* Zones 5 to 7. This mahonia spreads by rooting its creeping stems wherever they touch the ground. Growing only 1 foot high, creeping mahonia makes a nice ground cover for moist, shady situations. Its blue-green leaves turn purplish in the winter and it flowers in midspring.

✔ **Pacific wax myrtle:** *Myrica californica.* Zones 7 to 10. This California native has evergreen leaves and can attain tree heights up to 30 feet. Its versatile nature makes it at home at the beach, clipped into a hedge, or pruned to tree form. Give it moderate moisture.

✔ **Southern wax myrtle:** *M. cerifera.* Zones 8 to 11. This broadleaf evergreen grows throughout the southern United States in a wide range of soils and either sun or part shade. It tolerates salt and has elegant, narrow foliage; fragrant berries; and attractive grayish-white bark. You can train this 10- to 20-foot-tall shrub into a small tree. Individual shrubs are either male or female — you need at least one of each for production of the berries.

✔ **Heavenly bamboo:** *Nandina domestica.* Zones 6 to 9. Here's a tough, but graceful, plant for tough places and gardeners with brown thumbs. Heavenly bamboo forms spreading colonies of upright stems topped with pointed, blue-green, compound leaves. Spectacular clusters of red berries follow the long plumes of white flowers. It grows in sun or shade and puts up with any soil situation. To keep plants neat and compact, prune out old stems to the ground or head back new growth in the spring (see Chapter 14). Nandina has many cultivars. Some of the most popular include 'Harbor Dwarf', a compact 2- to 3-foot mound of fine foliage and 'Gulf Stream', which resists suckering and has metallic blue-gray foliage that turns red in the winter. 'Fire Power', 'Woods Dwarf', and 'Moon Bay' also have bright red winter foliage and grow to just 18 to 24 inches high.

✔ **Paxistima:** *Paxistima canbyi.* Zones 3 to 7. Small, glossy, deep-green leaves on spreading 12-inch plants give this ground cover a fine texture. Plant paxistima in moist, well-drained, calcareous or alkaline soil and watch it spread 3 to 5 feet or more. It takes full sun to dappled shade, is rarely bothered by pests or disease, and looks great in rock gardens or under high-branched trees.

✔ **Redtip photinia:** *Photinia × fraseri.* Zones 7 to 9. The bright, bronzy-red new growth on this vigorous shrub gives it its common name. The long oval leaves mature to dark green, and white flower clusters appear in the spring. You can train this shrub into a small 10- to 15-foot tree or as an espalier against a wall (see Chapter 14). Redtip photinia resists powdery mildew better than others in the *Photinia* species. Plant it in full sun and in fertile, moist, well-drained soil. Prune in early spring to keep the branches full and compact.

✔ **Tobira:** *Pittosporum tobira.* Zones 8 to 11. This widely used evergreen shrub is grown mostly for its dense, leathery, dark-green foliage, but it also has fragrant white flowers in early spring. It grows 10 to 15 feet high and makes an excellent hedge. 'Wheeler's Dwarf' grows only 2 feet high and can be massed as a ground cover. 'Variegata' grows 6 to 8 feet high and has handsome olive green leaves, edged with white. Plant in full sun or part shade in well-drained, moist soil. It tolerates seacoast conditions, but is subject to aphids and scale insects.

A CLOSER LOOK

Stuck on firethorn

Plant a firethorn hedge if you want to keep the kids from cutting across your lawn. This large group of densely branched shrubs sports sharp thorns along their limbs. Even if your castle doesn't need protecting, grow these shrubs for their outstanding, dense clusters of ornamental berries and for the birds that love them. The berries literally cover the shrubs of some cultivars. Firethorns enjoy full sun and well-drained to dry soil. Many species and cultivars are prone to fireblight, insect pests, and leaf spots (see Chapter 15).

✔ Cultivars that are hardy in zone 5 include 'Yukon Belle', which grows 6 by 6 feet and has orange berries; 'Gnome', a densely spreading shrub that's prone to leaf scab;

and 10-foot-tall 'Wyattii', which forms a 9- to 12-foot mass of orange-red fruit in zones 5 to 9.

✔ Cultivars hardy in zone 7 include 'Lalandei', which grows upright to 10 to 15 feet, has red-orange berries, and is scab and fireblight-resistant. 'Mohave' grows to 6 by 7 feet and flowers and fruits heavily. 'Graberi' and 'Cherri Berri' grow vigorously to 10 feet high and 8 feet wide and set red berries. 'Soleil D'or' also grows 10 feet by 8 feet, but has yellow berries. Smaller cultivars include 'Pauciflora', 'Red Elf', and 'Santa Cruz'. 'Ruby Mound' also stays low, but spreads as much as 10 feet wide — use it as a colorful ground cover.

✔ **Sweetbox:** *Sarcococca* species. Zones 6 to 8. A shade-loving plant for moist, well-drained, humus-rich soil, sweetbox forms a mounding colony of shoots up to 5 feet high. The long, pointed, leathery leaves remain green year 'round. The variety *S. hookerana* var. *humilis* grows only 18 to 24 inches high and makes an attractive ground cover for shady areas. It has insignificant flowers and fruit, suffers from few pests, and rarely needs pruning.

Chapter 8

Delightfully Deciduous Shrubs

● ●

In This Chapter

▶ Finding shrubs with colorful leaves

▶ Covering the ground with low-growing shrubs

▶ Turning tall shrubs into small trees

● ●

*S*ome deciduous shrubs finish the summer in a blaze of autumn glory as their leaves change from green to red, yellow, orange, and purple. Others carry their colorful fruit into winter, providing a feast for winter-weary eyes and a banquet for birds. Their bare branches shed snow and ice, and shrug off winter winds as if they were summer breezes. Their swelling green buds signal the return of spring.

Deciduous Shrubs from A to Z

The shrubs in this section are prized mainly for their leaf color, texture, or shape, although they may have attractive flowers or berries, too. Some of these shrubs also have unique growth habits, such as ground-covering ability or strongly horizontal branching. When you choose any of the following shrubs for these great characteristics, you can count any flowers that you see as an added bonus. If you want shrubs primarily for flowers, however, skip to Chapter 9.

Whether you're looking for a tall hedge, a ground cover, or something in-between, you can find it among these deciduous shrubs.

✔ **Japanese barberry:** *Berberis thunbergii.* Zones 4 to 8. Great for hedges, mass plantings, barriers, and specimen plantings, this thorny shrub has cultivars in a riot of foliage colors. The small, ½- to 1-inch, oval leaves and slender twigs give it a refined texture. In the autumn, the leaves turn bright red, orange, or purplish. The bright-red fruits — relished by birds — persist through the fall and winter, becoming especially attractive after the foliage drops.

A true brown-thumb gardener's plant, this barberry grows in soil from soggy to drought-prone, doesn't mind pollution or city conditions, and thrives in full sun. It rarely needs pruning, although you can shear it into formal shapes. Its only shortcoming is its tendency to collect windblown litter, which is difficult to fish out of the well-armed, prickly branches.

You can find dozens of cultivars at garden centers and nurseries around the country. Most have reddish-purple, yellow, or variegated foliage. The most common purple-leafed barberries include 'Atropurpurea', which grows 3 to 6 feet tall and 'Crimson Pygmy', a dwarf that grows 18 to 24 inches high. 'Rose Glow' has foliage that starts out pink, turns mottled reddish-purple, and finally matures to deep reddish-purple. It grows 5 to 6 feet high. Popular yellow-leaf cultivars include 'Aurea', which grows slowly to 3 to 4 feet, and 'Bonanza Gold', which only reaches 18 to 24 inches tall.

Some green-leafed cultivars have unique features, too. 'Kobold' has dark, glossy-green leaves and grows into a rounded shape 24 to 30 inches tall and wide. 'Sparkle' grows 4 to 5 feet high and has arching horizontal branches. 'Thornless' or 'Inermis' is an unarmed cultivar that grows up to 6 feet tall and has green leaves that change to bright orange in the autumn.

✔ **Tatarian dogwood:** *Cornus alba.* Zones 3 to 7. Bright red winter stems arch stiffly from the crown of this moisture-loving shrub. Pruning one third of the vigorous stems to the ground each spring keeps the shrub more attractive because the best color appears on stems grown in the current year. You can also remove all the stems to within 6 to 12 inches of the ground to keep the plant shorter and more compact. This species looks especially attractive in an informal shrub border, near a stream or pond or against a background of evergreens where it will form a spreading thicket of 6-foot stems. This dogwood grows in nearly any soil, but prefers a moist, well-drained situation and full to partial sun. Insects, such as borers and leaf miners, can cause quite a bit of damage, but keeping the shrubs vigorous can prevent serious attacks.

Walkin' the dogwood

Unlike the tree-sized dogwoods, these shrubby species are grown more for their attractive stems and foliage than ornamental flowers. These tough, North American natives grow in the harshest of winter conditions where their often brightly colored branches light up the snowy landscape. Many dogwood species provide valuable fruit for birds and other wildlife, as well.

In addition to colorful bark, some cultivars offer attractive foliage, giving these shrubs true three-season appeal. 'Argenteo-marginata', also known as 'Elegantissima', has pale green leaves with cream-colored edges — it looks wonderful in a partly shady spot. 'Gouchault' has green and pink leaves with cream and pink edges and dark red winter stems. 'Ivory Halo' grows 5 to 6 feet tall and has foliage with creamy white margins. 'Sibirica' has green leaves and coral-red winter stems. You may see other variegated cultivars with 'Sibirica' as part of their name. They range widely in height and spread.

✔ **Redosier dogwood:** *C. sericea.* Zones 2 to 7. This native American red-twigged dogwood looks very similar to the Tatarian dogwood, but is even more adaptable to different soils and climates and has fewer insect and disease problems. It's a great natural shrub for moist — even boggy — soils, but adapts to well-drained soil, too. Plant this dogwood in masses on erosion-prone embankments or stream banks to hold the soil or against an arborvitae hedge for outstanding winter color. More than 50 species of birds and animals enjoy the berries that follow the spring flowers. Care for this species as you would Tatarian dogwood. Most cultivars grow 5 to 8 feet tall.

'Baileyi' has red stems, dark-green leaves that turn purplish in the fall, and bluish fruits. 'Cardinal' has bright cherry red stems and is resistant to leaf spot. 'Flaviramea' has yellow stems instead of red, but is more disease prone than the species. 'Isanti' has bright-red stems and grows 5- to 6-feet tall, but is prone to leaf spot. 'Kelseyi' stays even shorter, reaching only 24 to 30 inches, but its stems are less colorful than the species and it's prone to leaf spot. 'Silver and Gold' has yellow stems and leaves with creamy white margins.

✔ **Harry Lauder's Walkingstick:** *Corylus avellana* 'Contorta'. Zones 4 to 8. Every plant catalog seems to offer this novelty cultivar of European filbert. Its twisted limbs make it look as if it came from the pages of a Dr. Suess book. The slim, brownish, contorted branches are most effective in the winter after the leaves fall, and make attractive additions to dried or fresh cut flower arrangements. Nurseries graft this cultivar onto the roots of noncontorted plants, so it's important to remove any noncontorted suckers that sprout from below the graft union to maintain its ornamental appearance. Plant this shrub in well-drained, humus-rich soil and full sun to dappled shade.

✔ **Creeping cotoneaster:** *Cotoneaster adpressus.* Zones 5 to 7. Growing only 12 to 18 inches high, this shrub is aptly named. Its branches root wherever they touch the ground allowing the plant to spread up to 6 feet in diameter. It has ornamental bright-red fruit and tiny, round leaves that turn red in autumn.

A CLOSER LOOK

Creeping cotoneaster, Batman!

Among the most widely used ground-covering shrubs, most of the deciduous cotoneasters (pronounced ka-TOE-nee-aster) have small leaves; attractive fruits; and distinctive, herring-bone-patterned branches. Their fine texture makes a nice contrast with shrubs with larger leaves. Often used in rock gardens and at the top of retaining walls, the stiffly arching branches soften the look of rough stone. The more upright-growing cotoneasters share the stiff habit and fine texture. They grow in a wide range of well-drained soils, including sandy, heavy clay, drought-prone, salty, and those with high or low pH. Cotoneasters prefer full sun and need little pruning. They are, however, prone to fire blight, leaf spots, canker, spider mites, and a few other insect pests.

- **Cranberry cotoneaster:** *C. apiculatus*. Zones 4 to 7. A great shrub for the front of the border, overhanging a rock wall, or covering a bank, cranberry cotoneaster grows up to 3 feet high, but spreads twice as far. Its glossy, dark-green, ½-inch leaves and slender branches give it a refined look. The ornamental red berries and reddish fall color keep it attractive through the autumn.

- **Spreading cotoneaster:** *C. divaricatus*. Zones 4 to 7. Despite its common name, this cotoneaster is actually an upright shrub that attains 5 to 6 feet in height and spread. It does, however, have the small, glossy, dark-green foliage, persistent red berries, and fine texture that makes plants in this genus so attractive. In the autumn, foliage turns yellow to red-purple.

- **Rockspray cotoneaster:** *C. horizontalis*. Zones 5 to 7. Although this cotoneaster grows well in only a narrow climate range, its unique layered branching effect is worth the effort. Snow cover or mulch helps protect it from winter damage where temperatures may drop to –20°. It has the typical cultural needs and habits of the other cotoneasters and grows 2 to 3 feet high and up to 6 feet wide. The cultivar 'Variegatus' has white-edged leaves that turn rosy pink in autumn. 'Perpusillus' grows only 12 inches high and spreads up to 7 feet, but is susceptible to fire blight.

- **Autumn olive:** *Elaeagnus umbellata*. Zones 4 to 8. Often sold in mail-order catalogs and by conservation services as a wildlife-attracting shrub, autumn olive is best suited to mass plantings along roadsides and other untended areas. Its spiny stems can form masses 12 to 18 feet high and 20 to 30 feet across. Although it has attractive silvery leaves and fragrant yellow flowers, its red fruits attract birds that spread the seeds everywhere, causing this plant to become a noxious weed in some parts of the country. It thrives in poor, drought-prone soil. The cultivar 'Cardinal' fruits heavily.

- **Burning bush, winged euonymus:** *Euonymus alatus.* Zones 4 to 8. This shrub has many qualities, including brilliant scarlet autumn foliage and ornamental, raised ridges or wings on the stems that give it a unique winter appearance. This shrub grows slowly into a dense horizontally spreading mound up to 20 feet high and wide. If you have such a large specimen, you can prune it into an effective small tree. Smaller shrubs make lovely hedges — both clipped and informal. If you want a burning bush that will remain smaller, try the cultivar 'Compactus', which grows to 10 feet, or seek out 'Rudy Haag', a dwarf at 4 to 5 feet. Prune in the spring to keep it compact.

- **Seabuckthorn:** *Hippophae rhamnoides.* Zones 4 to 7. Grown mostly for its spectacular bright-orange berries, seabuckthorn has other endearing characteristics. Its narrow, almost needle-like foliage, is bright, silvery-green and shimmers in the breeze. After the foliage drops in the fall, the showy berries become more obvious. The berries aren't attractive to birds, although they are edible, so they stay on the shrubs all through the winter. Plants are either male or female — only the females produce the ornamental berries. You need a least one male for every half dozen females for best fruiting. It actually prefers poor sandy soil and tolerates salt spray, making it ideal for planting by the shore or roadside and other difficult sites. Mature height is 8 to 12 feet tall, but it spreads wider by sending up shoots to form large billowy thickets. You can prune it into a small tree.

- **Winterberry:** *Ilex verticillata.* Zones 3 to 9. This deciduous holly thrives in cold climates that would kill most evergreen hollies to the ground and yet it retains many of the same ornamental characteristics. Like its cousins, winterberry has masses of stunning red berries that persist through the winter, if the birds don't eat them. Plants are either male or female — you need both to produce the showy fruit. The leathery, dark-green leaves are oval to oblong and lack spines. It ranges in size from 6 to 10 feet high and wide, but grows slowly and enjoys moist to wet, acidic soil. It's perfect for planting by a stream or pond or that low, damp spot out back. Although it tolerates light shade, it produces more fruit in full sun. Because winterberry has such a wide climactic range, buy plants that are genetically adapted for your climate. Individual plants native to the southernmost zones aren't as cold hardy as those native to the northern zones, for example.

  Cultivars include 'Jim Dandy', a male cultivar that acts as an excellent pollinator for female cultivars and is hardy to zone 4. 'Red Sprite' is a dwarf female cultivar that grows 3 to 5 feet high. It has large red fruits and shiny green leaves. Sometimes nurseries offer this cultivar under the names of 'Nana', 'Compacta' or 'Macrocarpa'. Use 'Jim Dandy' as a pollinator. 'Southern Gentlemen' is a male plant that grows to 8 feet. It pollinates 'Winter Red' and 'Sparkleberry'. It's also sold under the name of 'Late Male'. 'Winter Red' has tremendous crops of persistent berries and grows well in the southern and midwestern climates. 'Sparkleberry' grows upright to 15 feet tall.

- **Japanese kerria:** *Kerria japonica.* Zones 4 to 9. This pretty shrub grows next to my back steps where I can appreciate its fine, bright-green foliage. Its toothed, lance-shaped leaves gracefully cover the slender, arching green stems. Starting in midspring, bright yellow, 1½-inch flowers emerge at the tips of the branches and continue off and on throughout the summer. Kerria sends up vigorous, suckering new shoots that ultimately form large colonies up to 6 feet high. Plant Japanese kerria as a specimen shrub in the shade to part sun and give it well-drained, loamy soil. Prune to keep it looking neat and to remove excess shoots. The cultivar 'Pleniflora' grows more upright than the species and has double flowers that grow up to 2 inches in diameter.

- **Amur privet:** *Ligustrum amurense.* Zones 4 to 7. Commonly offered in mail-order catalogs as a cold-hardy hedge plant, this shrub does make a nice dense border if kept clipped. It grows rapidly to 12 to 15 feet tall and nearly as wide and requires at least two prunings a year, beginning at planting time, to keep it under control. It tolerates urban conditions and any soil except those with poor drainage.

- **Border privet:** *L. obtusifolium.* Zones 4 to 7. Winter hardiness, small leaves, and a horizontally spreading habit make this privet species attractive for northern hedges. It flowers in midsummer and grows 10 to 12 feet high and 12 to 15 feet wide. The variety *regelianum* has a distinct horizontal growth habit and grows only half as high as the species.

- **California privet:** *L. ovalifolium.* Zones 5 to 7. A semi-evergreen privet, this shrub keeps its foliage in warmer climates, but sheds them when winter temperatures drop towards 0°. It grows 10 to 15 feet tall and makes an excellent clipped hedge. Plumes of white flowers bloom in midsummer. Several cultivars have golden or variegated foliage.

A CLOSER LOOK

Hedging your bets with privet

One of the most common and popular shrubs for hedges and screens, privet has many species both evergreen and deciduous. Fast growth, relatively fine texture, and cast iron constitution contributes to its popularity. In addition, privets have plumes of small white flowers in summer, although not all have a pleasant smell. The persistent berries and all other parts of the plants are somewhat toxic when eaten. Privets are also prone to a number of blights, diseases, and insect pests, but usually manage to survive. Bare-root plants, available from nurseries and mail-order catalogs in the spring, are the most economical way to establish privet hedges. Plant them in any well-drained soil in full to part sun.

✔ **Common privet:** *L. vulgare.* Zones 5 to 7. Commonly used for clipped hedges, this privet grows rapidly to 12 to 15 feet if left unpruned. The key to growing an attractive, densely branched privet hedge lies in frequent shearing that begins when you plant the young shrubs. The foliage of this species is dark green and lance shaped. Flowers that appear in early summer have an unpleasant fragrance and are followed by persistent black berries. The cultivar 'Lodense' forms a dense hedge and matures at 4 to 5 feet, but is susceptible to disease. 'Aureum' has yellow foliage.

✔ **Northern bayberry:** *Myrica pensylvanica.* Zones 3 to 6. Native to the eastern United States, this aromatic shrub billows from sand dunes along the coast and sandy, dry roadsides. Birds relish the waxy gray berries, as do craftspeople who use them for scenting candles and potpourri. Shrubs spread in colonies and grow from 5 to 12 feet tall, depending on the climate and growing conditions. Plant bayberry in any well-drained soil and full sun to part shade. Use it as a hedge or mass planting, especially in difficult soils and along roadsides.

✔ **Ninebark:** *Physocarpus opulifolius.* Zones 2 to 7. This 10-foot-tall, suckering shrub forms thickets of upright, arching stems. Its most ornamental characteristics include peeling bark and small white flowers in the spring. The 2-inch foliage resembles small, lobed maple leaves. It grows in any soil (except poorly drained) and in full to part sun. You can cut it nearly to the ground to rejuvenate overgrown specimens. The cultivars are more attractive than the species and include 'Dart's Gold', a compact 4- to 5-foot plant with yellow foliage.

✔ **Purpleleaf sand cherry:** *Prunus × cistena.* Zones 3 to 7. An often-used and highly ornamental shrub, purpleleaf sand cherry has deep, reddish-purple foliage and fragrant pink flowers in early spring. It is cold hardy to temperatures as low as −30° to −35°. Although it grows 7 to 10 high, you can prune it to keep it smaller and more compact. It tolerates a wide range of well-drained soils and full sun. Plant it against a light-colored background or with variegated shrubs to accentuate its dark foliage.

✔ **Alder buckthorn:** *Rhamnus frangula.* Zones 3 to 7. Sometimes grown as a tall hedge, buckthorn grows up to 15 feet tall and about half that in width with an open, upright habit. It grows in sun to part shade and in any well-drained soil. Unfortunately, this shrub spreads rapidly by seeds dropped by birds and is considered an invasive noxious weed. Although the species is not particularly ornamental, the cultivar 'Tallhedge' or 'Columnaris' is commonly sold for windbreaks and screens. The less common 'Asplenifolia' has narrow, fern-like foliage.

✔ **Basket willow:** *Salix purpurea.* Zones 3 to 6. Unlike the tree-sized willow species, this one forms an 8- to 10-foot, mounded shrub. Its finely textured branches are used for basket making. This shrub, especially the cultivar 'Streamco', is used extensively by the Soil Conservation Service to plant along streams for soil stabilization because its fibrous roots form dense mats. The cultivar 'Nana' (Arctic Blue Willow) has narrow blue-green leaves and grows only 5 feet high.

- ✔ **Cutleaf stephanandra:** *Stephanandra incisa.* Zones 4 to 7. Excellent as a foundation shrub or for covering an embankment, this shrub has long, gracefully arching branches that root wherever they touch the ground. The fine foliage and small white spring flowers add to its interest. It grows about 5 feet high and spreads that much and more. Use it in front of tall or leggy shrubs. Plant in moist, acidic, fertile soil in full sun to part shade. The cultivar 'Crispa' grows only half as high as the species, and is commonly available.

- ✔ **Snowberry:** *Symphoricarpos albus.* Zones 3 to 7. Grow this shrub in the shade and enjoy its glowing-white berries. Snowberry grows into a dense mound, 3 to 6 feet across, and develops small pink flowers in early summer on new growth. Pruning in late winter to early spring can increase the bloom and berry production. It can grow on nearly any soil and in full sun to shade.

- ✔ **Chenault coralberry:** *Symphoricarpos × chenaultii.* Zones 4 to 7. This low-growing shrub has arching branches and a spreading habit. Its berries are white to pink and the leaves small and oval. 'Hancock' grows only 2 feet high and may spread up to 12 feet in width. It is more disease resistant and commonly available than the species.

Tall Shrubs to Prune into Small Trees

Some shrubs grow tall enough to consider as small trees, except that they have multiple stems or twiggy branches close to the ground that hide their trunks. Prune off the lower limbs and thin the stems to one to three main trunks and — voilà! — you can turn a large or overgrown shrub into an attractive specimen tree suitable for small landscapes or garden features. For flowering shrubs to prune into small trees, flip to Chapter 9. The following deciduous shrubs make especially nice small trees:

- ✔ **Cornelian cherry dogwood:** *Cornus mas.* Zones 4 to 7. This dogwood has pretty yellow flowers early in the spring before other flowers emerge. After the flowers drop, bright-red, cherry-like, edible fruits develop. You can use the fruit to make jelly or leave them for the appreciative birds. The summer foliage is deep lustrous green. It easily reaches the size of a small tree at 20 to 25 feet high and can be pruned to a single trunk. Plant this large shrub against a dark background, such as a brick building, where you can enjoy the mass of yellow spring flowers. It makes a good screen plant or tall hedge and grows well in any moist to well-drained soil in full sun to part shade. The cultivar 'Golden Glory' has more flowers than the species and grows more upright than spreading.

✔ **Pagoda dogwood:** *C. alternifolia.* Zones 3 to 7. This beautiful, large shrub actually looks more like a small, multistemmed tree as it matures. It grows 15 to 25 feet high and 20 to 30 feet wide. The horizontal branching habit mimics the flowering dogwood and gives the plant a layered look. The 10-foot specimen in my yard is covered with clusters of white flowers for a few days in late spring followed by berries on bright red stems. Cedar waxwings and catbirds readily eat the berries. Pagoda dogwood likes moist, acidic, well-drained soil and sun to part shade. It's prone to twig blight, which I prune out whenever I notice it.

✔ **Russian olive:** *Elaeagnus angustifolia.* Zones 2 to 7. My first exposure to this tough plant was along the interstate highways in New England where its salt, cold, and drought-tolerance and attractive willow-shaped, silvery foliage make it ideal for neglected mass plantings. The foliage shimmered and glowed on their spreading branches when they were young shrubs. As the plantings have aged, however, they look overgrown, messy, and unkempt with dead limbs lost to disease and insects. Occasional pruning to encourage vigorous growth is the secret to keeping this plant attractive (see Chapter 14).

Russian olive grows up to 20 feet tall and wide and can be pruned into a small tree if you remove all but one to three stems. Its stems are often thorny, making it useful for barrier plantings, as well. Although it tolerates nearly any soil, it grows most vigorously in well-drained, fertile soil and full sun. In summer, it produces fragrant but insignificant flowers followed by small silvery fruits eaten by birds. The cultivar 'Red King' has attractive red fruits.

✔ **Pussy willow:** *Salix caprea.* Zones 4 to 8. Silky-gray catkins emerge on the slender leafless branches in early spring and become yellow as they mature. This vigorous shrub quickly grows to 20 feet. Prune as soon as the catkins drop to control its size, or cut some branches just as the catkins swell to enjoy indoors. Although it prefers damp soil, it can grow in drier soil. It is also sold under the names of French, Goat, and Pink willow. The cultivar 'Pendula' is grafted on to an upright trunk from which it gracefully weeps downward.

A CLOSER LOOK

Here pussy, pussy willows

Unlike their tree-sized cousins, the willow shrubs fit into even the smallest yard where their ornamental flowering *catkins,* the "pussies" of pussy willow, brighten a late-winter landscape. Willows prefer moist — even flooded — soil and full sun to part shade. After the catkins fall, you can cut the stems back almost to the ground to rejuvenate them, if necessary. They have few pests.

✔ **Japanese pussy willow:** *S. chaenomeloides.* Zones 6 to 8. This species has huge 2½-inch, silvery-gray catkins, and stems long enough for cutting bouquets of the attractive, fuzzy flowers. The winter stems are mahogany red and grow to 20 feet.

✔ **Dragon's claw willow:** *S. matsudana* 'Tortuosa'. Zones 5 to 7. Also known as corkscrew willow, this cultivar has twisted branches that make interesting additions to cutflower and dry arrangements. This shrub will develop into a 20- to 30-foot tree if left unpruned. Heavy pruning not only keeps it smaller but also provides plenty of young branches, which show the most contortion.

Chapter 9

Falling for Flowering Shrubs

• •

In This Chapter

▶ Creating flowering focal points for your landscape

▶ Choosing shrubs with three seasons of color

▶ Selecting the best cultivars

• •

*F*lowers can jazz up your landscape with colors like wild red, orange, purple, and yellow or add serenity with white, pastel pink, lavender, and blue colors. From gaudy floral plumes and shrub-covering displays to tiny blossoms hidden among the leaves, flowers add color and fragrance to your yard.

The best flowering shrubs also have attractive foliage, stems, or ornamental berries. Disease resistance, hardiness, and tidiness count, too. If you have a small yard or room for only a few shrubs, look through this chapter for those with attractive features in several seasons.

Using Flowering Shrubs in the Landscape

Shrubs that feature flowers add colorful and fragrant accents to the landscape. Choose and plant them where you can enjoy their particular characteristics.

- ✔ **Fragrant flowers** belong where you can enjoy their perfume — by a window, porch, patio, or along a path.

- ✔ **Blooms from early spring to autumn** are possible with just a little planning. Extend the show by choosing shrubs that bloom at different times.

- ✔ **White or light-colored flowers** show best against dark backgrounds, and brighten shady spots.

- ✔ **Brightly colored blooms** focus your view from windows and streets.

Following a pruning and maintenance schedule for your shrubs can result in maximum bloom. To create a schedule, however, you need to know when shrubs start forming their flower buds. Deciduous shrubs fall into two groups:

- **Shrubs that bloom in spring** have buds that were formed during the previous summer or fall. These buds are said to be on old wood—the growth from last season. Examples include rhododendron, viburnum, and mock orange.

- **Shrubs that bloom in summer or fall** have buds that were formed earlier in the spring. These buds develop on shoots that grow in the spring, known as new wood or the current season's growth. Examples include shrub althea, crape myrtle, and summersweet.

Spring pruning or winter weather can remove or destroy flower buds on old wood (thereby reducing the number of flowers), but promotes buds on new wood. Chapter 14 has more details about how to prune shrubs for best flowering.

Shrubs That Feature Flowers

The shrubs in this section lose their leaves for the winter. Some bloom early in the spring before the new foliage emerges, while others brighten the summer landscape with both flowers and foliage.

- **Bottlebrush buckeye:** *Aesculus parviflora.* Zones 4 to 8. A handsome shrub for large landscapes, bottlebrush buckeye forms a spreading, 8- to 10-foot-high colony of upright branches clothed in large hand-shaped leaves. In midsummer, 10- to 12-inch-tall, brushy, exotic-looking flower spikes appear at the branch ends. The foliage of this American native turns yellow in the fall. Plant bottlebrush buckeye as a background for smaller shrubs, as an informal border, or for a summer screen. Buckeye grows in nearly any soil except poorly drained and can tolerate dappled shade under tall trees although it prefers full sun. Few pests or diseases bother it, and it crowds out weeds and other plants that may try to grow among its shoots. Although it rarely needs pruning, you can cut it back to the ground in late winter to rejuvenate overgrown plantings.

- **Red chokeberry:** *Aronia arbutifolia.* Zones 4 to 9. From early spring flowers to flaming fall color, red chokeberry has a lot to offer. The small, white blossom clusters develop into ornamental red berries that are relished by birds in autumn through early winter. Put this shrub in a mass planting or toward the back of a shrub border to hide its open, leggy habit. It grows 6- to 12-feet high and spreads slowly via suckering stems to half that in width. Native to swamps and fields, it tolerates a wide range of soils and light conditions. The cultivar 'Brilliantissima' has glossy dark green leaves that turn scarlet in the fall, and offers more flowers and fruit than the species.

✔ **Butterfly bush:** *Buddleia davidii.* Zones 5 to 9. Butterflies love this vigorous shrub. Although it dies to the ground in zone 5, it sprouts anew each spring and produces masses of lilac-like flowering trusses from summer through fall. In warmer climates, butterfly bush can retain its long, pointed leaves all winter. Depending on the cultivar and climate, shrubs may send their arching branches out 5 to 15 feet high and wide. Plant butterfly bush in moist, fertile ground in full sun and prune in the early spring before growth starts. It flowers on new wood.

Flower colors include white, cream, yellow, lavender, pink, purple, red, and shades in-between, some with a contrasting colored "eye" in the center of each blossom. Some butterfly bush flowers also offer fragrance, including the white cultivars 'Nanho Alba', 'Petite Snow' and 'White Bouquet', red-purple 'Nanho Purple', 'Royal Red' and 'Petite Plum', yellow 'Honeycomb', and pink-flowered 'Pink Delight'. 'Harlequin' has creamy-white, variegated foliage and fragrant reddish-purple flowers.

✔ **Beautyberry:** *Callicarpa* species. Zones 5 to 8. Jewel-like clusters of pink to violet berries all along their arching branches make several species and cultivars of these shrubs famous. Although the fruits are quite attractive, the shrubs tend to get rangy and unkempt-looking unless pruned early each spring. Beautyberries grow best in well-drained soil with plenty of moisture and in full sun to dappled shade. They flower on new growth.

One of the most commonly available beautyberries, *C. bodinieri* 'Profusion', benefits especially from pruning because it encourages plenty of purple-colored new growth and magenta berries. It can reach 8 feet high. Purple beautyberry, *C. dichotoma*, stays less than half that size and has arching branches. Its purple fruit remain attractive throughout the autumn. Japanese beautyberry, *C. japonica*, also grows 4 to 6 feet high and wide. Its fruits turn violet to metallic purple. The variety 'Leucocarpa' has white fruits.

✔ **Carolina allspice:** *Calycanthus floridus.* Zones 5 to 9. Grown in full sun to dappled shade and the moist, fertile soil it likes, Carolina allspice makes a lovely 6- to 9-foot by 6- to 12-foot specimen for a shrub border. It has lustrous, oval-pointed leaves and reddish brown, fragrant flowers that grow to 2 inches across in the spring. The fragrance varies considerably among individual plants, so sniff before you buy. Foliage turns yellow before dropping in the fall. Prune immediately after flowering, if necessary. It blooms on old wood.

✔ **Siberian peashrub:** *Caragana arborescens.* Zones 2 to 7. Native to Siberia, this hardy shrub can withstand winter temperatures to −50° and survive dry, windswept sites. Although it can become a bit rangy and unkempt in appearance, it serves well as an informal hedge or screen in situations where few other shrubs will grow. Pea shrub has bright yellow pea-like flowers in the spring and light green, compound leaves with small leaflets. The species, but not all of the cultivars, has spines on the stems at the base of the leaves. Shrubs grow quickly up to 20 feet tall and can spread nearly as wide, although you can train them into tree form. 'Pendula' is a weeping form with gracefully trailing branches grafted onto an upright trunk. Russian peashrub, C. *frutex,* (zones 3 to 7) lacks spines and stays more compact. It has an upright growth habit and grows to 8 feet tall and wide. Its cultivar 'Globosa' forms a compact 2 to 3 foot mound and performs well in cold, dry, windy locations. Pygmy peashrub, C. *pygmaea,* (zones 3 to 7) has refined, graceful foliage and branches and yellow flowers in late spring. It grows only 3 feet high, but spreads up to 5 feet, making an ideal low hedge plant for difficult sites.

✔ **Bluebeard:** *Caryopteris* × *clandonensis.* Zones 5 to 8. Bluebeard makes a nice, low, front-of–the-border shrub for sunny spots with well-drained soil. Its fine, narrow lance-shaped leaves are blue-gray, silver-gray, or golden yellow, depending on the cultivar. Tufts of small powder blue to purple-blue flowers cover plants in late summer. Bluebeard flowers on new growth, so you can prune it back in late winter to keep it neat and vigorous. It rapidly regrows into 2 to 3 foot mound. All parts of the plant are scented. The most common cultivars include 'Blue Mist' with powder blue flowers, 'Dark Knight' with deep blue-purple flowers, and 'Longwood Blue' with blue-violet flowers. 'Worcester Gold', which has golden foliage and blue flowers, is a real knockout in the late summer border.

✔ **Floweringquince:** *Chaenomeles speciosa.* Zones 5 to 8. This shrub's main feature is a one- to two-week-long display of ornamental flowers in late winter to early spring. Small rose-like blossoms open along the spiny stems before the glossy green leaves unfurl. Two-inch wide, hard, yellow fruits — suitable for jelly making — ripen through the summer. Planted in nearly any well-drained soil in full sun, floweringquince grows to 6 to 10 feet with a rambling or upright form. Use as a barrier planting, but avoid planting it where it may collect litter and debris — the sharp spines make it hard to clean. Prune after flowering to shape the plant and maintain its size.

✔ **Summersweet:** *Clethra alnifolia.* Zones 4 to 9. Fragrant, upright plumes of white flowers grace the new growth of this lovely native shrub in mid to late summer for several weeks. The lustrous green foliage changing to yellow in autumn and smooth, brown bark add to its attractiveness. It grows best in moist, acidic soil and part shade to full sun, but tolerates the less hospitable conditions by the seashore. It has few pests except for mites that bother stressed plants in overly dry sites. This species can grow 6 to 10 feet tall and wide, but some cultivars, such as 'Hummingbird' grow only 36 inches high. This outstanding cultivar blooms earlier and more heavily than the species and received the Pennsylvania Horticultural Society Gold Medal Award and the Georgia Gold Medal Award. It forms large colonies of upright shoots. 'Pink Spires' grows to 8 feet and has rosy pink flowers. 'Ruby Spice' is similar, but has darker pink blooms.

✔ **Fragrant winterhazel:** *Corylopsis glabrescens.* Zones 5 to 8. Fragrant clusters of pale yellow flowers hang from the branches of this winterhazel in early spring before the leaves emerge. Winterhazel's large, somewhat coarse leaves and open, spreading habit look most at home in a natural woodsy setting. An ideal spot would be against a group of evergreens that would give the shrub winter protection and serve as a foil for the flowers. It grows up to 15 feet tall and wide and needs moist, fertile, well-drained soil with plenty of humus. You can prune its tall stems into small trees. Buttercup Winterhazel, *C. pauciflora*, stays smaller at 4 to 6 feet. It's hardy in zones 6 to 8.

✔ **Smokebush:** *Cotinus coggygria.* Zones 4 to 8. This popular shrub has smoky clouds of flower stems all summer long. After the flowers fall in early summer, the pink-purple flower stalks remain effective for several months. The oval to nearly round leaves may be blue-green to dark purple, changing to yellow or yellow-orange in autumn, depending on the cultivar. Plant this shrub where it can spread out — it matures at 10 to 15 feet high and wide, although some cultivars may stay smaller. Smokebush grows in nearly any well-drained soil and full sun. Purple-leafed cultivars, such as 'Royal Purple' and 'Nordine' need a protected spot in zones 4 and 5 where they are less hardy than the green-leafed plants. Don't panic if your smokebush doesn't leaf out with the other trees and shrubs in the spring — their leaves emerge later than many others. Even plants that do die to the ground in cold winters usually grow back into fine, flowering shrubs as the weather warms. Prune out dead and undesirable wood in the spring as soon as the leaves emerge.

A CLOSER LOOK

Making a clean sweep with broom

The species in these groups of shrubs (*Cytisus, Genista,* and *Spartium* species, zones 4 to 10) have tiny leaves and slender, arching green stems that explode with color each spring. Pea-like flowers, usually yellow but also in white, rose, crimson, and every color in-between, cover the plants. Brooms make useful massing plants for low-maintenance areas and seaside locations because they prosper in poor, sandy, droughty soil in full sun to part shade. The smaller species also make good container plants. Although individual plants may live for only a few years, brooms tend to propagate themselves by spreading their seeds around. Choose from a variety of species, cultivars, and hybrids or any of the other cultivars available from your local nursery.

- **Scotch broom:** *Cytisus scoparius* and hybrids. Zones 5 to 8. Scotch broom can also survive in protected parts of zone 4 where it grows 5 to 6 feet high and spreads by seeds and root suckers into a rounded thicket. Many cultivars exist including 'Moonlight', a cream-white flowered plant. 'Lena' has red and yellow flowers and grows 3 to 4 feet high. 'Lilac Time' also remains smaller and has lilac colored blooms. 'Minstead' flowers are purple and white. 'Burkwoodii' has red blooms. *Cytisus × preacox* 'Allgold', has deep yellow flowers and grows to 4 feet tall. Sweet broom, *C. × spachianus* (zones 8 to 10) grows to 10 feet high and is covered with fragrant golden yellow flowers in late winter to early spring.

- **Broom:** *Genista lydia.* Zones 6 to 7. This low-growing plant forms a 12-inch-high mat that's covered with yellow, pea-like flowers in late spring to early summer. The green stems and tiny leaves make an attractive arching shrub through the summer. Silkyleaf woadwaxen, *G. pilosa.* (zones 5 to 7) forms a low-growing mat 12 to 18 inches high. Cultivar 'Vancouver Gold' is covered with yellow flowers when blooming and spreads to 3 feet. The hardiest of the brooms, woadwaxen, (*G. tinctoria,* zones 4 to 7) grows into a small arching shrub 2 to 3 feet high and wide. Yellow flowers cover the plant in June and continue all summer if you prune the spent flowering stems. The cultivar 'Royal Gold' forms an erect, 2-foot shrub with gold flowers at the branch tips.

- **Spanish broom:** *Spartium junceum.* Zones 8 to 10. This vigorous species grows up to 10 feet tall. It has loads of fragrant, bright-yellow flowers for most of the summer on its slender, nearly leafless, green stems.

Daffy for daphne

Sometimes you have to work a little harder for an especially rich reward — growing daphnes falls into that worthwhile category. All commonly grown species have fussy soil requirements, but their powerful perfume is worth any effort to achieve it. Most form neatly mounding low shrubs with very small, fine evergreen or deciduous leaves. The small, lilac-shaped flowers bloom from late winter through spring in white, pink, and deep rose colors. Look for the evergreen species in the "Evergreen Flowering Shrubs" section, later in this chapter.

Daphnes need moist, well-drained, acidic to neutral, humus-enriched soil and can't tolerate poor drainage. They grow in full sun or dappled to moderate shade. Daphnes don't like to be moved after they're established, either, so choose your planting site carefully. Depending on where you live, plant container-grown shrubs in the early spring or fall when the plants are not actively growing. Daphnes rarely need pruning. Choose from a variety of Daphne species to perfume your garden.

- **Burkwood daphne:** *Daphne* × *burkwoodii.* Zones 4 to 7. The most famous and common cultivar of this daphne is 'Carol Mackie', a beautiful 3- to 4-foot mound of variegated foliage. Each deep-green leaf has a creamy white border. The fragrant pinkish white flowers make their show in late spring on old wood. Although hardy to −30°, this shrub appreciates protection from winter wind and sun.

- **Caucasian daphne:** *D. caucasica.* Zones 5 to 7. This daphne grows to 4 feet and has a longer bloom period than other commonly available species. Flowering begins in late spring and continues off and on until the fall. Give it part shade to enjoy a summer full of fragrance.

- **Slender deutzia:** *Deutzia gracilis.* Zones 4 to 8. Clusters of fragrant starry white flowers, each ¾ inch across, light up the arching limbs of this small shrub in late spring to early summer. Of all the species of deutzia available, this one has the most refined character and compact habit. Slender deutzia grows 2 to 4 feet high and wider making it ideal for foundation plantings or in front of taller shrubs. Plant it in full sun in any well-drained soil. Prune out one third of the oldest stems in late winter every year or two to keep plants flowering vigorously. The cultivar 'Nikko' grows 24 inches high, but spreads up to 5 feet in diameter. Its deep-green leaves turn purple in the fall. 'Monzia', a Deutzia hybrid, grows 6 to 8 feet high and wide and has pink flowers.

- **Forsythia:** *Forsythia* species. Zones 4 to 8. Forsythia's cheerful, yellow, bell-shaped flowers welcome spring as few other flowering plants can. Long before the deep green leaves begin to emerge, golden flowers cover the stems from top to bottom. Forsythias become large, somewhat straggly shrubs, however, with few assets other than their spectacular spring bloom. All except for a few cultivars grow 8 to 10 feet tall and 10 to 12 feet wide. Plant forsythia in a shrub border or a mass planting where you can appreciate their spring display and then let them blend into the background for the rest of the year. They tolerate city conditions and just about any soil and prefer full sun. Prune forsythias each spring right after flowering and remove one fourth to one third of the oldest stems right to the ground. You can also renovate badly overgrown shrubs by cutting the whole plant back to a few inches. Look in Chapter 14 for more techniques and advice.

People in cold-winter regions often wonder why their forsythia shrub only blooms down around its feet while the upper limbs remain bare. The simple explanation is that the flower buds are less cold hardy than the branches and leaf buds. Snow often insulates the lowest flower buds from the coldest temperatures, so they survive while their exposed brethren perish. If you live where winters don't get below −10°, you can plant nearly any forsythia cultivar. The classic 'Lynwood Gold' has an upright habit and covers itself with flowers. 'Spring Glory' grows to

10 feet and performs especially well in zones 7 and 8. If your winter temperatures regularly drop to –30°, take heart. Plant breeders have developed cultivars that can take the cold and still bloom all the way to the top of the plant. Look for 'Northern Sun', 'Northern Gold', and 'Meadowlark' for zone-4 hardiness.

✔ **Fothergilla:** *Fothergilla gardenii.* Zones 4 to 8. If you want a true garden gem, stop right here. Dwarf fothergilla offers three seasons of interest beginning in midspring with fragrant white flowers that look like miniature bottlebrushes at the ends of each branch. One to 2-inch long, blue-green to dark-green leaves clothe the neat, compact 3- to 4-foot-high shrubs all summer, turning bright-orange, red, and yellow in autumn. Give this shrub, or a group of them, a place in your foundation planting, border, or along a path, or use them as a natural, unpruned low hedge. All they ask in return is moist, well-drained, acidic soil and full sun to dappled shade. They make excellent companions for azaleas, rhododendrons, daphnes, and pieris and require little pruning. The cultivar 'Mount Airy' has dark blue-green foliage, larger flowers, and better fall color than the species. It grows 5 to 6 feet tall with an upright habit. Large fothergilla, *F. major* (zones 4 to 8), grows to 6 to 10 feet high and wide and blooms just after the dwarf species has finished flowering.

✔ **Rose mallow:** *Hibiscus mutabilis.* Zones 7 to 11. Similar to the tropical hibiscus, rose mallow has large, funnel-shaped flowers and rich, green foliage. Although it is less famous than the tropical species (zone 11) or the hardier rose of Sharon, it fills the hardiness gap between them for gardeners in the southeast. In colder parts of its range, rose mallow may die back in the winter, but quickly regrows in the spring. It grows up to 12 feet tall and half that in width in a warm climate where it has well-drained, moist soil and full sun. The 4- to 6-inch-wide flowers appear in the summer in white, pink, or red.

✔ **Rose of Sharon:** *H. syriacus.* Zones 5 to 8. A tropical-looking shrub for the temperate-climate landscape, rose of Sharon displays huge 2- to 4-inch-wide trumpet flowers from late summer into fall. The fantastic color range includes white, red, pink, purple, and even sky blue. The lobed, dark green foliage emerges in late spring and persists into late fall. Depending on the cultivar, this shrub can grow up to 12 feet tall and nearly as wide. Plant it at the back of the shrub border or in a screen or hedge in well-drained, moist soil in full sun to part shade where it can enjoy the summer heat. Prune in the spring to remove dead wood and to encourage vigorous new growth on which the flowers emerge. Flowers may be single or double in one clear color or have a contrasting "eye" color in the center. Single-flowered cultivars include pink 'Aphrodite' and 'Minerva'; white 'Diana' and 'Helene'; and 'Bluebird', with huge, 5-inch wide sky blue flowers. Double-flowered cultivars include white 'Jeanne D'Arc' and pink to purple 'Blushing Bride', 'Ardens', and 'Collie Mullens'.

A CLOSER LOOK

Hooked on hydrangeas

Old-fashioned favorites from Maine to Mississippi and from California to the Carolinas, hydrangeas grew in every grandmother's garden and still find welcome in modern landscapes. Notable primarily for huge balls of white, pink, and blue flowers that decorate the yard in summer, the blooms dry easily for winter arrangements. Large blue-green to deep-green deciduous leaves and mounding growth habits also contribute to hydrangeas' appeal. They look great as informal borders and specimens, and the shorter plants make nice additions to foundation plantings, too.

As a group, hydrangeas aren't too fussy about their soil or sun conditions. They all prefer moist, well-drained soil with plenty of organic material worked in. They grow well in full sun in cooler climates, but prefer shade to part shade in hot summer areas and where the sun is especially intense. The less-hardy species benefit from a protected site, such as the north side of a building, that prevents them from leafing out too early in the spring when late freezes can damage their tender leaves and shoots. Generally, you don't have to worry too much about pests and diseases on hydrangeas. Some are prone to powdery mildew in humid climates. Aphids, mites, and scale can also cause some damage, but most hydrangeas are trouble-free.

Hydrangeas tend to be a confusing bunch on two issues: flower color and pruning. Flowers of most hydrangea species are white and change to pinkish brown as they age. The bigleaf or French hydrangea, however, has flowers that range from pink to blue depending on the pH of the soil. The genetics of each cultivar also determines the intensity of the colors. In this species, pink flowers occur when the soil pH is above 6.0. You get blue flowers when the pH drops to 5.0 to 5.5. Even if you purchase a blue-flowered shrub, its blooms will eventually become pink if you plant it in soil with a higher pH.

Lack of flowering is also a common complaint from many gardeners. The two main causes for this disheartening experience are lack of hardiness and improper pruning. Two popular hydrangeas, smooth and panicle, bloom on new wood grown in the current season. Pruning these hardy shrubs in the late winter or spring will lead them to bloom like crazy that same year. But, two other hydrangeas, bigleaf and oakleaf, bloom on wood that grew last summer. If you prune these more tender species in the spring or if the winter temperatures got too cold, you lose the flower buds for that year.

✔ **Smooth hydrangea:** *Hydrangea arborescens.* Zones 4 to 9. This tough shrub dies to the ground in the coldest climates, but comes back swinging in the spring to put on quite a display of white flower clusters all summer long. The leaves are 3 to 6 inches across and rounded with serrated edges. It grows 3 to 5 feet high in heavy shade and tolerates moist to somewhat dry soil from acidic to alkaline in pH. It's quite salt-tolerant, too, making it a valuable addition to seaside or roadside gardens as long as you keep it well watered. Although this low shrub grows rapidly, its life is often short. The most common cultivars include 'Annabelle', which has large round flower heads and a more compact habit than the species, and 'Grandiflora' or 'Hills of Snow'. 'Grandiflora' has smaller flower heads than 'Annabelle' does, but each individual flower is larger. Both cultivars have more compact and attractive growth habits than the species.

✔ **Bigleaf or French hydrangea:** *H. macrophylla*. Zones 6 to 9. Most popular for its pink and blue flowers, these shrubs grow quickly into mounds 3 to 8 feet high and wide that bloom from June to August, depending on the climate and cultivar. The potted hydrangeas often sold in florist shops, supermarkets, and garden centers belong to this species and won't survive the winter in cold climates. Bigleaf hydrangea has two flower types called *hortensias* and *lacecaps*. Hortensias, also known affectionately as *mopheads*, have globe-shaped flower heads of large, flat-petalled sterile flowers. Often the flower heads are so large that they bend the stems to the ground. Lacecaps have more delicate looking, flat flower heads with bead-like fertile flowers in the center surrounded by a ring of large, flat, sterile flowers. Both types have the full color range from deep pink to vibrant blue with plenty of variation in between.

'Nikko Blue' is the most popular cultivar. It grows vigorously to 6 feet and has blue mophead flowers in acidic soil. 'Blue Billow', a lacecap, received the Pennsylvania Horticultural Society Gold Medal in 1990 for its bright blue flowers and cold tolerance to 0°. 'Variegata mariesii' grows 3 feet high and has pink or blue lacecap flowers and white margined foliage. A related species, *H. serrata,* has the lovely cultivar, 'Bluebird', which blooms early in shades of pink or blue. The plant is more drought-tolerant than most others. 'Pia' (mophead) stays reliably pink and grows only 2 to 3 feet high. 'Forever Pink' (lacecap) also remains pink and 2 to 3 feet tall and blooms in early summer.

✔ **Panicle hydrangea:** *H. paniculata*. Zones 3 to 8. This species grows up to 20 feet high and flowers in late summer on new wood. Its flower heads are pyramid shaped and comprised of both sterile and fertile flowers. Panicle hydrangea, especially the very common cultivar 'Grandiflora', also known as 'PeeGee', has a coarse landscape habit and its stems tend to flop over when the heavy flower heads bloom. You can cut this one to the ground in late fall to keep it tidy and compact, or train it into a small, single-trunk tree.

✔ **Oakleaf hydrangea:** *H. quercifolia*. Zones 5 to 9. Offering three seasons of interest, this species has handsome, dark-green, oak-shaped leaves that turn various shades of red in the fall. Huge, creamy, pyramid-shaped, fragrant flower heads bloom in the summer and gradually change to pinkish tones as they age. In the winter, you can see the shaggy reddish brown bark after the leaves drop. Provide moist, well-drained, somewhat acidic soil and sun to shade conditions. They don't tolerate salt as well as some other hydrangeas, but I've seen them growing happily near the Atlantic Ocean around Cape Cod and Nantucket, Massachusetts. They grow 3 to 6 feet high and make good landscape companions for azaleas and rhododendrons. The cultivar 'Snow Queen' won the Pennsylvania Horticultural Society Gold Medal in 1989. 'Snowflake' has 12 to 15 inch long flower heads and rich burgundy fall color.

✔ **Sweetspire:** *Itea virginica.* Zones 5 to 9. This lovely little shrub has long, narrow streamers of fragrant white flowers trailing from its gracefully arching shoots in early-to mid-summer. It grows 3 to 5 feet high in sun to part shade and grows in all soils except those with high pH. The glossy foliage turns crimson red in the autumn. Prune out the old stems to keep the shrub vigorous and tidy. The cultivar 'Beppu' grows 24 to 30 inches tall. 'Henry's Garnet' has better autumn color than the species and a more compact habit and is hardy through zone 5.

✔ **Beautybush:** *Kolkwitzia amabilis.* Zones 4 to 8. Pink, bell-shaped flowers cover beautybush in late spring and really put on a show. It has few other decorative features, however, unless you count the exfoliating bark on mature plants. Growing to 6 to 10 feet high and nearly as wide, this shrub becomes leggy and open with most of the foliage near the top of the plant as it gets older. You can keep it more attractive by pruning out one fourth to one third of the oldest canes each year immediately after flowering and shortening overgrown shoots. It grows in nearly any well-drained soil in full sun.

✔ **Blueleaf honeysuckle:** *Lonicera korolkowii.* Zones 4 to 9. This shrub's common name comes from its attractive blue-green foliage. It also has pairs of pink flowers along its arching, spreading branches in midspring. Honeysuckles grow rapidly in nearly any well-drained soil and prefer full sun, but tolerate shade. Blueleaf honeysuckle is less commonly available than other species, but some cultivars are worth seeking out if you like honeysuckle and have trouble with aphids. 'Freedom' and 'Honey Rose' are aphid-resistant and grow about 6 to 8 feet high.

✔ **Tatarian honeysuckle:** *L. tatarica.* Zones 3 to 8. Scattered widely by berry-eating birds, tatarian honeysuckle is common along roadsides and in woodlands throughout its growing range. It has white, pink, or red flowers in late spring followed by red berries. Growing 10 to 12 feet tall, this shrub forms a mass of arching shoots that can be pruned into a hedge. Overgrown shrubs can be cut nearly to the ground and will rebound with new shoots. Aphids often infest this species and cause abnormal leaf and twig growth. 'Arnold Red' has dark red flowers. Other cultivars offer different flower and berry colors.

✔ **European fly honeysuckle:** *L. xylosteum.* Zones 4 to 6. This well-behaved honeysuckle has white to yellowish flowers and gray-green foliage on arching stems. These shrubs form mounds 6 to 10 feet high and wide. Improved cultivars include 'Emerald Mound' or 'Nana', which grows slowly to 3 to 4 feet and has blue-green foliage. 'Clavey's Dwarf' makes a natural 6-foot high hedge.

✔ **Mockorange:** *Philadelphus × virginalis.* Zones 4 to 8. Prized for their sweet-smelling, white blooms, mockorange has many fans. Many species, varieties, and cultivars of mockorange are available and the best combine fragrant blooms with a compact branching habit. They tolerate nearly any soil and light conditions, but grow best in moist, well drained, fertile soils, and full to part sun. Prune them right after flowering by cutting up to a third of the oldest branches to the ground. The most commonly available cultivars include 'Dwarf Snowflake', which has fragrant double flowers on an arching 3 to 4 foot shrub, and 'Natchez', which grows twice that high and has single, fragrant, white blooms. Not all cultivars have fragrant flowers, so try to buy them while they're in bloom or look for cultivars that are described as "fragrant."

✔ **Potentilla:** *Potentilla fruticosa* and hybrids. Zones 2 to 6. Count this among the brown-thumb plants for cold-climate gardeners. Potentilla combines so many virtues in one plant that you really can't go wrong with one or more of its scores of cultivars. They form finely textured, shrubby mounds that are 1 to 4 feet in height and width. Most cultivars have buttercup or rose-like 1-to 1½- inch, yellow flowers in various shades, although some have red, orange, or white blooms. The red and orange-flowered cultivars hold their bloom color best in part shade and cooler climates. Use potentilla in the shrub border, as a foundation plant, for massing in low-maintenance areas, or as a low, informal hedge. Although potentilla performs best in full sun in fertile, moist, well-drained soil, it also tolerates poor, dry soils. Prune out a few of the oldest stems in late winter to keep it neat and vigorous.

Yellow-flowering cultivars include 'Gold Star', 'Gold Finger', 'Gold Drop', 'Jackmanni', 'Katherine Dykes', and 'Klondike'. White-flowering cultivars include 'Abbotswood', 'McKay's White', and the 12-inch dwarf 'Frosty'. For flowers in the pink to orange range, try 'Princess' (yellow-centered pink flowers), 'Red Robin', 'Tangerine', 'Sunset' or 'Floppy Disc', which has double pink flowers.

✔ **Bumalda and Japanese spirea:** *Spirea × bumalda* and *Spirea japonica.* Zones 4 to 8, with some cultivars hardy to zone 3. These two spirea are so closely related that they share most of the same characteristics — both bloom on new wood and form compact mounds of attractive foliage. Prune heavily in the spring for best flowering. Unlike most other spireas, they have pink to deep-rose-colored flowers, and many of their cultivars have brightly colored yellow or golden foliage. The small, pointed leaves often emerge bronze or purple in color before turning dark green or golden, depending on the cultivar. Most also have good fall color.

Use the cultivars of these two species for foundation plants, ground covers, specimens for small spaces, and rock gardens. Cultivars include 'Alpina', which has pink flowers and grows 30 inches high and up to 6 feet wide; 'Little Princess', which has yellow foliage and pink flowers and grows to 2 feet high; and 'Shirobana', which has white, pink, and deep rose colored flowers on the same plant all at the same time. 'Magic Carpet'

A CLOSER LOOK

Spiffy spireas

No matter where you live, spireas are among the easiest to grow and most popular deciduous shrubs. Useful for foundation plantings, informal hedges, mass plantings, and mixed shrub borders, spireas have a lot to offer. Most species have small, toothed leaves and flat clusters of little white to pink flowers. Some cultivars even make the "three seasons of interest" list for their brilliant yellow foliage, floral display, and autumn color. Many bloom over a long period or bloom in spring and put on a repeat performance later in the summer. Spirea species have several specific growth habits. Some species, such as the bridalwreath spirea, have tall, arching shoots and mature into a vase shape. Others, like Japanese spirea, form tidy mounds. A few spread low and wide.

Spireas ask for little beyond well-drained soil, full sun, and adequate moisture. These tough characters are pretty hard to kill after they become established, providing reliable bloom for many years even if neglected. Most spireas need regular pruning to look their best because the shrubs tend to get full of crowded and unproductive shoots. The best time to prune spireas, however, depends on whether the plant blooms on the current year's growth or from buds developed on the previous year's wood. Most spirea species bloom on old wood, but bumalda and Japanese spireas and their cultivars bloom on new growth. Prune plants that bloom on old wood right after they finish flowering in the summer so that they have time to set next year's flower buds before the growing season ends.

grows 8 to 10 inches tall and has pink flowers and reddish young foliage that turns golden yellow. 'Anthony Waterer', 'Crispa', and 'Froebelii' grow 3 to 4 feet high and 4 to 5 feet wide and have bright pink flowers. 'Goldflame', 'Goldmound', and 'Limemound' have pink flowers and yellow to orange-red young leaves that mature to yellow or light green.

✔ **Double bridalwreath or Reeves spirea:** *S. cantoniensis.* Zones 5 to 9. This spirea forms an arching mound, 4 to 6 feet high and wide. The cultivar 'Lanceata' has a very graceful texture, double white flowers, and blue-green leaves. It's very heat-tolerant and blooms in early spring on old wood. In the warmest zones, it may remain evergreen; otherwise the foliage turns reddish before dropping in the fall.

✔ **Spreading spirea:** *S. decumbens.* Zones 5 to 7. Spreading spirea grows less than a foot tall and spreads wider into a ground-covering mat of mint green foliage and white flower clusters. It grows well in full sun and makes a great rock garden addition on well-drained soil.

✔ **Snowmound spirea:** *S. nipponica* 'Snowmound'. Zones 4 to 7. With upright, arching branches, this spirea grows up to 5 feet high. White flowers appear in early summer on old wood. The cultivar 'Halward's Silver' is a more compact version that grows about half the size of snowmound.

- ✔ **Thunberg spirea:** *S. thunbergii*. Zones 4 to 8. This plant has small, narrow, willow-like leaves and a twiggy, arching habit that gives it a graceful appearance. It blooms very early in the spring on old wood and has white flowers. The foliage is light green and changes to yellow-orange in the fall. 'Ogon' has yellowish leaves.

- ✔ **Vanhoutte spirea:** *S.* × *vanhouttei*. Zones 3 to 8. This spirea grows 8 feet tall and spread its arching limbs more than 10 feet wide. This fountain-shaped shrub blooms heavily in the spring on old wood and has white flowers.

- ✔ **Bridalwreath spirea:** *S. prunifolia* 'Plena'. Zones 4 to 8. Bridalwreath spirea has arching branches 5 to 9 feet high and 6 to 8 feet wide. It blooms in the spring on old wood. It tends to become leggy with most foliage at the top of the plant.

- ✔ **Common lilac:** *Syringa vulgaris*. Zones 3 to 9. Grown mainly for its huge clusters of fragrant flowers, lilac is as cherished as any family heirloom wherever it grows. Individual shrubs bloom for about 2 to nearly 3 weeks, but some bloom early in the season and others toward the end of the lilac season. By choosing early, midseason, and late cultivars you can have lilacs in bloom for six weeks! Flower colors include white, all shades of pink, lavender, purple, and even a bluish-lavender that's referred to as blue. Although both single and double-flowering cultivars exist, the singles tend to have the stronger perfume.

Plant breeders crossed common lilac with some other lilac species to create new hybrids, such as Chinese lilac (*S.* × *chinensis*) and early flowering lilac (*S.* × *hyacinthiflora*). These hybrids share the hardiness of common lilac. Chinese lilac has a more graceful habit with arching branches and loads of heavy fragrant purple flowers. The early flowering lilac closely resembles its parent, but blooms a week or two earlier, and its cultivars are often mixed with it in catalog listings. To distinguish the cultivars from those of common lilac, nurseries abbreviate the hybrid name as *S. h.* before the cultivar name, as in *S. h.* 'Angel White'.

To decide which of the hundreds of available cultivars to grow, choose which characteristics you want your shrub to have. If you live in either extreme of lilacs' growing range, first look at cultivars that will grow in your area. Next, choose the color and bloom season. Also keep in mind that some cultivars are more fragrant and disease and pest resistant than other cultivars. White-flowered cultivars include *S. h.* 'Angel White' (single, fragrant, and heat-tolerant), 'Mme Lemoine' (double, very fragrant, heat-tolerant, mid-season bloom), 'Primrose' (single, yellow buds open to creamy flowers, single, heat tolerant, mid-season bloom), *S. h.* 'Mount Baker' (single, very heavy flowering, early season bloom), *S. h* 'Sister Justina' (single, very fragrant, early season bloom), and 'Krasavitsa Moskvy', 'Pride of Moscow' (double, pink buds, very fragrant, mid season bloom).

Long live lilacs!

The common lilac, passed lovingly from family to family for generations, grows throughout temperate North America in zones 3 to 7. Plant breeders have added new hybrids and cultivars, however, that extend its range into zones 8, 9, and even 10 as long as they receive adequate water. With over 20 species of *Syringa* existent, you can find some that grow wherever you live. Lilacs have quite a range of sizes, too, from rock garden specimens to tree stature. Clusters of flowers, called *panicles*, bloom in shades of white to purple in spring through early summer from buds set the previous year.

For the best flowering and growth, lilacs need at least a few weeks of dormancy in the winter when they drop their foliage and prepare for a new season. In most of its growing range, cold weather and day lengths naturally trigger winter dormancy. In the warmest regions, however, some lilac fanciers have found a way to artificially trick the shrubs into becoming dormant and, in so doing, have extended lilac's growing range. The first step is to choose a heat-tolerant cultivar, such as 'Lavender Lady', 'Blue Skies', or 'Angel White'. Keep the soil around the shrubs moist throughout the dry summer months, but stop watering in August. The shrubs will become dormant for the winter. In late winter to early spring, fertilize the shrubs and begin irrigating again. The plants should bloom in early spring.

Most lilacs need regular pruning to look their best and to encourage vigorous bloom each year. Remove the faded flower panicles in spring and excessive suckering growth. If you have an overgrown lilac that's just tangle of crowded stems, you can prune it severely, leaving six to nine well-space trunks of various diameters in a clump about 2 to 3 feet in diameter (see Chapter 14).

Lilacs enjoy neutral to slightly acidic, moist, fertile soil and prefer full sun, but tolerate light shade. The only requisite they demand is well-drained soil — no wet feet for this group. A few pests and diseases cause serious trouble for lilacs, although some species and cultivars are more susceptible or resistant than others. Lilac borer and oystershell scale are the worst insect offenders. A disease called *yellows* causes reduced vigor, unusual growths and flowering, and leaf discoloration and death. Powdery mildew looks unsightly, but rarely kills a plant. See Chapter 16 for more on this disease.

For more information about lilacs, write to the International Lilac Society, Inc., Robert S. Gilbert, Assistant Treasurer, P.O. Box 83, Hyde Park, NY, 12538 or visit their Web site at `www.lilacs.freeservers.com/`.

For pink flowers, try 'Belle de Nancy', (double, bright-mauve-pink), *S. h.* 'Asessippi' (pinkish lilac, single, fragrant, heavy bloomer, very early season), 'James MacFarlane' (bright pink single, late-flowering), or *S. h.* 'Maiden's Blush' (vivid pink, single, early season, heat-tolerant). Purple-flowering cultivars include 'Lavender Lady' (single, fragrant, heat-tolerant), 'Ludwig Spaeth'(single, fragrant), 'Sensation' (deep purple with white rim, heat-tolerant, single, mid-season), *S. h.* 'Pocahontas' (heavy bloomer, single), and *S. h.* 'Excel' (double, fragrant, early season). 'Charles Joly' has very fragrant double, magenta red flowers and 'Monge' is a single red, mid-season bloomer. For blue flowers, look for 'President Grévy' (double, heavy bloomer) or 'President Lincoln' (single, fragrant, mildew resistant, early to mid-season).

✔ **Meyer lilac:** *S. meyeri*. Zones 3 to 7. This species grows into a small, mounded shrub about 4 to 8 feet high and 6 to 10 feet wide. The 1-inch-long leaves resist powdery mildew. This small, early, fragrant violet-colored flowers begin appearing when the shrubs are very young and small, making them ideal specimens for rock gardens, informal hedges, and borders. If you commonly experience late freezes, plant this lilac in a protected spot to prevent it from flowering too early when sudden cold can ruin the bloom. The most common cultivar of Meyer lilac, 'Palibin', grows into a very compact 4- to 5-foot mound and has reddish-purple buds that become a lighter pink as they open. Littleleaf lilac, *S. microphylla* (zones 4 to 7), has very similar habits to Meyer lilac. It flowers in May to June and sometimes again in late summer.

✔ **Manchurian lilac:** *S. patula*. Zones 3 to 7. The most common cultivar, 'Miss Kim', makes a nice dense shrub up to 8 feet high and has lilac-colored blooms in May about a week later than common lilac. I enjoy the fragrance of the ones planted under my office window every spring, especially when the swallowtail butterflies come to visit. Its foliage turns purplish in the fall.

✔ **Japanese tree lilac:** *S. reticulata*. Zones 3 to 7. This species grows 20 to 30 feet tall and 15 to 25 feet wide. One of its best assets is beautiful, shiny, reddish bark that's similar to cherry. It blooms in June and has huge white panicles of fragrant flowers. It also resists many of the pests and problems that beset common lilacs. Plant Japanese tree lilac under utility wires, near small homes, and streetside. You can train it to a single trunk or grow it as attractive multi-trunk clump. The cultivar 'Cameo's Jewel' has white variegated foliage.

✔ **Dawn viburnum:** *Viburnum × bodnantense* 'Dawn'. Zones 7 to 8. Grown mainly for its fragrant and bright-pink, early flowers, borne in late winter to early spring, this plant is best in the coastal areas. Give this plant a protected spot to protect these early flowers from spring frosts. It grows about 10 feet tall and has a rather coarse texture.

✔ **Burkwood viburnum:** *V. × burkwoodii*. Zones 5 to 8. This plant smells wonderful in the spring when the pink buds open to reveal white flowers. It grows and flowers in moist, slightly acidic soil, and reaches 8 to 10 feet high and 6 to 8 feet wide. Its foliage is actually *semi-evergreen,* meaning that it hangs on in warmer climates, but falls in colder zones. This excellent shrub makes a good informal hedge or addition to a mixed shrub border. The cultivar 'Conoy' is an evergreen hybrid grown as much for its lustrous dark green foliage and compact mounding habit as for the fragrance of its white flowers. It does especially well in zones 7 to 8.

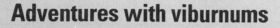

A CLOSER LOOK

Adventures with viburnums

I'm partial to plants that attract birds, live in tough situations, and offer year-round interest — many viburnum species fit the bill. Beautiful flowers, colorful fruit, and often-spectacular autumn foliage add to their appeal. Native to North America and other temperate regions of the world, viburnums grow from the coldest to the hottest zones. Species native to warmer areas have evergreen foliage, while those in the north drop their leaves in the fall. In size, viburnums range from 3-foot shrubs to 30-foot small trees. Although some species are grown primarily for their foliage, many produce clusters of flowers, usually white or pale pink and sometimes intoxicatingly fragrant. Use viburnums in woodland settings, shrub borders, mass plantings, informal hedges, and foundation plantings.

Some deciduous viburnums have powerfully fragrant flowers and many have ornamental fruit relished by birds. Use them as specimens or mass plantings, in informal hedges and screens. Some flower on new wood and others on old wood. The over-wintering flower bud clusters are usually obvious at the ends of the shoots and may need protection in the colder parts of each plant's hardiness range. (Many of the best deciduous viburnums are actually hybrids that plant breeders made by crossing related species. These hybrids have an "×" in their botanical name, such as *Viburnum × burkwoodii*.)

Most of these shrubs grow in any well-drained, but moisture-retentive soil. Some prefer acidic soil, while others are less fussy. Full sun to part shade suits them fine, depending on the species and climate. Most become established quickly after transplanting. In some species, male and female flowers occur on separate plants. When these kinds have desirable fruit, you must plant both sexes of shrubs to get the colorful or bird-attracting berries.

Pruning to thin out overgrown plants keeps them vigorous and neater-looking as new shoots quickly sprout to replace the old. Some species even make fine, clipped hedges. Most tolerate severe pruning and bounce right back with renewed vigor. Many insects, including aphids, scales, and plant bugs, bother viburnums, but most cause no permanent damage. The same holds true for diseases.

✔ **Fragrant viburnum:** *V. × carlcephalum.* Zones 6 to 8. This viburnum has fragrant, domed clusters of pinkish-white blooms in the spring, becoming a somewhat spreading, 6- to 10-foot shrub. The over-wintering flower buds may survive in warmer parts of zone 5. The cultivar 'Cayuga' is disease resistant and more compact.

✔ **Koreanspice viburnum:** *V. carlesii.* Zones 5 to 8. This plant grows only 4 to 5 feet high and wide and has fragrant blooms in the spring. It grows well in full sun to part shade in a wide range of soils. Use this attractive shrub in a foundation planting near a window where the perfume can waft in. This species has separate male and female plants — plant two different cultivars for berries. 'Compactum' has a dense habit and very dark green leaves that resist leaf spot disease. It grows 30 to 40 inches tall.

- **Arrowwood viburnum:** *V. dentatum.* Zones 3 to 8. This plant lacks the spectacular and fragrant blooms of many other viburnums, but it more than makes up for it with sheer tenacity: It grows in high pH soils, sandy soils, cold climates, and warm climates. Its shiny, dark-green, toothed leaves look good all summer, and its slender twigs have fine winter texture. Growing 6 to 15 feet high and wide, arrowwood makes an excellent screen shrub, especially for difficult sites and soils. The cultivar 'Autumn Jazz' has autumn color that ranges from yellow-orange to red. It grows to 8 by 10 feet in a vase shape with arching branches. 'Chicago Luster' also has reddish-purple fall color and has a more rounded habit.

- **Wayfaring tree:** *V. lantana.* Zones 4 to 7. This plant grows well in the U.S. midwest on dry, high-pH soils. It flowers on old wood and while the blooms look attractive, they have an unpleasant odor. Red to black fruits add to the fall color when the foliage turns purplish red. Use this 15-foot tall species as a screen, hedge, or mass planting. 'Mohican' grows only half as tall as the species and has orange-red fruit. A hybrid cross between this species and another viburnum resulted in 'Allegheny' and 'Willowwood' viburnums (*V. × rhytidophylloides),* shrubs superior to wayfaring tree in foliage, flower, and fruit. Hardy in zones 5 to 7, these hybrids have dark-green, disease-resistant foliage and bright-red fruit that turn black in the fall. They often bloom again in late summer as the berries from the spring bloom are turning red.

- **European cranberrybush:** *V. opulus.* Zones 3 to 8. This plant has foliage that resembles lobed maple leaves. It grows 8 to 12 feet high and spreads a few feet wider. In the spring, it bears 3- to 4-inch clusters of flowers that look like small lacecap hydrangeas, maturing into attractive, persistent red berries. The deep-green foliage lacks good fall color, unlike the similar North American native highbush cranberry described further on in this section. Several cultivars have improved characteristics over the species. 'Compactum' grows half the size of the species. 'Nanum' also stays dwarf, growing only 18 to 24 inches tall, but lacks showy flowers and fruit. 'Roseum' is an old cultivar also known as European snowball bush. Its flowers look very much like miniature mophead hydrangeas and cover the plants in spring, but it produces no fruit. 'Xanthocarpum' grows 8 to 10 feet high and has yellow berries.

- **Doublefile viburnum:** *V. plicatum tomentosum.* Zones 5 to 7. This plant is valued for its horizontal branching habit and white lacecap flowers borne in rows along the branches. It produces red fruit in the summer and doesn't require another shrub for pollination, unlike many other viburnums. It prefers well-drained, moist soil, and full sun to part shade. It grows 10 feet tall and 12 feet wide and makes a spectacular specimen plant against a dark background that shows off the bloom. It blooms on old wood. Cultivars include 'Mariesii', which has larger flowers that stand well above the foliage, and 'Newport', which has snowball-like flowers on a dense, mounded, 5-foot shrub with purple fall foliage. 'Shasta' spreads twice as wide as it grows tall (6 feet) and has a pronounced horizontal habit. 'Summer Snowflake' has a compact 6-foot habit and flowers sporadically throughout the summer.

Birches (*Betula*) **with white bark against evergreen trees and snow**

Chinese pistache *(Pistacia chinensis)* **in autumn**

Sweet gum *(Liquidambar styraciflua 'Gold Rust')* **leaf**

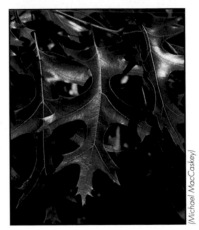

Scarlet oak *(Quercus coccinum)*

River birch *(Betula nigra)* **in summer**

Honey locust *(Gleditsia triacanthos inermis)*

(Positive Images)

(Positive Images)

(Michael MacCaskey)

(David Cavagnaro)

(Michael MacCaskey)

Tricolor European beech *(Fagus sylvatica 'Tricolor')* **with reddish foliage** (Michael S. Thompson)

Callery pear *(Pyrus calleriana)* **in autumn** (David Cavagnaro)

Gingko *(G. biloba)* **in fall color** (David Cavagnaro)

Sycamore *(Platanus)*

Indian laurel *(Ficus microcarpa)*

Sugar maple *(Acer saccharum)* **in fall**

Catalpa *(C. bignoides)*

(R. Todd Davis)

Flowering crabapples *(Malus)* **with white and red spring bloom**

(Michael MacCaskey)

Bailey acacia *(Acacia baileyana)* **with yellow flowers in early spring**

(David Cavagnaro)

Jacaranda *(J. mimosifolia)*

(R. Todd Davis)

Weeping cherry *(Prunus subhirtella)* **with white pine** *(Pinus strobus)*

(Michael MacCaskey)

Serviceberry *(Amelanchier canadensis)*
fruit in summer

(Crandall & Crandall)

Chinese flame tree
(Koelreuteria bipinnata)

(David Cavagnaro)

White flowering dogwood (*Cornus florida*)

(R. Todd Davis)

Flowering dogwood
(*Cornus florida*) **in fall color**

(Positive Images)

Pink flowering dogwood (*Cornus florida*)

(David Cavagnaro)

Southern magnolia *(Magnoila grandiflora)*

(Michael S. Thompson)

Hawthorn *(Crataegus 'Autumn Glory')* **with berries and snow**

(R. Todd Davis)

Witch hazel *(Hamamelis virginiana)* **branch with late-autumn flowers**

(Crandall & Crandall)

Pears *(Pyrus communis 'Duchess d'Angouleme')* **against brick wall**

(David Cavagnaro)

Eastern redbud *(Cercis canadensis)* **in bloom**

(David Cavagnaro)

Redwood *(Sequoia sempervirens)* **close up**

(Michael MacCaskey)

Atlantic cedar *(Cedrus atlantica)*

(Michael MacCaskey)

Colorado blue spruce *(Picea pungens 'Glauca')*

(David Cavagnaro)

Norway spruce *(Picia abies)* **with cones**

(David Cavagnaro)

Eastern redcedar *(Juniperus virginiana)*

(Michael MacCaskey)

Lemon-scented gum *(Eucalyptus citriodora)*

(David Cavagnaro)

White pine *(Pinus strobus)*

(R. Todd Davis)

Sawara false cypress *(Chamaecyparis pisifera)* **with blue spruce** *(Picea pungens 'Glauca')*

(David Cavagnaro)

Golden false cypress *(Chamaecyparis)* **with holly** *(Ilex aquifolium)* **in landscape**

(Michael S. Thompson)

Bird's nest spruce *(Picea abies 'Nidiformis')* **on wall with mugo pine** *(Pinus mugo mugo)* **and filbert** *(Corylus)*

(Michael MacCaskey)

Mugo pine *(Pinus mugo mugo)*

(David Cavagnaro)

Juniper *(Juniperus squamata 'Blue Star')*

(Michael S. Thompson)

Mixed conifers with red Japanese maple (*Acer palmatum*) **and heavenly bamboo**
(*Nandina domestica*)

(Michael S. Thompson)

Juniper (*Juniperus* 'Motherlode')

(David Cavagnaro)

Sawara false cypress (*Chamaecyparis pisifera*
'Filifera Nana')

Japanese floweringquince *(Chaenomeles speciosa)*

(R. Todd Davis)

Japanese camellia *(Camellia japonica* 'Pink Pagoda')

(David Cavagnaro)

Lowbush blueberry *(Vaccinium angustifolium)* **in fall color with rocks**

(R. Todd Davis)

Rhododendron 'PJM'

(R. Todd Davis)

Doublefile viburnum *(V. plicatum tomentosum* 'Shasta') **foliage and berries**

(David Cavagnaro)

Lemon bottlebrush *(Callistemon citrinus)* **and Japanese boxwood** *(Buxus)* **hedge**

(Positive Images)

Dwarf fothergilla *(Fothergilla gardenii 'Mt. Airy')* **bloom**

(R. Todd Davis)

Rugosa rose *(Rosa rugosa 'Linda Campbell')*

(R. Todd Davis)

Rugosa rose *(Rosa rugosa 'Henry Hudson')*

(David Cavagnaro)

Tropical hibiscus *(H. rosa-sinensis 'Mollie Cummings')*

(R. Todd Davis)

Butterfly bush *(Buddleia davidii 'Nanho Blue')*

(Michael MacCaskey)

(Michael MacCaskey)

Eastern ninebark *(Physocarpus opulifolius 'Diablo')*

Russian olive *(Elaegnus angustifolia)*

(R. Todd Davis)

Smokebush *(Cotinus coggygria 'Purple Robe')*

Rockspray cotoneaster *(C. horizontalis)*
in fall color

Oakleaf hydrangea *(Hydrangea quercifolia*
'Snow Queen') in bloom

India hawthorn *(Rhaphiolepis indica)*

Rockspray cotoneaster *(C. horizontalis)*
with summer berries

Spirea *(S. 'Limemound')* with smokebush
(Cotinus coggygria 'Royal Purple')

(David Cavagnaro)

Tobira *(Pittosporum tobira 'Wheeler's Dwarf')*, **rockspray cotoneaster** *(C. horizontalis)*, **and fountain grass**

(R. Todd Davis)

Lilac *(Syringa vulgaris)* **in a mixed bouquet**

(Crandall & Crandall)

Sweet mockorange *(Philadelphus coronarius)*

(David Cavagnaro)

English holly *(Ilex aquifolium)* **with berries**

(R. Todd Davis)

Rhododendron in wooded landscape

(R. Todd Davis)

Forsythia in early spring bloom

(R. Todd Davis)

Hydrangea *(Hydrangea macrophylla 'Nikko Blue')* **has pink flowers in alkaline soil**

Spirea *(Spirea japonica* 'Magic Carpet') **with Colorado blue spruce** *(Picea pungens* 'Glauca')

(David Cavagnaro)

Weigela *(W. florida* 'Red Prince')

(David Cavagnaro)

Japanese barberry *(Berberis thunbergii* 'Rose Glow')

(David Cavagnaro)

White and pink oleander
(Nerium oleander)

(David Cavagnaro)

Ceanothus *(C.* 'Julia Phelps')

(David Cavagnaro)

Unpruned boxwood
(Buxus sempervirens)

(David Cavagnaro)

(Michael S. Thompson)

Japanese spirea *(S. japonica 'Alpina')*

(David Cavagnaro)

Firethorn berries *(Pyracantha)*

(David Cavagnaro)

Wintercreeper *(Euonymus fortunei 'Canadale Gold')*

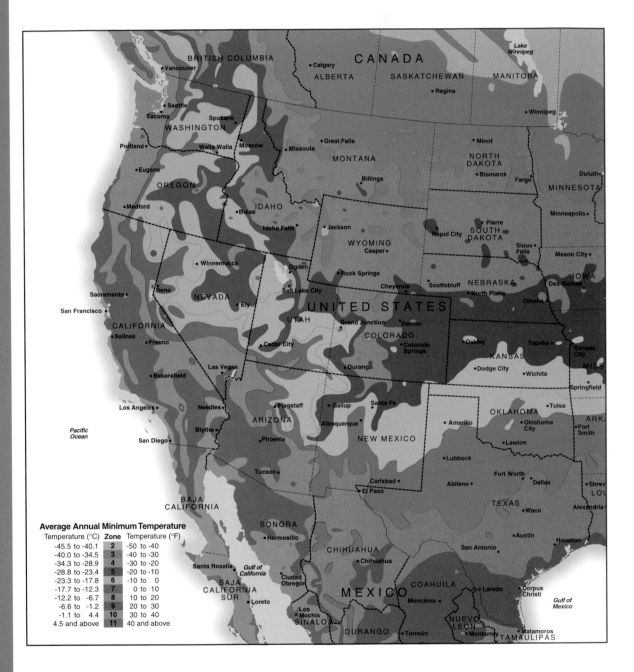

Average Annual Minimum Temperature

Temperature (°C)	Zone	Temperature (°F)
-45.5 to -40.1	2	-50 to -40
-40.0 to -34.5	3	-40 to -30
-34.3 to -28.9	4	-30 to -20
-28.8 to -23.4	5	-20 to -10
-23.3 to -17.8	6	-10 to 0
-17.7 to -12.3	7	0 to 10
-12.2 to -6.7	8	10 to 20
-6.6 to -1.2	9	20 to 30
-1.1 to 4.4	10	30 to 40
4.5 and above	11	40 and above

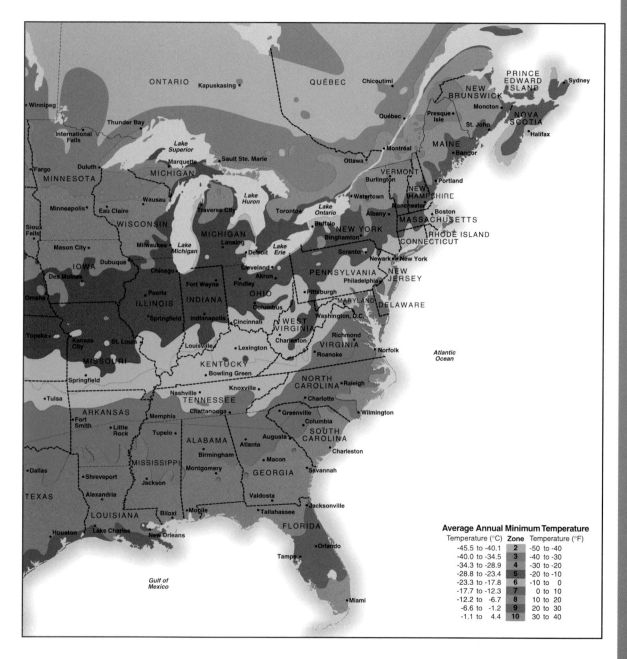

Average Annual Minimum Temperature

Temperature (°C)	Zone	Temperature (°F)
-45.5 to -40.1	2	-50 to -40
-40.0 to -34.5	3	-40 to -30
-34.3 to -28.9	4	-30 to -20
-28.8 to -23.4	5	-20 to -10
-23.3 to -17.8	6	-10 to 0
-17.7 to -12.3	7	0 to 10
-12.2 to -6.7	8	10 to 20
-6.6 to -1.2	9	20 to 30
-1.1 to 4.4	10	30 to 40

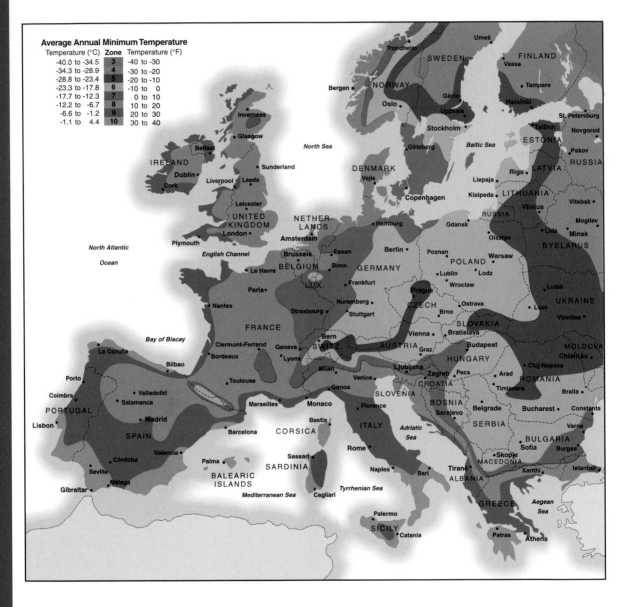

Average Annual Minimum Temperature

Temperature (°C)	Zone	Temperature (°F)
-40.0 to -34.5	3	-40 to -30
-34.3 to -28.9	4	-30 to -20
-28.8 to -23.4	5	-20 to -10
-23.3 to -17.8	6	-10 to 0
-17.7 to -12.3	7	0 to 10
-12.2 to -6.7	8	10 to 20
-6.6 to -1.2	9	20 to 30
-1.1 to 4.4	10	30 to 40

- **Blackhaw viburnum:** *V. prunifolium.* Zones 3 to 9. Blackhaw grows in nearly any soil, including dry, and in sun or part shade. The berries that develop after the midspring bloom are edible and relished by birds in the fall. Grow this plant as a tall shrub or prune into a small, 15- to 20-foot tree that resembles hawthorn.

- **Highbush cranberry:** *V. trilobum.* Zones 2 to 7. This plant grows in a seasonally flooded field between my house and the neighboring business' driveway. More of their customers ask the identity of those shrubs than any other plant in the border. Highbush cranberry tolerates wet to dry soils and frigid winters. It looks attractive all year 'round from the 3-inch clusters of white lacecap flowers in the spring and deep green lobed foliage in the summer to the fiery red fall foliage and huge bunches of red berries that persist until spring. Can you tell that I love this shrub? It grows up to 12 feet high and 8 feet wide and makes a great ornamental screen. Aphids sometimes distort its foliage, but a nontoxic horticultural oil spray takes care of the problem (see Chapter 15). 'Alfredo' grows about half the size of the species and has especially nice fall color. 'Compactum', growing only 6 feet tall, also stays small with more compact branching, but lacks 'Alfredo's' good autumn color. 'Wentworth', the cultivar I planted, is full-sized and has great reddish-purple fall color. Its berries turn from yellow to bright blood-red.

- **Weigela:** *Weigela florida* and hybrids. Zones 5 to 8. This old-fashioned shrub has seen a revival with an influx of new cultivars, many with attractively colored foliage. Long beloved for its rosy pink, funnel-shaped flowers borne in late spring, weigela now has white, red, and salmon-pink flowering cultivars, as well. Its arching branches grow into a 6 to 9 foot high and wider spreading mound. Pruning out a few of the oldest stems each year keeps the plant looking neater. Cold hardiness varies with the cultivar. Older cultivars grow through zone 5, but many newer ones can tolerate zone 4 with ease.

  Cultivars for zone 4, in order of hardiness from most to least, include 'Centennial'; 'Java Red', a compact 3 to 4 foot shrub with red flowers and purplish-green leaves; 'Minuet', a 30-inch dwarf with dark red flowers and purple-green foliage; and 'Pink Princess' and 'Red Prince', which grow to 5 to 6 feet. Good cultivars for zones 5 to 8 include 'Bristol Ruby'; white-flowered 'Bristol Snowflake'; and 'Variegata Nana', which has cream-edged, green leaves and rose-pink flowers.

A Rose By Any Other Name . . .

Roses rank as one of the most popular and beloved plants in the world. They have been grown for centuries, described by the world's greatest writers, painted by the most renowned artists, and possibly grown by more gardeners than any other plant. Roses are available in thousand of species and varieties, with flowers in almost every shade imaginable except blue. Flower forms range from single, five-petaled, dogwood-like blooms to the full-petaled, long-stemmed beauties from the florist shop (see Figure 9-1). Some roses lack fragrance, while others' scents range from intense and sultry to rich and fruity.

Figure 9-1:
Rose flower form ranges from single to semidouble to double.

Roses are also becoming more widely used as landscape plants. Newer varieties, and many of the old standbys as well, have exceptionally long blooming periods (on and off from spring to fall), and improved disease resistance so that they grow without frequent spraying. Don't feel that you have to confine roses to the rose garden, however. While growing roses for their charm alone has many rewards, their diversity of plant form — from low and spreading to tall and upright — makes roses useful in a variety of landscape situations including ground covers, shrubs, hedges, and climbing plants. The best roses for your landscape offer the following traits:

- Profuse and nearly continuous blooms
- Pest and disease resistance
- Hardiness to cold and heat in most regions
- Minimal pruning requirements
- Attractive plant shapes

A few landscape shrubs that meet these tough criteria include 'Royal Bonica' (ruffled pink flowers), 'Carefree Beauty' (mildly fragrant pink blooms), 'Carefree Delight' (pink with a white center), 'All That Jazz' (glowing orange blooms), 'Knockout' (red flowers), and 'Pillow Fight' (white flowers). These exceptionally colorful, carefree plants are perfect for many landscape situations.

For more formal landscapes, rose growers have turned some roses into trees called *standards,* which look like a regular rose, but on stilts. Standards cost more because it takes more time and effort to create one, but they're worth it. The secret? Growers have grafted desired roses on top of a tall trunk and you can buy almost any kind of popular rose this way. I like standards because they raise the flowers to nose height. So-called *patio* roses are the same idea, but smaller.

As you jump into the world of roses, be sure to check in with the American Rose Society. (Insiders refer to it as *The ARS.*) If you're searching for a particular rose, or for more information on any rose subject, write to The ARS at P.O. Box 30,000, Shreveport, LA 71130-0030; or call 800-637-6534 or visit their web site at www.ars.org. Annual membership in the ARS, which includes a one-year subscription to the monthly magazine, *American Rose,* costs $32. You can also locate rose varieties by visiting www.findmyroses.com on the Internet.

Got a rose question? Get an answer quick via the American Rose Society's Consulting Rosarians Online. Find the one nearest you at www.ars.org/cronline.html.

Growing roses

Given the right conditions, roses are tough plants. Purchase them as bareroot plants sold in winter to early spring, or as container-grown plants sold almost anytime (see Chapter 11 for more information on buying shrubs). They should be planted in full sun (at least six hours a day) and well-drained soil. Fertilize roses about every 6 weeks during the growing season, but stop about 6 to 8 weeks before the average fall frost date. Like most popular flowering shrubs, they need moist, well-drained soil.

Roses should be pruned annually, and in some cases, pretty severely. Hybrid teas, for instance, are usually pruned back to short stems in winter to keep them producing those huge, long-stemmed flowers in spring. The more you prune, the fewer — but bigger — flowers you get. Shrubs, floribundas, and other landscape roses are often just pruned back about halfway in winter. In any case, the nuts and bolts of pruning roses are covered in Chapter 14.

Aphids, Japanese beetles, cucumber beetles, rose chafers, and thrips are a few insect pests that sometimes bother roses. Diseases like powdery mildew, blackspot, and rust are often more serious but can usually be avoided by selecting disease-resistant varieties and providing the right growing conditions. Control measures for these and other pests are covered in Chapter 15.

Roses need winter protection anywhere colder than zone 8, and often even in zone 8. In zones 5 to 8, mulch the base of every plant to keep the base from freezing, thawing, and refreezing over and over. Wait until early winter, when the plant seems to be nodding into dormancy, and cut the canes back halfway.

Dump a cone of soil, sawdust, compost, or other insulating material, 6 to 10 inches deep, over the base of the plant. Encircle the base of the plant with a wire cage or cardboard box, and stuff it with shredded leaves or straw. The goal is to preserve the leaf buds on the bottom 8 inches of each cane. Protect climbing roses by removing them from their support, laying the canes on the ground and cover with soil or mulch. Remove whatever insulation you use in the spring, so that sun can reach the soil and warm it. If you live in zones 3 to 5, choose roses from the hardy roses information in the following section.

Selecting rose varieties

You can choose from literally thousands of kinds of roses, short to tall, big to little flowers, fragrant or not — you name it. To keep all these roses organized, rose growers divide them into classes or groups with similar characteristics or histories. You may be familiar with some of the groups, such as climbing roses or miniature roses, while other groups may be new to you. In this book, I discuss only the rose groups most commonly used for landscaping. You can find many more kinds of roses in *Roses For Dummies*, 2nd edition, by Lance Walheim and the Editors of The National Gardening Association (IDG Books Worldwide, Inc.)

When choosing a rose for your landscape, look first at the characteristics of the rose groups. If you want a low-growing rose to plant on a hard-to-mow slope, for example, start with the ground cover group. If you live in a cold-winter climate, look at the hardy roses first. The second characteristic to look for is disease resistance. Most roses are notoriously prone to disease, but some are resistant and are the best ones to choose. Cold hardiness varies widely among groups of roses and even between the different cultivars within a group. For this reason, I have not listed specific hardiness zones here. In general, most roses grow best in zones 7 to 10, while others survive in zones 5 to 6 with protection. The hardiest roses can tolerate zones 3 to 5. Read through the rose groups in this section to find the perfect plants for your landscape.

> ✔ **Hybrid tea roses:** Use hybrid teas as specimen shrubs in mixed flowerbeds or group them in a special rose bed. Hybrid tea roses bloom from spring through fall and have flowers that resemble florist roses. Many are fragrant. The best hybrid teas have earned consistently superior ratings from the ARS for their lovely flowers; their healthy, disease-resistant leaves; and their cold hardiness. Some of these include 'Dainty Bess', which has fragrant pink flowers; 'Double Delight' (very fragrant, white blushed with red), 'Mister Lincoln' (dark red, deeply scented flowers), 'Olympiad' (red, unscented blossoms), 'Peace' (ivory with pink blush, fragrant), 'Pristine' (white tinged with pink, fragrant), 'Tiffany' (soft pink, strongly scented), and 'Touch of Class' (coral pink, slight fragrance).

- **Floribunda roses:** This group has flowers grouped in clusters and they bloom on and off from spring to fall. The plants are mostly carefree and make great specimen shrubs or hedges. Some good and popular cultivars include 'Angle Face' (lavender, strongly scented), 'Betty Boop' (yellow and white, edged with red), 'Europeana' (deep red), 'Iceberg' (white), 'Nearly Wild' (pink, single flower), 'Red Ribbons' (dark red), 'Sexy Rexy' (light pink), 'Simplicity' (pink), and 'Trumpeter' (brilliant orange-red).

- **Grandiflora roses:** These large, vigorous roses make fine landscape shrubs. They have large, multipetalled flowers, either one to a stem or in clusters. Top-rated cultivars include 'Gold Medal', a colossal yellow rose; 'Love', which has petals that are bright red on top, silver beneath; 'Crimson Bouquet' (deep red), 'Caribbean'. Bright orange-yellow, 'Mt. Hood' (white), 'Prima Donna' (bright pink), 'Solitude' (brilliant orange), 'Tournament of Roses' (two-toned pink), and 'Fame' (pink).

- **Climbing roses:** These roses come from several other rose groups, but are distinguished by having long shoots that you can attach to a support structure. The supporting structure can be anything from a chain-link fence to an arbor or trellis. Tie climbing roses gently with pieces of stretchy cloth or old pantyhose. Some great climbers are 'Altissimo' (deep red), 'America' (bright pink), and 'Fourth of July' (red, white, and pink stripes).

- **Miniature roses:** These dainty shrubs have small leaves, short stems, and small flowers; they usually grow less than 2 feet tall. Miniatures fit easily into small beds and make great edging plants. You can also grow them in containers. The best are hardy, fragrant, disease-resistant, and long-blooming. Great cultivars include 'Jingle Bells' (bright red, 20 inches tall), 'Magic Carousel' (red edged in white, 18 to 24 inches), 'Party Girl' (apricot-yellow and salmon-pink, 12 to 14 inches), 'Rise 'n Shine' (yellow, 24 inches), 'Scentsational' (pink and nicely scented, 18 to 24 inches), and 'Starina' (orange-red, 12 to 18 inches).

- **David Austin roses:** Also called *English roses,* this group was created by a famous English rose breeder named David Austin. His goal was to mix the blossom shapes and fragrance of old garden roses with the disease resistance and everblooming qualities of newer types. More than 60 varieties currently exist and most are strongly scented. Plant size and hardiness varies, but most survive to zone 6. A few favorites include 'Emily' (pink flowers on a tall, spreading shrub), 'Gertrude Jekyll' (strongly fragrant, pink blossoms on a tall plant), 'Glamis Castle' (white, fragrant, and 3 feet high), 'Golden Celebration' (pinkish buds open to fragrant yellow blossoms, large shrub), 'Heavenly Rosalind' (soft pink simple flowers), 'Heritage' (pink rose, citrus scent; good landscape shrub), and 'Tradescant' (velvety red with strong, old-rose scent; tall climber).

- **Generosa roses:** This group is similar to David Austin roses, combining the best traits of modern roses (continuous bloom and disease resistance) — with the best of the old (old-fashioned flower shapes, strong scent primarily). Three of the best of these new roses include 'Claudia Cardinale' (bright yellow turning coppery red), 'Martine Guillot' (soft apricot and with a gardenia-like fragrance), and 'Sonyi Rykiel' (coral pink and very strongly perfumed).

- **Ground-cover roses:** The roses in this group produce long canes that remain close to the ground — usually no higher than about 2 feet. They make good covers for slopes when planted about 4 or 5 feet apart and thorny barriers for places where you don't want people to walk. Also use them in containers where they can spill over the sides. All are vigorous, very cold hardy (to zone 4), and produce many flowers; all grow 12 to 18 inches high and 36 to 48 inches wide. Some of the best include 'Flower Carpet' (pink, 12 by 42 inches), 'Magic Carpet' (18 by 36 inches), 'Pink Bells' (pink, 18 by 40 inches), 'Ralph's Creeper' (red, 12 by 48 inches), 'Rosey Carpet' (rose-red, 12 by 36 inches), 'Sea Foam' (white, 18 by 36 inches), 'Snow Shower' (white, 12 by 36 inches), and 'White Meidiland' (white, 12 by 36 inches).

- **Hardy roses:** If you live where winter temperatures dip down to −30°, you want to choose from this group of cold-tolerant roses. Most of these shrubs grow 3 to 5 feet tall, although some qualify as climbers. Red-flowering varieties include 'Captain Samuel Holland' (climber), 'Country Dancer', 'David Thompson' (climber), 'George Vancouver', 'John Cabot' (climber), 'John Franklin', and 'Morden Fireglow'. Those with pink flowers include 'Applejack', 'Morden Amorette', 'Morden Blush', 'Morden Centennial', 'Prairie Dawn', Prairie Princess', and 'William Baffin' (climber).

- **Rugosa roses:** If you need a tough shrub that can grow along the seashore, by the roadside, or nearly any other inhospitable place, take a long look at this group of shrub roses. Hardy from zones 2 to 8, these roses form dense thickets of thorny shoots in any well-drained soil, including beach sand. They do appreciate the addition of organic material to the soil for best growth, however. Most plants usually bloom just once a year, but many retain attractive red fruits, called *rose hips*, all winter long. Rose hips make good jelly and are a source of Vitamin C. Some hybrid rugosa roses bloom twice a year, including 'Buffalo Gal' (pink), 'Linda Campbell' (red), 'Snow Owl' (white), 'Frau Dagmar Hastrup' (pink), 'Thérèse Bugnet' (pink), and 'Topaz Jewel' (yellow).

Evergreen Flowering Shrubs

Count on most of these shrubs for year-round greenery, as well as spectacular seasonal bloom. Use them as ground covers, hedges, screens, and specimens wherever you want day-in, day-out foliage. In cold-weather climates, protect these broadleaf evergreens from drying winter winds.

✔ **Glossy abelia:** *Abelia grandiflora*. Zones 6 to 9. This handsome, arching plant has bright-green, glossy, oval foliage with bronzy-red new growth. Leaves turn reddish-purple in winter or may drop in cold climates. White or pink, fragrant, tubular flowers appear in the summer on new growth. Popular cultivars include 'Edward Goucher', which grows 5 by 5 feet; 'Francis Mason', which has variegated yellow and green foliage; and 'Prostrata', a semievergreen ground cover that grows 1½ to 2 feet high and 4 to 5 feet wide. Plant in full sun or light shade in moist, well-drained, acidic soil. Prune in early spring.

✔ **Japanese camellia:** *Camellia japonica*. Zones 7 to 9. When you mention camellia, most people think of this species, with its 2000-plus cultivars, blooms in every combination, and variegation of white, pink, rose, and red. Each bloom is borne alone on new growth from October through May. Camellia cultivars are described and organized by the American Camellia Society by their flowering characteristics as follows.

A CLOSER LOOK

Crazy about camellias

Camellias grow in mild climates, where they bloom from autumn through winter and into the spring, depending on the species and cultivar. Their leathery, deep evergreen, glossy foliage makes them attractive landscape shrubs for foundation plantings, specimen plants, hedges, ground cover, and borders. You can even plant them in containers, where they grow slowly and can thrive for many years.

Plant camellias from fall through spring in evenly moist, acidic, well-drained soil that's rich in organic matter — similar to what's preferred by rhododendrons and azaleas. As they grow and become established, they can tolerate more sun and drier soil. Shelter them from early spring frost and mid-day sun, and mulch them to protect the roots from winter cold. Camellias usually require little pruning because they grow slowly and most have a fairly compact habit. If you want to shape your plant, however, prune it right after flowering.

Several serious pests and diseases, including flower blight, canker, root rot, aphids, and scale insects, plague these elegant shrubs. To control flower blight, an unsightly browning of the flowers, remove all of the affected blossoms from the plant, pick up any that drop to the ground, and dispose of them all. Replace the mulch around the base of the plant to eliminate the disease spores. Contact a local nursery or your local extension service for advice if your camellias develop any other serious problems.

If camellias just won't survive in your climate, consider growing them in containers and moving them inside for the winter. They need high humidity, bright light, and night temperatures between 30° and 45° all winter. Unheated rooms and cool greenhouses make the best winter homes — keeping them in a heated house means certain failure. Water them sparingly through the winter months only adding more moisture as the soil dries out. Avoid softened and hard water, which may cause the soil to become too alkaline.

If you find yourself getting hooked on these winter-glorious shrubs, you can find a wealth of information by contacting the American Camellia Society at One Massee Lane, Fort Valley, GA 31030. Call them at (912)-967-2358, or visit their Web site at www.peach.public.lib.ga.us/ACS/.

- **Flower form:** Flowers occur as single, semidouble, rose-form double, formal double, anemone-form, and peony-form.

- **Flower size:** Miniatures have blooms up to 2½ inches across, small from 2½ to 3 inches, medium from 3 to 4 inches, large from 4 to 5 inches, and very large blooms over 5 inches.

- **Flowering season:** Early-blooming cultivars begin the show in the fall, midseason cultivars bloom from New Year's to March 1, and the late ones finish the season in the spring.

Most japonicas grow to 6 to 12 feet tall in the home landscape. A few common cultivars include 'Adolphe Audusson', a large, semidouble dark red, 'Alba Plena', a medium-sized, early, formal double white, and 'Betty Sheffield', a midseason, semidouble white with pink or red on the petal edges. 'Elegans' or 'Chandler' has very large rose pink, anemone-form flowers early to midseason. Other cultivars with 'Elegans' in their names have variegated blossoms or fringed petals. 'Glen 40', a large dark red, formal-double, mid-to late-season cultivar, is good for container growing and its blooms are prized for corsages. Look to your local nursery for cultivars suitable for your climate and mail-order catalogs for many more cultivars.

✔ **Reticulata camellia:** *C. reticulata.* Zones 8 to 10. This tender species has a less-attractive foliage and growth habit than the japonicas, becoming tall and lanky and developing into 30- to 50-foot trees in favorable conditions. They have huge flowers up to 9 inches across in late winter to early spring, and the flowers are mostly double with prominent yellow stamens in the center. Many reticulatas excel as espalier specimens (see Chapter 14) trained against a wall or building where they receive the winter protection and support for their large, heavy flowers. Common cultivars include 'Captain Rawes', one of the hardiest reticulatas with large rose pink, semi-double flowers, and 'Cornelian', a large vigorous shrub with variegated foliage and rose pink to red, semi-double blooms.

✔ **Sasanqua camellias:** *C. sasanqua.* Zones 7 to 8. This species has smaller, but more numerous, flowers and leaves than the japonicas and can tolerate more sun and less water. Shrubs grow 1½ to 10 feet high, making some cultivars good espalier, ground cover, or even hanging basket and bonsai subjects. Their fall flowering habit makes them especially valuable in the colder parts of their range, where winter freezes would otherwise destroy the blossoms. 'Mist Maiden' and 'Carolina Moonmist' are among the hardiest cultivars. 'Tanya', a red-flowered cultivar, has low-spreading growth that makes a good ground cover.

✔ **Camellia hybrids:** Many important hybrids between these species and others have increased the growing range of camellias. Dr. William Ackerman of the U.S. National Arboretum developed a number of camellias that bloom in the fall and live into zone 6. Some of his hybrids include pink 'Winter's Beauty', lavender-pink 'Winter's Interlude', red-purple 'Winter's Star', and white 'Winter's Waterlily'. His work also includes heat tolerant hybrids, such as rose-red 'Sunworshipper' and rose-pink 'Two Marthas', that can grow in the hotter parts of zone 10. Another plant breeder, Dr. Clifford Parks, also introduced some cold-hardy hybrids, including 'April Rose', 'Mason Farm', and 'Spring Promise'.

- ✔ **Heather:** *Calluna* species. Zones 5 to 7. This plant has hundreds of cultivars ranging in size from 4 to 24 inches in height, and spreading 2 feet or more. Flowers cover the spiky branches in colors from white to pale pink to deep carmine, and foliage may be colored golden yellow to minty green to deep green, depending on the cultivar. 'Gold Haze', for example, has golden-yellow foliage and white flowers, 'County Wicklow' offers double pale pink blooms and dark green foliage. 'Blazeway' starts the spring with yellow foliage that turns mint green in the summer and becomes bright red in winter. It has lilac-colored flowers. 'J.H. Hamilton', a 4-inch-high dwarf, has deep-pink double flowers.

- ✔ **Heath:** *Erica* species. Zones 4 to 6. These species and their cultivars form fine textured mats about 6 to 10 inches high and 20 inches wide. Spring heath *(Erica carnea)* tolerates more alkaline soils than others and flowers in shades of pink through white in winter to early spring. Its cultivars include 'Springwood White' and 'Springwood Pink'. *E. × darleyensis,* a hybrid of spring heath, becomes more shrub-like and tolerates higher summer temperatures than most others. Try this 2-foot high mounding heath in zones 6 to 7, including the midsouthern United States. It blooms in midwinter through spring in a range of pinks and whites. Twisted

A CLOSER LOOK

Covering ground with heaths and heathers

Covering the moors of northern England and Scotland, heaths and heathers set the fields ablaze with bloom nearly year 'round. These bright, finely-textured plants make outstanding ground covers and front-of-the-border shrubs for gardeners with the right soil and climate — both heather and heath require cool, moist, acidic, well-drained soil that's high in organic matter but low in fertility. They enjoy full sun to partly sunny sites. Best suited for cool, humid climates, such as the U.S. northwest and northeast, they excel as rock garden plants and make good companions for rhododendrons and azaleas, which share their cultural needs. You can grow heaths and heathers in warmer climates if you keep them out of hot, dry, alkaline soils. In

the northern zones, snow cover or mulch protects the plants from winter wind and sun.

If you're bitten by the collector's bug or just want more information, contact the North American Heather Society, c/o Karla Lortz, E. 502 Haskell Hill Road, Shelton WA 98584. Or visit their Web site at www.humboldt1.com/%7eheathers/ for information about regional heath and heather nurseries and societies located near you. The American Horticultural Society's book, *A-Z Encyclopedia of Garden Plants,* edited by Christopher Brickell and Judith Zuk, also describes and shows photographs of many heath and heather cultivars.

heath *(E. cinerea)* grows to about the same size in zones 5 to 7, but blooms June through September. About 150 or so cultivars exist. To keep heath and heather plants compact and neat, prune off the spent flower stalks immediately after bloom. Take care not to cut into the mature brown wood, though, because it may not produce new growth.

✔ **Mexican orange blossom:** *Choisya ternata.* Zones 8 to 10. As its common name indicates, this shrub claims kinship to the citrus family. Its glossy, oval, dark-green leaves; compact habit; and fragrant, white blooms earn it a place in any border where temperatures stay above 15°. It matures at 5 feet high when given fertile, well-drained soil and full sun. Protect it from cold, wintry weather.

✔ **Rose daphne:** *Daphne cneorum.* Zones 4 to 7. This small, spreading evergreen shrub grows only 6 to 12 inches high, but its scented rose-pink flowers more than makes up for its diminutive size. It blooms in late spring and may repeat bloom in late summer. Plant rose daphne in rock gardens or along the top of a retaining wall where it will receive excellent drainage. Protect it from harsh winter weather with evergreen boughs or good snow cover.

✔ **Fragrant daphne:** *Daphne odora.* Zones 7 to 9. Clusters of fragrant, pink flowers on this low, mounding, evergreen shrub will perfume your yard for weeks in late winter. It has glossy, lance-shaped leaves and grows slowly into a 4-foot mound. The cultivar 'Aureo-marginata' has leaves with creamy white edges and purple-red flowers. See the Daffy for daphne section earlier in this chapter for more growing information.

✔ **Escallonia:** *Escallonia × exoniensis.* Zones 8 to 9. A good shrub for coastal areas, escallonia has glossy, ¾-inch-long, oval-toothed leaves and clusters of apple-blossom-like flowers all summer long. The beautiful, fragrant pink, white, or carmine blooms appear on new growth at the branch tips. They enjoy fertile, well-drained soil in full sun and have few pests or diseases. The cultivar 'Frades', also known as 'Pink Princess', has deep carmine red blooms and grows 12 to 20 feet high and 10 to 15 feet wide.

✔ **Gardenia:** *Gardenia jasminoides.* Zones 8 to 10. Intoxicating fragrance is reason enough to grow this rather finicky broadleaf evergreen. The waxy white flowers, up to 4 inches across, appear in summer in climates where winter temperatures stay above 10°. The glossy, dark-green foliage is attractive in all seasons on the 4- to 6-foot shrubs. Gardenias require moist, fertile, acidic, well-drained soils that are high in organic matter, and full sun to light shade. Maintain moderate to high humidity when growing as a houseplant. In unsuitable conditions, gardenia develops many diseases including powdery mildew, leaf spot, and cankers, and attracts aphids, scale, white flies, mites, and other insect pests. Double-flowered cultivars include 'Aimee Yoshida', 'August Beauty', 'Mystery', and 'Vetchii'. 'Radicans' grows only 2 to 3 feet high and spreads to 4 feet. 'Radicans Variegata', which also grows 2 to 3 feet by 4 feet, has white leaf margins. 'Daisy' and 'White Gem' have single flowers with 6 to 7 petals.

✔ **Rockrose, sunrose:** *Helianthemum* species. Zones 5 to 10. This group of drought-tolerant, sun-loving ground covers grows 6 to 12 inches high and displays 1-inch wide, single or double flowers in a rainbow of pastel and bright colors in late spring to early summer. Their narrow leaves may be glossy green or gray-green. Plant them 2 to 3 feet apart on slopes, in rock gardens, or in planters for a dazzling display. Prune plants after blooming to encourage repeat flowering and to keep the plants compact.

✔ **St. Johnswort:** *Hypericum* species. Zones 5 to 8. A large genus with hundreds of species, the most commonly available St. Johnsworts have blue-green leaves and golden-yellow, buttercup-like flowers throughout the summer. Many thrive in heavy, dry soil after they're established, while others need regular moisture. All grow best in full sun to part shade. If you want to prune St. Johnswort do it in early spring because they flower on new wood. Hardiness and mature size depends on the individual species.

Some foolproof cultivars include golden St. Johnswort, *H. frondosum*, (zones 5 to 8) which forms a 3- to 4-foot mound and blooms in early to midsummer. The cultivar 'Sunburst' does especially well in the midwestern U.S. although it loses its leaves in cold climates. *Hypericum* × 'Hidcote' (zones 6 to 8), an award-winning hybrid, grows to 3 or more feet high and wide and shows off its 2- to 3-inch-wide golden flowers from late spring to early fall. *H.* × *moserianum* 'Tricolor' (zones 7 to 9), grows to only a foot high by 2 feet wide and has 2-inch long, bright-green leaves edged in white and pink, as well as reddish stems and yellow blooms. Kalm St. Johnswort, *H. kalmianum*, (zones 4 to 7) grows 2 to 3 feet high and blooms in midsummer. The cultivar 'Ames' is particularly hardy and compact.

✔ **Florida anise tree:** *Illicium floridanum*. Zones 6 to 9. The foliage of this upright, 5- to 10-foot high shrub releases the pungent odor of anise when crushed — hence its common name. Its dark green, glossy leaves grow 2 to 6 inches long and half as wide with red stems. Plants produce fragrant red flowers in mid to late spring. Prune anise tree only to maintain the plant's shape and grow it in shade to part sun in moist, rich soil. The cultivar 'Alba' has white blooms and stays more compact than the species.

✔ **Showy jasmine:** *Jasminum floridum*. Zones 7 to 9. Unlike the sweetly perfumed jasmine species, this species' flowers are unscented. The colorful yellow blooms appear from spring through autumn. The plant grows 3 to 4 feet tall and you can train it into a mounding ground cover or cascading vine. Give it full sun and regular garden soil and protect it from cold, drying winds in the winter. Prune it after flowering to keep it compact and within bounds.

✔ **Mountain laurel:** *Kalmia latifolia*. Zones 4 to 8. Trusses of white to rich-pink flowers, opening from attractive pink to red buds in spring, make mountain laurel an ideal companion for azaleas, rhododendrons, and other shrubs that enjoy moist, acidic, humus-rich soil. This shrub grows slowly to 5 to 15 feet, depending on the cultivar, and has shiny oval-pointed leaves in whorls around its stems. Grow it in full sun to light shade for the best flowering and mulch around its shallow roots to keep them cool and moist. Mountain laurel has many, many cultivars in all shapes, sizes, and flower colors. Some of the more commonly available include 'Elf', a 3-foot dwarf with pink buds and white flowers; 'Carousel', with white flowers sporting a pink circle inside each blossom; and 'Ostbo Red', which has bright red buds that open into pink flowers.

✔ **Lavender:** *Lavandula* species. Zones 5 to 9. The handsome, gray-blue to gray-green, needle-like leaves and 1- to 2-foot-high stature earn this group a place at the front of the perennial flower or shrub border. It also makes a valuable ground cover for sunny, well-drained, neutral to alkaline soils. The spiky fragrant flower stalks appear in mid to late summer, and bloom color ranges from white through purple, depending on the cultivar. Prune after flowering.

The most commonly grown lavender is English lavender, *L. angustifolia,* (zones 5 to 8). It can grow up to 3 feet high, but cultivars such as 'Munstead', 'Hidcote', and 'Loddon Pink' grow about half that height. Protect it in zone 5 and in the colder, windier spots of zone 6. Prune early in the spring to remove damaged foliage and keep plants compact. French lavender, *L. stoechas,* (zones 8 to 9) enjoys warmer climates and has 1-inch long, colorful bracts as well as purple blossoms on their flower spikes. They bloom in late spring and early summer and grow into compact 2-foot-high shrubs.

✔ **Chinese fringe-flower:** *Loropetalum chinense.* Zones 7 to 9. Grown for its spring floral display, fringe-flower really puts on a show with bouquets of spidery, long-petaled, white flowers against the dark green or reddish-purple foliage. Use it in foundation plantings and shrub borders, as specimen plants or screens. It can grow 5 to 10 feet tall and wide. Fringe-flower needs fertile, moist, well-drained, acidic soils, and sun to part shade to succeed. It's not happy in alkaline or droughty soil, but has few pests. A group of fringe-flowers (*L. chinense* var. *rubrum*) has purplish or reddish foliage instead of the normal green. One of these cultivars, 'Sizzling Pink', has more horizontal, layered branching and pink flowers. Many other cultivars exist with a wide range of variation in the foliage and flower colors. Prune, if necessary, right after flowering.

✔ **Oleander:** *Nerium oleander.* Zones 8 to 11. All parts of this plant are toxic, but that doesn't stop it from being one of the most widely used flowering landscape plants in hot, dry, and seaside climates. It grows quickly to 6 to 12 feet, making it useful for screening and hedges. Pruning and dwarf cultivar selection keeps oleander low enough for foundation plantings. You can also prune taller cultivars into small trees that are perfect for landscape accents. It tolerates salt, wind, and drought. Clusters of 1- to 2-inch flowers appear on new growth at the ends of branches all summer and into the fall. Flower colors run the gamut from single to double, fragrant and nonfragrant, white and cream to yellow, pink, salmon, and red. If you need to prune oleander, prune in early spring before flower buds begin to form. Scores of cultivars exist — if you can, see a plant in bloom or look for a full-color label with a photo before you buy, so that you know exactly what to expect. 'Calypso' has single red flowers, 'Hawaii' has single yellow blooms, and 'Casablanca' has single white flowers.

✔ **Fragrant olive:** *Osmanthus* species. Zones 9 to 10. Follow your nose to find this shrub when it blooms from late summer or autumn to spring. The species, *O. fragrans,* (zones 9 to 10) produces nodding clusters of tubular blooms all winter on vigorous, upright shrubs that grow to 6 feet or more. Its holly-shaped, spiny foliage becomes more oval and loses its spines on mature branches.

✔ **Pieris:** *Pieris* species. Zones 5 to 8. Great plants for the moist, acidic soil of the northwestern and northeastern United States, these shrubs sport bronze to brilliant-red new growth that changes to deep glossy green. Long, star-shaped sprays of small fragrant white to red flowers open in the spring. Plant pieris in shrub borders and foundation plantings with rhododendrons, azaleas, and other acid-loving plants, or use it as a specimen plant in full sun to dappled shade. Protect it from drought, wind, heavy snow and ice, and mid-day sun in hot climates.

Mountain pieris, *P. floribunda,* (zones 4 to 6) is the hardiest species for northern zones. It grows very slowly into a 2-to 4-foot-high mound and has sprays of white flowers in early spring. Japanese pieris, *P. japonica,* (zones 5 to 7) grows slowly to 4 to 8 feet tall and 4 to 6 feet wide over time. Popular cultivars include 'Forest Flame', with bright red new growth; 'Purity', which grows 3 to 4 feet high with white flowers; pink-flowered 'Valley Rose'; and red-flowered 'Valley Valentine'. Warm-climate gardeners can look for Prelude pieris, *P. taiwanensis* 'Prelude', which thrives in zones 7 to 9.

✔ **Cherry laurel:** *Prunus* species. Zones 6 to 8. Cherry laurel belongs to the large genus *Prunus*, which also includes cherries, almonds, peaches, plums, and nectarines. These evergreen shrubs and small trees have lustrous 5- to 6-inch, pointed, oval leaves and long, fragrant clusters of white flowers that are borne in spring. Plant cherry laurels in part to full shade in moist, well-drained soil that's high in organic matter. The species *P. laurocerasus* has numerous cultivars that are well-suited for foundation plantings because they grow slowly to compact 3- to 5-foot-high mounds. 'Mount Vernon' and 'Nana' fall into this category. 'Otto Luyken' also remains short, but spreads 6 to 8 feet wide and has narrow, finely textured leaves. 'Schipkaenisi' and 'Zabeliana' are hardy to zone 5.

✔ **Indian hawthorn:** *Rhaphiolepis* species. Zones 8 to 9. Choose this neat and tidy shrub for any spot that needs a low-maintenance, low-growing broadleaf evergreen. Its toothed and leathery foliage, dense habit, and white to red apple-like bloom in spring make it perfect for the front of the border, foundation plantings, informal hedges, or even a container plant. Indian hawthorn performs well in urban and coastal areas where it tolerates full sun and salt, but it prefers well-drained, reasonably moist, pH-neutral soil. Deer do love its foliage, however, and the plants are prone to fireblight and leaf spot. Protect it from wind in cold weather.

Indian hawthorn has a number of cultivars. 'Enchantress' and 'Spring Rapture' have rosy pink flowers and grow to compact 3 by 4- to 5-foot mounds. 'Pink Dancer' grows about half that size. Some cultivars have bronze green foliage, such as pink-flowered 'Springtime' and 'Hines Darkleaf' which turns purple and may rebloom in the autumn. Larger cultivars include 'Harbinger of Spring', which grows into a 5- by 5-foot mound, and 'Majestic Beauty' a vigorous 10-footer that can be pruned into a small tree.

✔ **Japanese skimmia:** *Skimmia japonica.* Zones 7 to 8. A beautiful plant for cool, moist climates, Japanese skimmia displays lilac-like trusses of creamy white to pink flowers in midspring. The tight clusters of red flower buds form at the ends of each stem in the winter. After blooming, they may develop into clusters of red or white berries, depending on the cultivar and whether the plant is male or female. The glossy, lance-shaped, dark green leaves are attractive all year round. The shrubs form compact 3- to 4-foot mounds in shady gardens with moist, well-drained, humus rich soil. They look great as a large mass or low hedge along a sidewalk or driveway and they do well in containers. Skimmia can't tolerate hot summer climates, and is prone to aphids and scale insects. The related species, *S. reevesiana,* can grow into zone 6 and grows only 18 to 24 inches high. It has a more open growing habit, but doesn't require male and female plants to set fruit.

✔ **Chindo viburnum:** *Viburnum awabuki.* Zones 8 to 10. One of the larger viburnums, this shrub can grow to 15 feet or more with lustrous, leathery, dark-green leaves. With plants of both sexes present, the females produce large clusters of bright-red berries.

✔ **David viburnum:** *V. davidii.* Zones 8 to 9, and protected parts of zone 7. David viburnum has lustrous, deep green, deeply ridged leaves. Flat clusters of white flowers, called *cymes,* cover the plant in late spring. Mounding shrubs grow 3 feet high and 5 feet wide. If you plant both male and female shrubs, the female bear attractive, blue fruits.

✔ **Leatherleaf viburnum:** *V. rhytidophyllum.* Zones 7 and 8, and protected parts of zone 6. This shrub's long, oval leaves are lustrous, dark-green, and heavily textured. It blooms on old wood in the spring and grows 10 to 15 feet high and wide. Temperatures below –15° may kill it to the ground, but it usually grows back from the roots. Protect it from severe winter cold to the best flowering. Prague Viburnum, *V. × pragense,* is a hardier hybrid of leatherleaf viburnum, surviving both colder and warmer climates from zones 5 to 8. It grows vigorously to 8 to 10 feet high and has wrinkly leaves, making it a useful, fast-growing screen.

✔ **Sandankwa viburnum:** *V. suspensum.* Zones 9 to 11. This viburnum thrives in sandy soil and grows best in the Gulf and Pacific coastal regions, where it grows 6 to 10 feet tall. Its fragrant rosy white flowers mature into red, and then black, fruits.

A CLOSER LOOK

Versatile evergreen viburnums

All of the evergreen viburnums naturally grow in the warmer climates of the world where their broad leaves won't be damaged by snow, ice, and drying winter winds. For more information on planting and caring for viburnums, see the "Adventures with Viburnums" sidebar, earlier in this chapter.

✔ **Laurustinus:** *V. tinus.* Zones 9 to 10. Laurustinus makes an excellent hedge plant, growing up to 10 feet high with attractive, 2- to 3-inch long, dark-green leaves and white flower clusters in mid-winter. It grows well in part shade and tolerates salt spray. Cultivar 'Compactum', also known as 'Spring Bouquet', grows only half the size of the species. 'Eve Price' also remains a compact dwarf and has pink flowers.

Rhododendrons and Azaleas

Both rhododendrons and azaleas belong to the genus *Rhododendron*. In general, most azaleas — but not all — are deciduous, while most — but not all — rhododendrons have evergreen leaves. In this section, when I refer to the whole genus, I use the word *Rhododendron* (uppercase italics) When I'm referring only to the group of mostly evergreen rhododendrons, I use the word rhododendron, with no italics.

Famous for their flowers, rhododendrons also have glossy, deep-green foliage that remains attractive through the summer. Some of the deciduous azaleas also have fiery autumn foliage. Flowers in every color except blue grace this group of plants. White, pink, crimson, and purple belong to the rhododendron and evergreen azalea species, while the deciduous azaleas offer yellow, orange, and apricot, in addition. The flower clusters, called *trusses*, emerge in the spring or early summer from buds developed the previous year.

Just as *Rhododendron* flowers inspire awe, growing them intimidates many gardeners. *Rhododendrons* grow naturally in cool, humid climates in loose, gravelly soil that contains lots of organic material. Frequent rain and humidity create the acidic soils that *Rhododendrons* enjoy. Many species grow wild under the high canopy of forest trees and, for that reason, appreciate partial shade and shelter from strong winds. To grow these outstanding shrubs, copy their natural environment as closely as possible. Add pine or fir bark and sphagnum peat moss to well-drained soil to provide the organic material and avoid planting them in clay soil. Take a soil sample to a local garden center or to a University soil-testing lab to find out your soil's pH. The lab can tell you how much sulfur or ferrous sulfate to add to your soil to bring the pH to between 4.5 and 5.5.

Find a place in your yard where the shrubs receive part shade and protection from the wind, especially if you live in a hot, sunny, or windy climate. Azaleas, with their naturally smaller leaves, are better suited to the sun than the species with larger leaves. As a general rule of thumb, the larger its leaves, the more shade a rhododendron requires. The kind of shade and protection most rhododendrons need exists on the north sides of buildings. In cold winter climates, rhododendrons often need protection from drying winter wind. See Chapter 15 for ways to protect them.

If you want to be sure that a rhododendron will grow in your yard, first choose one that is genetically adapted for your climate. Local nurseries that grow their own shrubs and chapters of the American Rhododendron Society can point you toward the best plants for your situation. Keep in mind that chain store garden centers often sell shrubs grown in climates that differ significantly from where you live. To contact the American Rhododendron Society, write to them at ARS, Executive Director, 11 Pinecrest Drive, Fortuna, CA 95540, phone: (707)725-3043, fax: (707)725-1217, or visit their Web site at www.rhododendron.org/. If you want information specifically about azaleas, write to Membership Chairman, Azalea Society of America, Post Office Box 34536, West Bethesda, MD 20827-0536 or visit their Web site at www.theazaleaworks.com/appl.htm.

Azaleas

Azaleas fall into two broad categories — deciduous and evergreen. The evergreen species require warmer winter temperatures than the deciduous species, with even the hardiest not tolerating temperatures much below 0°. The evergreen florist's azalea that's sold in supermarkets and florist shops is only hardy to 20°, for example. The deciduous azaleas, on the other hand, have species that can survive –40° without damage. Azalea species have been so interbred that more hybrids exist than species. These commonly sold species, hybrids, and cultivars represent only a fraction of the breadth of this group.

> ✔ **Exbury and Knap Hill azalea:** Zones 5 to 7. This is a large group of deciduous azalea cultivars that came from crossing several species in England in the 19th century. They bloom in spring, and have larger flowers than most azaleas in colors that include cream, pink, orange, red, and yellow. Their growth habit tends to be upright from 8 to 10 feet high and 6 to 8 feet wide. They don't grow well in climates with hot summers. 'Berryrose' has fragrant orange-red flowers and 'White Swan' is also fragrant with white and yellow flowers. More than 100 other cultivars exist, with varying cold hardiness.

- **Northern lights azalea:** Zones 3 to 7. As the hardiest group of deciduous azalea hybrids, these tough beauties can take temperatures all the way down to –40°. The fragrant flowers bloom in the spring in shades of yellow, apricot, orange, white, pink, and rose. They grow 8 to 10 feet high and wide, with a compact habit. Most of the ten or so cultivars have the word 'Lights' in their names. 'Rosy Lights' has fragrant dark pink flowers, 'Spicy Lights' has fragrant light orange blooms. 'Northern Hi-Lights' has white and yellow flowers, red fall foliage, and resists mildew.

- **Mollis hybrid azalea:** *Rhododendron × kosteranum.* Zones 5 to 7. Another hardy deciduous group similar to Northern lights, Mollis hybrid azaleas grow smaller. Most of the cultivars grow to 4 to 8 feet tall by 3 to 6 feet wide and have spring flowers in yellow, orange, and orange-red.

- **Girard hybrids:** Zones 6 to 9. Some of the cultivars in this group can take temperatures as low as –15°, which is unusual for evergreen azaleas. The hardiest evergreen cultivars include 'Girard Fuschia', 'Girard Chiara', and 'Girard Joshua'. They grow 4 to 6 feet tall. This hybrid group also includes some deciduous cultivars.

- **North Tisbury hybrids:** Zones 6 to 9. Developed primarily as ground covers, this group of evergreen azaleas remains quite low. Some cultivars may reach 4 to 5 feet, but most stay under 2 to 3 feet high. Flowers are pinks and reds, borne in the spring. Good snow cover improves their cold hardiness. 'Alexander' has salmon-red flowers in late spring, grows 18 inches high, and is hardy to zone 7. 'Michael Hill' also grows 18 inches tall and has light pink flowers.

Rhododendrons

When I think of rhododendrons, I picture huge shrubs with long, oval, dark, evergreen leaves framing bright red and pink trusses of flowers. True, some rhododendrons do look like that, but many others have smaller leaves and growth habits. A few even shed their foliage in the fall. The plants' broad evergreen leaves limit their range of hardiness: They're subject to winter drying and freezing in cold climates, and overheating in hot zones. They grow most comfortably in humid climates with mild winters and summers. The hardiest of the rhododendrons are referred to as *ironclad* because they tolerate the broadest range of heat and cold. These species and some of their cultivars survive temperatures down to –25° and include the following:

- **Rhododendron:** *R. catawbiense.* Zones 4 to 8. This species has the stature and bloom that I imagine all rhododendrons possess when I picture this genus. Although individual cultivars differ, the species can reach 10 high and 5 to 8 feet wide. This species has scores of cultivars. A few that remain cold hardy to –25° include 'Album' and 'Nepal' with white flowers, 'Boursault' and 'President Lincoln' with lavender flowers, and red-flowered 'Nova Zembla'.

✔ **Korean rhododendron:** *R. mucronulatum*. Zones 4 to 7. This deciduous rhododendron has smaller leaves and a smaller habit than *R. catawbiense*, reaching only 4 to 8 feet depending on the cultivar. Its flowers are naturally rosy purple and put on quite a show in early spring before the leaves emerge. To protect them from late freezes that may kill the swelling flower buds, locate them on the north or east sides of buildings. The most common and famous cultivar, 'Cornell Pink', has bright pink flowers.

✔ **P.J.M. rhododendron:** *R.* P.J.M. Zones 4 to 8. A group of hybrids rather than a single species, the P.J.M. rhododendrons are among the hardiest of the broadleaf evergreen types due, in part, to their small leaves. Most grow from 3 to 6 feet high and they bloom in early spring. Some of the hardiest cultivars include 'Popsicle', 'Pink and Sweet', 'Jane Abbott Pink' and 'Jane Abbott Peach', and 'Weston's Innocence'.

A CLOSER LOOK

Companion plants for rhododendrons and azaleas

Rhododendrons and azaleas are members of a larger group of plants that have very specific soil and climate requirements. They need moist, acidic soil that's high in organic material and drains quickly. Soil pH between 4.5 and 5.5 is ideal. Rhododendrons prefer cool, humid climates and can't tolerate windy conditions. The following shrubs and trees enjoy the same environment and make perfect companions.

Camellia: *Camellia japonica*. Zones 7 to 9.

Chinese fringe-flower: *Loropetalum chinense*. Zones 7 to 9.

Daphne: *Daphne* species. Zones 4 to 9.

Dogwood: *Cornus* species. Zones. 5 to 8.

Drooping leucothoe: *Leucothoe fontanesiana*. Zones 5 to 8.

Fir: *Abies* species. Zones 4 to 7.

Fothergilla: *Fothergilla* species. Zones 4 to 8.

Fragrant winterhazel: *Corylopsis glabrescens*. Zones 5 to 8.

Glossy abelia: *Abelia grandiflora*. Zones 6 to 9.

Heath and heather: *Calluna* and *Erica* species. Zones 4 to 6.

Japanese skimmia: *Skimmia japonica*. Zones 7 to 8.

Katsura tree: *Cercidiphyllum japonicum*. Zones 4 to 8.

Mahonia: *Mahonia* species. Zones 5 to 9.

Mountain laurel: *Kalmia latifolia*. Zones 4 to 8.

Oak: *Quercus* species. Zones 3 to 9.

Pieris: *Pieris* species. Zones 3 to 7.

Carolina silverbell: *Halesia tetraptera*. Zones 4 to 8.

Sour gum: *Nyssa sylvatica*. Zones 4 to 9.

Fruiting Shrubs

Even if you have just a small yard, you can grow these ornamental and tasty fruits. From spring bloom to summer fruit and fall foliage color, give them a place in your foundation planting or in an informal hedge for beauty and bounty.

Blueberries

Where they can be successfully grown, blueberries (*Vaccinium* species) make spectacular ornamental shrubs. From the white, bell-shaped blooms in spring to lustrous, green, oval leaves that turn scarlet in autumn, blueberries offer three seasons of interest. The delicious fruit is a bonus.

Blueberries must have moist, humus-rich, acidic soils with pH in the 4.0 to 5.0 range. Organic mulch keeps their shallow roots moist and weed free. If the soil is to their liking, blueberries are relatively carefree and long-lived. They can grow from zones 3 to 9, depending on the species and cultivar. Plant one these species to match your climate.

- ✔ **Lowbush blueberries** *(V. angustifolium)* grow in zones 3 to 6 and only reach 8 to 18 inches tall. They spread into wide mats by underground runners and produce small, intensely flavored fruits. They're most commonly found growing wild.

- ✔ **Highbush blueberries** (*V. corymbosum* and hybrids) grow from zones 4 to 10, although some cultivars are better suited to either extreme. These shrubs grow up to 6 feet tall and produce heavier crops of ½- to 1-inch fruits if you grow more than one cultivar. Cultivars for the north include 'Bluecrop', 'Blueray', Earliblue', 'Northblue' and 'Northland'. In warmer climates, try 'Gulf Coast', 'Misty', 'O'Neill', and 'Reveille'.

- ✔ **Rabbiteye blueberries** *(V. ashei)* grow up to 10 feet tall in zones 7 to 9 and have thicker skin than other species. They require cross-pollination from another cultivar with a similar bloom time, such as 'Beckyblue' and 'Bonitablue' or 'Powderblue' and 'Tifblue'.

Blueberries attract few diseases or pests except birds. You must completely surround and cover your shrubs with bird-proof netting if you hope to harvest your crop. Install the netting before the berries begin to turn blue for the best results. In winter to early spring, prune out the largest, oldest canes in the center of the shrub when they become less productive, and thin out older, twiggy growth.

Currants and gooseberries

These old-fashioned berries from the *Ribes* genus are making a comeback, both as ornamentals and for their fruits. Purple, red, white, and black currant fruits are traditionally used in wines, jams, pies, and juice. Green, yellow, and pink gooseberries are good fresh or made into jams and pies. The shrubs are hardy throughout North America and Europe. Their attractive early spring bloom, small lobed leaves, and arching shoots are especially ornamental.

Ribes species became unpopular and banned outright in some regions because they are an alternate host to white pine blister rust, a serious disease that affects five-needled pines. You can't buy or import these species in many states. If you do choose to grow them, plant them at least 300 feet from pines. Other diseases that affect *Ribes* species include powdery mildew and anthracnose. Aphids and currant fruit flies can also cause trouble.

Prune gooseberries and red and white currants by removing all shoots older than three years and thinning the remaining shoots to 3 or 4 each of one, two, and three year old wood. Prune black currants by removing all shoots older than three years and keeping 10 to 12 vigorous one- and two-year-old shoots.

Chapter 10

Shrubs That Beat the Heat

. . . .

In This Chapter

▶ Choosing shrubs for hot and dry climates

▶ Finding the best shrubs for tropical areas

. . . .

*T*he shrubs in this chapter find their homes in climates where summer temperatures range from mild to searing and where winter temperatures rarely fall more than 10 to 15 degrees below freezing. But, temperature alone doesn't determine the hardiness of plants within these climate zones. Rainfall and the availability of water are often the deciding factors.

In this chapter, I have divided the shrubs into two sections — those that survive in arid, drought-prone areas and those that require moist soil and humid weather.

Take a Walk on the Dry Side

Rainfall in arid climates amounts to only a few inches a year and water conservation is a primary concern for homeowners. Summer temperatures climb into the triple digits and winter lows may fall to 10° below freezing. But even in these challenging conditions, you can grow attractive shrubs in your landscape.

Many shrubs, once established, can survive where water is a scarce commodity. The secret to successfully growing them, however, is pampering them a bit for a year after planting until their roots have taken firm hold in the soil. Give them protection from strong winds and regular watering to speed their early growth. You can find more about weather protection in Chapter 15, planting in Chapter 12, and specific tips for establishing arid climate plants in Chapter 6.

If you live in an arid climate where winter temperatures fall below 20°, look through Chapters 7, 8, and 9 for shrubs that tolerate drought-prone soil. If you live in more balmy climate, you can choose from the popular plants in this section.

✔ **Blue hibiscus:** *Alyogyne huegelii.* Zones 10 to 11. Large lilac to violet, hibiscus-like flowers appear from spring through autumn on this 4- to 8-foot shrub. The dark-green leaves are hairy and deeply lobed. The cultivar 'Monterey Bay' has dark blue flowers and 'Santa Cruz' blooms are bright mauve-purple.

✔ **Cape mallow:** *Anisodontea × hypomadarum.* Zones 9 to 11. This fast-growing shrub produces an abundance of 1-inch, hollyhock-like, pink flowers almost year 'round. Cape mallow has small, lobed leaves and its fuzzy stems grow to about 6 feet high and 3 to 4 feet wide. 'Tara Pink' has larger pink flowers.

✔ **Dwarf coyote bush:** *Baccharis pilularis.* Zones 8 to 11. Widely used as a ground cover, this California native creates a tight cover of small, dark green foliage, 12 to 24 inches high and up to 6 feet wide. Prune in spring to keep the plants compact. Male and female flowers grow on separate plants and the females produce messy cottony seeds. Choose male plants, such as 'Twin Peaks', to avoid the seeds.

✔ **Lemon bottlebrush:** *Callistemon citrinus.* Zones 8 to 11. This large, tough, evergreen has bright-red, 2- to 6-inch, bottlebrush-like flowers sporadically throughout the year. Its narrow leaves emerge coppery red and mature to bright green. Bottlebrush grows 10 to 15 feet high and wide as a shrub, but can be pruned into a tree, as described in Chapter 15. 'Little John', which grows only 3 feet high, is one of several dwarf cultivated varieties. A related species, weeping bottlebrush, *C. viminalis,* has a weeping habit and is more treelike, up to 25 feet high. 'Captain Cook' is a dwarf form of this species, which reaches only 4 feet high.

✔ **Senna:** *Cassia* species. Zones 9 to 11. This airy deciduous or evergreen shrub is very useful in arid landscapes. Feathery cassia, *C. artemisioides,* has gray-green, needle-like, evergreen foliage on a 3- to 5-foot-high plant and clusters of deep-yellow flowers in early spring to summer. Golden wonder senna, *C. splendida,* an evergreen, can reach up to 10 feet high and wide, with orange-yellow flowers in winter. *Cassia armata* grows in zones 4 to 7 and has fuzzy silver stems, long leaves, and 6-inch flower clusters. All cassias benefit from pruning after bloom.

✔ **Wild lilac:** *Ceanothus* species. Zones vary. This large group of evergreen shrubs and small trees is mostly native to California. Most have dark-green foliage and blue or white spring flowers. Favorite cultivated varieties include 'Dark Star', which has dark blue flowers and grows 5 to 6 feet high by 8 to 10 feet wide; 'Concha', with dark blue blooms on a 6- by 6-foot shrub; 'Julia Phelps', with abundant blue flowers that grows 4 to 7 feet high by 7 to 9 feet wide; and 'Ray Hartman', which has medium-blue flowers, and can grow 15 to 20 feet tall and wide. For a good low, ground cover, try *C. griseus horizontalis* 'Yankee Point', which stays 2 to 3 feet high, but spreads over 10 feet wide. Many ceanothus are short-lived shrubs, rarely lasting more than 10 to 15 years. After they're established, they shouldn't be watered — summer watering kills them quickly. One exception to this rule is New Jersey tea, *C. americanus,* which grows in zones 4 to 8. It, too, tolerates drought, but doesn't mind regular watering.

✔ **Rockrose:** *Cistus species.* Zones 9 to 11. This dependable group of colorful evergreen shrubs has late spring to early summer flowers. *C. hybridus,* white rockrose, grows into a neat 2- to 5-foot-high mound with small, white flowers that have yellow centers. The foliage is crinkled, gray-green. Crimson-spot rockrose, *C. ladanifer,* has larger white flowers with crimson spots in the center and grows 3 to 5 feet high and wide. Orchid rock, *C. purpureus,* bears large, purple-red flowers on a 4-foot-high, mounded plant. Its leaves are green on top and hairy gray beneath. It grows particularly well in coastal areas. Sageleaf rockrose, *C. salviifolius,* is only 2 feet high but spreads up to 6 feet wide, with gray-green foliage. Its flowers are white with yellow spots at the base. 'Sunset' is a compact, spreading plant, 2 feet high and 6 to 8 feet wide.

✔ **Grevillea:** *Grevillea species.* Zones 9 to 11 for most common types. Grevillea is a large family of tough, Australian native evergreens with fine-textured foliage and flowers that usually bloom in spring. 'Noelli' grows to 4 feet high and a little wider, with bright green, needle-like leaves and pink and white flowers in spring. 'Canberra' is a nicely textured shrub that reaches 8 feet high and 12 feet wide with red flowers. *G. lanigera.*

Wooly grevillea, has gray flowers and deep-red, summer flowers that attract hummingbirds. It grows 3 to 6 feet high, spreads almost twice as wide, and is perfect for hot slopes. A lower-growing, prostrate form is called 'Mr. Tamboritha'. Rosemary grevillea, *G. rosmarinifolia,* has silver and green foliage that resembles rosemary and red and white flowers that bloom mostly in fall and winter, but can occur anytime.

✔ **Toyon:** *Heteromeles arbutifolia.* Zones 7 to 10. Grown mainly on the west coast of the U.S., this California native grows into a dense shrub or can be pruned to a small tree 10 to 25 feet tall — a nice form for a small yard. It has glossy, leathery, dark-green leaves. Clusters of white flowers in early summer, followed by bright red berries, give toyon its other common name — Christmas berry. Birds love the fruit. Plant toyon in full sun to part shade and give it well-drained, average soil.

✔ **Tea tree:** *Leptospermum species.* Zones 9 to 11. These evergreen shrubs and small trees come from Australia and New Zealand and are particularly useful near coastal areas. Although fairly drought-tolerant, most need some water to look their best. Most species have small, fine-textured foliage and a bright show of white, pink, or red flowers in spring.

Australian tea tree, *L. laevigatum,* can reach up to 25 to 30 feet high and almost as wide, but smaller cultivars like 'Compactum' (6 to 8 feet) and 'Reevesii' (5 feet) are more shrub-like. New Zealand tea tree, *L. scoparium,* has many cultivars available, which are more useful than the species. These include 'Helene Strybing', a 6 foot shrub with deep pink flowers; 'Ruby Glow', which also grows to 6 feet and has deep red flowers and dark foliage; and 'Snow White', a low growing, 2- to 4-foot-high plant with white flowers.

✔ **Rosemary:** *Rosmarinus officinalis.* Zones 8 to 11. This classic culinary herb is an evergreen shrub, which is also a very useful landscape plant in dry climates. Shiny, dark-green, aromatic leaves have silvery undersides. Blue flowers in late winter and early spring sometimes repeat in fall. 'Tuscan Blue' is upright to 6 feet high. 'Huntington Blue', 'Lockwood de Forest', and other prostrate forms grow less than 2 feet high, but spread up to 6 feet wide and will drape over walls.

✔ **Yucca:** *Yucca species.* Zones 8 to 11, but some are hardy to zone 4. This unusual group of stiff, sword-leafed plants fits nicely in arid gardens. You can choose from many species — some native to the U.S. southwest; others native to the southeast. Yucca range in size from 25-foot trees down to 2-foot shrubs. Most have huge spikes of white flowers in spring or summer. Plant in full sun. The Spanish dagger, *Y. gloriosa,* contrary to the name, doesn't do serious damage if you bump into it; it grows about 10 feet high.

Some Like It Hot

It's a jungle out there and these shrubs can take the heat. The shrubs in this section enjoy hot, sultry summers and mild, nearly frost-free winters. To look their best, they need moist, well-drained soil. Humidity helps, too.

Unlike shrubs in cold-winter climates, these tropical shrubs keep their foliage all year 'round. Commonly grown as landscape plants in Florida and the warmer parts of the southwestern United States, many of these shrubs also grow well as potted houseplants in cooler climates.

If you grow them indoors, keep their tropical preferences in mind and give them warm temperatures year 'round and 12 to 14 hours of light per day for best results. For more information on growing these and other tropical shrubs as houseplants, pick up a copy of *Houseplants For Dummies* by Larry Hodgson and the Editors of the National Gardening Association (IDG Books Worldwide, Inc.). Whether you grow them indoors or out in your yard, look to these shrubs for outstanding flowers and foliage.

✔ **Flowering maple:** *Abutilon × hybridum.* Zones 9 to 11. Grown mostly for their dangling, bell-shaped flowers in shades of white, pink, yellow, and red, flowering maples bloom in spring, but some flower year-round. Their common name comes from the maple-like shape of their leaves. Best grown in light shade, the flowering maple grows 8 to 10 feet high with arching branches, and can be grown indoors as a houseplant. Many cultivars with different flower colors and variegated foliage exist. Whitefly and scale often infest this plant.

✔ **Bougainvillea:** *Bougainvillea × buttiana* and *B. spectabilis.* Zones 10 to 11; protected parts of 9. Really more a vine than a shrub, but I include it because it's one of the most spectacularly colorful plants you can grow.

In warm weather, these plants cover themselves with shocking white, pink, yellow, red, and purple blooms. Most varieties are vigorous plants that can sprawl over 30 feet wide and 15 feet high with strong support. Heavy, frequent pruning can keep them within bounds. Smaller varieties like red-flowering 'Temple Fire', white-flowered 'Ms. Alice', and reddish pink 'Torch Glow' can easily be kept in the 3- to 6-foot high range. Plant carefully, disturbing their brittle roots as little as possible. It grows best in full sun.

✔ **Natal plum:** *Carissa macrocarpa.* Zones 10 to 11. Glossy, deep-green leaves and fragrant, white, star-shaped flowers grace this rugged shrub all year 'round. It has very thorny branches, however, which make it dangerous to plant near walkways, but useful for barrier hedges. Edible red fruit tastes somewhat like cranberries and can be made into jelly. Natal plum tolerates seaside conditions and grows best in full sun, but can take light shade. The species grows over 15 feet high, but lower-growing cultivars are commonly available. Look for 'Boxwood Beauty', which grows 2 feet high and is thornless; 'Fancy', which grows upright to 6 feet high; and 'Tuttle', which grows 2 to 3 feet high and wide. Upright types make excellent hedges, while spreaders can be used as ground covers.

✔ **False heather:** *Cuphea hyssopifolia.* Zones 10 to 11. Save a spot at the front of your border for this compact shrub. Rarely growing more than 2 feet high, it has small, glossy, bright-green leaves and rose-purple flowers produced over a long season. 'Compacta' stays under 12 inches high. Plant in full sun or part shade. In cold-winter climates, grow *Cuphea* in pots or plant in your flower garden as an annual.

✔ **Fatsia:** *Fatsia japonica.* Zones 8 to 10. A plant for moist, shady nooks, fatsia has boldly lobed leaves 6 to 12 inches across. It prefers moist, acidic, fertile soils, but tolerates a wide range of conditions as long as you give it part to full shade. Growing 6 to 10 feet tall and wide when planted in the landscape, it also fares well in containers and is grown as a houseplant in cold climates. Several cultivars are available, including one with variegated leaves.

✔ **Patty's purple hebe.** *Hebe* 'Patty's Purple'. Zones 9 to 11. This delightful evergreen shrub has dark green leaves on purplish stems, with purple flowers in summer. Plant in full sun in cool summer climates, but in part shade where summers are hotter. It needs excellent drainage.

✔ **Tropical hibiscus:** *Hibiscus rosa-sinensis.* Zones 10 to 11. When you think of the tropics, you probably picture these spectacular flowering plants first. Their huge single or double, trumpet-shaped flowers up to 8 inches across in bright shades of white, pink, red, yellow, and orange are legendary. Even when not in bloom, their glossy green foliage is attractive. Although it can reach 25 feet high in ideal climates, it usually grows 6 to 10 feet high and makes a good hedge or screen. Give it full sun, plenty of heat, water and fertilizer, and excellent drainage to keep it happy, but be on the lookout for aphids and whitefly pests.

Hundreds of cultivars of this shrub exist. You can find more information about hibiscus from the American Hibiscus Society, Executive Secretary, P.O. Drawer 321540, W. Cocoa Beach, FL 32932-1540; phone or fax (407) 783-2576; and Web site www.trop-hibiscus.com/dahs.html.

✔ **Banana shrub:** *Michelia figo*. Zones 9 to 11. This magnolia relative resembles its cousin with large, shiny leaves and white flowers with a banana-like fragrance in spring and summer. It grows 6 to 8 feet high, making it useful for small landscapes. Banana shrub can be grown in full sun in cool areas. Plant in light shade in hot climates.

✔ **Queensland umbrella tree:** *Schefflera actinophylla*. Zones 10 to 11. Commonly grown as a houseplant, *Schefflera* has large oval leaflets on long stalks that resemble the ribs of an umbrella. In the landscape, this shrub rapidly grows into a small, 20-foot tree, but can be pruned to keep it smaller and more compact. Three-foot long, spreading flower clusters start green and fade to pink or red and produce small purple fruit. Plant in full sun in cool areas, part shade elsewhere.

✔ **Yellow oleander:** *Thevetia peruviana*. Zones 10 to 11. Oleander has narrow, glossy-green leaves and fragrant, yellow to light orange flowers from spring to fall (some year 'round). Unfortunately, all parts of this lovely shrub are toxic if eaten. You can grow this 20-foot shrub as a small tree or prune it to half that height for hedges and screens. (See Chapter 14 for pruning tips.) Give oleander full sun, well-drained soil, and protection from the wind.

✔ **Princess flower:** *Tibouchina urvilleana*. Zones 10 to 11. This shrub has widely spaced branches covered with reddish-purple, velvety foliage. Large bright purple flowers bloom sporadically almost all year 'round. Princess flower usually grows 5 to 10 feet high, but can reach nearly 20 feet. It appreciates full sun on its leaves and shaded roots.

Part IV

Buying, Planting, and Caring for Your Trees and Shrubs

The 5th Wave   By Rich Tennant

"I considered planting maple trees or oak trees, but shoe trees just seemed to make the most sense."

In this part . . .

Imagine this. You're standing in a garden center looking at a jillion junipers. Your mission, should you choose to accept it, is to pick the best one to buy, get it safely home, plant it, and nurture it into adulthood. Feeling a little lost? No worries! This part is the plant world's answer to a child-rearing, self-help book. In this part, I walk you through choosing healthy trees and shrubs, planting them as individuals or groups, feeding, watering, and tucking them into a bed of mulch at night.

If you're a runs-with-scissors type, take Chapter 14 with you on the journey. It covers the two basic techniques you need to know and when and where to use them. From sawing a limb to renovating a hedge, by the time you dash through this chapter, you'll be a regular Edward Scissorhands. Of course keeping everybody happy and healthy as they grow is important, too. Turn to the last chapter in this part to get the jump on pests, diseases, and other problems that can ambush your trees and shrubs.

Chapter 11

Buying Trees and Shrubs

- -

In This Chapter

▶ Choosing trees and shrubs with good structure

▶ Shopping for healthy bare-root, root-balled, and container-grown plants

▶ Keeping your plants healthy until planting time

- -

*B*uying healthy trees and shrubs is an important step in ensuring that they will thrive in your landscape for many years without excessive maintenance. The shape of the young shrub or tree, its source, and care in the nursery or garden center play a large part in your success. The arrangement and attachment of branches becomes especially important as trees get larger. Weak limbs and trunks create hazards and become a liability in your landscape. Strong, well-placed branches create a healthy structure for future growth.

Nurseries sell trees and shrubs in several different forms — each has benefits and cautions. You can buy trees and shrubs from so many sources — from local nurseries and garden centers to mail-order nurseries across the United States. Where you decide to make your purchase depends on your needs and the size and quality of the plants offered. In addition, your responsibility for your plants begins when you take them home. How you transport and care for them before planting makes a difference in how they grow after you plant them.

Deciding Where to Buy

You can buy trees and shrubs from many different sources and each has its benefits and drawbacks. Consider the size, number, and variety of plants you desire, as well as your budget, climate, and the time of year you intend to plant when you select your source. Also let your level of plant expertise and need for expert advice guide your decision about where to buy your trees and shrubs.

Guarantees also vary from one business to another. Many reputable companies offer up to a one-year replacement of failed merchandise, but if you choose healthy, well-grown trees and shrubs and plant them properly and in the right place, you shouldn't have any plants to return.

Local nurseries

Nurseries grow many, if not all, of the trees and shrubs they sell. Some nurseries specialize in a particular type of plant, such as fruit trees, while others grow a wide and diverse selection of locally adapted plants. You can be fairly certain that the plants local nurseries offer will grow in your climate. Plants undergo less stress, too, when they avoid lengthy transport and storage. Local growers are familiar with the soil and growing conditions in their area. Experienced tree and shrub growers can also give you valuable advice about selecting the plants most suitable for your situation and how to plant and care for them.

A good-quality nursery guarantees the health of the plants it sells. Some offer replacement plants, while others will give you your money back. The length of the warranty varies, too, but up to a year or at least a full growing season is not uncommon. When evaluating a nursery, look for healthy, well-formed plants, as described in the "Choosing Strong Foundations for the Future" section later in this chapter, and helpful, knowledgeable staff.

If you want large trees and shrubs, buy them from a local nursery that offers delivery and planting, although this service may cost extra. Don't wait for the season to be in full swing, however, if you want the nursery to plant your trees or shrubs for you. Long waits are common during the busy season. Some nurseries also allow customers to buy plants still growing in the field for digging and delivery at the proper time. If you seek a specimen plant for a landscape focal point or have other special needs, head out to the nursery several weeks before the planting season begins to have the best selection — the choicest plants will be gone first!

Garden centers

Garden centers range from small, locally owned seasonal businesses to departments in mass merchandising and home improvement stores. The range of goods and services — and often the plant quality — varies just as widely. When you shop for trees and shrubs at a garden center, look for the following qualities:

✔ Clean sales area with plants neatly arranged and well labeled.

✔ Evidence of regular watering, such as overhead sprinkler system or irrigation tubing and moist soil in the containers. No wilted plants.

✔ Root balls and containers protected from overheating or freezing with mulch or covering, if necessary.

✔ Plants offered are suitable for your climate and hardiness zone. Refer to Chapter 2 and the map in the color section of this book for climate and zone descriptions. Parts II and III give specific plant requirements.

✔ Knowledgeable and helpful sales staff.

✔ Delivery and professional planting service, if you need it.

Garden centers buy some, if not all, of their trees and shrubs from wholesale nurseries, either locally or from some distance away. Be aware that trees and shrubs grown in a cold or heat hardiness zone significantly different from where you live may be less hardy than plants grown closer to home. Ask a salesperson where the plants came from if you have questions about their cold or heat tolerance.

The price of trees and shrubs can differ greatly among garden centers. Lower price, however, does not always mean better value. Instead, choose your plant source for the quality of its merchandise. Well-cared-for plants recover from transplanting more quickly and grow more vigorously than plants that received poor care. Sometimes neglect, such as drought stress from lack of water, doesn't show up until a year after you take your purchase home and plant it. Even if the plant lives, it may never look as attractive or grow as vigorously as one that received adequate care. As in most home-improvement projects, the materials are cheap compared to your time and labor. Many garden centers offer a one-year warranty on their plants, but failed plants can cost you a year or more in fulfilling your landscape plan.

Mail order

Many specialty nurseries sell their plants by publishing catalogs and shipping their plants through the mail or by commercial carrier. If you seek unusual or uncommon trees or shrubs or less expensive bare-root plants for a hedge, ground cover, windbreak, or orchard, try mail-order catalogs.

Like garden centers, mail-order nurseries vary in size and quality of their merchandise. Many of their catalogs offer a great variety of trees and shrubs, but with the following caveats:

✔ Mail-order companies usually offer only bare-root or small potted plants because heavy soil costs too much to ship. Potted plants usually are much smaller than those available at local nurseries or garden centers.

✔ Plants grown in other parts of the country may not be hardy in your area. (See Chapter 2 for more information on climate.)

Gardening by Internet and mail

Hundreds of mail-order catalog companies exist and they sell every kind of plant from seeds to trees. The World Wide Web offers a wealth of information about these companies and the products that they sell. The Mailorder Gardening Association, a membership organization of mail order and garden magazine companies, has a list of its members at their Web site at www.mailordergardening.com/index.htm.

Some Web sites have compiled huge lists of landscape-, nursery-, and garden-related mail-order catalogs but don't send out catalogs themselves. Some, such as Gardenscape, offer comprehensive lists that include catalog companies' addresses, phone numbers, and Web addresses. This site also has an AT&T toll-free telephone number directory that allows you to search by category, company, or location. Find Gardenscape at www.gardenscape.com/GSCompaniesWWW.html.

At Plants By Mail, their large catalog list comes complete with customer and catalog company owner comments and ratings. They encourage customers who order from any garden-related mail-order catalog company to comment about the plant quality, customer service, and other experiences for inclusion in their database. They update the information regularly. The Web site is www.pbmfaq.dvol.com/index.html.

✔ You can't inspect the plants before you buy them. Returning unsatisfactory plants may be difficult or inconvenient. Many companies go by the honor system, however, and if you report an unsatisfactory plant, they will simply replace it.

✔ Shipping conditions can damage your plants. Mail order companies pack plants carefully and ship them at the most appropriate times of year, but they can't control the temperature that plants may experience in transit or how shippers treat your package.

Avoid ordering from catalogs that don't give adequate information about the plants that they sell. Look for descriptions that give both common and botanical names, hardiness zones, cultural requirements, plant size at time of shipping, and mature height and width. The most useful catalog photographs show the growth habit of mature specimens, not just close ups of ornamental features. Catalog plant descriptions also tend to praise the virtues of the merchandise without mentioning the faults. Flip to Chapter 18 for lists of problem trees.

Compare the shipping size, price, and guarantee of the catalog plants to those of locally available trees and shrubs before ordering.

Other sources

Many states' tree nurseries and conservation or charitable organizations offer trees and shrubs for sale. If you wish to plant native trees and shrubs for wildlife, habitat restoration, erosion control, or other conservation use, watch for these opportunities to purchase inexpensive plants. Many garden clubs and arboretums also hold plant sales where you may find rare and unusual trees and shrubs.

Digging plants from the wild is the least desirable source of trees and shrubs. Although considered a source of free plants, I caution you against digging trees and shrubs from the wild for several reasons:

✔ You may be breaking the law unless you obtain the plant from your own property or from someone else's land with permission. Moving endangered or protected plants or taking anything from federal or state property can carry heavy penalties and fines.

✔ Unless you dig only small plants with large root balls, you risk injuring or killing the plant by damaging too many of its roots.

✔ Wild plants often carry pests and diseases that domesticated plants resist.

✔ Trees and shrubs collected from the wild don't easily adjust to growing conditions that are significantly different from their native habitat. If you take a tree out of the woods where it grew in shade and plant it in your sunny yard, for example, it may perish.

Transplanting trees and shrubs from the wild is best done in situations where construction or other habitat loss may destroy them anyway. Always get permission from landowners before digging. See the Chapter 12 for transplanting tips to help ensure your plants' survival.

Choosing Strong Foundations for the Future

"As the twig is bent, so grows the tree," goes the old proverb. Like the foundation of a house, a young tree's framework of limbs and shape of its trunk determine the integrity of the structure built upon it. Although you can solve some defects with pruning and training (see Chapter 14), structurally sound trees require less maintenance, live longer and healthier lives, and cause fewer hazards as they age. Although shrubs vary more in form, you can select plants with structures that best meet your landscape needs. Go to Chapter 1 for more on tree and shrub anatomy.

When you shop for trees, compare all of the available specimens of the same type to find those with the most desirable branching and trunk habits. If you don't find any that meet your requirements, look at plants in a different garden center or nursery. Trees with a healthy structure have the following characteristics:

- ✔ Strong trunk that stands straight without a stake and is free of wounds, streaks, and sunken spots.

- ✔ Trees and shrubs with multiple stems have trunks that don't crowd or rub against one another.

- ✔ Branches evenly spaced around and along the trunk and properly attached with wide, V-shaped crotches, as shown in Figure 11-1. Avoid trees with narrow crotches.

- ✔ Dense, evenly colored foliage, if present. Dormant buds undamaged.

- ✔ Trunk that tapers evenly from top to bottom and flares gently at the soil surface.

Avoid trees with the following defects, as shown in Figure 11-1:

- ✔ Trunk divides into two or more roughly equal-size *leaders* or trunk shoots. One or more branches are the same diameter as the leader.

- ✔ Branches squeeze against the trunk, forming a narrow V-shaped crotch.

- ✔ Branches spaced close together, clustered near the top of the trunk, or unevenly distributed on one side of the trunk.

- ✔ Dead or broken branches.

- ✔ Bark damage on trunk or branches.

- ✔ Leaves smaller or lighter color than other specimens or show evidence of insects or disease. (See Chapter 15 for pest and disease identification.)

- ✔ Trunk flare buried so that the trunk appears to come straight out of the soil like a telephone pole. Trunk flare is more obvious with larger trees than with small ones.

Shrubs, too, need healthy structures right from the start to develop into long-lived, trouble-free plants. The "right" structure for shrubs varies among species more than among trees because shrubs differ more in their growth habits (Figure 11-2 shows a shrub with characteristics to avoid). The way you intend to use your shrub also makes a difference in the structure you should choose. Multistemmed plants that branch close to the ground make better hedges. Plants that branch higher up on their stems can be pruned to resemble small trees (see Chapter 14). The following guidelines for choosing healthy shrubs generally hold true:

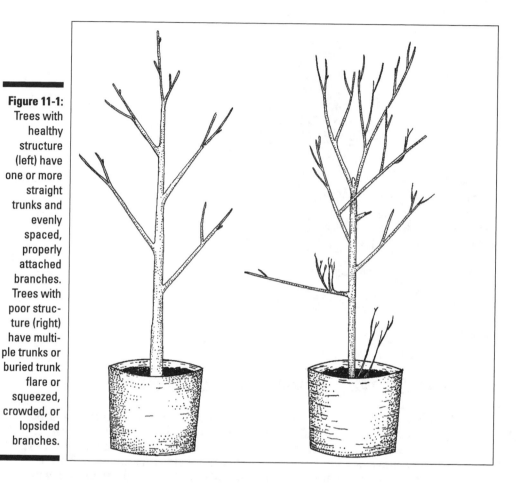

Figure 11-1: Trees with healthy structure (left) have one or more straight trunks and evenly spaced, properly attached branches. Trees with poor structure (right) have multiple trunks or buried trunk flare or squeezed, crowded, or lopsided branches.

- Stem or stems of approximately the same size arising from roots at or just beneath the soil surface.
- Shrubs for hedges or ground covers of uniform size and habit.
- Branches evenly distributed, not lopsided.
- Foliage and shoots appear vigorous without wilting, dead spots, or broken limbs.
- Few, if any, shoots rubbing against one another.

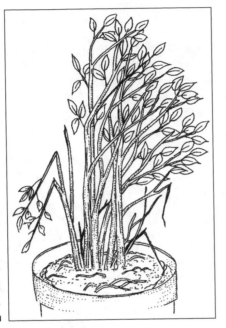

Figure 11-2:
Avoid shrubs with crowded shoots or dead, broken, or lopsided growth.

Getting to the Root of the Matter

Plant nurseries grow and sell trees and shrubs several different ways. Some plants grow in the ground in nursery fields and are called *field-grown* stock. When field-grown stock grows large enough to sell, growers dig the trees and shrubs and sell them either with or without field soil around their roots. Those without soil are called *bare-root* plants. Trees and shrubs dug with balls of soil around their roots are called *root-balled* or *balled and burlapped (B&B)* stock.

Plant nurseries also grow trees and shrubs right in the plastic containers in which they are sold. *Container-grown* stock is sold by the container size in which it grows, such as 1 gallon, 2 gallon, or 5 gallon.

Bare-root and fancy free

Nursery workers dig bare-root trees and shrubs during the autumn after the plants become dormant or in the early spring before the plants begin growing. Fall-dug plants spend the winter in cold storage and are ready to ship in late winter. These dormant plants are lightweight and easy to transport, making them the plant of choice for mail order nurseries. They also cost relatively less than either container-grown or root-balled stock and recover quickly from transplanting. If you plan to plant a hedge or cover a large area of ground, bare-root shrubs offer the best value, but plan ahead — they are usually available only in late autumn or late winter to early spring. In zones 5 and colder, plant bare-root trees and shrubs in spring. If you live in zones 6 and warmer, fall planting gives roots time to become established before the hot summer weather returns.

When choosing bare-root stock, look for moist, evenly distributed roots spreading out around the base, and avoid the following, as shown in Figure 11-3:

- ✔ Plants with mushy or dry, broken or torn roots or those with very few small feeder roots (see Chapter 1).

- ✔ Roots that wrap around the trunk, thus preventing vigorous growth.

Figure 11-3:
Look for bare-root plants with moist, unbroken, evenly distributed, spreading roots, avoiding those with lopsided or broken roots.

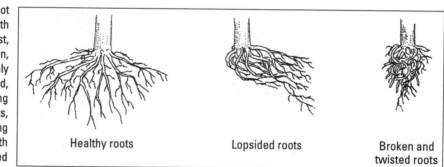

Healthy roots · Lopsided roots · Broken and twisted roots

Root-balled stock

Nurseries also dig root-balled or balled and burlapped (B&B) stock from the field in winter or early spring. Plants can lose up to 90 percent of their roots when dug for B&B stock, depending on the nursery's methods of growing and harvesting its plants. After digging, workers wrap the root ball in plastic or natural fiber burlap and twine or wire to hold the soil and roots together for transport. Although nurseries can ship root-balled or B&B stock long distances safely, it's heavy and expensive. Large trees and shrubs most often come as root-balled stock.

TIP

When you shop for B&B trees and shrubs, look for the following (see Figure 11-4):

- ✔ **Solid, well-proportioned root balls:** The diameter of the root ball should be at least 10 to 12 times the diameter of the trunk measured 6 inches above the soil. Flattened sides or lopsided balls, loose soil, or a trunk that shifts easily in the soil indicates that the plant may have been dropped — a bad sign that could mean broken roots.

- ✔ **A flat-topped ball with the trunk centered and the flare at soil level:** If the grower used trunk wrap to prevent damage to the bark during shipping, ask to have it removed so that you can inspect the trunk for wounds and pests.

- ✔ **A moist and fresh-looking root ball, and dense, full-sized, and normally colored foliage (if present).**

Figure 11-4:
Healthy root-balled stock has moist, unbroken soil without flattened sides or loose trunk (left). Lopsided root-balls and loose wrapping many indicate root damage (right).

Container-grown

Most shrubs and many trees grow directly in the pots or containers in which they reach the market, making them easy to transport and store for long periods of time. Container-grown stock retains all of its roots, unlike bare-root or B&B stock, which has been dug from the field. Nurseries and garden centers can sell container-grown stock throughout the gardening season — year round in warm climates.

Growers start the young plants in small containers and transplant them to larger pots each year as they grow. Trees and shrubs in larger pots usually have grown longer in the nursery and so cost more to produce — I say "usually" because sometimes nurseries take field-grown, bare-root stock and plant it into containers for sale. If transplanted from the field into a container, the plant needs a season or more of growth to rejuvenate its roots before you transplant it again. Regardless of which method the grower used, trees and shrubs should be well-rooted in their pots, and not shift easily around in the potting soil.

Well-grown trees and shrubs have roots that fill their container evenly, but don't circle around inside the pot, creep out the top, or grow out the bottom drainage holes. If you can slip a shrub out of its pot, inspect it for tangled, circling, or matted roots. These *root-bound* plants, such as shown in Figure 11-5, may not recover from transplanting as quickly as those plants with straight, unmatted roots. Look for moist soil and healthy foliage without dead limbs or leaves.

Figure 11-5: Container-grown trees and shrubs should fill pots evenly with straight roots that don't circle or grow out of the drainage holes.

Root-bound shrub   Shrub with healthy roots

The price is right

The prices that different companies charge for seemingly similar trees and shrubs can vary widely. A juniper in a one-gallon pot at one store costs $5.99, while the same plant costs $10.99 at another. Often, plants of equal size, but different species or cultivated varieties have price tags that differ considerably. When you compare prices between different plants and companies consider these factors:

✔ **Plant size:** Shrubs in larger pots usually have spent more time in the nursery and cost the nursery more to grow than those in smaller pots. Trees also vary in age, but are most often measured and sold by *caliper size*, which is the diameter of the trunk 6 inches above the ground. (If trees are more than 4 inches in diameter, the caliper is measured at 12 inches above the ground.)

✔ **Bare-root, container, or B&B:** The way that plants are offered for sale affects their price due to shipping costs of heavy soil and the labor required to grow, harvest, and handle them.

✔ **Species and cultivated varieties:** Unusual plants sell for more than common ones. The newest rose varieties always cost more than the old standbys. Plants that grow very slowly, such as dwarf conifers, (see Chapter 7) cost nurseries more to produce. Colorado blue spruce 'Globosa', for example, costs more than a plain Colorado blue spruce. A fast-growing Leyland cypress costs less than a slower-growing Black Hills spruce in the same size container.

✔ **Plant source:** Very large garden centers buy and sell tractor-trailer loads of shrubs and trees in a single weekend during their busy season. Wholesale nurseries charge these big retail companies a lower price for their plants because they buy in large volumes. Smaller garden centers often pay more for the plants that they sell to you. Don't confuse price with value, however, as many smaller stores offer excellent service. Another option — buying directly from a nursery that grows its own plants — can save you money by eliminating the "middleman."

Transporting and Safekeeping Your Purchase

After buying your tree or shrub, you have to get it home and in the ground. The way you transport and care for them until planting time can literally mean the difference between life and death or, at the very least, health and harm.

Getting your tree or shrub home safely

The greatest threats to plants' health come from mechanical injuries and environmental extremes. Caring for your new tree or shrub begins with how you carry it. Although stems and trunks look like perfect handles by which to grab and lift a plant, that method may break the plants' roots or separate them from the soil in the root ball. Instead, lift trees and shrubs by their root balls or containers so that you support their roots. If a plant is too heavy to lift, drag it on a tarp.

Extreme heat and cold can quickly damage plants' living tissue. Trees and shrubs enjoy the same temperature comfort range that you do. Closed vehicles parked in the sun, even on cool days, can reach temperatures that are fatal to trees and shrubs. Some car trunks, too, overheat, even when the passenger compartment feels comfortable. If you have plants in your car, make your garden center or nursery stop the last one of the day or plan to keep your car cool while you complete your other errands.

Wind also damages plants by shredding and drying out their foliage. Putting a tree in the back of your pick-up truck and driving it down the highway is the equivalent of subjecting that tree to a hurricane. Although dormant plants without foliage can tolerate some wind, evergreens and other plants with foliage can be severely injured, even if you drive just a short distance and at relatively low speed. Remember that 30 miles per hour is slow in a car, but feels like strong wind to a tree. If you must transport plants in an open truck, wrap their canopies in Kraft paper, a tarp, or shrink wrap to protect them from wind damage.

Take care to protect the trunk and branches from torn or crushed bark when you secure them in your vehicle. Pad the plant with cloth or other soft material before tying ropes around it. Do wrap it and tie it securely, though — abrasion from rubbing on your tailgate or trunk lid also damages the bark and branches. If you can't get your tree or shrubs home safely in your own vehicle, ask the nursery for delivery service. Delivery usually costs extra, but may be well worth it, especially for large, heavy, and expensive plants. Inspect the delivered plants carefully before the driver leaves, however, to ensure that the bark, roots, and limbs are undamaged.

Caring for your purchase until planting time

If you can't plant your shrubs or trees for a day or two after you get them home, store them where they will remain cool and moist, but not freeze or get waterlogged. Good temporary storage areas include the shady north side of a building or well-ventilated garage. For longer keeping, follow these guidelines:

- ✔ **Bare-root plants:** Dig a trench or hole that can accommodate the plant roots. Lay the plants in the trench at an angle, as shown in Figure 11-6. (This process is called *heeling in* a plant.) Water thoroughly. Transplant to their permanent home as soon as possible or before the plants begin active growth.

- ✔ **Root-balled and container-grown plants:** Place plants where they will not receive hot midday sun. Cover their root balls or containers with bark or other loose mulch to keep their roots cool, shaded, and moist, as in Figure 11-6. Keep them well watered.

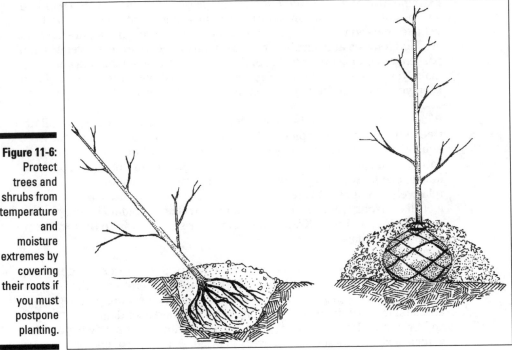

Figure 11-6:
Protect trees and shrubs from temperature and moisture extremes by covering their roots if you must postpone planting.

Chapter 12

Putting Down Roots

● ●

In This Chapter

▶ Figuring out the best time to plant

▶ Spacing your trees and shrubs for healthy growth

▶ Planting trees and shrubs as hedges and ground covers

▶ Staking and protecting trees and shrubs

▶ Transplanting shrubs and small trees

● ●

*P*lanting a tree is a weighty matter. How and where you plant it can affect the life of the tree and generations of people who may live and work in its shade. The season of planting, how you dig the hole, and the care you give the tree after setting its roots into the ground determine its success or failure.

Shrubs, although usually not as long-lived as trees, benefit from proper planting, too. Those used for hedges need the right amount of space between them so that they can grow to their potential size, but fill the space quickly. And low-growing shrubs that cover rocky slopes and other impossible areas need a little extra preparation and care to help them thrive and become well-established, carefree ground covers.

It's All in the Timing

The right time to plant your new shrubs and trees depends on where you live and the kinds of plants you intend to install. The best time to plant is when the shrub or tree will have an opportunity to grow new roots without the additional stress of severe weather. Let your climate and the type of tree or shrubs that you're planting — both covered in the next two sections — be your guide.

Climate

Autumn planting gives the best results in the warmer parts of the United States because it marks the beginning of the cool rainy season — a boon that lessens your watering chores and decreases transplant distress. If the rainy season comes at a different time of year where you live, plan to plant trees and shrubs whenever it occurs.

In climates with freezing winter temperatures, early spring planting gives trees and shrubs a full growing season to adjust before winter. Evergreens and bareroot plants especially appreciate early planting. You can also plant container-grown plants in the early autumn as they prepare for *dormancy* (the time when the above ground plants parts cease growing). At this time of year, roots continue to grow as long as the soil temperature remains above 40°.

Unless roots have a chance to become firmly established before winter sets in, however, the plant may be pushed partially out of the ground. *Frost heaving* occurs when the soil expands and contracts throughout the winter and spring freeze-and-thaw cycles, and can damage or even kill newly planted trees and shrubs. Protect fall-planted trees and shrubs from frost heaving with a 4- to 6-inch-thick layer of loose, organic mulch, such as shredded leaves or bark. Remove excess mulch in the spring, leaving a 2- to 3-inch layer.

Plant type

Nursery workers dig and sell bare-root deciduous trees and shrubs only during the dormant season — they must be planted immediately after purchase. Balled and burlapped stock, also dug from the field while dormant, should be planted as soon as possible after it has been dug. Container-grown stock, on the other hand, has not suffered the root loss that characterizes field-dug stock. You can plant trees and shrubs grown in containers at nearly any season except as limited by your climate and length of growing season. (See Chapter 11 for more information on choosing bare-root, balled and burlapped, and container-grown plants.)

Conifers and broadleaf evergreens recover more quickly after spring planting in frigid northern climates because they lose water through their foliage during the dormant winter months and can become dehydrated. Planting early in the spring allows them to grow feeder roots and store water during the summer. In areas with hot, windy summers, however, plant evergreens in late summer through September. Except in areas where frost heaving damages plants, also plant deciduous trees and shrubs in the late summer through autumn months when they have little, if any, foliage to support.

Space Case

Trees and shrubs need enough space to stretch their mature limbs and roots without creating a nuisance or crowding nearby plants. Before you buy a tree or shrub, read its plant label or description to find out how tall and wide the plant could grow. Its rate of growth — whether slow or vigorous — tells you how quickly the plant will reach its mature size. You need this information in order to dig the planting hole, too.

Trees

Planting a tree carries with it a long-term responsibility because trees have the potential to live for decades, if not centuries, right where you plant them. Future generations may curse or bless the decisions you make when you plant a tree.

Before you decide where to plant a tree, you need to know how big it will get. Genetics, climate, and specific site conditions have a significant impact on the ultimate size and life span of the tree. A white oak tree growing in an open field can expect to live for centuries and spread its branches in a canopy 75- to 100-feet wide. Imagine another white oak tree planted in a 4-foot wide patch of ground between the street and sidewalk in a city. Although soil compaction, air pollution, and vandalism may prevent the oak from growing as large as its country cousin, you still must consider its possible size when you decide where to dig the planting hole. Even a 50- to 60-foot tall oak can disrupt overhead wires, crack pavement, and hang its branches across the adjacent road.

To find the best place to dig a hole and plant your tree, first find out the potential height and width of the plant. Flip to the chapters in Part III for tree descriptions and be sure to look at Chapter 2 to help you choose the right tree for your site.

After you buy your tree (see Chapter 11), follow these guidelines to find the spot to start digging:

- **Measure the width of the mature canopy on the ground from the nearest obstacle using a tape measure.** If you want to plant a flowering crabapple tree near your house that will grow 20 feet wide, for example, measure 20 feet from the house out through your proposed planting site.

- **Mark the center of the measured canopy on the ground with an X and adjust the location of the digging spot as needed.** In the crabapple tree example, the digging spot is 10 feet from the house.

✔ **Check for conflicts.** Measure all around the digging spot to check for other potential conflicts, such as other plants, buildings, driveways, roads, sidewalks, and utilities. Adjust your digging spot accordingly.

✔ **Check the overhead clearance, too.** Use the method for estimating height given in Chapter 2 to get an idea of how tall your tree will grow. Remember not to plant trees under or near utility wires if they'll grow taller that 20 feet. You also want to avoid having limbs hang over your house or driveway. Visit Northern States Power Company's Web site at www.mpelectric.com/treebook/ for more tree size and planting location recommendations.

✔ **Check the underground clearance.** Tree roots usually spread from 2 to 5 times wider than the width of the branch canopy. That means that your 20-foot-wide crabapple could have roots that stretch from 20 to 50 feet away from its trunk. Avoid planting where tree roots can damage septic systems or paving or become damaged themselves from soil compaction, digging, or chemicals. See Chapter 18 for more information.

Shrubs

Shrubs, by definition, don't grow as large as trees, but their planting is no less significant. You've invested in healthy plants and want them to grow to their full landscape potential. Shrubs grow three different ways in the landscape — as specimen plants, as hedges, and as ground covers — and the space requirements differ for each.

✔ Plant specimen shrubs as you would a tree, giving each plant enough space to mature without interfering with other plants or causing a nuisance. Consider shrub height especially when you plant them under windows or near road intersections where they could interfere with drivers' sight.

✔ Shrubs planted as ground covers or hedges should grow together closely enough to create a uniform wall or carpet, but not so close that they compete excessively for available light, water, and nutrients.

Planting shrubs becomes a balance between the shrubs' long-range needs and your short-term goals. When you plant a hedge for privacy, you want it to fill in quickly so that it can do its job. But, if you plant your shrubs too close together, hoping for quick results, the long-term health of the plants will suffer and your hedge may become unsightly or unable to fulfill its potential as the plants begin to crowd each other. Correct spacing is critical to the success of your hedge or ground cover.

Shrubs as hedges

You can plant hedges in a single line or as an offset double row depending on your available space, patience, budget, and style of hedge you desire. The single-row method requires fewer plants and takes up less space than the double row, but the hedge takes longer to fill in. Plant single rows of shrubs either in a trench or in individual holes, as shown in Figure 12-1. Trenches work best for bare-root shrubs and in soils that require amendments. Use individual holes for container-grown and root-balled stock. If you're planting windbreaks and sound barriers, consider planting double or even triple rows. When you dig holes for double rows, offset the holes so that plants form a zigzag pattern.

You can grow your hedge in either a sheared, formal style or allow the shrubs to retain their natural form (see Chapter 14 for more information on pruning hedges). The number of plants you need and their spacing depends on which style you choose. Generally, sheared plants can grow closer together so you need more of them to make a hedge.

Regardless of the style, space plants in the row(s) so that their limbs will overlap as they mature. You won't find any absolute best planting distance between plants because it varies by species and cultivar of plant, size at planting time, and the height and width of the hedge. Use the following guidelines, however, to get you started. Ask experienced nursery staff for specific recommendations.

Figure 12-1:
Plant hedge shrubs in a single row or staggered double row depending on desired density of the hedge. Dig a trench for bare-root plants.

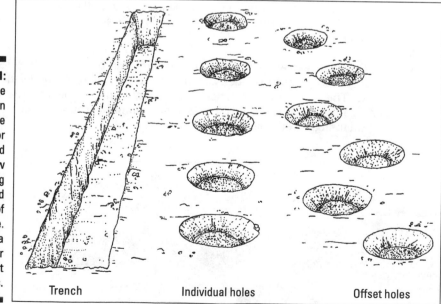

Trench   Individual holes   Offset holes

✔ For a formal, low-growing hedge less than 3 feet high, plant small, bare-root shrubs 12 to 18 inches apart.

✔ For formal hedges 4 to 6 feet high, plant larger container or root-balled plants 24 to 36 inches apart.

✔ Plant shrubs for an informal style hedge about 25 percent farther apart than those in a formal hedge.

Remember to leave space on either side of your hedge, too. A mature hedge can be 3, 5, or even 8 feet across, depending on the plants and style you choose. Plant it far enough from boundaries so that you can maintain the hedge from your own property and away from fences and buildings that will shade or restrict its growth.

Shrubs as ground covers

Shrubs protect soil from eroding and make an attractive alternative to grass on slopes and terrain too steep, rough, or arid to grow a lawn. The correct spacing between plants is very important, but again depends on the species you choose. The rule for spacing, though, is that you want the ground to be covered by the end of the third growing season after planting. Closer spacing may compromise the plants' health as they become crowded and compete for moisture and nutrients. It also costs more money.

Evenly space ground-covering shrubs in staggered rows as shown in Figure 12-2. You have to control weeds until the shrubs fill in, so plan to lay down a landscape fabric or organic mulch before planting (see Chapter 13). If you use mulch, cut holes in landscape fabric and pull organic mulch away from the hole at planting time. When you dig, pile soil on a tarp to keep the mulch clean.

Small shrubs, like wintercreeper *(Euonymus)*, can be spaced 12 to 18 inches apart, but larger shrubs, such as junipers, require 48 to 60 inches between plants. The spacing varies depending on your climate, soil, and the size of plant you start with. Table 12-1 lists some common ground-covering shrubs and their suggested spacings.

Figure 12-2:
Space ground-covering shrubs in staggered rows.

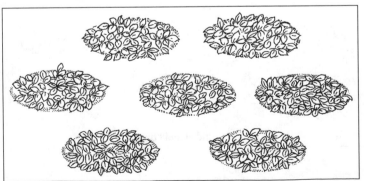

Table 12-1   Suggested Spacing for Ground-Covering Shrubs

Shrubs Planting	Distance Apart
Bearberry: *Arctostaphylos uva-ursi*	3 to 4 feet
Marlberry: *Ardisia japonica*	18 to 36 inches
Dwarf coyote bush: *Baccharis pilularis*	3 to 5 feet
Heather: *Calluna* species	12 to 18 inches
Japanese yew plum: *Cephalotaxus harringtonia*	2 to 3 feet
Rockspray cotoneaster: *Cotoneaster horizontalis*	3 to 5 feet
Willowleaf cotoneaster: *C. salicifolius*	3 to 5 feet
Heath: *Erica* species	12 to 18 inches
Wintercreeper: *Euonymus fortunei*	24 inches
Broom: *Genista lydia*	18 to 36 inches
Rockrose: *Helianthemum* species	2 to 3 feet
Spreading junipers: *Juniperus* species	4 to 5 feet
Lantana: *Lantana montevidensis*	3 to 4 feet
Oregon grape holly: *Mahonia aquifolium*	24 inches
Russian cypress: *Microbiota decussata*	5 to 8 feet
Paxistima: *Paxistima canbyi*	3 to 5 feet
Potentilla: *Potentilla fruticosa*	12 to 24 inches
Rosemary: *Rosmarinus officinalis* 'Huntington Blue'	3 to 4 feet
Japanese spirea 'Alpina': *Spirea japonica* 'Alpina'	3 to 5 feet
Cutleaf stephanandra: *Stephanandra incisa*	3 to 5 feet
Snowberry: *Symphoricarpos albus*	3 to 5 feet
Coralberry: *S.* × *chenaultii*	5 to 6 feet
Dwarf European cranberrybush: *Viburnum opulus* 'Nanum'	3 to 4 feet
Lowbush blueberry: *Vaccinium angustifolium*	18 to 24 inches

To calculate the number of plants you need to cover an area, use Table 12-2:

Table 12-2	Area Covered by 100 Ground-Covering Shrubs
Planting Distance Apart	*Area Covered*
12 inches	100 sq.ft.
18 inches	225 sq.ft.
24 inches	400 sq.ft.
30 inches	625 sq.ft.
36 inches	900 sq.ft.
48 inches	1600 sq.ft.
60 inches	2500 sq.ft.

Step-By-Step Guide to Planting

Get your tools together and put on your digging clothes. It's planting time! To dig a proper hole for your tree or shrub, you need a shovel or spade and a measuring stick or tape measure. Other tools that may come in handy include a spading fork or mattock (for loosening the soil) and pruning shears (to trim broken roots). If your plant is wrapped in burlap and twine or wire, keep a knife or scissors and a pair of sturdy wire cutters on hand, too. Don't forget water and mulch for the plant (see Chapter 13 for more information).

I need to dispel a common planting myth before you start digging and planting. Notice that, in the list of tools and supplies, I don't mention fertilizer or soil amendments, such as peat moss or topsoil. Tree and shrub experts do not — I repeat, do not — recommend adding anything to the soil in which you plant your trees or shrubs. When you put all those extra goodies into the planting hole, the roots stay in the hole and don't venture out into the surrounding soil. As a result, the plants become more prone to drought stress and toppling in the wind. If you have chosen plants that are suitable for your site (see Chapter 2), they don't need that stuff anyway. The only exceptions to this rule are in situations where the natural soil is severely disturbed by construction fill or you are attempting to grow plants not naturally suited to your soil conditions. To speed plant growth, you can fertilize them after they begin growing (see Chapter 13 for information).

Remember to keep your plants out of the hot, dry sun while you dig. And one last thing before you get started — be sure that you have located any underground utilities before you start digging — see Chapter 2.

Digging the hole

Two factors determine the diameter of the planting hole — the diameter of the plant's root ball or spread of its bare roots and your soil's structure (see Chapter 2).

> ✔ Measure the width of the root ball, container, or bare-root spread and multiply that measurement by 3 times to find the diameter of the planting hole. For example, if the root ball measures 12 inches across, the basic planting hole diameter is 36 inches.

> ✔ If your soil is compacted from construction or if you are working with a hard layer of impenetrable soil, break up or loosen the soil in a circle up to 5 times the diameter of the root ball to improve the drainage and ability of roots to penetrate.

You only need to consider one factor when determining the depth of the planting hole — the height of the root ball from the bottom of the container or root ball to the base of the trunk flare on a tree (where the trunk widens near the soil, see Chapter 1) or the crown of a shrub. If the trunk flare is buried in the soil in the container or covered by burlap, uncover it before measuring. The trunk flare must be planted just at the ground level or up to one inch above it. If planted too deeply, the roots, which usually grow within 6 inches of the soil surface, may suffocate. Young trees and shrubs commonly fail to thrive for this reason. In poorly drained soils, you can plant shrubs and trees a few inches higher than usual. Add and slope soil around the plant so that it blends with the surrounding soil.

To prevent your shrub or tree from settling lower in the soil after planting, never dig the center of the planting hole deeper than the height of the root ball. If you must break up hard soil in the bottom of the planting hole, leave a mound of undisturbed soil in the center on which to place the root ball. Leave the mound a little higher than you think you will need it — it's easier to reduce its height than to add soil back. With bare-root plants, leave a firm cone-shaped mound of soil on which to set the roots at the proper height. See the following section for more on planting bare-root stock.

Slope the sides of the planting hole from the bottom out to the sides to form a saucer shape, as shown in Figure 12-3. If your soil has a lot of clay in it, rough up the sides to help the plant roots penetrate the soil.

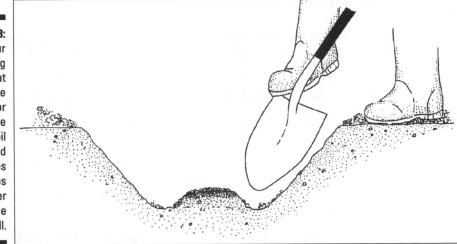

Figure 12-3: Dig your planting hole so that trunk flare sits at or just above the soil surface and sloped sides are 3 times the diameter of the root ball.

Planting bare-root trees and shrubs

Bare-root plants need extra attention and careful handling from the time you receive them until you plant them safely in the ground because they have no soil to protect their roots from drying out and temperature fluctuations. When they arrive in the mail or come home from the nursery, check the packing material for moisture around the roots. If it feels dry, add enough water to moisten the material, as shown in Figure 12-4, but don't completely saturate the roots or leave them in a puddle — excessive moisture can rot the roots. Soak the roots in the packaging or a bucket of tepid or air-temperature water for an hour just prior to planting. Don't add fertilizer to the water.

Planting roses

Rose bushes require special attention at planting time because they have an upper and a lower part that join at a *graft union* just above the roots. Rose growers graft the fancy rose cultivars onto a vigorous set of roots. Where the top meets the bottom, the stem bulges.

The depth at which you plant the graft union depends on your climate. Grafts unions are easily damaged by severe cold and need protection in the coldest climate zones. In climates with harsh winter temperatures (zones 5 and colder), plant the graft union 4 to 6 inches below ground. In zones 6 and 7 where winter minimums reach 0° or just a bit colder, set the union slightly below soil level. In warm climates (zones 8 and above), you can plant the union at or just above the soil surface.

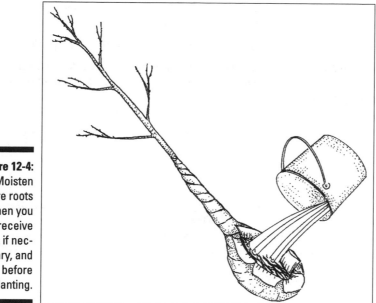

Figure 12-4:
Moisten
bare roots
when you
receive
them, if nec-
essary, and
before
planting.

Always work with bare-root plants on cloudy, cool, calm days, whenever possible, or protect them from sun and wind while you work. To plant them,
follow these instructions:

1. **Gently remove the packaging from your tree's roots.**

2. **Prune off any broken or crushed roots close to the damaged area, as
in Figure 12-5.**

   Preserve as many roots as possible.

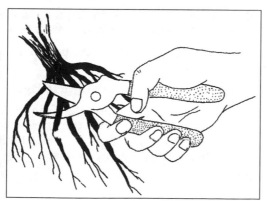

Figure 12-5:
Prune
broken
and
crushed
roots with
sharp
shears.

3. **Set the tree in the planting hole and drape the roots over the cone-shaped mound of soil in the middle.**

   Adjust the plant so that it has its best face forward, so to speak.

4. **Lay a yardstick across the hole at the normal ground level, as shown in Figure 12-6, and adjust the tree so that its trunk flare is at (or an inch above) the ground.**

Figure 12-6:
Use a yardstick laid across the planting hole to set the trunk flare at the proper depth.

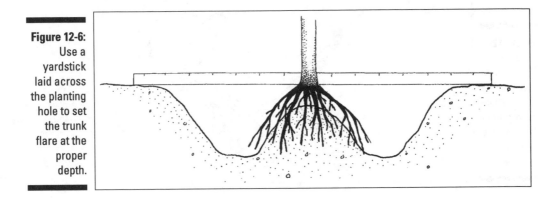

5. **Add or remove soil from the mound so that the tree remains at the proper planting height.**

6. **Holding the tree at the proper height with one hand, add soil to the planting hole, working it around the roots to fill air pockets.**

   Keep the tree centered and straight as you fill the hole.

7. **When the hole is about three-quarters full, add water to the hole carefully to settle the soil and eliminate air, as in Figure 12-7.**

   Hold the tree at the right level until the water soaks into the soil.

8. **Finish filling the planting hole with soil, bringing it up to the trunk flare and settle it firmly, but not too heavily, with your foot.**

9. **Make a 3- to 4-inch-high soil ring just outside the perimeter of the planting hole to create a watering basin.**

10. **Fill the basin with water and let it drain, as shown in Figure 12-8.**

    Bare-root plants usually don't require further watering until they begin growing actively. Over-watering dormant plants can cause root disease. Skip to the "After-planting protection and care" section, later in this chapter, for tips on mulching, staking, and protection.

Figure 12-7:
Partially backfill the planting hole, holding the tree at the proper height. Water to settle the soil.

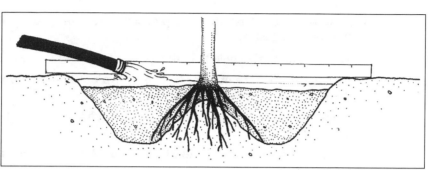

Figure 12-8:
Finish backfilling and form a watering basin just outside the perimeter of the planting hole. Fill basin with water.

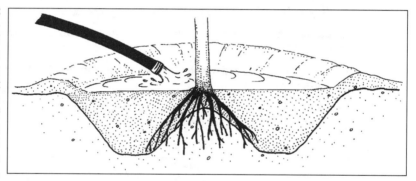

Planting balled and burlapped trees and shrubs

The day before you plant your balled and burlapped (B&B) plant, give the root ball a thorough soaking. Take care not to dislodge any of the soil, however. You can water it closer to planting time, but the soil will be heavier and more likely to break away from the roots when you handle it. Remember to always carry B&B stock by the root ball and not the trunk or stems. Drag heavy plants on a tarp.

Follow these instructions:

1. **Remove the ties from the burlap around the trunk, but don't unwrap the root ball just yet.**

   The ties and burlap help hold the root ball together.

2. **Find the trunk flare on your tree or crown on shrubs, and measure the height of the root ball from this point.**

   Adjust the depth of the planting hole to match the root ball height, as shown in Figure 12-9.

4. **Set the plant on a shovel and lift it into the hole, as shown in Figure 12-10.**

   If you're planting a small shrub, remove the burlap and twine covering before setting the plant into the hole. For larger plants, cut away the wire or twine around large root balls — without disturbing the root ball — before lifting them into the planting hole. Find a buddy or two to help you lift it by holding onto the burlap covering.

5. **Set the ball onto a mound of firm, undisturbed soil, as shown in Figure 12-11.**

6. **Use your yardstick laid across the planting hole to check the depth of the trunk flare.**

   It should be just at or up to an inch above the soil surface. Adjust the plant and soil mound as necessary.

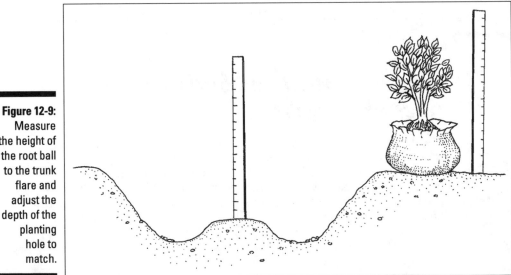

Figure 12-9:
Measure the height of the root ball to the trunk flare and adjust the depth of the planting hole to match.

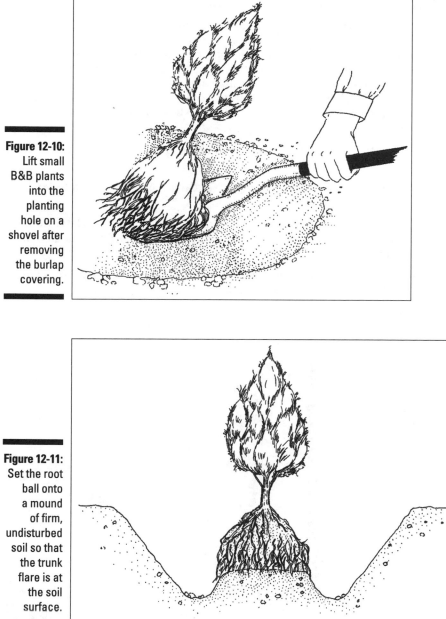

Figure 12-10:
Lift small B&B plants into the planting hole on a shovel after removing the burlap covering.

Figure 12-11:
Set the root ball onto a mound of firm, undisturbed soil so that the trunk flare is at the soil surface.

7. **Remove the burlap and ties or wires.**

You may need heavy-duty wire or bolt cutters to cut away the wire baskets on large trees. Burlap may be either plastic or a natural, biodegradable material. Often the natural burlap is treated with preservative, however, that prevents it from rotting. Remove or cut away as much of plastic burlap as possible. It's best to remove natural burlap, too, or at least cut it back so that none of it remains above or near the soil surface after planting. Otherwise, the burlap can wick moisture away from the roots.

8. **Fill the planting hole with soil until about three-quarters full and tamp it down firmly.**

9. **Holding the tree or shrub upright, fill the hole with water and let it drain. See Figure 12-12.**

Add a stake, if necessary (see the "Staking a claim" section, later in this chapter). Continue filling the hole to the trunk flare. Add an inch or two more soil to the planting hole, if the tree settles after watering.

10. **Form a watering basin just outside the perimeter of the planting hole by making a 6-inch-high soil ring, as shown in Figure 12-13.**

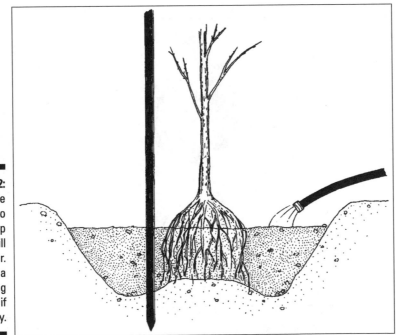

Figure 12-12:
Backfill hole nearly to the top and fill with water. Insert a planting stake, if necessary.

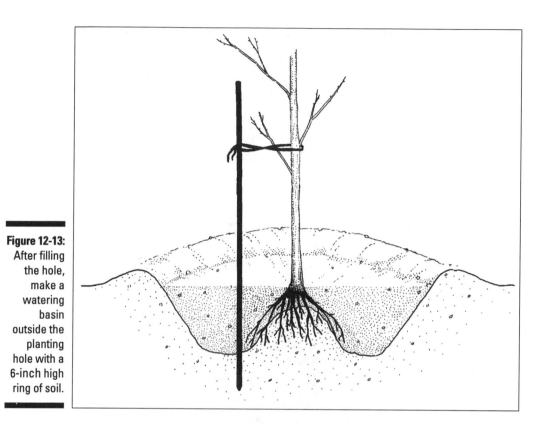

Figure 12-13:
After filling the hole, make a watering basin outside the planting hole with a 6-inch high ring of soil.

11. **Fill the ring with water and let it drain.**

Continue to water your newly planted tree or shrub for the next two growing seasons whenever the soil feels dry a few inches under the soil surface. B&B plants need a year or two to regrow their roots before making many branches. Don't water them during their dormant season.

Planting container-grown trees and shrubs

Unlike bare-root or balled and burlapped stock, container-grown trees and shrubs have all of their roots intact inside their container. Unfortunately, the plants often become root-bound with roots winding around inside the pot, becoming so tangled that they don't grow easily out into the soil after planting. Roots that circle the root ball can eventually strangle the plant. Before you plant a root-bound shrub or tree, loosen and spread the roots carefully to avoid as much damage as possible, following these steps:

1. **Water the root-bound shrub so that the soil is like mud.**

2. **Slip the plant carefully out of its pot onto the ground.**

3. **Use your fingers or a garden fork to loosen matted roots and straighten circling roots, as in Figure 12-14.**

Figure 12-14:
Tease circling roots away from the root ball with your fingers or a garden fork.

4. **If the roots are tightly wound, wash some soil from the roots to extricate them, as shown in Figure 12-15.**

5. **Prune off broken roots and those that circle the trunk.**

6. **Spread the roots as much as you can so that they drape over the mound of soil in the planting hole.**

Well-grown shrubs and trees aren't root-bound and don't need this untangling treatment. You can simply slip them out of their pots and put them right into the planting hole, doing the following:

1. **Set your prepared plant into the planting hole and adjust its height so that the trunk flare or crown is at or up to an inch above the soil surface.**

   Use a yardstick laid across the hole to check the level.

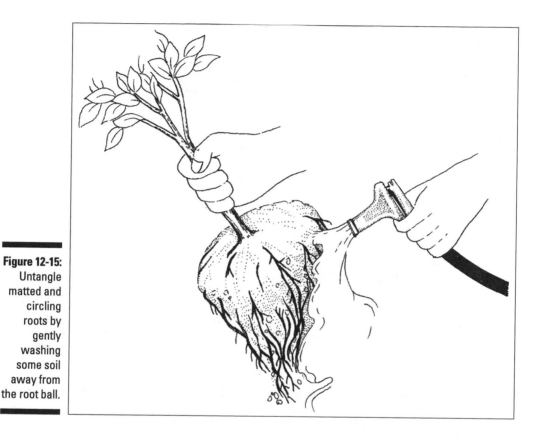

Figure 12-15:
Untangle matted and circling roots by gently washing some soil away from the root ball.

2. **Holding the plant level and straight, add soil to the hole until it's nearly full.**

3. **Press the soil firmly, but don't stomp on it, which could compact the soil. Fill the hole with water to eliminate large air pockets. Let it drain, and then finish filling the hole, mounding the soil gently away from the trunk.**

4. **Build a low ring of soil to form a shallow watering basin around the outside of the planting hole.**

   See Figure 12-16.

5. **Water the plant gently to keep the basin intact.**

   Water weekly, if you don't receive adequate rainfall, for the remainder of the growing season. The soil should feel damp, but not saturated, several inches under the surface. Too much water drives the air out of the soil and suffocates the roots.

6. **Knock down the soil ring after a few months, especially in wet climates, so that it doesn't collect more than the plant needs.**

Figure 12-16:
Plant container-grown plants with their crown or trunk flare at or slightly above the soil surface.

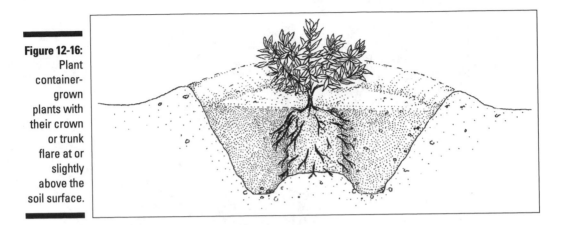

Planting hedges

Planting a row of shrubs for a hedge is similar to planting individual shrubs, with the main difference in the number and uniformity of the plants being installed. If you're working with container-grown or balled and burlapped shrubs, simply plant them in individual holes using the spacing suggested in Table 12-1.

Large bare-root shrubs can be planted in individual holes, but if plants are small and closely spaced, planting them in a trench saves you time and gets the plants off to a better start. Here's how to do it:

1. **While you dig the trench, soak the bare roots in a bucket of tepid to cool water for up to an hour.**

2. **Dig the trench the length of the hedge you intend to plant and at least twice the width of the root spread.**

3. **Determine the depth by measuring the length of the roots to the crown where the roots join the stems.**

   Leave a mound of soil down the center of the trench over which to drape the roots.

4. **Set the first plant into place at one end of the trench.**

5. **Laying a yardstick across the hole to help you determine ground level, adjust the plant so that its crown is at or slightly above ground level, as shown in Figure 12-17.**

6. **Cover the roots with enough soil to hold the plant in place and prevent them from drying out while you plant the others.**

7. **Set the next shrub in place at the correct distance from the previously planted shrub.**

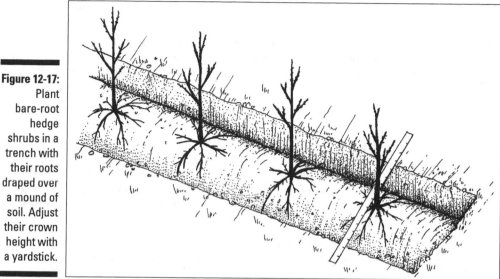

Figure 12-17:
Plant bare-root hedge shrubs in a trench with their roots draped over a mound of soil. Adjust their crown height with a yardstick.

Refer to Table 12-1 for suggested spacing.

8. **When you finish placing all the shrubs in the trench, backfill it with the soil you removed until it is nearly full.**

9. **Fill the trench gently with water to settle the soil.**

10. **Fill the trench with the remaining soil and mound it slightly away from the crown of the shrubs.**

Care for your newly planted hedge as described in the "After-Planting Protection and Care" section, later in this chapter.

Planting ground covers

Many shrubs make excellent ground covers for difficult slopes and other areas where you can't or don't want to grow grass. The best ground-covering shrubs grow no more than 2 to 3 feet tall and have a spreading habit. Some shrubs spread quickly by growing additional roots where their branches touch the ground.

Before digging holes, you must eliminate all competing vegetation from the site to be covered by shrubs. Weeds compete for light, moisture, and nutrients and are difficult to control after you plant your shrubs. Prepare for your ground cover planting well in advance of the actual planting date because ridding an area of weeds and grass takes time. The methods mostly commonly used to vanquish weeds include:

- ✔ **Hand pulling and digging:** Use this method for small areas with big weeds.

- ✔ **Rotary tilling:** These powerful machines work best on large, level areas with few rocks. After tilling, rake up the weeds and dispose. If you're tilling near established trees and shrubs, don't dig more than an inch or two deep to avoid disturbing their roots.

- ✔ **Sod stripping:** If you plan to plant over an existing lawn, you can rent a mechanical sod stripper for large areas or strip it by hand with a spade.

- ✔ **Suffocation and sun sterilization:** Mow or cut the weeds close to the ground and place a sheet of black plastic over the area. Seal the perimeter with soil to hold in the heat and place rocks or other heavy objects on the plastic to prevent the wind from picking it up. Use this method during the hottest, driest season. It may take from several weeks to several months to eliminate the weeds, depending on your climate.

- ✔ **Herbicide:** Consider chemical controls on rough terrain where none of the other methods is practical. Use a herbicide that kills all vegetation, but does not remain active in the environment for more than a few days, such as glyphosate, commonly sold as RoundUp. Plants absorb this herbicide through their leaves and, from there, the chemical travels throughout the plant, disrupting its growth and finally killing it. It may take days or even weeks to completely kill all the weeds. Follow all the label instructions carefully.

When you finish preparing the ground, cover the area with weed barrier or landscape fabric. Spread about 2 inches of mulch (see Chapter 13) over the ground or fabric, and then establish the spacing for your shrubs. See Table 12-1 in this chapter for spacing suggestions. Mark each spot where you want to plant a shrub and pull the mulch away from the digging site. Dig and plant as described in the section "Step-by-Step Guide for Planting" for the appropriate type of shrub, piling the soil on a tarp to contain the soil and keep the mulch clean. When planting on a slope, make a little terrace for each plant to hold the soil and water in place. Build a water moat around the perimeter of each hole.

After-Planting Protection and Care

After you plant your tree or shrub, it needs your continued care until its new roots grow out into the soil and its leaves and branches resume normal growth. It can take a year or two for plants to reestablish themselves after planting. Moisture, mulch, and protection from weather and other hazards are a plant's most critical needs during this period. Look at Chapter 13 for tips on how to mulch and water. Chapter 15 has more information about pests, diseases, and weather hazards. Be sure to visit Chapter 14 for tips on pruning to establish your new plant's branching structure.

Staking a Claim

I don't recommend routinely staking trees because trees that are allowed to sway naturally grow stronger and faster than those staked at planting time. Shrubs rarely need staking. If you plant where wind may blow over your new trees or large evergreen shrubs, however, well-placed stakes can support them until the roots become established.

Staking small trees and shrubs

Trees up to 3 inches in diameter and large evergreen shrubs usually need only one or two stakes. Cut sturdy stakes equal to half the height of the tree plus 18 inches. Drive the stakes 18 inches into the ground outside the root ball. If using one stake, place it on the *windward* side of the tree — the direction from which the prevailing wind blows. If using two stakes, place them opposite each other and perpendicular to the prevailing wind, as illustrated in Figure 12-18. Loop soft, wide strips of cloth or plastic loosely around the trunk and secure it near the top of the stakes. The tree should be able to sway in the wind after staking.

Check the ties frequently and remove them if they chafe or constrict the bark. Remove the ties and stakes after one year.

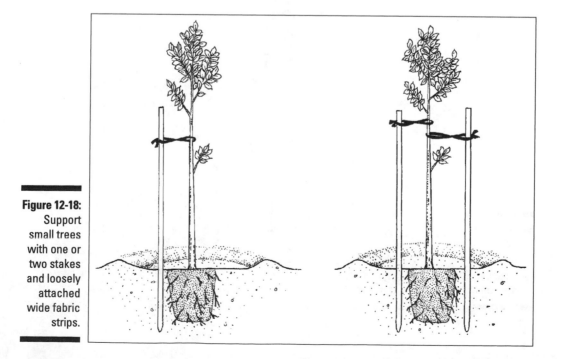

Figure 12-18: Support small trees with one or two stakes and loosely attached wide fabric strips.

Staking large trees

Trees larger than 3 inches in diameter, as well as large, dense evergreens planted in very windy sites, need support staking until they can establish strong roots. Trees of this size have very heavy root balls that may require special equipment or several people to move. If you need large trees, consider hiring professionals to deliver and plant them.

If you choose to do the planting yourself, you need three ground anchors or stakes about 18 inches long with a shallow notch cut into one side 2 to 3 inches from the top, wire cable and cable clamps to fit, and soft rubber hose. You can also buy staking kits from most tree nurseries and many garden centers. Install the wire cables as follows:

1. **Drive the anchors into the ground outside the planting hole and equidistant from each other.**

   Angle the anchors or stakes as shown in Figure 12-19, with the notched side away from the tree.

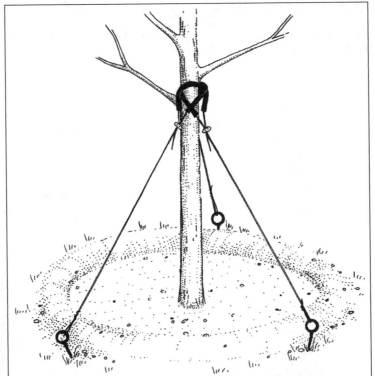

Figure 12-19: Use guy wires to support large trees.

2. **Wrap one end of a length of cable firmly around a stake.**

    Slip a cable clamp and a piece of soft hose onto the wire. Adjust the hose in a loop around the trunk securing it above a branch.

3. **Snip off excess cable and run the end of it into the cable clamp.**

    Tighten the clamp to hold it in place.

4. **Repeat Steps 2 and 3 for the remaining cables.**

    Adjust the tension so that the tree remains upright, but can sway an inch or so in any direction.

5. **Tie white or brightly colored strips of cloth or plastic on the wires as a warning.**

    Keep in mind that guy wires can be dangerous near walkways and playgrounds because they're hard to see and people may trip on them.

Leave the guy wires in place for a year, but no more than two. Check frequently to ensure that the wires are not digging into or squeezing the bark.

Using tree guards

Environmental hazards are the leading cause of premature tree death. Trunk injuries come from gnawing rodents, weather, lawnmowers and weed whips, dogs, bicycles, and vandals. The sun, too, can damage trees by heating up the bark. When this happens in the winter, the bark may split when the temperature outside the bark drops rapidly. You can avert most of this unnecessary damage by protecting the tree trunk with a *tree guard*. Tree guards wrap loosely around the trunk and prevent animals and people from hurting the tender bark. *Tree wrap*, on the other hand, is usually paper or plastic wrapped tightly around the trunk to protect it during shipping. Remove this after planting because it holds moisture against the trunk and can harbor insect pests.

You can buy plastic tree guards that wrap around the trunk or make your own from wire mesh. Both store-bought and handmade have benefits and drawbacks.

✔ **Plastic guards.** Readily available and easy to install (see Figure 12-20), light-colored plastic guards help prevent sun injury and damage from rodents, dogs, and people. They may become too tight, however, and restrict the growth of the tree. They should always have holes punched in them for air and heat exchange, but even so, they tend to hold moisture against the trunk, which can lead to decay. Some damaging insects also like to hide inside plastic guards.

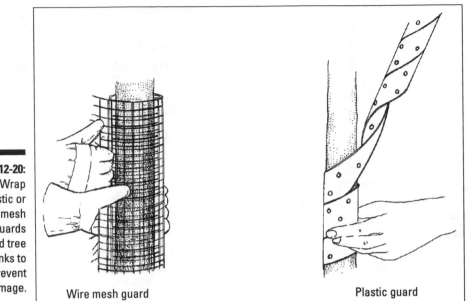

Figure 12-20:
Wrap plastic or wire mesh tree guards around tree trunks to prevent damage.

Wire mesh guard   Plastic guard

✔ **Wire mesh guards.** You have to make these yourself from half-inch wire mesh, available from hardware stores. Cut the mesh to the circumference of your tree trunk plus about 6 inches and high enough to reach above any expected snow cover or below the lowest branch. Wrap the mesh around the trunk loosely and fasten the ends with wire, as shown in Figure 12-20. Wire mesh guards allow air to circulate freely around the trunk and don't give insects a place to hide. They also prevent mechanical damage from machines, but don't protect from the sun.

Regardless of the guard you choose, you must remove it before it begins to restrict the growth of the tree trunk (also called *girdling*). Remove plastic guards after two years, but leave wire mesh in place to prevent rodent injury as long as necessary.

In some areas, deer and other large browsers eat shrubs, young trees, and the lower limbs of some mature trees. They especially favor fruit trees, azaleas and rhododendrons, arborvitae, yew, fir, dogwood, hybrid tea roses, and euonymus. If Bambi visits your yard regularly, consider caging your trees with a circle of wire fencing. Make the fence high enough or install it far enough from the plants so that the animals can't reach inside. Stake it to the ground so that they can't knock it over.

Transplanting Established Trees and Shrubs

You can move many trees with trunks up to an inch in diameter, or shrubs with several stems that, when measured together, equal about an inch. Larger trees and shrubs need a large root ball, which can weigh several hundred pounds or more — too heavy and awkward for most people to handle. Moving large shrubs and trees with trunk diameters of 2 inches or more calls for an expert with special digging equipment.

Some trees have long taproots, which grow down deeply into the soil. These trees rarely survive or flourish if moved after they become established. Shrubs and some shallow-rooted trees with horizontally growing or very fibrous root systems make the best candidates for transplanting. The best time of year to transplant trees and shrubs is the same as the best time to plant them in your area. See the "It's All in the Timing" section, earlier in this chapter.

Preparing trees and shrubs for the move

The goal in moving established plants is to disturb as few roots as possible so that the plant recovers quickly and resumes vigorous growth in its new location. Some advance preparation helps you achieve that goal. If you have six months to a year to prepare, you can prune the tree's roots to encourage fibrous roots to grow closer to the trunk within the future root ball — an especially important step when moving larger trees and shrubs. Here's how to do it:

1. **Calculate the size of the root ball.**

   For trees, measure the trunk diameter 6 inches above the trunk flare and multiply it by 12 to determine the minimum diameter of the root ball. The larger the root ball, the more roots you can preserve. For shrubs, use the outer tips of the branches, known as the *drip line,* as the outside of the root ball.

2. **Prune the roots by pushing a spade straight down into the soil around the calculated perimeter of the root ball.**

   See Figure 12-21. Do this 6 to 12 months before you intend to transplant.

The day before you dig and move your tree or shrub water it thoroughly to a depth of at least 12 inches. Let the soil drain thoroughly before digging, however, to avoid losing too much soil from the root ball.

Figure 12-21:
Prune roots
6 to 12
months
before
transplant-
ing a tree.

Digging and moving day

If possible, choose a cool, cloudy day to transplant your tree or shrub, and follow these instructions:

1. **Tie up the branches of shrubs, especially thorny ones, with burlap and twine prior to digging, as shown in Figure 12-22.**

   This makes your job easier.

2. **Cut down around the root ball with a spade in the same way as described in Steps 1 and 2 in the "Preparing trees and shrubs for the move" section.**

3. **Make a second cut about 9 inches outside the first one.**

4. **Remove the soil from the trench between the two scored circles, digging as deep as the main roots, usually 18 inches or more as shown on the left in Figure 12-23.**

   Pile the soil on a tarp to preserve as much soil as you can and to keep the digging area neat.

5. **When you reach the bottom of the root ball, excavate under it to free it from the surrounding soil, as shown on the right (refer to Figure 12-23).**

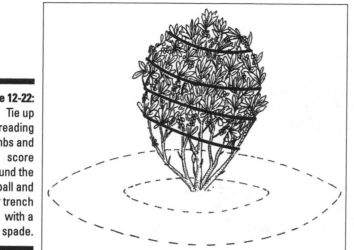

Figure 12-22:
Tie up
spreading
limbs and
score
around the
root ball and
outer trench
with a
spade.

6. **Lift the plant by the root ball onto a tarp.**

   Wrap it carefully to avoid breaking up the soil or damaging the roots. Get help lifting heavy plants out of the hole or drag them on a tarp, as shown in Figure 12–24.

7. **Replant the shrub or tree as soon as possible — preferably within a few minutes.**

   Use the method described in the "Planting balled and burlapped trees and shrubs" section, earlier in this chapter.

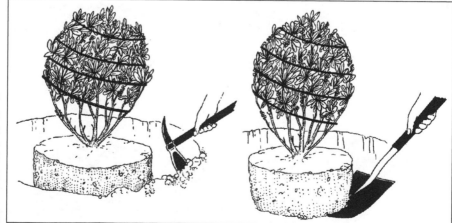

Figure 12-23:
Dig a trench
around the
shrub and
undercut
the root ball
to free it.

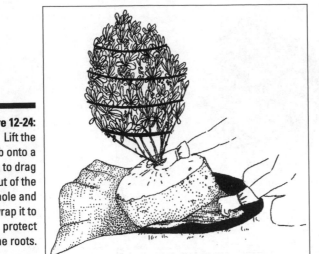

Figure 12-24:
Lift the shrub onto a tarp to drag it out of the hole and wrap it to protect the roots.

Chapter 13

Fertilizing, Watering, and Mulching

· ·

In This Chapter

▶ Recognizing nutrient deficiencies

▶ Understanding fertilizers and how to use them

▶ Determining when to water trees and shrubs

▶ Choosing and applying mulch correctly

· ·

*W*hether your tree or shrub is newly planted or a decades-old specimen, it needs adequate water, nutrients, and a healthy soil environment in order to thrive and grow. Each plant has unique requirements, however, so it can be tricky to figure out just what your particular plant needs. This chapter gives you plenty of tips on fertilizers, watering, and mulching to keep your trees and shrubs growing vigorously.

Feeding Frenzy

Trees and shrubs growing in their natural habitat get their nutrients from decaying leaves and other organic material that earthworms and other creatures work into the soil. When you plant them in unnatural places, however, such as lawns, alongside streets, in containers, or near buildings, your trees and shrubs may need more nutrients than the soil can provide. Soil around newly constructed homes and buildings and in planting strips near roads and in parking lots may be especially infertile and compacted, making plant growth difficult. Adding fertilizer to the soil, as well as providing adequate moisture, can really boost tree and shrub vigor.

Knowing when to supplement

One way you can determine when your trees and shrubs need extra nutrients is by looking carefully at their growth and vigor. When you examine them, look at the following plant parts and possible symptoms.

✔ **Leaves** smaller, lighter green, or off-color compared to others of the same species growing nearby.

✔ **New twig growth** is much shorter on established plants than in previous years or compared to others of the same species and cultivar.

Note that newly planted trees and shrubs often have shorter than normal growth for 1 or 2 years until their roots become established and that some cultivars naturally have short growth.

✔ **Dead twigs** at the ends of branches.

Before you rush out to buy fertilizer, however, pause to consider other factors that can cause symptoms that look like nutrient deficiency: Disease, insects, damaged roots and bark, drought, flooding, environmental pollution, and other stresses can also decrease the growth and vigor of your plants. See Chapter 15 to rule out these problems before deciding whether or not your plants need feeding. After you find out what's ailing your plants, additional nutrients may help trees and shrubs recover from the stress more quickly.

Take a soil test, too, before you try to guess at what your plant needs. When you know the current pH and nutrient levels of your soil, you can better judge what's needed to correct any deficiencies. Flip to Chapter 2 if you need a course on soils and pH. Good garden centers test your soil for you, sell you a do-it-yourself soil test kit, or have mailers and instructions for sending away samples to soil testing labs. Testing labs give you the most accurate information, including the amount of each nutrient and soil amendment needed for your specific soil and plants.

Testing labs can also perform a *tissue analysis* by testing leaves from your tree or shrub and determining which, if any nutrients are deficient. Tissue analysis is the most accurate way to detect a perennial plant's nutritional status and professional tree and fruit growers use it regularly. Contact a testing lab or your Agricultural Extension System agent for more information about how and when to collect the leaves for your particular plant and where to send them.

Reading the label

Plants need sixteen different elements or nutrients to stay healthy. They get three of them — oxygen, carbon, and hydrogen — from air and water, but the rest come from the soil.

The three nutrients that plants use in large quantities, called *macronutrients,* are nitrogen, phosphorus, and potassium. Fertilizer labels always list these nutrients prominently on the packages in the same order. The numbers give the percentages of each nutrient in the bag. For example, a bag labeled 10-10-10, as shown in Figure 13-1, contains 10 percent each of nitrogen; phosphoric acid, a form of phosphorus; and potash, a form of potassium. Therefore, a 20-pound bag of 10-10-10 contains 2 pounds of each nutrient. That's why a bag of 20-20-20-analysis fertilizer costs more than a bag of 10-10-10 — it contains twice as many nutrients! The rest of the stuff in the bag or bottle is inert filler that helps distribute the nutrients evenly when you apply the fertilizer.

Each of these macronutrients plays an important role in plant growth.

Figure 13-1: Fertilizer bags always list the percentage of nitrogen, phosphorus, and potassium, known as N-P-K, first on the label. Micronutrients, if added, are listed next.

- ✔ **Nitrogen (N).** This nutrient, represented by the chemical symbol N, is responsible for the healthy green color of your plants. Deciduous trees and shrubs with a nitrogen deficiency develop smaller than normal, yellowish-green leaves that drop earlier and have brighter color in the fall. Conifers also show smaller, yellowish needles. Nitrogen leaches readily out of the soil and is the nutrient most likely to become deficient.

- ✔ **Phosphorus (P).** Phosphorus (chemical symbol P) is associated with good root growth, increased disease resistance, and fruit and seed formation. If deficient, leaves and needles may remain dark green, but become purplish, especially with older foliage. The plant may produce fewer and slightly smaller leaves and fruits that drop early in the fall. Most soils between pH 5 and 7 contain enough available phosphorus.

- ✔ **Potassium (K).** This nutrient, represented by the chemical symbol K, promotes vigorous growth and disease resistance. Deficiency symptoms include yellow areas along the leaf veins and leaf edges, crinkled and rolled up leaves, and dead twigs. Conifer needles may become dark blue-green before turning yellow to reddish-brown. Florida palms are especially prone to deficiency of this nutrient. Their leaves develop yellow to orange spots on the oldest foliage first and then the leaf edges turn brown and die. Most soils contain enough potassium for woody trees and shrubs, however.

Plants need other nutrients, too, such as calcium, magnesium, and sulfur, the three *secondary nutrients*. In areas of high rainfall, where the soil tends to be acidic, adding calcium and magnesium in the form of lime raises the pH closer to neutral. In areas of low rainfall, the soil tends to be alkaline. Adding sulfur lowers the pH. I don't recommend changing the soil pH for most trees and shrubs. Instead, plant trees and shrubs that are adapted to the existing soil.

Iron, manganese, copper, boron, molybdenum, chlorine, and zinc are the *micronutrients,* which plants need only in very small quantities for good health. Most soils contain enough of these nutrients for plant growth, but they sometimes become deficient because the soil pH makes them unavailable. When soils are too acidic or too alkaline, the nutrients change into chemical forms that plant roots cannot absorb. Some fertilizers contain some of these additional nutrients. The most common additives include iron, zinc, and manganese. These elements are usually *chelated,* or chemically attached to other nutrients, so that plants can absorb them better. A soil test or tissue analysis is the best way to determine if these nutrients are deficient.

Choosing fertilizers

Plant fertilizers come in different forms and each benefits your trees and shrubs in different ways. The two basic kinds of fertilizers are *synthetic* and *organic.* Organic fertilizers come from plant, animal, and rock sources, such as blood meal, alfalfa meal, fish emulsion, and manure. Soil organisms break down the material into nutrients that plants can use. Although organic fertilizers usually contain significant amounts of only one of the major nutrients, such as phosphorus in bone meal, they often have trace amounts of many other beneficial nutrients. In addition, some add organic material that improves soil structure. The nutrients become available more quickly in warm weather when soil organisms are most active. As a general rule, organic fertilizers release about half their nutrients in the first season.

Synthetic fertilizers are made from chemicals that don't come directly from plant, animal, and rock sources. They usually cost less to buy than organic fertilizers, but they release their nutrients quickly and do nothing to build the health of the soil and organisms that live in it. The kind that you choose depends on your needs and those of your plants. Fertilizers also come in different forms, such as liquid or granular. The most common fertilizer forms for tree and shrubs include the following.

- ✔ **Granular:** These commonly available and most widely used fertilizers come in boxes or bags as 10-10-10, rose food, and the like. They dissolve in moist soil, some quickly and some over a period of time. Apply these with a lawn fertilizer spreader or by hand.

- ✔ **Liquid:** These fertilizers may come ready-to-use or in concentrated form. Although usually more expensive than dry fertilizers, they are useful for injecting directly into the soil through special applicators and for adding to irrigation systems.

- ✔ **Spikes:** Easy-to-use spikes made of compressed granular fertilizer are available in many formulations for specific plants, such as evergreens, roses, and fruit trees. You place them into holes in the ground throughout a tree's root zone. They are expensive compared to granular fertilizers, however, and tend to concentrate all the nutrients in a small area around the spike.

- ✔ **Slow-release:** These fertilizers release nutrients at specific rates in specific conditions over an extended period of time. For example, Osmocote brand fertilizers release nutrients in response to soil moisture. Other types rely on soil microorganisms to slowly release their nutrients. Use slow-release fertilizers especially for plants growing in tubs or planters.

- ✔ **Foliar:** Spray these liquid fertilizers directly on a plant's leaves for a fast transfer of nutrients. Don't apply foliar fertilizers in hot weather, though, because they can damage heat-stressed leaves. Fertilizer sprayed on the foliage gives a fast nutrient boost, but doesn't give a long-lasting effect.

Using fertilizers

Tree and shrub roots grow most actively in the early spring and autumn and that's when they need available nutrients the most. Apply fertilizer during these months and avoid fertilizing from midsummer until after the plants become dormant in midautumn. Extra nutrients in the late summer can stimulate growth that will be less cold hardy than shoots that grew in the spring.

Scattering granular fertilizer over the root zone of trees and shrubs is the easiest and most effective method of applying nutrients to tree and shrub roots. To fertilize a tree using the scatter method, follow these steps.

1. **Calculate the size of the root zone in square feet.**

   Tree roots usually spread at least twice as far as the edge of the leaves. So, a tree that measures 10 feet from the trunk to the edge of the end of the longest branch has a root zone that extends 20 feet from the trunk. To calculate the root zone area, use this formula: 3.14 × (root radius) × (root radius). In this case, 3.14 × 20 × 20 = 1,256 square feet.

2. **Determine the amount of fertilizer needed.**

   Using a 20-pound bag of 10-10-10 fertilizer as an example, you know that the bag contains 2 pounds each of nitrogen, phosphorus, and potassium (ten percent of 20 pounds equals 2). If your soil test indicates that you need 1 pound of nitrogen per 1000 square feet, then you know that your 20-pound bag contains enough nitrogen to cover 2,000 square feet or .01 pounds per square foot. Therefore, you only need 12½ pounds of 10-10-10 to cover 1,256 square feet.

3. **Calibrate your lawn fertilizer spreader.**

   Follow the instructions on the fertilizer bag for calculating the correct setting on your spreader, if possible. You can also calibrate your spreader by trial and error using a smooth, dry, clean surface, such as a driveway or garage floor, where you can mark out a 100 square foot area (10 feet × 10 feet). Determine the amount of fertilizer needed to cover 100 square feet by dividing the amount needed for 1000 square feet by 10. For example, 20 pounds divided by 10 equals 2 pounds. Put 2 pounds of fertilizer in the spreader and apply it over the marked area. Adjust the spreader until you can cover the area evenly with the correct amount of fertilizer, sweeping up and reusing the sample between trials.

4. **Mark the root zone of the tree.**

   Using a hose or stakes in the ground, mark the outside boundary of the root zone of the tree you intend to fertilize, in this case, a circle 40 feet from the trunk of the tree. Now mark the inner boundary of the zone 3 to 4 feet from the trunk. Don't apply fertilizer close to the trunk.

5. **Apply the fertilizer.**

   When the grass is dry, evenly distribute the fertilizer throughout the marked root zone, as shown in Figure 13-2. Applying fertilizer to wet grass can burn its leaves. After applying the fertilizer, water the soil thoroughly to a depth of 12 to 18 inches to wash the nutrients into the soil.

As a rule, it's safe to apply up to 1 pound of nitrogen fertilizer per 1000 square feet per application. More than that could damage plant roots. Apply nitrogen once a year, if needed, and phosphorus and potassium only once every 3 to 5 years unless a soil test indicates otherwise (see the "Knowing when to supplement" section, earlier in this chapter). If you regularly apply lawn fertilizer around your trees, they probably don't need any supplemental feeding.

When you fertilize your lawn, do not use "weed and feed" products that contain herbicides or weed killers near tree and shrub roots. Many trees and shrubs are sensitive to these toxic chemicals and can decline in health from repeated exposure. Fertilizers can damage plants, too, if used incorrectly. Applying too much leads to *fertilizer burn*, when plant tissues, such as the leaves or roots, die. Using more fertilizer than the plants really need is also bad for the environment. Synthetic fertilizers, especially nitrogen, leach through the soil quickly and can cause water pollution. Organic fertilizers, such as manure, can also pollute the environment if applied to frozen soil or near water sources.

Figure 13-2:
Scatter fertilizer evenly over the root zone of a tree, which extends at least twice as far from the trunk as the edge of the tree canopy.

Still Waters Run Deep

Roots need adequate moisture to grow, but give them too much and they drown. Soil has spaces between its particles that hold either air or water —

plant roots need a balance of both. Newly planted shrubs and trees need extra water during their first two growing seasons while they adjust and regrow their lost roots.

I can't give you exact recommendations about the amount of water to give your trees or shrubs nor can I tell you how often to water. Each situation is unique and depends on a number of factors. When you're deciding whether or not to water, consider these circumstances:

- ✔ **Weather:** Plants use more water in hot, dry weather, especially in sunny situations. Wind also dries the soil and causes plants to take up more water. Cool, rainy weather may give the plants as much moisture as they need without your help.

- ✔ **Season of the year:** Trees and shrubs planted just prior to the rainy season need less frequent watering than those planted during times of drought. Actively growing plants need regular watering or rainfall, but dormant plants need only a little, because they take up minimal moisture from the soil during the cold winter months.

- ✔ **Soil:** Clay soils and those with an impenetrable crust below the surface may hold plenty of water and be very slow to drain. Sandy soil, on the other hand, drains so quickly that you must water frequently.

- ✔ **Tree or shrub species:** All newly planted trees and shrubs need extra water, but some species tolerate more drought or flooding as they become established in their second growing season. Some plants also use more water than others, especially those with lots of soft new leaves and stems. Adjust your watering habits to suit your individual plant's needs. See Parts II and III for detailed information about plants' needs.

The best way to determine if your plant needs water is to dig down about 6 to 10 inches with a shovel within the drip line of established trees and feel the soil. If it feels dry, water the plant until the soil is moist to a depth of at least 6 to 8 inches. For newly planted shrubs and trees, push a paint stick or other piece of narrow, untreated wood into the soil of the rootball and leave it in place for an hour. When you pull it up, water the soil if the stick feels dry. Be sure that the rootball and not just the surrounding soil is moist.

 How you water matters just as much as when you water. The water must penetrate the soil deeply to reach the roots at the bottom of the planting hole. If you water only the top few inches of soil, you encourage roots to grow close to the surface. Shallow-rooted trees and shrubs suffer more from droughts and soil compaction than deeply rooted plants. Trees with shallow roots can also become a liability because they blow over more easily in high winds.

Let the water trickle slowly so that the soil can absorb it. Turn down the hose if the water puddles to the point of runoff. Check the depth of water penetration again with either a digging or stick method. Let the soil dry somewhat between waterings. It should still feel slightly moist, but not wet, before you water again. Too much water in the soil can suffocate the roots and actually prevent them from taking up water, resulting in wilted or yellowing foliage and root diseases.

Thank You Very Mulch

Mulch is something you put on the ground to control weeds, conserve moisture, moderate soil temperature, and make the yard look good. You can use *inorganic mulch,* such as stones, or *organic mulch,* like shredded bark, depending on where you live, where you're putting the mulch, and the landscape look you want to achieve. *Organic mulch* eventually decomposes into the soil, but *inorganic mulch* stays inert for a long, long time.

It doesn't sound very glamorous, but spreading mulch around the yard is one of the most important things you can do for your trees' and shrubs' health. Mulch helps trees and shrubs grow healthier in several different ways:

- ✔ **Reduces weed and grass competition.** Trees and shrubs grow faster and larger when they don't have to compete for water and nutrients.

- ✔ **Maintains consistent soil climate.** Mulch prevents moisture from evaporating and keeps the soil an even temperature.

- ✔ **Improves soil environment.** Organic mulches decay and contribute organic material and nutrients to the soil and promotes the growth of earthworms and other beneficial organisms.

- ✔ **Prevents mechanical damage.** Mulch eliminates the need to mow or use a weed whip near easily damaged trunks and stems. Mechanical damage is a leading cause of tree death (see Chapter 15). Mulch also helps prevent soil compaction.

Inorganic mulches

Mulches that don't readily decay or break down in the environment are called *inorganic.* Use inorganic mulch around buildings in areas where damaging termites and carpenter ants are a problem. They include stone, gravel, sand, and landscape fabric. Each material has its own benefits and drawbacks.

- ✔ **Stone and gravel.** Use these around buildings where you need low-maintenance, fireproof, and insect resistant materials. They don't add nutrients or organic material to the soil. Choose colors and textures that complement your landscape.

- ✔ **Sand.** It's fireproof, but may attract ants and cats and weed seeds looking for a place to germinate. Use in climates where sandy landscapes naturally occur, or in specialty gardens. Rake frequently to keep it looking fresh.

✔ **Landscape fabrics.** These materials allow water and air to pass through and are often used underneath gravel or organic mulches and on slopes to help prevent erosion. Unfortunately, they prevent beneficial organic material from reaching the soil.

I need to say a word about plastics — don't. Plastic mulch works great to eliminate weeds because it prevents water from reaching the soil and it helps the sun's energy heat the soil to root-killing temperatures. The same characteristics that make plastic mulch so effective at controlling weeds, however, makes it deadly for trees and shrubs, too. Save the plastic for the vegetable garden and for eliminating grass and weeds when preparing the soil for planting. If you must use something under your gravel or bark mulch to prevent weeds, use landscape fabric instead.

Organic mulches

Mulch that decays and adds organic matter and nutrients to the soil is called *organic* or *fertile mulch*. Mulches decay at different rates, depending on the size and composition of the pieces and the climate. Some last a single season or less, while others remain effective for a year or more. The most commonly available organic mulches fit into several categories.

✔ **Bark.** The most long-lasting organic mulch, bark is available either shredded or in chunks. Large bark chunks generally last longer than finely shredded bark. Look for bags labeled "bark" to get the highest percentage of actual bark and longest landscape life.

✔ **Wood chips and shavings:** These inexpensive materials may be dyed to mimic bark. They decay faster than bark, however, and use up nitrogen in the soil. You may need to apply fertilizer to replace the nitrogen.

✔ **Shredded leaves and pine needles:** These materials decay quickly, but add valuable nutrients and organic matter to the soil. Whole leaves may mat down and prevent water from easily reaching the soil, so it's best to shred them before using. Use pine needles and shredded oak leaves around acidic-soil-loving trees and shrubs.

✔ **Seed hulls:** Locally available cottonseed, buckwheat, cocoa bean, peanut hulls, and others make good mulch, but may need frequent replenishing. Lightweight materials blow around in the wind and may wash away in heavy rain.

✔ **Lawn clippings:** It decomposes quickly, but it's usually free. Use dried clippings to prevent matting, which can keep water from penetrating. Don't use clippings from lawns that have been treated with pesticides or weed-and-feed fertilizers.

Not all organic materials make good mulches. Avoid peat moss because it repels water when it dries. Manure, straw, and hay often contain weed seeds — compost them before applying around established plantings.

Organic mulches can go "sour" and actually harm trees and shrubs. Piles of wet, densely packed mulch, such as sawdust, shredded bark, and grass clippings, can heat up and begin to decay. Sour mulch smells like vinegar, ammonia, sulfur, or silage and is very acidic. It can burn any plant part it contacts. Aerate mulch piles by turning them with a garden fork to prevent souring.

Some fresh mulches made from toxic trees can harm sensitive plants. Avoid mulch made from eucalyptus sawdust and leaves, redwood and cedar sawdust, and Douglas fir and spruce bark as well as any mulch containing sawdust from pressure-treated lumber or any portion of walnut trees.

Mulching methods

Mulch trees and shrubs when you first plant them and renew or replace the mulch as needed. The traditional time to replace old mulch is midspring, after the soil has begun to warm. Removing and replacing old mulch is especially important around insect- and disease-prone trees and shrubs because that's where some insects, such as plum curculio, and disease spores, such as apple scab and leaf spot, hang out. Simply rake up the old mulch and compost or dispose of it and put down a fresh layer.

Where and how you place the mulch depends on several factors:

- **Young trees:** Mulch an area at least 3 feet in diameter around the trunk or to the outside of the planting hole, whichever is larger.
- **Mature trees:** Spread mulch from the trunk to the drip line, if possible, for the most benefit. At a minimum, extend mulch to at least the turning radius of your lawn mower.
- **Specimen shrub:** Mulch to the drip line.
- **Group of shrubs:** Mulch them as a group to visually tie them together and make your maintenance tasks easier. Cover all the ground out to the drip line of the outermost shrubs.

Apply loose organic mulches, such as shredded bark, about 2 to 4 inches deep. Stone, gravel, and sand spread over landscape fabric only needs to be an inch or two deep.

It's very important that you don't pile mulch against the trunks and stems of your trees and shrubs. Mulch holds moisture against the bark and gives damaging insects and rodents a place to hide. Properly applied, mulch should resemble a flattened doughnut with the tree trunk or shrub at the center of the hole. Incorrectly mulched trees resemble volcanoes with their trunks erupting from cones of mulch.

Follow these steps to mulch trees and shrubs correctly.

1. **Remove the weeds or grass from a circle around the tree.**

   The diameter of the circle depends on the turning radius of your lawnmower and the *drip line* or outer branch perimeter of the tree.

2. **Lay landscape fabric, if you desire.**

   Cut it a few inches smaller than the diameter of the circle and keep it at least 6 inches away from the tree trunk.

3. **Cover the circle with mulch.**

   Rake it into a flattened doughnut shape to the outer edge of the circle. Rake the mulch 6 inches away from the tree trunk.

Chapter 14

Pruning 101

· ·

In This Chapter

▶ Knowing when, why, and what to prune

▶ Mastering the basic techniques

▶ Using the tools of the trade

▶ Pruning plants with special needs

· ·

*I*f the art and science of shaping and training trees and shrubs looks like alchemy to you, you've come to right chapter. Pruning isn't so mysterious after you get familiar with a few terms, basic techniques, and tools. The trick is in knowing where to cut, how to do it, and when to call in a pro.

Pruning for a Reason

I'm not sure which causes more plant damage — random acts of pruning or outright neglect. If you're someone who gets the urge to cut something, anything, when you get a pair of clippers in your hand, pause here for a minute before you head out into your yard. Have a pruning goal in mind — a reason why you want to snip off a limb! Like checking a map before setting out into unfamiliar territory, knowing your destination and the best route before pruning will give you better results.

Plants change and grow constantly and that's why they need pruning. You usually prune trees and shrubs for the following reasons:

✔ **Establishing a healthy frame.** Selecting well-placed, healthy limbs when plants are young prevents major corrective surgery as they mature.

✔ **Controlling growth and rejuvenating overgrown shrubs.** Keeping trees and shrubs within bounds, shaping them, and helping them start over when they get too big and tangled is a regular part of yard maintenance.

✓ **Increasing flowers and fruit.** Removing spent flowers after they bloom encourages the plant to make more flowers. Some fruiting trees and shrubs produce more and better quality fruit when pruned properly.

✓ **Removing dead, diseased, and damaged wood.** These three "D"s keep trees and shrubs healthy and safe by removing infected and injured limbs before the problems spread or the branches become a hazard.

As a rule, the less you prune your trees and shrubs the better, because every time you cut into the bark you risk introducing disease or attracting damaging insects. Your well-intentioned cuts may also have unintended consequences, including unsightly or weakened growth and delayed or decreased flowering. Many plants grow without ever needing pruning. Plants for special purposes, such as fruit trees, formal hedges, topiary, and some flowering shrubs are the exceptions.

Parts is Parts

When you know a little about how plants grow, you can make better pruning decisions. The time of year, size and location of the pruning cut, and the plant species all affect how trees and shrubs respond to your surgery.

Oh, shoot

Plants produce hormones that control how they grow. Many of those growth-regulating hormones occur in the *apical buds* or *tip buds* at the ends of branches. The hormones in these buds stimulate shoot growth and suppress the growth of buds lower down on the stem, which are called *dormant shoot buds*. When you cut off the tip bud, the dormant buds can begin growing and producing hormones themselves. Often, several dormant buds sprout into vigorous shoots, competing to become the new dominant tip bud. Pruning just before growth begins in the spring results in the most vigorous sprouting. Pruning in early to mid-summer, when most shoot growth has stopped, yields the least amount of new growth.

Some tree and shrub species grow undesirable *suckers* and *water sprouts,* which are vigorous shoots that grow from dormant buds, usually in response to pruning or damage. See Figure 14-1. Suckers grow from the base of the tree near or below the soil line. Water sprouts grow vertically from horizontal limbs or close to a pruning cut.

Figure 14-1:
Suckers (left) and water sprouts (right) grow vigorously upright in response to pruning or damage.

Budding genius

The angle at which a branch grows also affects bud growth. Those with 45° to 60° *crotch angles*, where the limb joins the trunk, tend to develop more flower buds — an important factor when you want to maximize flowering or fruiting.

Trees and shrubs also grow different kinds of buds — *shoot buds* and *flower buds*. New leaves and twigs come from shoot buds. These buds are usually covered with small overlapping scales that protect them. Each year, when the tip bud expands into a shoot, the scales fall off and leave little scars around the twig, as shown in Figure 14-2. Rings of scars separate each year's growth. You can determine how much a branch grew by measuring the distance between scar rings.

Flower buds only produce flowers. Some flower buds grow on new shoots and open in the same year that they developed, which is called *blooming on new wood*. Other flower buds develop one year, but don't open until the next year. These plants are referred to as *blooming on old wood*. Usually, you can tell which kind of plant you have by looking at where the flowers are located on the branches. Flowers appear on the branch tips of plants that bloom on the current year's growth, as shown on the left in Figure 14-3. Flowers that bloom from previous year's buds usually do so further down the branch, as shown on the right. Some early bloomers, however, such as lilacs and rhododendrons, produce their flowers on the branch tips.

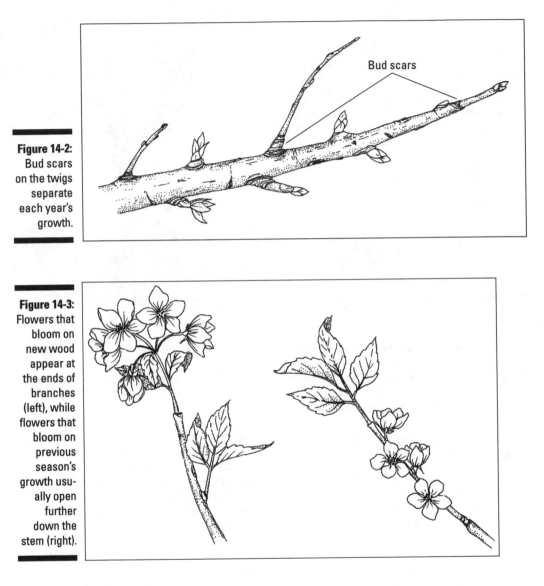

Figure 14-2:
Bud scars on the twigs separate each year's growth.

Figure 14-3:
Flowers that bloom on new wood appear at the ends of branches (left), while flowers that bloom on previous season's growth usually open further down the stem (right).

Most trees and shrubs are one kind or the other, but some plants flower on both kinds of wood. Plants that bloom on new wood usually do so in the summer or fall, while those that flower on old wood are typically spring bloomers. The different types are pruned at different times of the year to maximize flowering (see the "Pruning Techniques for Every Situation" section, later in this chapter, for the lowdown).

Ring around the collar

The *branch collar* and *branch bark ridge* occur where a branch attaches to the tree trunk or a twig meets a limb. The branch collar is located at the base of the branch, while the branch bark ridge is usually a bulge or a series of raised rings in the crotch between the limb and trunk or two limbs. Scar tissue develops around the branch collar and bark ridge, so you don't want to remove this part of the limb when pruning — never cut a branch flush with the trunk. Leaving a stub also delays healing, which increases the plant's exposure to pests and diseases. The best pruning cut is made just outside this zone (see Figure 14-4).

When a limb dies or is removed from a woody plant, the tree or shrub heals itself by forming a barrier around the damaged area. The barrier that shows on the outside of the tree is called a *callus*, as shown in Figure 14-5. A healthy callus forms a complete ring around the wound. If the branch bark ridge or branch collar is damaged, the wound may form an incomplete or unhealthy callus, resulting in further decay or damage to the tree.

Figure 14-4:
Make pruning cuts just outside the branch bark ridge in the crotch and branch collar under the limb.

Figure 14-5: A complete callus forms around a healthy pruning cut (left). Improper cuts can lead to an incomplete callus and wood decay (right).

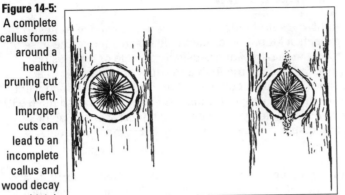

Tools of the Trade

For most pruning jobs, you need only a few basic tools. It pays to buy the best tools that you can afford because quality tools stay sharp longer, are more comfortable to use, cause less plant damage, and should last for many, many years. These five tools, shown in Figure 14-6, will get you through pruning jobs that you can safely tackle without a professional. If your pruning job is bigger than you can safely handle, see the "Who ya gonna call?" section, later in this chapter. For tips on sharpening your tools, see "Maintaining tools" section.

✔ **Hand pruners.** Use these for cutting limbs up to ¾ inch in diameter. Professionals prefer bypass pruners that have curved blades and a scissors-like action. Bypass pruners make a cleaner cut than anvil pruners, which can crush the stems between the blade and the "anvil" or bar that the blade presses against. Sharp anvil pruners work well for removing dead flowers and limbs under ½ inch in diameter, but may twist and cause stem damage on larger branches or when dull. Price is usually a good indicator of tool quality — light duty bypass and anvil pruners generally cost $5 to $15, while heavy duty professional models cost $20 to $40. Left-handed pruners are available.

Snipping small twigs and flowers with a pair of hand pruners isn't much more dangerous than using a pair of scissors, but I wear leather gloves and safety goggles when I prune, anyway. This basic equipment, which keeps my hands and eyes safe from accidental cuts, thorns, and sharp twigs, has paid off many times.

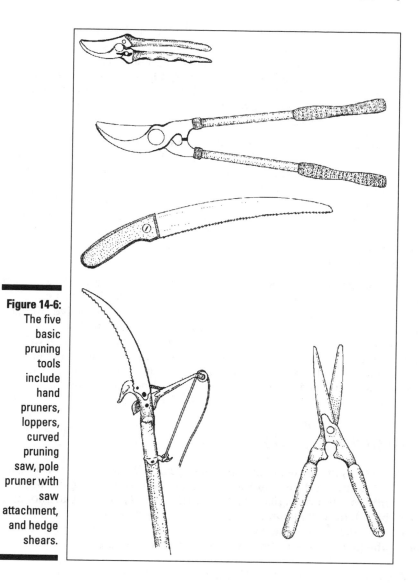

Figure 14-6:
The five basic pruning tools include hand pruners, loppers, curved pruning saw, pole pruner with saw attachment, and hedge shears.

✔ **Loppers.** For cuts between ¾-inch and 1½-inches in diameter or limbs that are just out of arm's reach, choose a bypass-type lopper (rhymes with copper) with curved blades. Lightweight aluminum or fiberglass handles with cushioned grips and a rubber stop between the handles make this tool more comfortable to use. Some have gears or compound action (more than one pivot point) that reduces the amount of strength needed to make heavy-duty cuts. Loppers also come in anvil style, but these have the same drawbacks as the anvil hand pruners. Expect to pay $25 to $40 for high quality, bypass loppers with compound action and cushioned grips.

✔ **Pruning saw.** Choose one with a curved 8- to 12-inch blade and tri-edge teeth. Each tooth of these so-called Japanese blades is sharpened on three angles or bevels for smooth, fast cutting. These saws cut as you pull them toward you and make quick work of limbs up to 4 inches in diameter. Saws that fold into their handle must lock securely open when in use to prevent injury to the operator. A folding saw with a Japanese blade costs $15 to $30.

✔ **Pole pruner.** When you need to make a pruning cut near the top of an apple tree, a long-handled pole pruner is the tool to reach for. Aluminum or fiberglass telescoping handles extend up to 14 feet. A hook at the top holds the pruner in place while the blade slices through limbs up to 1-inch in diameter. A pruning saw attachment for cutting larger limbs comes in handy and is usually included with the pruner. The best quality pole pruners operate with a chain-and-gear mechanism and generally cost over $50. Light duty pole pruners, adequate for most home users, range from $25 to $40.

✔ **Hedge shears.** The quiet swish and snick of manual shears won't disturb the tranquility of the day nor make irreversible gouges in your hedge, seemingly of their own volition the way that gas-powered hedge clippers can. Straight blades make the smoothest cuts, but look for those with a notch or serration near the base of a blade for snipping stems up to ½-inch in diameter. Choose lightweight handles that are long enough to allow you to comfortably reach all parts of your hedge. Prices range from under $20 to $40, depending on manufacturer and features.

Maintaining tools

Clean, sharp tools make clean, healthy pruning cuts. Disease travels from one tree or shrub to the next on your tools, so to prevent transferring diseases, clean the blades (after each plant that you prune) with isopropyl alcohol or a mild 1:10 bleach to water solution between plants. Rinse and dry the blades after each use and rub them lightly with household oil before storing them. Lubricate the pivot points where the two handles join regularly.

Dull blades crush plant tissue, making healing more difficult and providing a greater opportunity for insects and diseases to move in. Sharp blades are also safer to use because they cut instead of slip or twist when you apply pressure. Keep your tool blades sharp by rubbing them on an oilstone or whetstone, which are available from any hardware store. Here's how to get a good sharp edge.

1. **Take your pruners or loppers apart, if possible.**

   If not possible, use a medium-fine flat file or small handheld whetstone to sharpen the blades.

2. **Hold the edge of the blade against a whetstone (or flat file) at a 45° angle or existing bevel with the sharp edge away from your body.**

   The *bevel* is the slope between the flat blade and the sharp edge. It is important to maintain the angle of this slope.

3. **Slide the blade gently along the stone away from your body, as shown in Figure 14-7, maintaining the angle.**

   Lift the blade between strokes. Sharpen only the beveled side of a blade unless it is beveled on both sides. Wear leather gloves and handle the sharp blade carefully to avoid cuts.

Take pruning saws to a professional saw sharpener. Check the Yellow Pages in your telephone directory or ask for a recommendation at a nursery, hardware store, or landscape service.

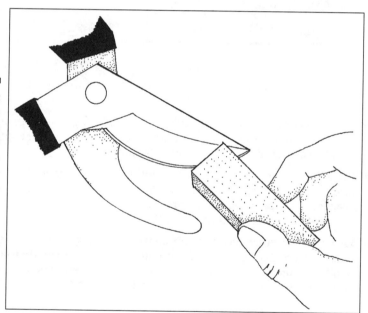

Figure 14-7: Hold the sharp edge of the blade against a whetstone and, maintaining the bevel angle, slide the blade away from you to sharpen it.

Who ya gonna call?

As the size of the limb and power of the equipment increase, so does the hazard. Getting hit by falling branches, sustaining cuts from a saw blade, or tumbling off a ladder or out of a tree can cause serious injury. Call a professional arborist (see the "Consulting the professionals" sidebar) when the pruning job involves the following feats:

Consulting the professionals

Qualified arborists should have proof of insurance, a list of references (check them), and certification from a professional organization. Avoid tree companies that offer tree topping (see the "Topping hurts trees" sidebar) or that climb trees with spikes, unless the tree is being removed. The largest arborist organizations and their addresses follow.

✔ **The International Society of Arboriculture,** P.O. Box 3129, Champaign, Illinois 61826, phone 217-355-9411, or web site at www.ag.uiuc.edu/%&Eisa/.

✔ **The American Society of Consulting Arborists,** write to them at 15245 Shady Grove Road, Suite 130, Rockville, MD 20850, phone: 301-947-0483, or web site at www.asca-consultants.org/.

✔ **National Arborist Association,** Inc., P.O. Box 1094, Amherst, NH 03031-1094, phone: (603) 673-3311, or web at www.natlarb.com/.

✔ **Limbs are too high to reach from the ground.** If you can't cut a branch from the ground with a pole pruner, don't climb the tree or go up a ladder with a saw.

✔ **Branches or trees are near utility wires.** A falling limb or pruning equipment that touches an electric utility wire can kill you (see Figure 14-8). Don't risk your life: Call the utility company.

✔ **Branches or trees could fall on building or into street.** Big, heavy branches can damage roofs or block traffic when they fall. Leaning, cracked, and damaged trunks are unstable and dangerous to remove. Arborists can take them down safely.

✔ **Large cuts require power equipment.** Removing big branches can cause severe damage to a tree and must be done correctly to ensure tree health. Chain saws are dangerous in inexperienced hands and should never be used above chest height, while on a ladder, or when in a tree.

If you're unsure about how to proceed, let an experienced arborist suggest strategies for removing, saving, or improving the health of your trees. Trained professionals know which limbs to cut and why.

Figure 14-8:
Call a professional arborist or utility company to prune trees near utility wires to avoid injury from electricity.

Topping hurts trees

Cutting back large tree branches to stubs or small branches is called *topping* or *tipping*. When a tree becomes too tall or large for the available space, inexperienced pruners may consider reducing the size of the tree's crown by topping. Unfortunately, topping trees creates more problems for you and the tree.

When you cut major branches back to stubs, the tree can't heal properly and may begin to decay. Trees also respond to topping by growing many vigorous, weakly attached shoots near the pruning cut. As the shoots become larger with age, they split easily from the trunk, damaging the tree and causing hazards as they fall. Topped trees become an ugly liability instead of an asset to your property because their natural branching habit is destroyed.

If the tree height must be reduced, a professional arborist can remove branches to the branch collar or to a limb that's at least one-third of its diameter. See "Hiring a professional" in this chapter for professional arborists.

Pruning Techniques for Every Situation

Proper pruning should always retain the plant's natural form and reduce hazards, not create them. The Golden Rule of pruning is "good pruning doesn't show."

Pruning involves only two basic kinds of cuts — heading and thinning. A *thinning cut* removes a branch back to its origin or to a lateral branch that's at least one-third of the removed limb's diameter. The simplest thinning method is rubbing off an undesirable bud. Other thinning cuts, shown in Figure 14-9, leave the pruned plant with a natural appearance and a more open branching structure. Plants usually don't respond to proper thinning by producing vigorous new growth.

Heading cuts, shown in Figure 14-9, remove shoots or branches back to stubs, buds, or lateral branches less than one-third the removed limb's diameter. Plants respond to heading cuts by producing vigorous new growth from buds growing below the cut. When you shear a hedge, you are removing the tips of the twigs, resulting in denser growth. *Deadheading*, which results in increased flowering, involves pinching or snipping off the flower stems as soon as flowering finishes, but leaving any developing buds on the plant, as shown in Figure 14-10.

Figure 14-9:
Thinning cuts remove a limb to its point of attachment or to a large lateral branch. Heading cuts remove shoots back to buds; stubs; or small, lateral branches.

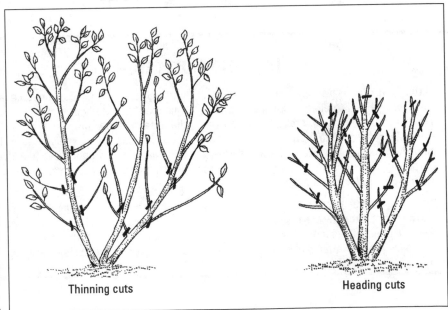

Thinning cuts

Heading cuts

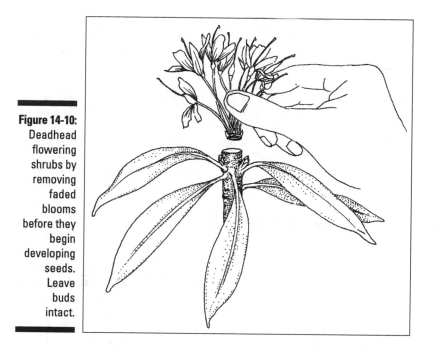

Figure 14-10:
Deadhead
flowering
shrubs by
removing
faded
blooms
before they
begin
developing
seeds.
Leave
buds
intact.

When you make a thinning pruning cut, position the blade so that it cuts upward into the wood and the hook is just outside the branch bark ridge. Make heading cuts about ¼-inch above the uppermost bud or lateral branch at a 45° angle and slope it away from the bud, as shown in Figure 14-11.

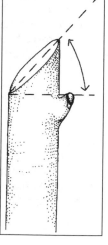

Figure 14-11:
Make
heading
cuts ¼-inch
above and
sloped away
from the
uppermost
bud at a
45° angle.

Using just heading and thinning pruning cuts, you can shape and maintain your trees and shrubs to keep them healthy, productive, attractive, and safe. The rest of pruning is mostly a matter of timing and techniques that are specific to different groups of plants.

 I need to debunk a myth about what to do after pruning. People used to believe that painting or smearing tar over pruning wounds helped trees heal more quickly. Actually, the opposite is true. Paint and tar slow the healing process and can harm the tree by sealing in moisture and disease organisms. The exceptions to this rule are oaks and elms, which benefit from wound dressing that helps seal out oak wilt and Dutch elm disease-carrying beetles.

Shaping flowering shrubs

To get the most flowers from your trees and shrubs, it helps to know whether they bloom from buds that grew in the previous year or from buds grown in the current season on new wood. (See the "Budding genius" section, earlier in this chapter, for a complete overview.) The best time of year to prune flowering shrubs depends on whether they bloom on old or new wood.

- **Bloom on the current season's wood.** To encourage lots of vigorous new growth and flowers, prune them in late winter just before they begin growing.

- **Bloom from previous year's buds.** Prune these shrubs right after they finish blooming to give them time to develop new flower buds for next year.

Removing flowers after they finish blooming (called "deadheading" — see the "Budding genius" section, earlier in this chapter) helps increase flowering later. When plants don't have to spend their energy developing seeds, they can use their resources to grow more roots, stems, and flower buds. Roses bloom more prolifically and grow stronger shoots when you deadhead them back to a healthy leaf with 5- to 7-leaflets, as shown in Figure 14-12. Use hand pruners to snip the stem at a 45° angle about ¼-inch above the leaf. Angle the cut so that water will flow away from the leaf (refer to Figure 14-11).

In addition, roses bloom most vigorously on strong new growth, which you can encourage by pruning out weak shoots, root suckers, and old unproductive canes, as shown in Figure 14-13. Remove suckers where they originate at the base of the shrub. Cut all other canes back to a large bud that points toward the outside of the shrub to encourage a more open branching habit. Prune in early spring as the buds begin to swell, but before they expand into shoots.

Figure 14-12:
Prune off
spent rose
flowers by
cutting the
stem back
to a healthy
5- to 7-
leaflet leaf.

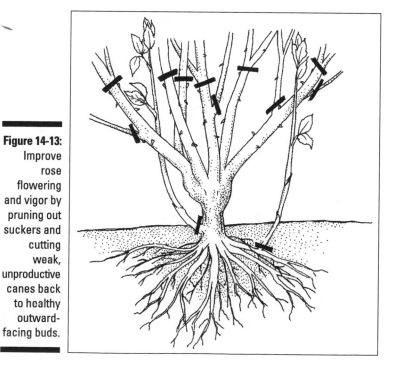

Figure 14-13:
Improve
rose
flowering
and vigor by
pruning out
suckers and
cutting
weak,
unproductive
canes back
to healthy
outward-
facing buds.

Shaping hedges

Hedges come in two styles — formal and informal — and they are pruned differently. In a *formal hedge,* the goal is to create a smooth, even surface by trimming all of the hedges as one plant. *Shearing* or trimming the ends of the limbs causes them to branch into dense, vigorous twigs.

To grow a densely branched formal hedge, begin pruning and training the shrubs at planting time. Snip the ends of the limbs and the central trunk, if present, back, as shown in Figure 14-14, to encourage branching. (The shrubs on the left show pruning cuts made in the first year. The shrubs on the right show the resulting growth and the second-year pruning cuts.)

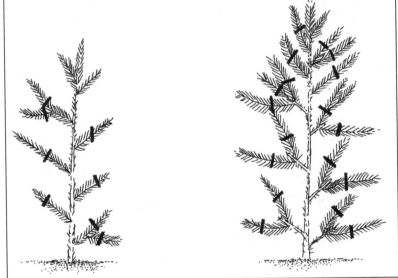

Figure 14-14:
Prune newly planted shrubs (left) to encourage dense branching. Prune the resulting growth again the following year (right).

The shape of your hedge determines its long-term health. Always prune so that the bottom of the hedge is wider than the top, as shown in Figure 14-15. If the top is wider than the bottom, the lower limbs receive less sun and will become sparse and thin. If your existing hedge is pruned incorrectly, you can change the shape over several years. Each year, cut the sides at the top a little more than the bottom until the hedge assumes the correct shape.

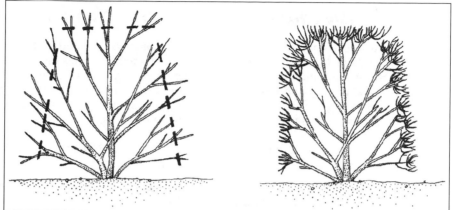

Informal hedges may consist of plants all of one or of more than one species. Instead of making heading cuts to create a smooth wall as in formal hedges, however, informal hedges require thinning cuts that allow each shrub to retain its natural form. Because you allow the shrubs to keep their natural shapes, they usually need far less pruning. Prune informal hedges only to remove dead, diseased, damaged, or undesirable shoots. If you wish to reduce their height or width, cut the longest shoots back to a desirable limb or strong bud.

You can help a formally pruned shrub regain its natural habit by using thinning cuts over a period of several years, as shown in Figure 14-16. Gradually eliminate the dense, twiggy growth at the ends of the limbs and encourage a more open branching habit by pruning twigs back to an outward growing limb.

Figure 14-16:
Return a
shrub to its
natural form
by thinning
twigs back
to outward
growing
limbs over a
period of
several
years.

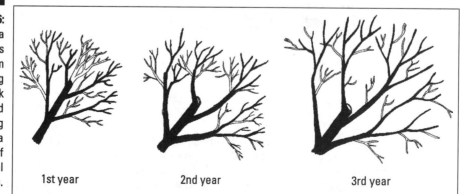

1st year   2nd year   3rd year

Rejuvenating hedges and shrubs

As shrubs mature, their shoots may become so crowded that light and air can't easily reach the inner limbs. The shaded branches die or become prone to disease and insect infestation and, after a while, the whole shrub starts looking ratty and unkempt. You can return shrubs to their former glory by removing crowded, unhealthy shoots and encouraging strong new growth. Follow these steps for a gradual rejuvenation plan.

1. **Remove all dead, damaged, and diseased limbs by cutting them back to healthy wood or to the ground.**

2. **Cut one-third of the oldest shoots back to the ground or as close as possible, as shown in Figure 14-17.**

   Use loppers on any large and hard-to-reach shoots.

3. **Repeat the process each year to keep the shrub vigorous and healthy.**

   Never remove more than one-third of the living wood in one year. Doing so can weaken the plant by eliminating too many food-producing leaves.

Figure 14-17: Cut one-third of the most crowded shoots off close to the ground to allow more light and air to reach into the shrub.

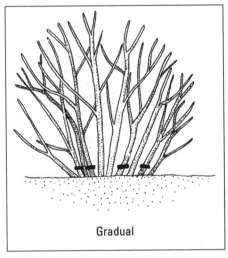

Gradual

Some shrub species can tolerate severe pruning and still bounce right back with renewed vigor. Instead of removing a few shoots each year, you can cut the whole plant back to within 6 to 12 inches of the ground all at once, as shown in Figure 14-18. As the shrub begins to grow back, choose strong, well-spaced shoots to form the framework of the new shrub and remove the less desirable shoots. Use this treatment to bring overgrown shrubs back to a more manageable size. Severe annual pruning, however, could significantly reduce the vigor of the plant.

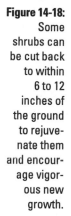

Figure 14-18: Some shrubs can be cut back to within 6 to 12 inches of the ground to rejuvenate them and encourage vigorous new growth.

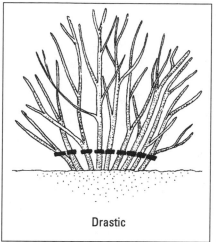

Drastic

Formal hedges, too, sometimes need rejuvenation. If your hedge has grown too large or become thin, weak, and leggy, you usually can cut it back. Some species, such as yew, holly, firethorn, barberry, and many deciduous shrubs, can take more severe pruning than others. Follow these steps.

1. **Determine mature width and height that you desire.**

2. **Cut back all the limbs on one sunny side of the hedge back close to the main stems or within the desired width range, as shown in Figure 14-19.**

   Do this in late winter to early spring.

3. **Prune back the top growth to lower than the desired mature height.**

   The hedge may grow an inch a year, depending on your pruning.

4. **Give the hedge an application of fertilizer in the spring and keep it well watered to help it overcome the shock of pruning.**

   See Chapter 13 for more information.

5. **Cut the other side of the hedge, as described, the following spring.**

   Trim back vigorous growth from the previously pruned side and top.

Not all hedge plants will survive such hard pruning. Use more moderate pruning techniques on broadleaf evergreens, conifers, and slow-growing shrubs.

Figure 14-19:
Rejuvenate a formal hedge by shearing the limbs on one side early in year one. Shear other side and trim vigorous growth in year two.

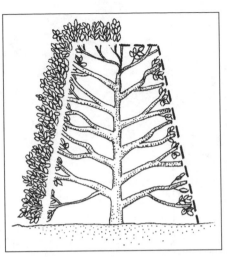

Shaping and rejuvenating shade and ornamental trees

If you select a healthy young tree with good branching structure, as described in Chapter 11, your mature tree will rarely need pruning except to remove dead, damaged, and diseased wood and branches that become unsafe or unsightly. As the tree grows, prune undesirable limbs as they appear and when they're small because trees can heal from a small wound more quickly than a large one. Remove limbs that rub, have narrow, V-shaped crotches, and those that interfere with mowing or traffic.

Most trees should be pruned in early spring before active growth begins. This timing ensures that new wounds heal quickly and lessens the chance of disease infection. Some trees, however, bleed excessive amounts of sap unless pruned later in the season — I call these *bleeders*. Bleeding causes unsightly stains on the tree bark and invites insects and disease. Prune bleeders, such as maple, birch, walnut, hemlock, fir, and horse chestnuts, in midsummer. Oaks shouldn't be pruned from April through June because pruning at this time exposes them to infection by oak wilt disease. You can, of course, take out deadwood anytime.

If your trees are already mature, I recommend that you call a qualified arborist to prune them (see the "Consulting the professionals" sidebar, earlier in this chapter).

Incorrect pruning, especially of large overhead limbs more than a few inches in diameter, is dangerous work and can lead to the decline and eventual death of the tree. If you can reach the limb from the ground, however, you may want to tackle it yourself. Here's how to prune a large limb safely. Figure 14-20 shows the three cuts.

1. **Using a pruning saw, cut about one-third of the way through the limb from the underside, towards the top, about 6 to 12 inches from the trunk.**

   This undercut prevents the bark from tearing down the trunk. If the branch is very long, trim off sections near the end of it to lighten the limb before making the final cuts near the trunk.

2. **Next, saw through the limb from the top a few inches further out on the limb from the undercut.**

   Take care when the limb breaks loose and falls.

3. **Support the remaining stub with your free hand and saw from top to bottom at outer ring of branch collar or bulge where the branch joins the trunk.**

Figure 14-20: Remove heavy limbs using a 3-step method. Undercut the limb first, cut from the top further out, and remove the stub at the branch collar.

Keeping conifers healthy

Most conifer trees and shrubs don't need pruning except to remove the dead, damaged, and diseased wood and to prune out undesirable growth, such as competing main leaders. If you want to keep these plants smaller or more compact than their normal size, however, you can prune them in early spring or as the shoots expand in late spring to early summer. Conifers with differing branching habits require different pruning methods.

✔ **Pine, spruce, and fir with whorled branches.** These species have layers of branches that form a whorl or circle around the trunk. Prune tip growth only to a lateral shoot or pinch the expanding new growth, called *candles,* before the needles elongate and harden. See Figure 14-21. Don't cut into old wood because these species don't have dormant buds.

✔ **Arborvitae, false cypress, cypress, juniper, and yew with random branching.** These species may sprout new growth from older, foliage-bearing wood if pruned. Prune to a lateral shoot or to foliage-bearing wood. Pinch new growth in spring as it elongates.

Figure 14-21: Shorten the new growth of pine, spruce, and fir by pinching candles before the needles harden.

Conifer trees generally grow with one central leader or trunk. If the bud on the tip of that leader is damaged or killed, the tree may sprout two or more competing leaders. To maintain the tree's natural and desirable shape, remove all but one upright-growing leader. If no upright growth exists, tie a lateral branch from the uppermost whorl into an upright position, as shown in Figure 14-22. Remove the tie when the shoot can stand on its own.

Don't remove the lower branches of pyramid and column-shaped conifers, if it's possible to save them. They add balance and grace as they sweep the ground.

Espalier, topiary, and other formalities

Using special pruning and training techniques, you can turn trees and shrubs into decorative forms. Plants trained to these forms require frequent maintenance and attention to detail to achieve and maintain their unique shapes.

Topiary is the practice of shearing plants into geometric and fanciful shapes, such as animals. Small-leafed evergreens make the best plants for turning into topiary. Stiff wire is often used to hold developing branches in place, especially in elaborately shaped forms. You can achieve a similar effect by training a small-leafed, finely textured vine over a wire frame.

Training trees and shrubs into flat, two-dimensional forms, usually against a wall or trellis, is called *espalier*, shown in the following figure. This very formal style is used not only for decorative effect, but also for producing large quantities of high quality fruit in a small space. Apples, pears, and firethorn *(Pyracantha)* make especially good subjects for espalier training.

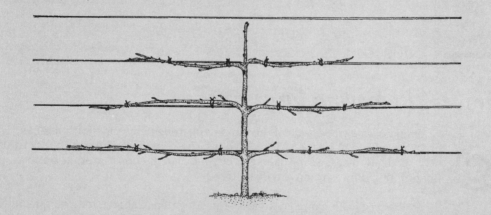

Pleaching involves weaving the branches of closely planted trees together to form a tunnel, called an *allée*. Trees with supple branches, such as beech *(Fagus)*, apple, pear, peach, and hornbeam *(Carpinus)*, are trained to a wire trellis and woven together as they grow.

Bonsai are miniature trees that are highly trained to resemble mature trees in a natural landscape. In this ancient art form, small-leafed trees are root-pruned to fit into small, shallow containers. The developing limbs and trunks are held in place with wire and pruned to achieve special effects, such as a wind blown landscape, a grove of trees, or a gnarled old specimen.

Figure 14-22:
Train a lateral shoot to become the new central leader if the old leader dies.

Timber! Removing large trees

Taking down a tree is one of the most dangerous landscape jobs you can tackle and is a permanent decision not to be considered lightly. Unless the tree is dead, diseased, or damaged beyond repair, consider other options before deciding to remove a living tree.

- If a tree is blocking your view or casting dense shade, for example, an arborist can thin the limbs or reduce the size of the canopy (don't confuse this with topping, which I discuss in the "Topping hurts trees" sidebar, earlier in this chapter).

- Trees growing into utility wires can be pruned to grow around the lines.

- If you're planning a building project, try to leave as many existing trees as possible and protect them during construction (see Chapter 16). Mature trees add considerable value to your property, and provide shade, wildlife habitat, and privacy.

If a tree really must go, determine if it's a job that you can handle before you proceed. Consider these factors.

- **Height and size of the tree:** Can the tree fall full length without hitting anything, including another tree? If not, an arborist can remove the top first and take it down in sections. See Chapter 2 for estimating tree height. Also never try to cut down a tree that has a trunk wider than the bar length of your chain saw, usually 12 to 14 inches.

✔ **Condition of the trunk:** Is it split, decayed, hollow, twisted, forked, or leaning? Is the canopy lopsided? These trees may fall in unpredictable ways and cause serious harm.

✔ **Location of the tree:** If the tree doesn't fall where you expect, can it hit a building, utility lines, or fall across a road or into a neighbor's yard? Do you have room to move quickly away from the tree when it falls?

✔ **Weather:** Wind can affect the direction in which the tree falls.

✔ **Appropriate tools and your experience in their use:** Saws and chainsaws are extremely dangerous tools in inexperienced hands. Using a tool too small for the job increases your danger because the saw blade may become stuck in the tree. Hire an expert if you're inexperienced with these powerful machines.

✔ **Your physical fitness:** Do you have the strength and stamina to get out of the way quickly when the tree falls and to cut it into manageable pieces? Do you want the stump removed? Don't underestimate the size of the job. A tree service can handle these chores for you.

If your tree-felling project passed the litmus test and you feel comfortable cutting it down, here's how to proceed.

1. **Choose the direction of the fall.**

   The tree should be able to fall without hitting anything. Leave plenty of room for error on both sides of your chosen landing site. If the tree leans or has lopsided branching, it will naturally want to fall where gravity pulls it.

2. **Choose your escape routes and clear the area.**

   Trees often fall in unpredictable ways. Be sure you can get away quickly when the tree starts to move. The safest route is at a 45° angle from where the tree will land. Keep bystanders at least three tree lengths away.

3. **Make the first cut on the side facing the direction where you want tree to fall.**

   Cutting from top to bottom, make a 50° to 60° angle cut off the horizontal, ending about ⅕ to ¼ into the diameter of the trunk, as shown in Figure 14-23.

4. **Make the second cut to form a 90° wedge.**

   Cutting from bottom to top, make the second cut about 30° to 40° off the horizontal. Aim the cut so that it will meet the end of the first cut perfectly. This is important.

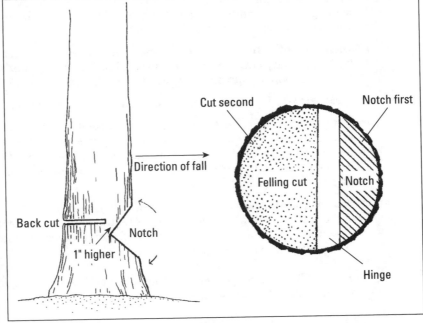

Figure 14-23:
Starting with the top cut in the direction of the fall, remove a 90° wedge. Back cut at or just above the notch and leave a 1½ inch hinge.

5. **Make the back cut.**

   Starting at or one 1 inch above the center of the notch on the opposite side, cut the trunk straight across. Don't cut all the way through, however. Leave a hinge about 1 to 1½ inches, or ⅒ the diameter of the trunk, intact to help control the fall, as shown in Figure 14-23.

6. **Use wedges to start the tree falling.**

   Drive one or two plastic wedges into the back cut to prevent the saw blade from getting stuck and to get the tree moving in the right direction. Chainsaw dealers sell wedges.

7. **Move!**

   When the tree starts to go over, move away fast and shout a warning to spectators. Stay out of the zone directly behind the tree. Three tree lengths away is a safe distance.

Chapter 15

Battling Pests, Diseases, and Weather

- -

In This Chapter

▶ Preventing tree and shrub problems

▶ Controlling common tree and shrub pests

▶ Curing tree and shrub diseases

▶ Outwitting greedy animals

▶ Withstanding cold weather and other calamities

- -

*E*very tree and shrub, no matter how tough and rugged, is susceptible to some pest or disease, and even perfectly healthy plants aren't immune to the effects of severe weather, hungry animals, or human error. Choosing the right plant for the right place (Chapter 2), buying a healthy tree or shrub (Chapter 11), and planting it correctly (Chapter 12) can forestall many of these potential problems. But if you suspect that your shrub or tree already has a problem, flip through this chapter to find descriptions and illustrations of many common insect pests, diseases, and environmental injuries. After you know which symptoms to look for, you can get your plants back on the road to health with the safe and effective treatments in this chapter. Some disease and pest puzzles are more difficult to solve, however, and if that's your situation, you need to know when to call an expert for help — this chapter shows you how.

Using an Ounce of Prevention . . .

Research suggests that plants emit a chemical signal when they're under stress, and insects hone in on this chemical signal like a landing pattern from air-traffic control. Diseases are similarly opportunistic, causing the most trouble when plants are already weakened. So, what can you do to give your plants the best possible chance at a healthy life? Here are some suggestions:

✔ **Choose the proper site and soil.** Azaleas planted in full sun, for example, are more apt to be ravaged by azalea lace bugs than those planted in their natural woodland. Shrubs and trees that prefer well-drained soils are more prone to root diseases when planted in wet soils. (See Chapter 2 for more information and look at the plant descriptions in Parts II and III.)

✔ **Care for plants properly.** Plant that are stressed from lack of water or improper care are more susceptible to insects and diseases. But too much of a good thing can also cause problems. Too much nitrogen fertilizer, for example, attracts aphids and encourages soft, weak branches and shoots.

✔ **Choose plants well-adapted to where you live.** Plants grown outside of their normal range of adaptation are susceptible to all types of calamities from winter-kill to sunburn to voracious insects. See Chapter 2 and the Plant Hardiness Zone maps in the color section near the center of this book for more information.

✔ **Keep your yard clean and tidy.** Rake up fallen leaves and fruit from under your trees and shrubs and dispose of it in your compost pile. For composting information, see *Gardening For Dummies*, 2nd Edition, by Michael MacCaskey, Bill Marken, and the Editors of The National Gardening Association (IDG Books Worldwide, Inc.). Debris from diseased or insect infested plants should go in the trash to eliminate sources of infection. Clean your pruning tools (see Chapter 14) between working on plants to prevent the spread of disease.

✔ **Choose resistant plants when possible.** Many tree and shrub species or cultivated varieties (*cultivars,* for short) within a species resist plant pests and certain diseases. The species river birch is less bothered by borers than European white birch, for example, and the lilac cultivar 'President Lincoln' resists powdery mildew. Throughout the plant descriptions in Parts II and III, I list disease and pest resistant plants whenever possible.

✔ **Encourage beneficial insects.** Good insects eat the bad insects that damage your trees and shrubs. See the "A leg up for good insects" section, later in this chapter, for tips on identifying the good guys and helping them win.

✔ **Mulch to reduce insects, weeds, and disease.** Mulch also moderates the soil temperature and moisture, which helps keep roots healthy. See Chapter 13 for the lowdown on mulching.

Knowing When To Call for Help

When a problem does occur, correctly identifying the cause is essential. Some pests are easy to spot — Japanese beetles munching on your roses and leaf miners tunneling patterns on the birch leaves. But sometimes, tree and shrub problems can be especially difficult to diagnose, so you may want to get outside help. The symptoms, for example, may be high in the canopy, but the cause may be in the roots. Often, more than one pest, disease, or environmental factor affects a troubled tree or shrub at one time. Professionals have the tools and resources to identify the problems and recommend solutions.

You can often get help identifying tree and shrub problems from your county cooperative extension service or local nurseryman, but you'll probably still need someone else to execute control measures. Some garden maintenance companies, pest control operators, or landscape contractors can spray shrubs and small trees or help with cultural problems. A certified arborist (see Chapter 14 for more information) is the most highly trained, commercial specialist for tree care.

Tree professionals aren't cheap, but they can save you money — the money you'll lose in property value if your big trees die; the money you'll save if you don't have to remove the dead tree (big bucks); and the money you'll save if you don't have to repair the neighbor's garage that gets crushed when your sick tree falls (even bigger bucks).

How do you know when its time to call for help? Your shrubs and trees will probably let you know with one or more of the following signs:

- ✔ **Dropping leaves:** You shouldn't be raking leaves and pine needles in midsummer.

- ✔ **Dropping goop:** You shouldn't have to wash the sticky gunk off your car or sidewalk everyday.

- ✔ **Thinning canopy:** Leaves aren't dropping, but the canopy of leaves looks thinner.

- ✔ **Dead limbs:** A sure sign of trouble.

- ✔ **Oozing wounds:** Wet or sticky stuff oozes from wounds on the trunk, stems, or large limbs.

- ✔ **Changes in foliage color:** No, not in fall; in spring or summer. If the plant was green last week, and yellow today, get on the phone.

Diagnosing and Managing Pest Problems

Before you can cure what ails your tree or shrub, you have to figure out whether it has a pest, a disease or an environmental problem. (For nonpest problems, see the "Preventing and Reducing Shrub and Tree Diseases" and "Reducing Environmental Stresses" sections later in this chapter.)

Some problems are simple to diagnose because you can see the pest crawling or flying around. Other insects, however, are so tiny that you need a magnifying glass to find them. Luckily, all these pesky pests cause tell-tale symptoms that help you identify the culprit when you know what to look for. The following section describes the most common tree and shrub pests and how to control them.

Rounding up the usual suspects

Use the following descriptions of common insect pests to find out what's eating your trees and shrubs and what to do about them. The "Managing pests" section, later in this chapter, has more specific information about how to control these pests.

✔ **Aphids.** These tiny, soft-bodied, pear-shaped pests (shown in Figure 15-1) suck plant sap with their needle-like noses. They vary in color from black to green, red, or even translucent. Aphids leave behind sticky sap droppings that attract ants and may turn black if covered with sooty mold. Aphids can proliferate quickly on weakened plants and tend to congregate on the newest leaves and twig tips. Blast them off with a hose, control with beneficial insects or sticky yellow traps, or spray with insecticidal soap. The beneficial insects green lacewings and ladybird beetles are also excellent controls.

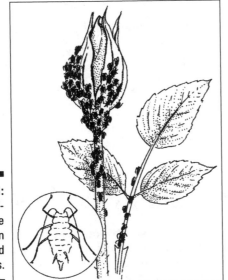

Figure 15-1:
Aphids pro-
liferate
quickly on
weakened
plants.

✔ **Apple maggot.** Slightly smaller than houseflies, these pests spend the winter in soil, and then appear in June or July to begin laying eggs in apples, crabapples, plums, and other fruits. (Apple maggots are a problem mostly for northern gardeners.) To control these pests without pesticides, rake up and dispose of infested fruit in the fall before the maggots emerge and become established in the soil for the winter. Trap adult flies with red, apple-like spheres coated with sticky goo (Tangle-Trap is a common brand) and baited with a special apple-scented lure. Begin trapping three weeks after the petals begin falling from the blossoms in spring and continue through August, cleaning and refreshing the sticky stuff every two weeks or as needed. Use one or two traps in young or small, 6- to 8-foot high trees and six traps in mature 10- to 25-foot trees.

To make it easier to renew the sticky stuff on apple maggot traps, enclose the trap in a plastic sandwich bag before you smear on the goo. Cover the bag with the trapping material instead. Then, when it's time to renew the goo, dispose of the old plastic bag and replace it with a new one.

You can find apple maggot traps and other nontoxic pest controls at many garden centers and nurseries. Mail-order catalogs usually offer the widest selection, however, and several sources are listed in the "Finding safe and effective pest controls" sidebar, later in this chapter.

✔ **Borers and bark beetles:** Several kinds of beetle and caterpillar larvae or grubs tunnel into the wood or stems of fruit trees, needled evergreens, white birches, dogwoods, shade trees, rhododendrons, and recently planted trees, as shown in Figure 15-2. Their tunneling weakens the plant and allows easy access for diseases to invade. The holes can also cut off nutrient flow to the affected limb. Prevention is the best defense against borers: Methods include choosing plant species that are less susceptible (see the "Beetles and borers and weevils, oh my!" sidebar in this chapter, along with Chapter 4, for more information) and wrapping the trunks of young trees to prevent sunburn or other wounds where borers can attack. Watch for signs of borer or beetle damage — dead bark, sawdust piles, dead limbs, and poor performance. If you find borers or bark beetles, cut off and destroy the severely infested limbs, inject parasitic nematodes into the remaining borer holes, and remove dead or dying trees.

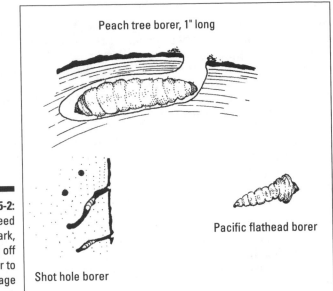

Peach tree borer, 1" long

Pacific flathead borer

Shot hole borer

Figure 15-2: Borers feed under bark, cutting off water to foliage

A CLOSER LOOK

Beetles and borers and weevils, oh my!

Beetles damage all parts of trees and shrubs: They tunnel through the wood and eat the roots, leaves, twigs, and flowers. Adult leaf-eating beetles are usually easy to see as they munch their way through a rose bush, but those that do their dirty work inside the plant, under the bark, or underground are harder to identify. Immature beetle larvae or grubs cause plenty of destruction as well, by tunneling through wood and fruits and eating roots. Weevils — beetles with a long snout or nose — lay their eggs in fruit and under bark, which the hatching larvae destroy.

The wounds that beetles make to shrubs and trees leave the plants more vulnerable to disease infection. Some beetles also spread plant diseases themselves, adding insult to injury. Elm-leaf beetles, for example, can completely defoliate American elm trees, weakening them and making them more susceptible to bark beetles that transmit Dutch elm disease.

Controlling beetles and grubs requires prevention methods and vigilance. Some trees and shrubs resist these pests, while others seem to invite them. Japanese beetles and rose chafers, for example, consider rose bushes their food of choice, but rarely bother lilacs. The wood-tunneling bronze birch borer attacks European white birch with reckless abandon, but usually causes less damage to river birch. Choose insect-resistant plants whenever possible. Vigorously growing plants also attract fewer pests and recover from damage more quickly than slower-growing plants. Rake up insect-infested fruits, twigs, and leaf debris regularly and dispose of it by burning or taking to the landfill.

If you spot beetle damage, take action quickly. Several methods are effective, including spraying with *Bacillus thuringiensis* or Bt for short. This bacteria is toxic only to certain insects, but is safe for animals and the environment. See the "Managing pests" section later in this chapter for this and other safe controls.

✓ **Leaf-feeding beetles:** Many beetles and their larvae feed on the foliage of trees and shrubs. Some common ones include black vine weevil, which is a dark, crawling, 1- to 2-inch-long beetle that chews on the foliage of evergreen trees and shrubs, such as rhododendrons and yews. Its larvae eat the roots, but can be controlled with beneficial nematodes (see "Managing pests" in this chapter). Japanese beetles, shown in Figure 15-3, are ½ inch long, metallic blue-green beetles with coppery wing covers. They eat almost any plant with gusto. Their fat, white, C-shaped, ¾-inch-long larvae consume grass roots. To control, treat your lawn with milky spore disease, which takes several years to spread through the lawn, or with beneficial nematodes, a quicker-acting helper. Inspect your garden in the evening or early morning for the beetles, knocking them off plants into a can or bucket of soapy water. You can also spray with neem, a pesticide made from the neem tree. Other leaf-eating beetles include the elm leaf beetle and rose chafer.

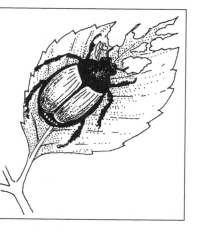

Figure 15-3:
Japanese beetles consume almost any plant.

✓ **Curculio:** The damage that these ¼-inch-long weevils do is easier to spot than the beetles themselves. The female beetles make crescent-shaped cuts in young apple, pear, and cherry fruit right after the petals fall from the flowers, and then lay their eggs in the wound. When the grubs hatch, they eat through the fruit and cause it to drop prematurely from the tree. To control the adult beetles, spread out a tarp or old sheet underneath the tree and shake it to knock the beetles off and then step on them. Rake up and destroy prematurely fallen fruit, which may contain larvae.

✓ **Spruce budworm:** These orange-yellow to brownish caterpillars cause significant damage to spruce and fir forests throughout North America and can severely disfigure or kill landscape trees, too. Caterpillars spin webs around and eat the mature and newly developing needles in the spring, usually April to June. Control the pest by cutting off and destroying the affected branch tips, spraying with Bt, or releasing parasitic trichogramma wasps.

A CLOSER LOOK

Creepy, crawly caterpillars and mischievous moths

Moths and butterflies can be beautiful additions to the flower garden and landscape, but their caterpillars are voracious eaters that consume the leaves, twigs, wood, and fruit of many trees and shrubs. Some, such as tent and gypsy moth caterpillars, attack in groups that can eat all the leaves off a young tree within days. Others, like codling moth caterpillars, are solitary feeders that tunnel through fruit.

Controlling these pests is tricky because most chemicals and even some less toxic methods used to kill damaging the pests also destroy harmless moths and butterflies. One of the most effective controls for caterpillars is *Bacillus thuringiensis* (Bt for short), which is a bacteria that is harmless to animals, but is toxic to many insect pests. Horticultural spray oil and sticky traps baited with scent work against many of these pests. (See the "Managing pests" section later in this chapter.)

SOURCE

✔ **Bagworms:** These small caterpillars feed on the leaves and twigs of many trees and shrubs and are especially fond of arborvitae and juniper. After hatching in late spring, bagworms use pieces of the tree or shrubs to construct a 1- to 2-inch long, dangling, silken, bag-like structure as a home. Remove and destroy bags whenever seen and spray with Bt, as described in "Managing pests" later in this chapter.

✔ **Codling moth:** This ½-inch-long, brown moth lays its eggs on the leaves and twigs of apples and other fruits starting when the trees' flower petals begin falling in the spring and continuing through the summer. When the caterpillars hatch, they tunnel inside the fruit, usually ruining it. The most effective way to control codling moth is to prevent the moths from laying eggs by trapping, killing, or confusing them. This insect spends the winter as an immature larvae or grub under the loose bark of fruit trees. Spray trees with horticultural oil in early spring before the leaves emerge to smother the larvae. You can also trap the larvae by wrapping corrugated cardboard around the tree trunks in summer and then destroying it after the insects crawl inside. Monitor and replace every 1 to 2 weeks.

LEAF LINGO

Sticky traps baited with powerful insect-attracting scents are the safest way to eliminate the adult moths. These scents, called *pheromones,* are the perfumes of the insect world. Undetectable to humans, the tiny amounts of these chemicals released by female butterflies and moths are a siren song to males of the same species. They flock to the artificial lure and then become stuck to the sticky white cardboard. Hang the baited traps just before the trees bloom. See the "Finding safe and effective pest controls" sidebar in this chapter for sources of lures and traps.

✔ **Gypsy moths:** These 2-inch-long, gray (with brown hairs), foliage-eating caterpillars (see Figure 15-4) and their egg clusters hitchhike across the country on cars, campers, and trains. They eat foliage on a number of shade trees, including oaks, and can defoliate trees when their population gets large enough. Monitor their population with pheromone traps (see the previous bullet point). Catch caterpillars as they attempt to crawl up tree trunks by using a sticky pest barrier, which is a band of plastic or paper covered with sticky TangleTrap and wrapped around the tree. Spray the caterpillars with Bt or neem. Call an arborist for help, if the pests are severely damaging any trees that are too tall for you to treat yourself.

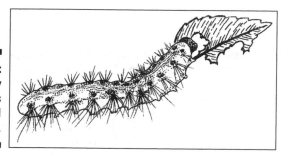

Figure 15-4:
Gypsy moths larvae feed on leaves.

✔ **Oriental fruit moths:** These small moths produce ½-inch-long, white to pink larvae that tunnel into the young wood or fruit of ornamental and fruit trees. In spring, work the soil shallowly around infested trees to kill larvae spending the winter there. Catch adult males in pheromone traps as described in the codling moths bullet point. You can kill moth eggs with horticultural oil spray.

✔ **Pine shoot moth:** The larvae of these moths tunnel through new shoots of pines. Look for yellow needles and wilted, distorted branch tips. Eventually, the affected branches die as the tunneling insects cut off food and water to the limbs. Call an arborist or your local extension service for help.

✔ **Tent caterpillars:** These caterpillars, shown in Figure 15-5, form tent-like webs full of teeming caterpillars on trees and shrubs. In large numbers, they can defoliate an entire tree. Prune the tents out of the tree before the caterpillars disperse and destroy by burning. Knock caterpillars off severely infested branches with a broom or pole. Spray with Bt.

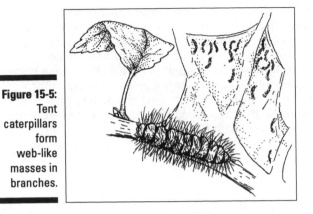

Figure 15-5:
Tent caterpillars form web-like masses in branches.

✔ **Gall-producing insects:** Galls are abnormal growths that appear as warts, bumps, or balls on leaves or twigs. Their growth is stimulated by mites, flies, aphids, or wasps laying eggs on the leaves or twigs. The young hatch and feed inside the gall that forms around them. Leaf galls usually don't damage plants, although they may detract from its appearance. Woody galls may sometimes kill twigs. Although unsightly, galls are something you live with or prune out. Spraying isn't required.

✔ **Lace bugs:** These tiny insects, smaller than an "i" on this page, suck the sap out of leaves. They attack the underside of the foliage, giving the leaves a whitish or yellow blotchy appearance. Look under the leaves for their brown, sticky droppings. Firethorn, mountain laurel, cotoneaster, and rhododendron are often attacked. Spray with horticultural spray oil to suffocate the pests or use a botanical pesticide.

✔ **Leaf miners and sawflies:** The larvae of tiny sawflies, moths, beetles, and flies tunnel through the leaves of plants, such as holly, pine, boxwood, birch, and lilac, and leave discolored patches on the foliage. They're hard to eliminate when they're protected inside the leaf. Remove and destroy infested leaves and rake up any that fall. Spray with neem in spring when adults begin to lay eggs.

✔ **Scale:** Looking like bumps on plant stems and leaves, these tiny sucking insects cling to plant branches, hiding under an outer shell that serves as a shield (see Figure 15-6). These pests suck plant sap and can kill plants if present in large numbers. Look for sticky, honey-like sap droppings, one clue that scale may be present. Remove and destroy badly infested stems. Indoors or on small plants, clean light infestations off with a cotton ball soaked in rubbing alcohol. Spray larger plants with horticultural oil in early spring or summer.

Aliens invade!

The speed and convenience of modern travel and mail has been a boon to insects and diseases, too. That's how pests such as the Asian longhorn beetle, gypsy moth, Japanese beetle, Mediterranean fruit fly, and silverleaf whitefly got to North America. Historically the spread of pests has been blocked by geography. Not so anymore. In the United States, the 1,800 inspectors and 62 canine teams (the "beagle brigade" of international airport fame) of the Animal and Plant Health Inspection Service — APHIS —

lead the defense. Do farmers and fellow gardeners a favor and don't mail fruits home from foreign locations, and follow U.S. Customs and APHIS regulations when traveling overseas. If you intend to bring plants home, first call APHIS: 301-734-8645. To find out more about APHIS and U.S. Customs regulations see the Web sites at www.aphis.usda.gov/oa/new/pe.html, and www.customs.ustreas.gov/travel/kbygo.htm#Food/Plants.

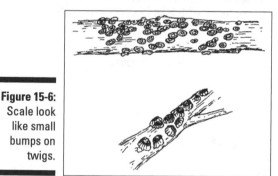

Figure 15-6: Scale look like small bumps on twigs.

✔ **Snails and slugs:** These soft-bodied mollusks, shown in Figure 15-7, feed on tender leaves during the cool of night or in rainy weather. Sometimes they're hard to spot: All you see is the slime trail they leave behind and holes chewed in leaves. They proliferate in damp areas, hiding and breeding under rocks, mulch, and other garden debris. Take advantage of this habit by making a slug trap by placing a few boards or rolled-up newspaper in the garden. In the early morning, lift the traps and destroy the slugs by sprinkling common table salt on them. Make another effective trap by setting a saucer with the rim at ground level and fill the saucer with beer — slugs crawl in and can't get out. You can also surround plants with copper barriers — metal strips that seem to shock slugs if they attempt to crawl across. Diatomaceous earth also deters them. Look for new, nontoxic baits that contain iron phosphate. See the "Finding safe and effective pest controls" sidebar in this chapter.

Figure 15-7:
Slugs are common garden pests.

✔ **Spider mites:** These tiny arachnids (shown greatly enlarged in Figure 15-8) are almost microscopic, but when they appear in large numbers, you can begin to see the fine webs that they weave. They suck plant sap, causing leaves to discolor and plants to lose vigor. They are especially active in arid conditions. You find spider mites on fruit trees, miniature roses, citrus, and pines. Wash plants with a strong blast of water, or use dormant oil in early spring or light horticultural oil or insecticidal soap in summer. Encourage beneficial insects, many of which prey on spider mites.

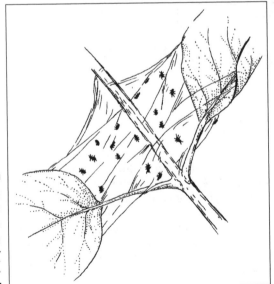

Figure 15-8:
Spider mites form fine netting under leaves.

✔ **Thrips:** Thrips are tiny flying insects that damage all soft parts of plants, including leaves, flowers, and roots. Infested flowers look distorted and leaves have silvery or white discolored patches on them. Spray with horticultural oil or botanical pesticide.

✔ **Whiteflies:** Whiteflies look like small, white gnats, but they suck plant sap and can proliferate in warm climates or greenhouses. They can also spread diseases with their sucking mouthparts. Trap whiteflies with yellow sticky traps. Cure infestations with insecticidal soap, light horticultural oil, or pyrethrin. Be sure to treat leaf undersides where whiteflies and their larvae reside.

✔ **Wooly adelgid:** Canadian and Carolina hemlocks *(Tsuga canadensis, T. caroliniana)* are the hosts for this small (⅟₁₆-inch), but deadly, pest. The insect sucks the sap out of the needles, which causes the needles to turn yellow and drop from the tree. Look for tiny, cottony masses at the base of the needles in March. Spray with horticultural oil in spring and summer.

Managing pests

Think of pest management as a staircase. On the first step are the least-disruptive, innocuous actions, and on the top step are the most toxic and the most potentially harmful measures. The best approach is to start at the bottom and move up the stairs only when absolutely necessary. This strategy, called *integrated pest management* or *IPM,* takes advantage of the complex interrelationships between insects and plants to find the least toxic ways to reduce damage to plants.

The following list outlines the actions you can take to keep a pest from getting the upper hand. The measures move from the least aggressive and potentially harmful to the most aggressive.

✔ **Strong blast from a hose** knocks small pests such as aphids and spider mites off your plants. Spraying daily can provide good control.

✔ **Barriers** prevent pests from getting to your trees and shrubs. Try barriers, such as a ring of sticky goop (sold as Tanglefoot) around the trunk of a tree to keep caterpillars from migrating into the canopy; metal barriers to keep animals from climbing into trees, nets to keep birds away from fruits, and copper strips that encircle plants to give slugs an electric shock. See the "Finding safe and effective pest controls" sidebar in this chapter for sources of barriers.

✔ **Beneficial insects** prey upon other, plant-damaging insects. See "A leg up for good insects" section in this chapter for more information and sources.

✔ **Insect traps** use chemical attractants and colors to lure pests, such as sticky, red balls for apple maggots, and slug bait for slugs. See the "Finding safe and effective pest controls" sidebar in this chapter for mail-order catalog sources.

✔ **Biological insecticides** are diseases that kill damaging insects. You can find more information about them in the "Natural pest controls" section, later in this chapter.

✔ **Least toxic controls,** such as insecticidal soaps and horticultural oils, kill pests but cause minimal impact on the environment. Flip to the "Natural pest controls" section, later in this chapter, for more information.

✔ **Botanical insecticides,** such as neem, and rotenone. Check out the "Natural pest controls" section, later in this chapter, for more information.

A leg up for good insects

The average square yard of garden contains more than a thousand insects, but very few of them actually damage your trees and shrubs. Some pollinate plants and some help break down organic matter. Others, called *beneficial insects,* prey upon garden, tree, and shrub pests. In nature, beneficial insects keep plant-eating pests under control. Here are some beneficial insects that you'll want to keep around your yard:

✔ **Ladybugs:** Ladybugs have a voracious appetite for aphids. Both larva and adult stages prey on these pests, eating as many as 40 to 50 aphids a day. Ladybugs also prey on mites and other soft-bodied insects.

✔ **Green lacewing:** Larval-stage lacewings feed on aphids, thrips, mites, and various other insect eggs, making it the most useful insect for controlling common landscape pests. The adult-stage lacewing is also beneficial.

✔ **Trichogramma wasps:** These tiny wasps help control caterpillars by laying their eggs in the eggs of moths and butterflies. The wasp larvae feed on the moth and butterfly eggs, reducing the number that develop into caterpillars. They attack (but will probably not eliminate) tent caterpillars, Oriental fruit moths, and other pests of trees and shrubs. They don't attack people in any way.

✔ **Beneficial nematodes:** These tiny worm-like creatures feed on many soil-dwelling and burrowing insects, such as Japanese beetle grubs, borers, and weevils.

All these beneficial insects are available from mail-order gardening companies, such as the ones listed in the "Finding safe and effective pest controls" sidebar in this chapter. They each have special requirements about the best time to release them into the garden. Whether you choose to buy beneficial insects or rely on the ones already present in your yard, you can take steps to encourage them to stick around:

✔ **Avoid indiscriminate pesticide spraying, which kills beneficial insects as well as pests.** If you must spray, choose a product that specifically targets the pests you want to eliminate, and use it when it will be least harmful. For example, sprays that are harmful to bees can be used in the evening after bees have returned to the hive.

✔ **Make sure that the beneficial insects have plenty to eat by allowing small numbers of pests to reside in your garden.** If you release ladybugs before you've even spotted aphids, they may move elsewhere to find food.

✔ **Provide beneficial insects with shelter.** Grow a variety of plants — tall, short, spreading, and upright — to give the insects many potential homes.

✔ **Many beneficial insects also feed on nectar and pollen, so grow flowers such as Queen Anne's lace and evening primrose.** Lacewings love fennel, caraway, and dill. Goldenrod has been found to attract more than 75 different species of beneficial insects.

Natural pest controls

A handful of pesticides exists that come from natural sources, such as flowers, seeds, or the earth. All of them decompose within days after you spray them and effectively control some insect pests. They leave no harmful residue in the environment. But they are pesticides, nonetheless, and should be used with respect. Some are completely harmless to all but their targets; others are deadly to fish, birds, and beneficial insects.

✔ ***Bacillus thuringiensis:*** This bacteria, called Bt for short, exists naturally in most soils — different strains of it are toxic to certain insects. The strain that kills most caterpillars (but, has no effect on adult butterflies or moths) is called *B. t. kurstaki*. Remember, however, that not all caterpillars are pests. Strains of Bt also have been developed for a few other pests — for example, some leaf-feeding beetles (including elm leaf beetle) are now susceptible to *B. t. tenebrionis*.

Finding safe and effective pest controls

Local garden centers and nurseries sell many different chemicals, traps, repellants, and other pest control methods. But often, you need to seek a more specialized company when you want to try some of the natural and less toxic controls or beneficial insects listed in this chapter. The following mail-order catalog companies can meet your needs.

✔ **Gardens Alive!:** Phone (812) 537-8650, write to 5100 Schenley Place, Lawrenceburg, IN 47025, or visit their Web site at www. gardens-alive.com. Their catalog is packed with good information and products, including beneficial insects.

✔ **Gardener's Supply Company:** Call (800) 863-1700, write to 128 Intervale Road, Burlington, VT 05401, or visit their Web site

at www.gardeners.com for a variety of nontoxic pest controls.

✔ **Harmony Farm Supply:** Phone (707) 823-9125, write to Box 460, Graton, CA 95444, or visit their Web site at www.harmony-farm.com for beneficial insects and other supplies.

✔ **IPM Labs:** Phone these folks at (315) 497-2063 or write to Box 300, Locke, NY 13092-0300 for beneficial insects.

✔ **Peaceful Valley Farm Supply:** Phone (916) 272-4769, write Box 2209 #NG, Grass Valley, CA 95945, or visit their Web site at www.groworganic.com, for a wide variety of pest controls and beneficial insects.

- **Advantages:** One advantage is safety — Bt has no affect on humans, other mammals, or birds. Bt also affects only specific pests and is easily incorporated with existing natural controls.

- **Disadvantages:** It takes awhile for Bt to kill the target pest. After pests consume it, their feeding slows down, but their deaths may not occur for two to five days. Bt also breaks down quickly — if the caterpillars don't eat some while it's fresh, it probably won't work.

Because Bt is a near-perfect insecticide, there is danger of overuse. Any overused insecticide gradually becomes less effective as insects evolve defenses to it. Some insect pests, such as the diamondback moth and Indian meal moth, were once susceptible and are now at least partially immune.

- **How to use:** Use *B.t. tenebrionis* against elm leaf beetles (entire neighborhoods must be sprayed for effective control). The bacterial toxin causes caterpillar death two to five days after its eaten; the toxin dissipates in two days or less. It is available as liquid spray or dust. Apply in late afternoon and reapply after rain. Repeat applications as needed. Mix with insecticidal soap for greater effectiveness.

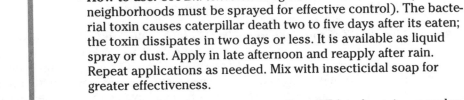

- **Diatomaceous earth:** *Diatomaceous earth,* or DE for short, is a powder-like dust made of the silicate skeletons of tiny water creatures called *diatoms.* Millions of years ago, as they died, their skeletons gradually accumulated into deep layers that are mined today from deposits where oceans or large lakes once covered the land. DE acts like ground glass, cutting into the waxy coat of many kinds of insects and causing them to dry out and die. DE is often combined with the botanical insecticide, pyrethrin (described later in this chapter). The addition of pyrethrin makes DE more lethal for many insects.

- **Advantages:** Easy to handle and apply. DE isn't toxic and leaves no residue.

- **Disadvantages:** DE is not selective and kills spiders and beneficial insects as well as pests. DE is available in two forms. One, which is used primarily in swimming pool filters, is not an effective insecticide and is dangerous to inhale (can cause a lung disease called silicosis). In your garden, use only the natural grade of DE. Always wear goggles and a dust mask during application because the fine particles can irritate your throat and lungs.

- **How to use:** Dust DE onto leaves and stems to control pests such as aphids, ants, immature forms of some beetles, and whiteflies. Sometimes a band of DE makes an effective slug and snail barrier. It works best in dry situations; reapply after rain.

One of the most convenient applicators of small amounts of DE is the Spritzer *tube duster*. This applicator holds a small amount of dust and dispenses it with a pump action. It's available from Perma-Guard, Inc., 115 Rio Bravo SE, Albuquerque, New Mexico 87105. Or call (505) 873-3061. The Cadillac of dust applicators is the Dustin-Mizer. It holds a pound of dust in a canister and dispenses with a hand crank. (See the "Finding safe and effective pest controls" sidebar in this chapter for sources.)

✔ **Horticultural oils:** Horticultural oils are most often highly refined extracts of crude oil. (Some vegetable oils, such as cottonseed and soybean oil, are also sometimes used.) They kill insects by plugging the pores through which the insects breathe. Two basic kinds of oils are available — those used on dormant plants and those for use when plants are growing actively. Dormant oils are effective at smothering the eggs of overwintering insects and reducing problems in the next growing season. Lighter weight summer oils are sprayed on plant foliage during the growing season.

- **Advantages:** These oils present few risks to either gardeners or beneficial insects and integrate well with natural biological controls. Also, oils dissipate quickly through evaporation, leaving little residue.

- **Disadvantages:** Oils can damage plants if applied at excessive rates, on particularly hot (above 100°) or cold (below 40°) days, or in combination with other pesticides, such as sulfur.

- **How to use:** Spray any time of year to kill aphids, scales, spider mites, and whiteflies.

Use highly refined horticultural oils and dilute according to label directions. Do not apply oils to drought-stressed plants, or on hot, cold, or very humid days. Don't apply horticultural oils to green plants at rates recommended for leafless, dormant plants.

✔ **Insecticidal soaps:** Insecticidal soaps are specific fatty acids that are toxic primarily to soft-bodied insects like aphids, spider mites, and whiteflies. Adult Japanese beetles are also susceptible.

- **Advantages:** Insecticidal soap is one of the safest insecticides. Most nontarget insects are unaffected, and the soaps are not toxic to animals. Soap insecticides act fast and leave no residue.

- **Disadvantages:** Soaps readily burn some plants, especially during hot weather, and the effectiveness of the soap diminishes greatly when mixed with hard water (water high in dissolved minerals). Soaps only kill pests they contact directly.

- **How to use:** Use against aphids, grasshoppers, Japanese beetles (adults), leafhoppers, spider mites, and whiteflies. To improve effectiveness, mix with warm, soft water and be sure to cover both sides of leaves. Apply when the air is still and reapply after rain.

✔ **Neem:** Neem is an extract derived from the crushed seeds of the tropical neem tree *(Azadirachta indica)*. Although it's been intensely studied for many years now, it is still a new botanical insecticide. The primary active ingredient is the compound azadirachtin, for which two forms are available. One is a 3 percent solution of azadirachtin, the most insecticidal component, and the other is "clarified hydrophobic extracts of neem seeds," — usually sold as a syrupy oil (make sure it's warm before mixing with water).

Both forms of neem work as both an insecticide and as an agent that prevents insects from feeding. They also kill insects in the juvenile stage by thwarting their development and are most effective against aphids, thrips, and whiteflies. Neem oil is also fungicidal and can control black spot of roses, powdery mildew, and rust diseases.

- **Advantages:** Neem has no measurable toxicity to mammals. (In some countries, neem extract is considered healthful to people and is added to various food and personal products.) The U.S. Environmental Protection Agency (EPA) stipulated that neem was exempt from food crop tolerances because it is considered nontoxic.

- **Disadvantages:** Neem doesn't have a quick "knock-down" effect, but a week or so after application, you notice a steady decline in the number of pests. It is not as effective against adult insects, especially large populations (although it may interfere with egg production).

- **How to use:** To mix neem oil with water, the oil needs to be a least room temperature. But, neem mixes even better when you warm it first. Set the pesticide container in hot water on the stove or microwave the container for about 30 seconds. If you try the latter, be sure to remove the aluminum seal under the cap first, and then seal the cap. After it's diluted, neem sprays degrade very quickly in water, so mix only the amount you need and apply all of it immediately. Apply liquid spray morning or evening when humidity is highest. Repeat weekly or after rainfall; spray lasts on plants about one week.

On the plant, neem retains its activity against juvenile insect pests for about one week. Use neem to kill juvenile aphids and thrips, and to repel whiteflies and Japanese beetles. As a toxin, apply when pests are young.

✔ **Pyrethins:** This natural insecticide, made from the pyrethrum flower, belongs to a groups of pesticides called *broad-spectrum insecticides*. These products kill a wide range of insects — damaging pests and beneficial ones alike. Use them with caution to avoid harming beneficial insects. *Pyrethroids*, such as cypermethrin, permethrin, and resmethrin, are synthetic chemicals that resemble pyrethrins, but are more toxic and persistent in the environment and, therefore, less desirable for home landscape use than the natural pyrethrins.

- **Advantages:** Pyrethrins are only mildly toxic to mammals, but kill insects quickly. In sunlight, they break down and are harmless to even insects within a day or less.

- **Disadvantages:** Pyrethrins are toxic to honeybees — apply it in the evening after bees are in their hives.

- **How to use:** It's useful against many pests, including hard-to-kill beetles and tarnished plant bugs, but pyrethrins degrade within one day. For best results, apply in the late afternoon or evening.

✔ **Rotenone:** Rotenone is often recommended for organic gardeners because of its botanical origin (derived from the roots of tropical legumes).

- **Advantages:** It is approved for use in organic gardens and becomes nontoxic quickly in sunlight.

- **Disadvantages:** Rotenone is toxic to pests and beneficial insects alike. It is toxic to fish and birds and must be used with caution.

- **How to use:** Use this broad-spectrum insecticide as a last resort against fruit worms, Japanese beetles, and weevils. Apply in calm, wind-free weather in early evening when bees are inactive. It remains effective against pests for up to one week.

Many pesticides, even the ones from the garden center, are dangerous to you and to the environment, especially when treating large plants, like trees. Instead of spraying landscape trees yourself, I recommend that you call a professional arborist who can diagnose your tree problems and take the appropriate steps to return it to health. If you need assistance with smaller trees and shrubs, call your cooperative extension agent for advice.

Preventing and Identifying Diseases

Some plant diseases are difficult, if not impossible, to cure, but many can be prevented. Healthy, vigorously growing trees and shrubs are less likely to become infected by disease and keeping them growing strong is your first and best defense. Use the tips in this section to prevent disease in other ways, too. But, when disease does strike, try to identify the problem with the help of reference books or personnel at a local nursery, garden center, botanical garden, or county extension office. Use the disease descriptions in this chapter and look up the affected plant in Part II or III of this book to get further clues about the diseases most likely to infect your trees and shrubs.

Nifty ways to avoid plant diseases

Some of the most aggravating plant diseases are easier to avoid in the first place than to cure later on. Here are some of the simple measures you can take to sidestep a good portion of disease problems:

- **Choose disease-resistant plants.** 'Liberty' apple resists apple scab fungus, for example. Flip through Parts II and III, for descriptions of disease-resistant plants.

- **Mulch to prevent soil-borne diseases from splashing onto flowers and foliage.** But, to discourage fungus that attacks tree trunks and stems, keep mulch a few inches away from plants. See Chapter 13 for more about mulching.

- **Choose plants that are adapted to your site.** If your soil drains poorly, for example, don't plant shrubs that require well-drained soil. See Chapter 2 for more about soil and the plant descriptions in Parts II and III for specific plant requirements.

- **Space and prune plants to provide good air circulation.** Some fungus diseases described in this section thrive on moist leaves, but not on dry foliage. Fresh air helps leaves dry quickly and thwarts diseases.

- **Water the soil, not the plants.** Early morning watering is best because the sun will evaporate any water on the leaves. Avoid evening watering because the foliage stays wet all night, giving fungus spores a chance to grow and infect plants.

- **Don't walk amid plants when the foliage is wet because you could spread disease spores from plant to plant.**

- **Keep your yard clean.** Dispose of diseased leaves, fruit, and wood in the garbage, not the compost pile. If necessary, sanitize pruning shears between cuts by spraying with isopropyl alcohol or a 1 to 10 bleach to water solution. Some insect pests — such as aphids, bark beetles, and tarnished plant bugs — can spread diseases. Keep them under control, and you'll help prevent disease.

Dastardly diseases: What to do

Tree and shrub diseases are often harder to diagnose than insect pests because the symptoms of some diseases resemble each other or those of an environmental problem. Yellowing leaves, for example, can indicate nitrogen deficiency, root rot, or other diseases. The following diseases are among the most common in trees and shrubs. Ask an experienced arborist, nursery worker, or your local extension agent for help in identifying diseases — and in treating them, if necessary.

✔ **Anthracnose:** These fungi (many different species of fungi cause anthracnose) can attack many trees, including dogwoods, ash, and sycamores. The first symptoms are small, discolored leaf spots or dead twigs, which can spread to kill branches and eventually the tree. Choose resistant plants. Destroy fallen diseased leaves and dead branches and twigs. Hire an arborist to spray trees that have been disease-ridden for three consecutive years. Consider removing susceptible trees and replanting with resistant varieties.

✔ **Apple scab:** This fungus attacks apple and crabapple trees, producing discolored leaf spots and woody-brown fruit lesions or scabs. Plant scab-resistant varieties, such as those described in Chapter 5 (crab-apples). Rake and destroy fungus-infected leaves in fall to prevent the fungus from living through the winter and reinfecting the trees in spring. Susceptible varieties need a preventive spray program during wet spring and summer weather to prevent reinfection.

Spray sulfur, copper, or Bordeaux mixture (a mixture of copper sulfate, lime, and water) as a protective spray at the beginning of scab season (after flower buds in spring), and then two or three more times at approximately weekly intervals.

✔ **Black spot:** This rose disease causes black spots on the leaves (see Figure 15-9) and can spread, causing the shrub to lose all its foliage. Avoid problems by growing disease-resistant roses and cleaning up and destroying any diseased leaves that fall to the ground. To prevent black spot on susceptible roses, use a preventive fungicide spray during damp or humid weather. Sprays of copper or lime sulfur are best. Also try potassium bicarbonate (or baking soda — sodium bicarbonate) at the rate of 1 tablespoon per gallon of water, weekly or after rain. Apply in morning and not during periods of hottest weather. Neem oil is also effective.

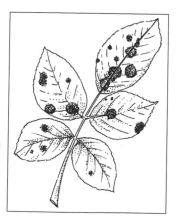

Figure 15-9:
Blackspot
on roses.

✔ **Botrytis blight:** This fungus attacks a wide variety of plants, especially in wet weather. It causes discolored patches on foliage, browning and droopy stalks on flowers, and premature rotting of fruits. Discourage botrytis by allowing air to circulate freely around susceptible plants. Remove and destroy any infected plant parts.

✔ **Cytospora canker:** This bacterial disease attacks woody stems on susceptible plants, such as fruit trees, spruces, and maples, forming cankers that can kill infected branches. Cankers appear as sunken or very swollen areas on the bark, depending on the bacteria and plant affected. Plant resistant or less-susceptible plants and avoid bark injuries that provide an entrance for infecting bacteria. If possible, remove and destroy infected branches.

✔ **Dutch elm disease:** This catastrophic disease has devastated American elm trees and is spread by bark beetles throughout the United States. The first symptom is yellowing leaves that soon wilt. An infected tree can die within a season or two as the disease destroys the tissue that moves water and nutrients through the tree. If you have elm trees, keep them healthy and vigorous. Contact your local extension office or a certified arborist for ways to prevent and treat infection. The lacebark elm (see Chapter 4) resists the disease.

✔ **Fireblight:** This bacterial disease, shown in Figure 15-10, attacks apple, cotoneaster, crabapple, hawthorn, pear, and pyracantha. Fireblight causes young shoots to turn black and scorched-looking, hence the name. It's spread by insects through blossoms during rainy or wet weather. The best prevention is to choose fireblight-resistant varieties, such as those in Chapter 5. After infection takes place, prune out damaged wood, cutting well back (at least 6 to 12 inches) into healthy tissue. Burn prunings to prevent reinfection and sterilize pruning equipment with isopropyl alcohol. Fireblight can also be prevented by frequent sprays of fixed copper or agricultural streptomycin (which is hard to find) during bloom.

Figure 15-10:
Fireblight
makes
shoots
looked
scorched.

✔ **Mildew (downy and powdery):** These two fungi produce similar symptoms: white, powdery coating on leaves. A variety of plants are susceptible, including roses, sycamores, euonymus, and lilacs. A different kind of mildew attacks each kind of plant. A mildew that attacks lilacs, for example, won't harm roses. The fungi disfigure plants, but may not kill them outright. Instead, they weaken plants, making them unattractive and susceptible to other problems. Downy mildew attacks during cool, wet weather; powdery mildew (shown in Figure 15-11) comes later in the season during warm, humid weather and cool nights. Avoid mildew by planting resistant plants and by not getting the leaves wet. Rake up infected leaves and destroy. Treat plants with fungicide or baking soda spray (1 tablespoon per gallon water.)

Figure 15-11:
Powdery
mildew
thrives
during
warm,
humid days
and cool
nights.

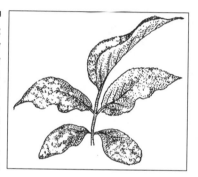

✔ **Peach leaf curl:** This fungal disease overwinters on peach tree twigs and migrates to the emerging leaves in humid, wet weather when temperatures are between 50° and 60°. The leaves curl, turn red and eventually die. Typically, the disease develops early the first year and the tree may grow through it and appear fine. But when the disease becomes established, the leaf curl returns and gets progressively worse each year. Eventually, the tree becomes debilitated. When you see the symptoms, it's too late to stop the organism that season.

You can control peach leaf curl with one — or at most two — applications. First, spray a fungicide such as lime sulfur or Bordeaux mixture in fall when the trees are dormant (leafless). For extra insurance, spray again in early spring before leaves emerge.

✔ **Phytophthora blight:** This bacterial disease attacks a variety of plants, including rhododendrons. It causes leaves to discolor and stems to die, often killing the entire plant. Another form can cause root rot and rapid plant death. Start with healthy plants and provide them with well-drained soil. Work the bark into the soil — this appears to discourage the fungus. Try not to wet the foliage in the afternoon or evening.

✔ **Rust:** Many different fungi cause rust, and the symptoms of this disease vary widely, depending on the kind of plant they infect. Some rusts, such as white pine blister rust, have complicated life cycles and must infect two different plants — in this case, white pines and *Ribes* species, such as currant and gooseberry. Symptoms include yellow, orange, reddish-brown, or black powdery spots or masses on leaves, needles, or twigs — see Figure 15-12. On juniper, cedar-apple rust appears as yellow to orange jelly like masses in the spring. Rust-susceptible trees and shrubs include juniper, fir, hemlock, pine, spruce, apple, hawthorn, and roses. Avoid susceptible plants or look for disease-resistant varieties. Provide good air circulation. Remove and destroy infected parts. Control with Bordeaux mix and copper-based fungicides.

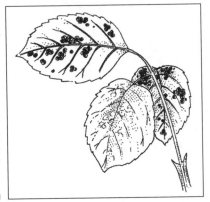

Figure 15-12:
Rust takes a
variety of
forms.

✔ **Slime flux:** Oozing and often bad-smelling sap running from old wounds or pruning cuts is caused by a bacterial rot inside the tree. Contact an arborist for control measures.

✔ **Sooty mold:** Insect pests, such as aphids, that release sticky drops of honeydew encourage this harmless but unattractive fungus disease. The black-colored mold grows on the honeydew, a sure sign that sucking insects are at work. Rinse off the mold and sap with soapy water, and then control the insect pests.

✔ **Root rots:** A number of diseases of plant roots are often lumped together under the term *root rots*. These soil-borne fungus diseases cause susceptible plants to turn yellow, wilt, and sometimes die, often a branch at a time. The fungi survive many years in the soil without a host, and usually become a problem when plants are overwatered or are growing in heavy clay soils. Some susceptible plants can be infected even under ideal conditions. After an infected plant shows severe symptoms, it's difficult to save.

The best way to avoid root diseases is to plant species that are resistant to locally known problems. In the southern and western United States, choose plants resistant to Armillaria root rot (known as *oak root fungus* in the western U.S. — see Figure 15-13), and in the southwest watch out for Texas root rot. Verticillium wilt can occur almost anywhere and is particularly troublesome on Japanese maples, olives, and cherries.

Mycelial plaques

Figure 15-13:
White strands under bark and mush-rooms at the base of plant are signs of Armillaria root rot.

Armillaria on tree bark

Least-toxic disease remedies

Use the following fungicides to make a protective coating on susceptible plants. Most are certified by organic gardening groups and are widely available at nurseries and garden centers. The following list is arranged from least to most toxic.

- ✔ **Remedy fungicide:** Baking soda is the key ingredient in this spray, which helps control a range of fungal diseases on ornamental plants and fruit trees. It is effective mostly only on powdery mildew and black spot on roses.

- ✔ **Sulfur:** This naturally occurring mineral is nontoxic but is a potential skin and eye irritant. You can buy sulfur in powder or liquid form. Powders can be applied with a dust applicator, or mixed with water according to label directions.

- ✔ **Lime sulfur:** Powerful and caustic but highly effective for some problems, lime sulfur can burn the leaves of some plants.

- ✔ **Bordeaux mixture:** A mix of copper and sulfur, this old-time fungicide is less toxic than pure copper but has the same limitations.

- ✔ **Copper:** This strong, broad-spectrum spray can be toxic to some plants, especially when overused. Use only as a last resort.

When you use any disease-control remedies on food crops, be sure to wash your harvest well — with soap — before eating it.

Outwitting Animals

It's maddening to plant trees and shrubs and nurture them carefully only to have a herd of deer chew them to the ground or hungry mice and rabbits munch the bark. The irony is that the nearby woods or fields or open space that attracted you to living in your home in the first place also provides habitat for many of the animals that plague you. You may, in fact, have moved into their territory. When trying to coexist with wild animals, the first priority is to keep your sense of humor. Beyond that, you can use a few techniques to protect your landscape trees and shrubs. If you don't succeed with one method, try another.

If you're at wit's end dealing with marauding deer, consult your local animal control officer. Normally, you can find these folks listed under the city, county, or state listings in the telephone book.

A couple of other resources are the books *Outwitting Critters: A Humane Guide for Confronting Devious Animals and Winning* by Bill Adler, Jr., and *Deer Proofing Your Yard and Garden* by Rhonda Massingham Hart.

- ✔ **Deer:** Deer are creatures of habit. They often travel along the same routes day after day, moving between two locations. Deer avoid some plants, although they are notorious for changing their minds. In general, pungent or fuzzy-leafed plants are safe, but some trees and shrubs attract them. Apple and crabapple trees, yew, rhododendron, roses, arborvitae, and others are practically an invitation to dinner. Avoid planting these deer-attractive plants if deer are a problem in your area. See Chapter 17 for a list of deer-resistant shrubs.

  Try surrounding your yard with a heavy fishing line attached to posts at about 3 feet high. This can startle deer because they don't see it, and they may retreat. This wouldn't be a method to try with young children around who could injure themselves on the line. Otherwise, build a deer-excluding fence, which has to be about 8 feet high (deer have been known to jump 10-foot fences). Surrounding individual shrubs and trees with a fence can also exclude deer. Wrap chicken wire or other wire fencing around the tree or shrub to protect it as high as a browsing deer can reach and anchor it to the ground. Cover the top if you are enclosing a small shrub.

Repellants, such as chemicals and startling sights and sounds, have a short-term effect because deer are smart. It doesn't take them long to figure out that the blaring radio, shiny tinfoil blowing in the breeze or bags of hair you tied to the trees can't hurt them.

✔ **Gophers:** These are burrowing rodents that are able to carve out 700 square yards of elaborate underground tunnels. While they tunnel, they work up quite an appetite and any plant roots that happen to be in the way turn into lunch. Stop them by installing underground barriers made of hardware cloth around trees and shrubs at planting time. You can also buy premade wire cages that you can use to line the planting hole. Install barriers at least 2 feet deep to block their burrowing. Various traps are available to catch gophers dead or alive, and traps are the only method used by orchardists and others who are serious about limiting gopher damage. Traps work best when set inside the tunnels.

✔ **Rabbits and rodents:** They may be small, but don't underestimate their ability to destroy your trees and shrubs. These creatures eat bark and young branches within their reach. When they chew off the bark, the plants lose the ability to move water and nutrients through their stems and die. Protect newly planted trees and shrubs with a circle of hardware cloth as described in Chapter 12.

Reducing Environmental Stresses

Many insects and diseases gain a foothold in your plants only after the trees and shrubs are already weakened by environmental stress. Stress may come from natural conditions, such as weather, or be the result of human activity — nearby construction, digging, or de-icing salt, for example. (See Chapter 19 for human-induced stresses.) This section describes the most common environmental stress symptoms and how to prevent them.

Winter damage

Winter injury describes several types of plant damage caused by environmental conditions during late fall, winter, or spring. Damage ranges from scorching on leaf edges to killed plants, based on the type of winter injury. Winter-injured plants often leaf out normally in the spring only to collapse later in the season after stored food reserves have been totally used up by the plant. Occasionally, damage doesn't become apparent until one or two years after the injury occurs. Strong winds and drought can often accentuate winter injury, described in more detail in the four following sections.

Frost

Late spring and early autumn frosts injure plants that aren't sufficiently dormant and able to withstand cold temperatures. Plants growing in colder zones than those in which they are adapted are usually the most vulnerable. Late spring frosts, for example, can kill expanding flower buds on magnolia or cherry. Early autumn frosts can damage young, succulent, actively growing shoots that are not yet prepared for freezing weather. Prune off damaged plant parts. The plants rarely suffer any long-term effects.

Frost cracks

Frost cracks are splits in the bark and wood of a tree that occur when winter sun causes an expansion of wood beneath the bark. The initial crack is often accompanied by a loud snap. In winter, the crack may become wider and narrower during colder or warmer periods. Such frost cracks often close and callus during the summer, only to open again in subsequent winters.

In midautumn, wrap the trunks of young trees with commercial tree wrap paper or burlap to protect against frost cracks. White, water-based paint applied to exposed trunks also prevents the sun from heating up the bark and wood. Frost cracks in trees are ideal sites for the entrance of wood decay organisms. Affected trees should be checked regularly to ensure that they are free from serious decay, and therefore not a hazard to surrounding buildings and living things.

Low temperature

Cold temperatures damage plants in several ways. Damage is most common in early fall or late spring, when there is little or no snow cover to insulate plant roots and moderate the soil temperature. Plants are also likely to be damaged during winters of little snow cover, and during periods of prolonged low temperatures. Rapid fluctuations in temperature are dangerous for plants no matter what time of year they occur.

Plants injured or killed directly by low winter temperatures are those planted in areas colder than their minimum hardiness zone. For instance, if a plant rated as hardy in USDA zones 5 through 9 is planted in zone 4, it will likely suffer in an average zone 4 winter. Such plants can't harden off at an appropriate rate or to an extent sufficient to withstand prevailing winter temperatures. However, even hardy plants can suffer injury during unusually cold periods or when temperatures drop rapidly or change frequently.

Plants in containers are particularly vulnerable to low winter temperatures — the roots lack below-ground protection. Roots are much less hardy to cold than trunks and branches. Roots of even the hardiest shrubs and trees die at temperatures between 0 and 10°. Avoid low-temperature injury to roots by any of the following methods:

- ✔ Place container plants in protected areas.
- ✔ Sink containers, plant and all, into the ground.
- ✔ Add a heavy layer of mulch to the container.

To prevent winter damage to your plants, avoid plants that aren't hardy where you live. To allow proper hardening of plant tissues, avoid fertilizing and pruning plants in late summer, which can promote new growth that won't mature before freezing occurs. Mulch around the bases of root-tender plants to help protect the crowns and roots from freezing temperatures. Even with good management, injury to young growth or insufficiently hardened tissues may still occur as a result of unusual weather patterns. Little can be done to prevent injury in these instances. After growth resumes in the spring, prune injured and dead stems and branches.

Snow and ice

Heavy snow or ice on weak or foliage-bearing limbs (as with evergreens) can result in breakage.

Prune trees and shrubs to reduce the amount of snow or ice they collect, and to eliminate weak branches. Branches with a wide angle to the main stem are generally stronger and can support more snow and ice than can those with a narrow or acute angle. Plant trees and shrubs away from places where snowmelt from roofs will drip on them. Wooden barriers may be built over small shrubs (see Figure 15-14) to allow snow and ice to slide off rather than accumulate. Narrow evergreens can be protected by encircling them with rope.

Figure 15-14:
Wood covers prevent snow build-up on shrubs.

Drought

Drought damage usually appears in late winter or very early spring on evergreen plants and in summer on trees and shrubs with broad leaves. The injury occurs during sunny and/or windy winter weather when plants lose water from their leaves faster than it can be replaced by roots that are frozen in soil. Broad-leaf evergreens, such as rhododendron, are especially vulnerable to winter drought damage. Needle-bearing evergreens, such as white pine, exhibit browning needle tips when injury is slight. Extensive injury may result in browning and premature drop of entire needles. In summer, horsechestnuts and Japanese maples typically suffer from lack of water. The damage first appears as brown edges on the leaves — called leaf scorch — and may result in the death of the entire leaf.

You can take several steps to avoid drought damage on your plants:

✔ Water plants thoroughly, especially during dry periods when plants are actively growing and in late autumn before the ground freezes.

✔ Mulch around the root zones to maintain moisture.

✔ Place a protective barrier of burlap over or around plants to protect them from winter winds and sun.

✔ For winter protection of broad-leaf evergreens, apply a waxy spray, such as Wilt-Pruf, that reduces water loss through the foliage: once in late autumn and again in midwinter. You can find Wilt-Pruf and similar sprays at garden centers and nurseries.

Sunscald

This type of injury occurs when the sun heats tree bark during the day, and cooler evening weather chills the bark rapidly after sunset. These abrupt fluctuations are most common on south or southwest sides of tree trunks and branches, and they may kill the inner bark in those areas. Apply white paint to the trunks and exposed limbs of susceptible species, such as citrus trees.

Eliminating Other Threats to Trees and Shrubs

A number of human-caused calamities can threaten trees and shrubs, but you can avoid most of them with a little care. Here are some things to watch out for:

✔ **Lawn mower and line trimmer disease:** Thrashing from weed whips or banging from lawn mowers (or from any equipment) can seriously damage tree trunks by interrupting the flow of water and nutrients through the trunk and opening wounds that invite insects and diseases. To protect trees growing in lawns, use a plastic tree collar sold in most nurseries, or keep a 3-foot, grass-free ring of mulch around the trunk. See Chapter 13 for more on mulching.

✔ **Grade changes:** Raising or lowering the soil level beneath the canopy of trees and around shrubs can seriously damage their roots and often kills large trees. Retaining walls (see Figure 15-15) or tree wells are good ways to protect roots, but you may need the help of a landscape contractor or arborist to construct them properly.

✔ **Soil compaction:** Cars, construction equipment, and even a lot of people walking beneath the canopy of a tree can compact soil, driving all the air out and suffocating the roots. During construction, protect tree roots by fencing off an area twice the diameter of the tree canopy. Don't park cars under trees. Mulch areas that receive heavy foot traffic.

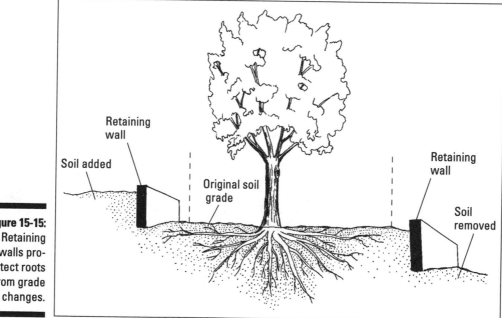

Figure 15-15: Retaining walls protect roots from grade changes.

Retaining wall

Soil added

Original soil grade

Retaining wall

Soil removed

✔ **Road salts:** De-icing salt poses a serious threat to trees and shrubs that grow near roads. As water drains off the roads, salts in the water accumulate in the soil, burning foliage and possible killing plants. Salts that splash onto foliage can also damage or kill trees and shrubs. You can leach road salts out of the soil with heavy irrigation, but a better solution is avoid planting within 20 feet of a frequently iced road, and to divert drainage water from the road away from plants. See Chapters 16 and 17 for lists of trees and shrubs that tolerate salty soil.

Part V

Part of Tens

The 5th Wave

By Rich Tennant

Oh, those silly things? They've been blooming every June since anyone can remember. We just stay out of the backyard for about a month and keep the dog on a leash.

In this part . . .

Lists reduce big concepts into bite-sized chunks. I love lists — so this part is pure indulgence. I've included lists of trees and shrubs for special places and lists of plants with special features. Because you may be killing your plants unintentionally, I wrote up a list of probable causes. And if you don't have any trees and shrubs to kill yet, flip to the last chapter for some landscape design ideas.

Chapter 16

Ten Sets of Terrific Trees

In This Chapter

▶ Finding the right tree for common situations

▶ Trees with special features

▶ Choosing trees for difficult growing sites

*W*hether you have a small urban lot, a few rural acres, or an estate, you can find the right size tree to fit your needs. Wet soil, salt breeze, strong winds, dusty roadside conditions — no problem. Some trees will thrive there. If you want a special tree for a garden specimen, consider ones with weeping limbs, horizontally spreading branches, or attractive bark that keep the tree interesting all year 'round.

Trees for Small Yards

In a pinch for space? These trees stay under 30 feet tall. Plant them in yards near single-story homes, under utility wires, or anywhere you want a small, well-behaved tree. Also take a look at Chapter 8 for a list of tall shrubs that can be pruned into small trees.

✔ **Maple:** Trident *(Acer buergeranum)*, Fullmoon *(A. japonicum)*, Japanese *(A. palmatum)*. Zones 5 to 8.

✔ **Serviceberry:** *Amelanchier species.* Zones 3 to 7.

✔ **Brazilian butterfly tree:** *Bauhinia* species. Zones 9 to 11.

✔ **Gray birch:** *Betula populifolia.* Zones 3 to 6.

✔ **Hornbeam:** *Carpinus caroliniana.* Zones 4 to 9.

✔ **Redbud:** *Cercis canadensis.* Zones 5 to 9.

✔ **Dogwood:** Flowering *(Cornus florida)*, cornelian *(C. mas)*, kousa *(C. kousa)*. Zones 5 to 9, depending on species.

✔ **Hawthorn:** *Crataegus* species. Zones 4 to 7.

- **Australian willow:** *Geijera parviflora.* Zones 9 to 11.
- **Crape myrtle.** *Lagerstroemia indica.* Zones 7 to 9.
- **Magnolia.** Star *(Magnolia stellata),* saucer *(M. × soulangiana).* Zones 4 to 8.
- **Flowering crabapple:** *Malus* species. Zones 4 to 7.
- **Persian ironwood:** *Parrotia persica.* Zones 5 to 8.
- **Carolina cherrylaurel:** *Prunus caroliniana.* Zones 7 to 10.
- **Mountain ash:** *Sorbus* species. Zones 3 to 7.
- **Japanese stewartia:** *Stewartia pseudocamellia.* Zones 5 to 7.
- **Japanese snowbell:** *Styrax japonicus.* Zones 5 to 8.

Large Trees for Large Spaces

These trees grow at least 50 feet tall and many have large, spreading canopies. Plant these big guys where their branches have room to roam.

- **Maples:** Sugar *(Acer saccharum),* Norway *(A. platanoides),* red *(A. rubrum),* silver *(A. saccharinum).* Zones 3 to 9, depending on species.
- **Birches:** *Betula,* many species. Zones 2 to 9, depending on species.
- **Cedar:** *Cedrus* species. Zones 6 to 9, depending on species.
- **Katsura tree:** *Cercidiphyllum japonicum.* Zones 4 to 8.
- **Yellowwood:** *Cladrastis lutea.* Zones 4 to 8.
- **Beech:** *Fagus* species. Zones 4 to 7.
- **Ash:** *Fraxinus* species. Zones 3 to 9, depending on species.
- **Sweetgum:** *Liquidambar styraciflua.* Zones 5 to 9.
- **Bull bay or southern magnolia:** *Magnolia grandiflora.* Zones 6 to 9.
- **Dawn redwood:** *Metasequoia glyptostroboides.* Zones 5 to 8.
- **Tupelo:** *Nyssa sylvatica.* Zones 4 to 9.
- **Spruce:** *Picea* species. Zones 2 to 8, depending on species.
- **Pine:** Austrian *(P. nigra),* white *(Pinus strobus),* Scotch *(P. sylvestris).* Zones 3 to 7, depending on species.
- **London planetree:** *Platanus × acerifolia.* Zones 5 to 8.
- **Oak:** *Quercus* species. Zones 4 to 9, varies with species.
- **Lacebark elm:** *Ulmus parvifolia.* Zones 5 to 9.

Street Trees

Life on the street is tough, but these contenders have what it takes — the ability to adapt to air pollution; road salt; full sun; and often dry, compacted soil. Some stay short enough to stay out of the utility wires, while others will mature into majestic road-shading specimens.

- **Maple:** Trident *(Acer buergeranum)*, hedge *(A. campestre)*, amur *(A. ginnala)*. Zones 5 to 8.

- **Hornbeam:** *Carpinus betulus*. Zones 5 to 8.

- **Hackberry:** *Celtis* species. Zones 4 to 9, depending on species. Large tree.

- **Hawthorn:** *Crataegus* species. Zones 4 to 7.

- **Maidenhair tree:** *Ginkgo biloba*. Zones 4 to 8. Large tree.

- **London planetree:** *Platanus × acerifolia* 'Bloodgood'. Zones 5 to 8. Large tree.

- **Callery pear:** *Pyrus calleryana* 'Bradford', 'Chanticleer'. Zones 5 to 8.

- **Oak:** Pin *(Quercus palustris)*, willow *(Q. phellos)*, English *(Q. robur)*. Zones 5 to 9, depending on species. All large trees.

- **Lacebark elm:** *Ulmus parvifolia*. Zones 5 to 9. Large tree.

- **Zelkova:** *Zelkova serrata* 'Green Vase'. Zones 5 to 8.

Trees that Tolerate Salt Spray

Whether it comes naturally from the sea or as a de-icer from a wintry road, salt spray causes significant injury to many trees. Salt spray can travel 100 feet or more from busy roads, but the following species can take whatever the highway department dishes out.

- **Silk tree:** *Albizia julibrissin*. Zones 6 to 9.

- **Shad:** *Amelanchier* species. Zones 3 to 7.

- **Birch:** Paper *(B. papyrifera)*, gray *(Betula populifolia)*. Zones 3 to 6.

- **Common hackberry:** *Celtis occidentalis*. Zones 3 to 9.

- **Cockspur hawthorn:** *Crataegus crus-galli*. Zones 4 to 7.

- **Carrot wood:** *Cupaniopsis anacardioides*. Zones 10 to 11.

- **Red flowering gum:** *Eucalyptus ficifolia*. Zones 9 to 11.

- **Honey locust:** *Gleditsia triacanthos*. Zones 4 to 9.

- ✔ **Eastern red cedar:** *Juniperus virginiana.* Zones 4 to 9.

- ✔ **Tupelo:** *Nyssa sylvatica.* Zones 4 to 9.

- ✔ **White spruce:** *Picea glauca.* Zones 2 to 6.

- ✔ **Pine:** Limber *(Pinus flexilis),* Japanese black *(P. thunbergii),* Japanese white *(P. parviflora).* Zones 4 to 8, depending on species.

- ✔ **White poplar:** *Populus alba.* Zones 3 to 8.

- ✔ **Cottonwood:** *Populus deltoides.* Zones 3 to 9.

- ✔ **Black locust:** *Robinia pseudoacacia.* Zones 4 to 8.

- ✔ **Willow:** *Salix* species. Zones 4 to 8, depending on species.

Flood-Tolerant Trees

If you need trees that live where seasonal flooding occurs, choose from these species. They can tolerate flooded soil for as long as 30 to 40 percent of the growing season. In other words, if your growing season is 180 days long, these trees can live with their roots in soggy ground for 7 to 10 weeks a year.

- ✔ **Deciduous trees** include Italian alder *(Alnus cordata)* and common alder *(A. glutinosa),* green ash *(Fraxinus pennsylvanica),* river birch *(Betula nigra)* and gray birch *(B. populifolia),* sweetgum *(Liquidambar styraci-flua),* swamp oak *(Quercus bicolor)* and pin oak *(Q. palustris),* white poplar *(Populus alba)* and cottonwood *(P. deltoides),* and most willows *(Salix* species). Some maples, including red *(Acer rubrum),* boxelder *(A. negundo),* and silver *(A. saccharinum)* also adapt to flooding.

- ✔ **Deciduous conifers** include baldcypress *(Taxodium distichum),* dawn redwood *(Metasequoia glyptostroboides),* and larch *(Larix decidua).*

- ✔ **Evergreens** include balsam fir *(Abies balsamea),* eastern white cedar *(Thuja occidentalis),* white spruce *(Picea glauca),* and black spruce *(P. mariana).*

Trees with Outstanding Fall Foliage Color

Choose deciduous trees with colorful autumn foliage to light up the land-scape as the summer comes to a close. As the green leaves give way to yellow, orange, red, and purple, look to these species for a fiery spectacle.

- ✔ **Yellow to orange-foliaged trees** include birch *(Betula* species), katsura tree *(Cercidiphyllum japonicum),* larch *(Larix* species), maidenhair tree *(Ginkgo biloba),* maple *(Acer* species), mountain ash *(Sorbus* species), persian parrotia *(Parrotia persica)*, sassafras *(Sassafras albidum)*, serviceberry *(Amelanchier* species), sourwood *(Oxydendrum arboreum)*, stewartia *(Stewartia* species), sweetgum *(Liquidambar styraciflua)*, and tupelo *(Nyssa sylvatica)*.

✔ **Red to purple foliage** occurs on dogwood *(Cornus* species), maple *(Acer* species), oaks *(Quercus* species), sassafras *(Sassafras albidum)*, stewartia *(Stewartia* species), sweetgum *(Liquidambar styraciflua)*, white ash *(Fraxinus americana)*, and zelkova *(Zelkova serrata)*.

Trees with Decorative Bark

Think year 'round ornamental value when you choose trees with decorative bark. These trees have peeling, flaking, or smooth bark that add interest and color to the landscape in all seasons of the year.

✔ **Smooth, gray barked** trees include beech *(Fagus* species), hornbeam *(Capinus* species), and yellowwood *(Cladrastis lutea)*.

✔ **Smooth reddish-brown barked** trees include cherry *(Prunus* species) and Japanese tree lilac *(Syringa reticulata)*.

✔ **Flaky, mottled bark,** often in red-orange, gray, green, brown, and cream, occurs on sycamore maple *(Acer pseudoplatanus)*, gum *(Eucalyptus* species), stewartia *(Stewartia* species), lacebark elm *(Ulmus parvifolia)*, Persian ironwood *(Parrotia persica)*, and planetree *(Platanus* species). Some pines, including Scotch *(Pinus sylvestris)*, Japanese red *(P. densiflora)*, and lacebark *(Pinus bungeana)* also have flaking, orange-red and gray bark.

✔ **Peeling white or red bark** occurs on birch *(Betula* species) and paperbark maple *(Acer griseum)*.

Column-Shaped Trees

Tall and narrow, these trees sometimes stand out like exclamation points in the landscape. Use these trees where you need a vertical accent in the landscape, such as at entrances and as contrast to horizontal trees and buildings. They often look best in groups of three or more. Cultivars are often named 'Columnaris' or 'Fastigiata'.

✔ **Norway maple:** *Acer platanoides* 'Columnare'. Zones 4 to 7.

✔ **Hornbeam:** *Carpinus betulus* 'Frans Fontaine'. Zones 5 to 8.

✔ **Leyland cypress:** *Cupressocyparis leylandii*. Zones 6 to 10.

- **Italian cypress:** *Cupressus sempervirens.* Zones 7 to 9.
- **Maidenhair tree:** *Ginkgo biloba* 'Fastigiata', 'Princeton Sentry'. Zones 4 to 8.
- **Dawn redwood:** *Metasequoia glyptostroboides.* Zones 5 to 8.
- **Lombardy poplar:** *Populus nigra* 'Italica', 'Afghanica'. Zones 3 to 9.
- **Black locust:** *Robinia pseudoacacia* 'Pyramidalis'. Zones 4 to 8.
- **Baldcypress:** *Taxodium distichum.* Zones 4 to 11.
- **Linden:** *Tilia cordata* 'Corinthian'. Zones 3 to 7.

Weeping Trees

Many trees with weeping or pendulous branches are grafted onto an upright trunk that keeps the otherwise prostrate limbs off the ground. Use weeping trees as specimens in places where their unique forms suggest falling water. Some tree species, including the following, have weeping cultivars, usually called 'Pendula' or 'Pendulum'. Check your local nurseries for more.

- **Japanese maple:** *Acer palmatum* var. *dissectum.* Many cultivars. Zones 5 to 8.
- **Weeping birch:** *Betula pendula* 'Youngii', 'Dalecarlica'. Zones 2 to 6.
- **Peashrub:** *Caragana arborescens* 'Pendula'. Zones 2 to 7.
- **Katsura tree:** *Cercidiphyllum japonicum* 'Pendulum'. Zones 4 to 8.
- **Beech:** *Fagus sylvatica* 'Pendula', 'Purpurea Pendula'. Zones 4 to 7.
- **Flowering crabapple:** *Malus* 'Red Jade', 'White Cascade', 'Molten Lava'. Zones 4 to 7.
- **Weeping cherry:** *Prunus subhirtella* 'Pendula'. Zones 5 to 8.

Chapter 17

Ten Lists of Super Shrubs

In This Chapter

▶ Shrubs for special situations

▶ Attracting and discouraging wildlife

▶ Flowers and foliage for the senses

*Y*ou know what you want — a shrub that lives in full sun on dry soil, feeds the birds, and has colorful foliage, but how can you find such a plant? When you need a shrub for a special purpose, look to the lists in this chapter. Whether you have a difficult shady or soggy site, want to attract or discourage wildlife, or just smell the roses, you can find a winner among the shrubs listed here. Turn to the shrub description chapters in Part III for more specific information about each of these problem-solvers.

Shrubs with Berries for Wildlife

Birds and small animals animate the landscape and bring cheer to dreary autumn and winter landscapes. The following shrubs provide food that attracts these hungry critters.

✔ **Bearberry:** *Arctostaphylos uva-ursi.* Zones 2 to 6. Evergreen.

✔ **Dogwood:** *Cornus* species. Zones 3 to 9, depending on species. Deciduous.

✔ **Holly:** *Ilex* species. Zones 4 to 10, depending on species. Deciduous, evergreen.

✔ **Juniper:** *Juniperus* species. Zones 2 to 6. Evergreen.

✔ **Bayberry:** *Myrica* species. Zones 3 to 10, varies by species. Deciduous.

✔ **Firethorn:** *Pyracantha* species. Zones 5 to 10. Evergreen.

✔ **Elderberry:** *Sambucus canadensis.* Zones 3 to 9. Deciduous.

✔ **Blueberry:** *Vaccinum* species. Zones 3 to 7. Deciduous.

✔ **Viburnum:** *Viburnum* species. Zones 3 to 9, varies by species. Deciduous.

Shrubs with Fragrant Flowers

Plant one of these delightfully scented shrubs near a window, bench, or entrance to your home and enjoy the perfume.

✔ **Glossy abelia:** *Abelia grandiflora*. Zones 6 to 9. Evergreen.

✔ **Summersweet:** *Clethra alnifolia*. Zones 4 to 9. Deciduous.

✔ **Winter hazel:** *Corylopsis* species. Zones 6 to 9. Deciduous.

✔ **Broom:** *Cytisus* species. Zones 5 to 8, depending on species. Deciduous.

✔ **Daphne:** *Daphne* species. Zones 4 to 9, depending on species. Deciduous.

✔ **Gardenia:** *Gardenia jasminoides*. Zones 8 to 10. Evergreen.

✔ **Sweetspire:** *Itea virginica*. Zones 6 to 9. Deciduous.

✔ **Lavender:** *Lavandula* species. Zones 5 to 9, depending on species. Evergreen.

✔ **Spicebush:** *Lindera benzoin*. Zones 5 to 8. Deciduous.

✔ **Star magnolia:** *Magnolia stellata*. Zones 4 to 8. Deciduous.

✔ **Fragrant olive:** *Osmanthus* species. Zones 9 to 10. Evergreen.

✔ **Mock orange:** *Philadelphus* × *virginalis*. Zones 4 to 8. Deciduous.

✔ **Cherry laurel:** *Prunus* species. Zones 6 to 8. Evergreen.

✔ **Rose:** *Rosa* species. Zones 3 to 9, depending on species. Deciduous.

✔ **Lilac:** *Syringa* species. Zones 3 to 9, depending on species. Deciduous.

✔ **Viburnum:** *Viburnum* species. Zones 4 to 9. Deciduous and evergreen.

Shrubs with Colorful Foliage

Flowers are nice, but foliage lasts all season long. Choose a cheerful specimen from among these showy ornamentals.

✔ **Glossy abelia:** *Abelia grandiflora* 'Francis Mason'. Zones 6 to 9.

✔ **Flowering maple:** *Abutilon* × *hybridum*. Zones 8 to 9.

✔ **Gold dust plant:** *Aucuba japonica*. Zones 7 to 10.

✔ **Japanese barberry:** *Berberis thunbergii* 'Crimson Pygmy', 'Rose Glow', 'Aurea', 'Bonanza Gold'. Zones 4 to 8.

✔ **Heaths and heathers:** *Calluna* and *Erica* species. Zones 4 to 6.

✔ **Falsecypress:** *Chamaecyparis* species. Zones 4 to 8.

✔ **Tatarian dogwood:** *Cornus alba* 'Argenteo-marginata', 'Gouchault', 'Ivory Halo' and **Redosier dogwood:** *Cornus sericea* 'Silver and Gold'. Zones 3 to 7.

✔ **Smokebush:** *Cotinus coggygria* 'Royal Purple'. Zones 4 to 8.

✔ **Daphne:** *Daphne* × *burkwoodii* 'Carol Mackie'. Zones 4 to 7.

✔ **Wintercreeper:** *Euonymus fortunei* 'Emerald Gaiety', 'Sunspot'. Zones 5 to 9.

✔ **Hypericum:** *Hypericum* × *moserianum* 'Tricolor'. Zones 7 to 8.

✔ **Juniper:** *Juniperus* species 'Old Gold', 'Icee Blue', others. Zones 3 to 8.

✔ **Pieris:** *Pieris japonica* 'Forest Flame'. Zones 5 to 7.

Shrubs for Soggy Sites

Gardeners in arid climates would gladly trade for some of your surplus moisture. Take advantage of your bounty with these water-loving shrubs.

✔ **Atlantic white cedar.** *Chamaecyparis thyoides*. Zones 4 to 8. Evergreen.

✔ **Bottlebrush buckeye:** *Aesculus parviflora*. Zones 4 to 8. Deciduous.

✔ **Red chokeberry:** *Aronia arbutifolia*. Zones 4 to 9. Deciduous.

✔ **Carolina allspice:** *Calycanthus floridus*. Zones 4 to 9. Decidous.

✔ **Summersweet:** *Clethra alnifolia*. Zones 4 to 9. Deciduous.

✔ **Redosier dogwood:** *Cornus sericea*. Zones 2 to 7. Deciduous.

✔ **Seabuckthorn:** *Hippophea rhamnoides*. Zones 3 to 7. Deciduous.

✔ **Winterberry:** *Ilex verticilata*. Zones 3 to 9. Deciduous.

✔ **Sweetspire:** *Itea virginica*. Zones 6 to 9. Deciduous.

✔ **Leucothoe:** *Leucothoe fontanesiana*. Zones 5 to 8. Evergreen.

✔ **Spicebush:** *Lindera benzoin*. Zones 5 to 8. Deciduous.

✔ **Swamp azalea:** *Rhododendron viscosum*. Zones 4 to 9. Deciduous.

- **Willow:** *Salix* species. Zones 2 to 8, depending on species. Deciduous.
- **Elderberry:** *Sambucus canadensis.* Zones 3 to 9. Deciduous.
- **Eastern white cedar:** *Thuja occidentalis.* Zones 3 to 7. Evergreen.

Shrubs for the Shade

These shady characters go undercover to avoid the heat. Some prefer light shade, while others lurk in the shadows.

- **Gold dust plant:** *Aucuba japonica.* Zones 7 to 10. Evergreen.
- **Camellia:** *Camellia japonica.* Zones 8 to 10. Evergreen.
- **Falsecypress:** *Chamaecyparis* species. Zones 4 to 8. Evergreen.
- **Summersweet:** *Clethra alnifolia.* Zones 4 to 9. Deciduous.
- **Daphne:** *Daphne* species. Zones 4 to 7. Deciduous.
- **Wintercreeper:** *Euonymus fortunei.* Zones 5 to 9. Evergreen.
- **Fothergilla:** *Fothergilla* species. Zones 4 to 8, Deciduous.
- **Hydrangea:** *Hydrangea* species. Zones 3 to 9, Deciduous.
- **Mountain laurel:** *Kalmia latifolia.* Zones 4 to 8. Evergreen.
- **Kerria:** *Kerria japonica.* Zones 4 to 9. Deciduous.
- **Leucothoe:** *Leucothoe fontanesiana.* Zones 5 to 8. Evergreen.
- **Fringe flower:** *Loropetalum chinense.* Zones 7 to 9. Evergreen.
- **Mahonia:** *Mahonia* species. Zones 5 to 9. Evergreen.
- **Bayberry:** *Myrica* species. Zones 3 to 10, varies by species. Deciduous.
- **Pieris:** *Pieris japonica.* Zones 5 to 7. Evergreen.
- **Pittosporum:** *Pittosporum* species. Zones 8 to 9. Evergreen.
- **Rhododendron:** *Rhododendron* species. Zones 2 to 8. Deciduous, evergreen.
- **Sweetbox:** *Sarcococca* species. Zones 6 to 8. Evergreen.
- **Skimmia:** *Skimmia japonica.* Zones 7 to 8. Evergreen.
- **Yew.** *Taxus* species. Zones 4 to 7, depending on species. Evergreen.
- **Viburnum:** *Viburnum* species. Zones 3 to 9, varies by species. Deciduous.

Shrubs for Seaside Conditions

A day at the beach is no picnic for most shrubs, but these salty dogs can take the heat.

- **Deciduous shrubs** include bearberry *(Arctostaphylos uva-ursi)*, red chokeberry *(Aronia arbutifolia)*, cotoneaster *(Cotoneaster* species), Russian olive *(Elaeagnus angustifolia)*, seabuckthorn *(Hippophae rhamnoides)*, hydrangea *(Hydrangea macrophylla)*, northern bayberry *(Myrica pensylvanica)*, purpleleaf sand cherry *(Prunus* × *cistena, P. maritima)*, and beach rose *(Rosa rugosa)*.

- **Evergreens** include heaths and heathers *(Calluna* and *Erica* species), broom *(Cytisus* and *Genista* species), escallonia *(Escallonia rubra)*, Japanese euonymus *(Euonymus japonicus)*, common juniper *(Juniperus communis)*, lavender *(Lavendula angustifolia)*, oleander *(Nerium oleander)*, rosemary *(Rosmarinus officinalis)*, and yucca *(Yucca* species).

Roadside Survivors

It's a dirty job, but somebody's got to do it. These shrubs can take the heat, cold, drought, salt, air pollution, and neglect that go with the territory. In other words, these are some of the toughest characters you'll ever plant.

- **Deciduous shrubs** include Siberian peashrub *(Caragana arborescens)*, Russian olive *(Elaeagnus angustifolia)*, forsythia *(Forsythia* species), seabuckthorn *(Hippophae rhamnoides)*, Tatarian honeysuckle *(Lonicera tatarica)*, northern bayberry *(Myrica pensylvanica)*, potentilla *(Potentilla fruticosa* and hybrids), beach rose *(Rosa rugosa)*, and Vanhoutte spirea *(Spiraea* × *vanhouttei)*.

- **Evergreen shrubs** include Scotch broom *(Cytisus* species), Chinese holly *(Ilex cornuta)*, juniper *(Juniperus communis* and *J. sabina)*, heavenly bamboo *(Nandina domestica)*, and oleander *(Nerium oleander)*.

Deer-Resistant Shrubs

If four-footed browsers view your yard as one big salad bar, consider the plants on this list. Although not guaranteed to deter the most determined foragers, most deer find these shrubs distasteful.

✔ **Deciduous shrubs** include barberry (*Berberis* species), buddleia (*Buddleia davidii*), cotoneaster (*Cotoneaster* species), Russian olive (*Elaeagnus angustifolia*), forsythia (*Forsythia* species), potentilla (*Potentilla fruticosa* and hybrids), lilac (*Syringa* species), and viburnum (*Viburnum* species).

✔ **Evergreen shrubs** include glossy abelia (*Abelia grandiflora*), boxwood (*Buxus* species), heaths and heathers (*Calluna* and *Erica* species), Japanese yew plum (*Cephalotaxus harringtonia*), St. Johnswort (*Hypericum* species), juniper (*Juniperus* species), heavenly bamboo (*Nandina domestica*), and oleander (*Nerium oleander*).

Shrubs for Coldest Climates

When your min/max thermometer reads −40°, be glad that you planted some of these cold-hardy survivors. Hailing from some of the coldest regions on the planet, the following shrubs should tolerate whatever Jack Frost throws at them.

✔ **Hardy to zone 2** shrubs include bearberry (*Arctostaphylos uva-ursi*), Siberian pea shrub (*Caragana arborescens*), redosier dogwood (*Cornus sericea*), Russian olive (*Elaeagnus angustifolia*), potentilla (*Potentilla fruticosa* and hybrids), and cranberry (*Viburnum trilobum, V. opulus*).

✔ **Hardy to zone 3** shrubs include hydrangea (*Hydrangea arobrescens*), juniper (*Juniperus communis, J. chinensis, J. sabina*), purpleleaf sand cherry (*Prunus* × *cistena*), alder buckthorn (*Rhamnus frangula*), rose (*Rosa glauca, R. rugosa*), Russian cypress (*Microbiota decussata*), basket willow (*Salix purpurea*), spirea (*Spirea japonica*), eastern white cedar (*Thuja occidentalis*), and lilac (*Syringa* × *henryi, S. hyacinthiflora, S. patula* 'Miss Kim').

Shrubs Worthy of Greater Attention

When you just want something different, give these shrubs a try. Although not as commonly used as some other shrubs, they deserve far greater consideration.

✔ **Deciduous shrubs** include bottlebrush buckeye (*Aesculus parviflora*), small-leafed lilacs (*Syringa microphylla, S. meyeri, S. patula*), viburnums (*Viburnum* species), highbush blueberry (*Vaccinium corymbosum, V. ashei*), summersweet (*Clethra alnifolia*), and fothergilla (*Fothergilla* species).

✔ **Evergreen shrubs** include yew plum (*Cephalotaxus haringtonia*) and Russian cypress (*Microbiota decussata*).

Chapter 18

Ten Types of Troublesome Trees

In This Chapter

▶ Avoiding trees that damage septic systems

▶ Preventing extra yard cleanup

▶ Keeping your home and car safe from disaster

*S*ome guests wear out their welcome more quickly than others. You know the ones I mean. They use up the hot water and leave wet towels on the floor. They don't offer to help with the dishes. They have one affliction after another.

Well, some trees are like that, too. But unlike houseguests, these big guys stick around for a long time and can cause more than a strained friendship. Think twice before you invite any of these trees onto your property.

Leach-Field Saboteurs

LEAF LINGO

Invasive tree roots are one of the leading causes of leach field failure. A *leach field* is the drainage area for a private septic system and is composed of perforated pipes laid in a gravel bed. The following moisture-seeking trees grow vigorous roots that plug the holes in the pipes. Most of these trees also have shallow roots that can crack pavement and heave patio stones.

- ✔ **Maple species:** Red *(Acer rubrum)*, boxelder *(A. negundo)*, and silver *(A. saccharinum)*. Zones 3 to 9.
- ✔ **Birch species:** *Betula* species. Zones 2 to 6, varies by species.
- ✔ **Beech:** *Fagus* species. Zones 4 to 7.
- ✔ **Ficus:** *Ficus* species. Hardiness varies, but is generally not frost hardy.
- ✔ **Honey locust:** *Gleditsia triacanthos.* Zones 4 to 9.
- ✔ **Sweetgum:** *Liquidambar styraciflua.* Zones 5 to 9.
- ✔ **Poplar species:** *Populus* species. Zones 3 to 9, varies by species.

- ✔ **Black locust:** *Robinia pseudoacacia.* Zones 4 to 8.
- ✔ **Willow:** *Salix* species. Zones 4 to 8, varies by species.

Weak-Wooded Home Wreckers

Remember the story about the tortoise and the hare? The rabbit was faster, but the turtle won the race. A slow, but steady pace is a virtue when it comes to trees, too. Slow growers build strong, dense wood. Vigorous trees that seem to grow while you watch have weaker wood that can't hold up to strong wind, ice, and snow. Plant these weak-wooded wonders only where they can't do any damage.

- ✔ **Boxelder:** *Acer negundo.* Zones 2 to 9.
- ✔ **Red maple:** *Acer rubrum.* Zones 3 to 9.
- ✔ **Silver maple:** *Acer saccharinum.* Zones 3 to 9.
- ✔ **Horsechestnut:** *Aesculus hippocastanum.* Zones 4 to 8.
- ✔ **Catalpa:** *Catalpa* species. Zones 5 to 8.
- ✔ **Eucalyptus:** *Eucalyptus* species. Zones 9 to 11, varies by species.
- ✔ **Poplar:** *Populus* species. Zones 3 to 9, varies by species.
- ✔ **Willow:** *Salix* species. Zones 4 to 8, varies by species.

Messy Guests

These trees drop leaves, flowers, pollen, sap, fruit, twigs, the kitchen sink — you name it. If you enjoy a day out in the yard with a rake, by all means, plant one of these untidy trees. These species do have a place in the landscape — just be sure it's not too close to your house or driveway. Although not listed here, note that nearly all fruit and nut trees drop messy fruits.

- ✔ **Boxelder:** *Acer negundo.* Zones 2 to 9. Dead twigs, leaves, and seeds.
- ✔ **Horsechestnut:** *Aesculus hippocastanum.* Zones 4 to 7. Fruit, weak branches, and large foliage.
- ✔ **Catalpa:** *Catalpa* species. Zones 5 to 8. Flowers, twigs, large seed pods, and huge leaves.
- ✔ **Honey locust:** *Gleditsia triacanthos.* Zones 4 to 9. Fruit pods — buy fruit-less cultivars.
- ✔ **Walnut:** *Juglans* species. Zones 4 to 9, varies by species. Large nuts dent cars and stain concrete and wood. Large foliage in autumn.

✔ **Sweetgum:** *Liquidambar styraciflua.* Zones 5 to 9. Messy fruit.

✔ **Pine:** *Pinus* species. Zones 3 to 7. Sticky sap.

✔ **Planetree, sycamore:** *Plantanus* species. Zones 5 to 8. Drops leaves throughout summer; messy fruit.

✔ **Oak:** *Quercus* species. Zones 3 to 8, varies by species. Hard, messy acorns and abundant foliage and pollen.

✔ **Willow:** *Salix* species. Drop twigs and leaves and have brittle wood. Zones 4 to 8, varies by species.

Chronic Complainers

"My tummy hurts. A mosquito bit me. I need a Band-Aid. Can you take my temperature?" Ack! If it's not one thing, then it's another. The plants on this list have some fine ornamental features, but they come at a price. Pests and diseases just seek these plants out and make their lives — and yours — miserable. Flip to Chapter 15 for more information.

✔ **European white birch:** *Betula pendula.* Zones 2 to 6. Bronze birch borer, leaf miner.

✔ **Flowering dogwood:** *Cornus florida.* Zones 5 to 9. Borers, fungus diseases.

✔ **Hawthorn:** *Crataegus* species. Zones 4 to 7. Borers, scab, aphids, scale, fireblight, cedar hawthorn rust, fungus diseases.

✔ **Ash:** *Fraxinus* species. Zones 4 to 9. Borers, scale, and cankers.

✔ **Honey locust:** *Gleditsia triacanthos.* Zones 4 to 9. Borers, webworm, canker, rust, powdery mildew.

✔ **Flowering crabapples:** *Malus* species. Zones 4 to 7. Aphids, borers, fireblight, apple scab, canker, cedar apple rust. Plant resistant cultivars.

✔ **Spruce:** *Picea* species. Zones 3 to 7. Spruce budworm, bagworms, white pine weevil, aphids, canker.

✔ **Pine:** *Pinus* species. Zones 3 to 7. White pine weevil, webworm, scale, rusts, canker, blights.

✔ **Planetree, sycamore:** *Platanus* species. Zones 5 to 8. Borers, bagworms, scales, moths, anthracnose, canker.

✔ **Poplar:** *Populus* species. Zones 3 to 9, varies by species. Borer, caterpillars, several cankers, rusts.

✔ **Willow:** *Salix* species. Zones 4 to 8, varies by species. Aphids, weevils, borers, blight, canker, anthracnose.

✔ **Mountain ash:** *Sorbus aucuparia.* Zones 3 to 6. Borer, fireblight, canker.

Chapter 19

(Must be) Ten Ways to Lose Your Cover

In This Chapter

▶ Using food, water, and pesticides wisely

▶ Preventing tree and shrub damage from pets and machines

▶ Mowing and maintaining your landscape for tree safety

Trees and shrubs withstand harsh weather, inhospitable climates, and impossible soils only to meet their demise at the hands of well-meaning humans. Help your valuable landscape plants survive to ripe old ages by avoiding the common scenarios in this chapter.

Wrong Plant, Wrong Place

You risk failure when you plant a big tree in a small space, a cold-sensitive shrub in a frigid climate, or an acid-loving plant in alkaline soil. Your trees and shrubs depend on you to make informed decisions about their future, to use your best judgement in their selection and planting. Check out Chapter 2, and then read the plant descriptions in Parts II and III when deciding which trees and shrubs to choose and where to plant them.

Withholding Food and Water

Every living thing needs food and water — that's a pretty basic concept. Most soils contain enough nutrients for trees and shrubs to get by, but if the soil pH is too high or too low, the roots can't absorb those nutrients. Without available nutrients, the tree goes hungry and grows slowly, if at all. Take a soil sample to a testing lab and apply the amendments your tree needs.

And what is it with the weather? It's too wet; it's too dry. How is a tree supposed to cope? Mature trees have seen it all and can handle nearly anything the weatherman throws at them. Young trees, however, need a helping hand. Keep their root zone moist, but not saturated, until they can go it alone — at least two to three years after planting. In a prolonged drought, consider watering the thirstiest trees, regardless of their age.

The Ties That Bind

As any Thanksgiving dinner survivor can attest, too much of a good thing can hurt. That goes for trees, too. When you give a tree a sturdy start by tying it to a stake, you have to remember to untie it. The tree guard that you wrapped around the trunk to keep the bark safe from gnawing animals needs to expand with the growing girth. Check each tie and wrap at least twice a year and remove or loosen any tight ones before they become a strangling noose.

Running With Scissors

Bad pruning is much worse than a bad haircut. Not only is it unattractive, it can cause the plant's early demise. Leaving stubs and cutting branches flush with the trunk are bad practices that make healing difficult for the tree. While the tree struggles to close its wounds, insects and diseases can easily enter. Done right, pruning can improve the tree's health or at least not injure it. See Chapter 14 for proper pruning methods.

Substance Abuse

Herbicides are chemicals designed to kill plants and they can damage more than your intended target. Herbicides hurt trees and shrubs two ways — through the soil and roots or by leaf and bark contact. Products that you spread on the soil, such as "weed and feed" lawn products, contain herbicides that trees and shrubs can absorb through their roots. Liquid products that you spray can drift through the air and land on sensitive nontarget foliage and tender, new shoot growth.

Insecticides can hurt, too. Some plants are sensitive to certain chemicals and suffer damage if sprayed accidentally. Read pesticide labels carefully and apply the chemical only to approved plants. Pesticides also kill beneficial insects that ordinarily help keep damaging insects in check. When the good guys are gone, the bad guys may come back stronger than before.

Too much fertilizer also damages trees and shrubs by burning their roots and causing rapid, weak-wooded branch growth. In cold-winter climates, fertilizer-induced growth that occurs in late summer often freezes and dies.

Me, Tarzan

Build a tree house, hang a swing, and live like the king of the jungle — until the tree limbs and trunk begin to decay. Every nail you drive into your tree opens a wound that invites infection. Trees may never heal the wounds around nails, which are frequently jarred and shifting under the weight and movement of young Tarzans. Bark damage from construction and playtime activity adds further insult to the injury.

Tying a rope swing around a limb presents another set of problems. The rope constricts and abrades the bark, disrupting the flow of food and water. The weight and strain of someone swinging also weakens the limb's attachment to the tree and can eventually damage both branch and trunk.

Spot, Stay!

Chaining Spot to a tree in the backyard not only annoys the dog, it may kill the tree. Anything that damages the bark, such as a constricting rope or chain, prevents food and water from flowing between the leaves and roots. Watch out for horses, goats, sheep, and cattle, too. If their brunch includes bark, your trees are doomed. Put Spot behind a fence and wrap the trunks of trees with wire mesh if grazing beasts can reach them.

Lawn Cowboys

Yee-haw! Ride 'em cowboys. But watch where you drive that mower and what you lasso with your weed whacker. Bark damage interferes with the tree's food and water supply, and gives insects and disease an easy opening. Maintain a wide circle of weed-free mulch around plants so you and your trusty steed can keep your distance (see Chapter 13 for more information on mulching).

Parking the Car

Plants don't like anyone stepping on their toes any more than you do — and they have really big feet. Roots can extend twice the diameter of the crown's spread, living mostly in the top 12 inches of soil. When you regularly drive over their roots, you compact the soil, squeezing out air and water and making eating, drinking, and breathing difficult for the roots. Your car's fluids can also injure sensitive roots. And, before you use a handy branch to winch the engine out of your project vehicle, see the "Me, Tarzan" section, earlier in this chapter.

Construction Ahead

Big machines mean big trouble for trees and shrubs. Bashing, crashing, crushing, and compacting are only part of the story, however. Construction often involves changing the amount of soil around tree roots and that can be fatal to plants. Piling soil on top of the root zone suffocates the tree. Removing soil also removes roots. It's a lose-lose situation.

Keep construction equipment far away by erecting a temporary fence around the tree root zones, which extend about twice the diameter of the tree's canopy.

Chapter 20

Ten Winning Combinations for Common Landscape Needs

• •

In This Chapter

▶ Choosing plants for common situations

▶ Practical considerations for landscaping

▶ Plans you can use at home

• •

*E*very homeowner faces similar landscaping situations at one time or another: covering the gap between the house and the yard, decorating the front entrance, planning a hedge, planting around a pool, or finding something that grows in the shade. Use the tips in this chapter to help solve your landscape challenges. For additional tips, pick up a copy of *Landscaping For Dummies,* by Philip Giroux, Bob Beckstrom, Lance Walheim, and the Editors of The National Gardening Association (IDG Books Worldwide, Inc.).

Welcoming Entrance

Think of your front door as a personal statement — a reflection of your style and personality. The arrangement of shrubs and small trees around your home's entrance should invite and welcome visitors to your door. Keep the plan practical, though, with the following considerations in mind:

- **Use low-maintenance plants.** Shrubs that require frequent pruning or cleaning get messy looking too quickly. Untidy plantings send the wrong message.

- **Avoid nuisance plants.** Don't plant shrubs that have thorns to catch on your clothing, bee-attractive flowers, or messy fruit close to the sidewalk or entrance.

- **Think layers.** Plant the short shrubs in front of the taller shrubs. Put the tallest plants, such as small trees, near the corners of the house.

- ✔ **Consider plant width.** Choose shrubs that won't encroach on your sidewalk, driveway, or porch as they grow.

- ✔ **Combine ornamental features.** Use plants with decorative foliage, fruit, flowers, and growing habits. Plant shrubs with different bloom times for displays throughout the season.

- ✔ **Use plants to blend your house into the landscape.** Use repeating elements, such as color, texture, and specific plants to connect the entrance to the yard (see Chapter 2 for more information).

- ✔ **Consider the house style.** Asymmetrical plantings look more casual and informal than mirror-image plantings on either side of the front steps. Symmetrical plantings, on the other hand, look better with formal architecture. See Chapter 2 for more design ideas.

Hiding Your House Foundation

I think homeowners must use more shrubs to hide the joint between their house and the lawn than for any other single purpose. But the biggest mistake most people make is using too few plants. A single row of evergreen "soldiers" across the front of the house is just too boring. For better effect, layer the plants from low ground cover plants out near the sidewalk or lawn up to the tallest shrubs closest to the house. As you choose plants to cover your foundation, ponder these tips:

- ✔ **Widen the border.** Make the planting area wide enough to accommodate two or three rows of mature shrubs. Taller homes and buildings need wider beds than single-story homes.

- ✔ **Consider mature size.** Choose shrubs that won't cover your windows as they grow. Slow-growing shrubs need less maintenance than vigorous ones.

- ✔ **Vary the textures and colors.** Mix evergreens and deciduous species as well as light and dark, large and small foliage. Use accent plants, such as those with unusual foliage, sparingly. Choose shrubs predominantly for their texture and foliage and add flowering plants for seasonal bursts of color.

- ✔ **Give them room to grow.** Give each plant enough room to spread without growing against the siding or creating a fire hazard. Avoid placing shrubs directly under the drip line of the roof or where snow slides may fall on them in the winter.

- ✔ **Add fragrance.** Choose shrubs with fragrant flowers to plant under windows and by entrances.

- ✔ **Match the scale of the house.** Avoid massive shrubs and trees around small homes. Look for small trees and lower growing shrubs instead. Plant tall trees and use bold textures and shapes near larger homes.

Boundary Beautifiers

Marking the boundary between your yard and the neighbors' serves several purposes — privacy screening, windbreak, defining property lines, and providing a foil for garden plants. The plants that you choose to delineate your space depend on whether you want to completely block the view or provide a low background for your flower garden, and on your personal style. Use the following pointers to select the best shrubs or trees for your needs.

- ✔ **Flaunt your style.** Let the outside walls of your landscape reflect your personal style. Tightly clipped hedges say "formal." Loosely billowing shrubs say "casual." Look around the neighborhood and your own landscape for inspiration.

- ✔ **Think about the maintenance.** Clipped hedges need more frequent grooming than informal plantings.

- ✔ **Consider your needs.** Choose tall, dense evergreens for year-round privacy and windbreaks. Shorter shrubs and those with deciduous foliage or loose habit beautify the boundary without shutting out the neighborhood.

- ✔ **Look at both sides of the fence.** Plant high-maintenance shrubs far enough from the actual property line so that you can prune them without trespass. Use narrow-growing shrubs, if space is tight.

Shady Situations

Many trees and shrubs thrive in shade, but each has specific tolerance from deep to part shade. Consider the following tips when you choose plants for the shade.

- ✔ **Determine the shade density.** Deep shade occurs on the north sides of buildings and under trees with dense canopies. Partial shade exists under high-branched or loose-crowned trees and on the east and west sides of buildings.

- ✔ **Note the season and time of day when the shade occurs.** The amount of sun and shade in any given spot changes throughout the day and seasons of the year as the earth moves around the sun and the leaves fall from trees.

- ✔ **Consider the soil moisture.** Soil around shallow-rooted trees, under building overhangs, and on hillsides tends to be dry. Low spots and soil near streams and ponds and downspouts stays moister.

- ✔ **Choose plants to brighten the darkness.** White, yellow, and silver stand out in the shade. Use shrubs with silvery or white variegated foliage and plants with white or yellow flowers to brighten a dark area.

Poolside Potential

When you landscape around your pool, choose plants that fit your design theme whether it's formal, tropical, or relaxed. Consider the following tips when you choose the trees and shrubs to plant near your pool.

- ✔ **Keep it sunny.** Sunbathing and shade don't mix in northern climates, but southern swimmers welcome cool shade on a hot day. Plant tall trees and shrubs either far away or north of the pool in cool climates and use low-growing shrubs around the perimeter instead. In the south, choose nonshedding trees that cast dappled shade, and plant them on the west or south side of the pool.

- ✔ **Avoid messy plants.** Trees and shrubs that drop leaves, fruit, flowers, and twigs create extra work. Plant deciduous trees downwind so that their leaves with blow away from the pool. Keep those with damaging roots, such as the trees listed in Chapter 18, far away from pool liners.

- ✔ **Stay away from wildlife-attracting plants.** Avoid bee-attracting blooms as well as trees and shrubs that produce nuts and fruit, because berry-eating birds can really cause a nuisance.

- ✔ **Use low-maintenance plants.** Use your pool time to relax, not to garden.

- ✔ **Consider containers.** Dwarf trees and pot-size shrubs add décor without taking up lots of space. Bring tender container-grown shrubs into a sheltered garage for the winter in cold climates.

Index

Notes